Anxiety Disorders and Phobias

By Aaron T. Beck

Depression: Causes and Treatment (1967, 1972)

Diagnosis and Treatment of Depression (1973)

Prediction of Suicide (1974)
(with other editors)

Cognitive Therapy and the Emotional Disorders (1976)

Cognitive Therapy of Depression (1979)
(with other authors)

Love Is Never Enough (1988)

Prisoners of Hate (1999)

Cognitive Therapy of Personality Disorders (2004)
(with other authors)

By Gary Emery

Cognitive Therapy of Depression (1979)
(with other authors)

New Directions in Cognitive Therapy (1981)
(with other editors)

A New Beginning (1981)

Own Your Own Life (1984)

Rapid Relief from Emotional Distress (1985)
(with James Campbell)

Overcoming Depression (2000)

ANXIETY DISORDERS AND PHOBIAS

A Cognitive Perspective

Aaron T. Beck and Gary Emery
with Ruth L. Greenberg

BASIC
BOOKS
A Member of The Perseus Books Group

Revised paperback edition published in 2005

Published by Basic Books,
A Member of the Perseus Books Group

Books published by Basic Books are available at special discounts for bulk purchases in the United States by corporations, institutions, and other organizations. For more information, please contact the Special Markets Department at the Perseus Books Group, 11 Cambridge Center, Cambridge, MA 02142, or special.markets@perseusbooks.com.

Library of Congress Cataloging in Publication Data
Beck, Aaron T.
    Anxiety disorders and phobias
    References: p. 325
    Includes index.
    1. Anxiety. 2. Phobias. 3. Cognitive therapy.
I. Emery, Gary. II. Greenberg, Ruth L. III. Title
[DNLM: 1. Anxiety Disorders. 2. Behavior therapy.
3. Cognition. 4. Phobic Disorders.   WM 172 B393a]
RC531.B37   1985
616.85'223   84-42849
ISBN-13 978-0-465-00384-6 ISBN-10 0-465-00384-2 (cloth)
ISBN-13 978-0-465-00587-X ISBN-10 0-465-00587-X (paper)

Printed in the United States of America

10 9 8 7 6 5 4

Contents

PART I

Theoretical and Clinical Aspects

BY AARON T. BECK

PART II

Cognitive Therapy: Techniques and Applications

BY GARY EMERY

The names, locales, and other identifying details

of individual case histories

have been changed in the interest

of protecting privacy.

Preface to the 2005 Edition

Since the first publication of this book, a great deal of work has provided empirical support for the theory and therapy of anxiety disorders. Although our approach was based largely on clinical observation, the principles have found solid and extensive support in the research literature. Continuing research has further refined the therapeutic approach. In addition, cognitive therapy has been shown to be effective in a broad range of anxiety disorders: Generalized Anxiety Disorder (GAD), Panic Disorder (PD), Post-traumatic Stress Disorder (PTSD), Social Phobia (SP), and Health Anxiety (Hypochondriasis). It is now generally accepted that individuals with anxiety disorders have cognitive biases toward threat which make them hypervigilant for danger in their environment and lead them to interpret ambiguous situations as threatening (selective abstraction) or to exaggerate minor threats (magnification). Research has now demonstrated that underlying these cognitive errors is a system of dysfunctional beliefs relevant to danger.

A paper by myself and David A. Clark extended our original model by proposing a three-stage sequence of information processing.[1] The processing, driven by the activation of cognitive schemas, moves from being automatic and unconscious to conscious and strategic. A further feature in the evolution of the cognitive approach has been the development of elaborate models for each of the specific anxiety disorders. The British investigators such as David M. Clark, Anke Ehlers, Paul Salkovskis, and Adrian Wells have extended these models further and increased their specificity. For example, Clark refined the original cognitive model of panic with the concept of "catastrophic misinterpretation of bodily sensations."[2] Our own work has demonstrated that the total fixation of attention on physical and psychological experiences precludes realistic reasoning regarding their benign nature.[3]

Understanding Anxiety Disorders and Phobias

Our cognitive perspective on anxiety disorders and phobias has stimulated over twenty years of theoretical and empirical work. Newer cognitive models of anxiety disorders have drawn on the central features, such as a cognitive schema, or beliefs, that predispose individuals to process information in a biased manner, attentional focus on threat, and catastrophic misinterpretations of ambiguous stimuli. The original model consequently generated numerous testable hypotheses, and its longevity speaks to its significant explanatory power in accounting for the phenomenology of anxiety disorders.

Memory Biases: Several empirical lines of research have been designed to validate aspects of the biased information processing described in this volume. For example, Emery and I described the manner in which anxious individuals narrow their attention on threat and ignore safety cues. Experiments using Emotional Stroop and probe detection tasks have found that anxious individuals selectively attend to threatening semantic and pictorial stimuli.[4] Moreover, studies employing masked stimuli of threatening and neutral contents have revealed that attentional biases occur outside of awareness.[5] These studies confirmed our concept that these biases are automatic and often not under conscious control. In addition, we proposed that anxious individuals *inaccurately* appraise neutral situations as dangerous. This thesis has been confirmed by many studies that demonstrate that when anxious individuals are presented with ambiguous scenarios that involve potential harm, they rate negative or catastrophic explanations for the events as being more likely than do nonanxious individuals.[6]

Our theory also suggested that the activation of a maladaptive cognitive set should bias the entire sequence of information processing, from perception to retrieval from long-term memory. Some researchers examining the intentional recall of threat-relevant information generally have found a memory bias in Generalized Anxiety Disorder, although others using different research strategies have not.[7] But consistent memory biases have been found in Panic Disorder and Post-traumatic Stress Disorder.[8] Other researchers have examined implicit memory, or instances in which previously presented stimuli influence a person's behavior when he or she is not consciously trying to retrieve that information. Implicit memory is demonstrated when participants complete word stems with the previously rated words at a higher rate than would be expected by chance, and research demonstrates that anxious individuals do so particularly when they are completing stems of threat-relevant words.[9] Such biases in implicit memory have been found in all the anxiety disorders.[10]

Imagery: Recent studies confirm our thesis that imagery is an important cognitive mechanism that maintains anxiety symptoms. We reported that patients with panic disorders experience frightening imagery that accompanies their negative automatic thoughts during instances of acute anxiety.[11] Wells, Clark, and Ahmed reported that patients with social phobia recall memories of social situations primarily from an observer perspective, which limits the degree to which they attend to aspects of others' behavior in these memories that potentially would disconfirm negative beliefs about their performance.[12] Hirsch, Clark, Mathews, and Williams demonstrated that anxious symptoms increase and objective performance decreases when individuals with social phobia hold negative, rather than neutral, images in their minds during social interactions.[13] Thus, results from the body of studies examining anxiety-relevant imagery raise the possibility that the activation of threatening images plays a substantially different role in different pathologies.

Implicit Associations: Anxiety researchers have applied the Implicit Association Task to examine fear-related cognitive structures, or schemas, in individuals with specific phobias.[14] The IAT is a reaction-time computer task that measures the strength of associations between concepts in memory, which is another indicator of schematic processing. The rationale behind the task is that stimuli are classified more quickly when the target and adjectives match participants' automatic associations (e.g., spiders and bad) than when they are mismatched (e.g., spiders and good). Teachman, Gregg, and Woody found that spider-fearful participants reacted faster to associations between spiders and negative descriptors than between snakes and negative descriptors, and snake-fearful participants demonstrated the opposite pattern.[15] In a follow-up study, Teachman and Woody reported that these implicit associations are attenuated following psychotherapy, suggesting that the structures of anxiety-relevant schemas are changed with successful psychosocial interventions.[16] Thus, the Implicit Association Task has the potential to yield data that defines the parameters and structure of maladaptive schemas associated with anxiety disorders.

Self-Focused Attention: There is robust empirical evidence to suggest that anxious individuals exhibit attentional biases toward threat in their environment, so that they detect potential danger more quickly than non-anxious individuals and focus their attention on threat at the expense of neutral or safety stimuli. When socially anxious individuals are in a potentially embarrassing situation, they turn their attention onto themselves instead of monitoring their environment.[17] This shift of attention impairs performance in some instances, increases negative affect, and activates negative cognitions.[18] This line of research raises the interesting notion that more than one type of attentional bias is at work in social phobia, each of which may be amenable to treatment with cognitive therapy.[19]

Thought-action fusion is the belief that unacceptable thoughts and beliefs have a tangible influence on the world.[20] *Likelihood* thought-action fusion is the belief that having an unacceptable thought increases the probability of the adverse event occurring, whereas *moral* thought-action fusion is the belief that having an unacceptable thought is almost the equivalent of having carried out that act. According to Shafran and Rachman, instances of thought-action fusion reflect an inflated perceived responsibility for harm. Moreover, the importance of these thoughts is interpreted in an exaggerated manner. Although empirical work with clinical samples in this area of research is sparse, the studies that have been conducted suggest that thought-action fusion is relevant to many anxiety disorders, including obsessive compulsive disorder and generalized anxiety disorder, as well as depression.

Panic Disorders

To date, the cornerstone of cognitive theories of panic has been the fearful cognitions triggered by physical and psychological experiences as described in this volume or, alternatively, by the catastrophic misinterpretation of these sensations as described by D. M. Clark.[21] While this kind of reaction to physiological sensations constitutes an important characteristic of panic disorders, it represents only one of the cognitive processes that are at work in this disorder. Maladaptive beliefs make up another layer of cognition that predisposes anxious individuals to misinterpret ambiguous feelings and process this information in a biased manner. Recently, our group provided evidence suggesting that panic patients indeed endorse these beliefs even when they are not in a state of acute anxiety and that the degree to which these beliefs are characteristic of them declines over the course of cognitive therapy (CT).[22] When a belief such as "A rapid heartbeat means I'm having a coronary attack" is activated, the individual then is likely to experience anxiety or possibly panic, provided that a necessary *third component* occurs. This necessary third component consists of the total *fixation* of the patient's attention on the sensations and their interpretations. A study by Wenzel, Sharp, Sokol, and Beck using the Attentional Fixation Questionnaire (AFQ), an objective self-report measure, provided validation for this approach to panic.[23]

In an expanded presentation of our cognitive theory of panic, I proposed that individuals with panic disorder are characterized by a relatively unique cognitive problem—they fixate on their subjective experience (faintness, palpitations, etc.). This fixation results in their inability to access corrective information, to reason, and to use a rational approach to evaluate their fearful thoughts.[24] Attentional fixation is a processing disturbance that is independent of specific thoughts and instead disrupts the ability to reappraise hypervalent cognitions. I described this phenomenon as a "dissociation of the higher-level reflective processes from automatic cognitive processing" (p. 101) and noted that panic patients lack the ability to reflect on what is happening and to distance themselves from their fears in the midst of an attack.[25] Their self-absorption with their fear preempts their ability to use techniques to make realistic appraisals.

Thus the complete model of panic consists of (a) fearful cognitions regarding ambiguous physical or mental experiences, (b) underlying dysfunctional attitudes regarding medical threats, and (c) total fixation on the *meaning* of these experiences.

Social Phobias and Other Conditions

Cognitive models of social phobia have built on our notion of the "vicious cycle" by proposing that socially anxious individuals narrow their attention on their own anxiety symptoms during evaluative situations.[26] This focus on the self causes them to miss important social cues and to experience an objective decrement in their social performance. Wells has added to our understanding of social phobia by distinguishing between two types of worry.[27] Type I worry refers to worry about external events, whereas Type II worry refers to negative beliefs about their worrying; for example, "If I worry, bad things will happen." Further, Riskind has provided empirical support for his concept of the "looming" aspect of the impending threat in anxiety.[28] Specific cognitive models have been proposed for other anxiety-related conditions. These include a formulation of compulsive checking and post-traumatic stress disorder.[29]

Cognitive Therapy of Anxiety Disorders

Since the publication of this volume, numerous investigations of the application of cognitive and behavioral techniques to anxiety disorders have been conducted. A number of these studies drew their theoretical framework and many of their techniques from relevant chapters in this book. Other studies, such as those by Barlow and Borkovec and their colleagues, were conducted from a behavioral perspective but used many of the cognitive strategies described here. These researchers applied the term "Cognitive Behavior Therapy" to describe their approach. The reviews of the literature have generally lumped together the varying approaches, including Cognitive Therapy, under the label of Cognitive Behavior Therapy (CBT). The use of the term Cognitive Behavioral Therapy is somewhat misleading since at times it is used to denote treatment based on the cognitive model and at other times to describe a package of cognitive and behavioral techniques based on a behavioral model or no specific theoretical framework at all.

There have been a sufficient number of studies of these consolidated approaches to warrant meta-analysis, in which the samples from each of the studies are combined to yield a large enough number of cases to ascertain the statistical significance of any superiority of CBT over the controls. These studies also yield "effect sizes." An effect size of 1.0, for example, means that 87% of the patients in the CBT group improved more than did those in the control group. Meta-analyses by Chambless and Gillis (1993) and Chambless and Peterman (2004) as well as Gould, et al. (1997) indicate that CBT was superior to controls in Generalized Anxiety Disorder and Panic Disorder.[30]

In order to evaluate the clinical impact of cognitive therapy of anxiety disorders in the clinical trials, we attempted to segregate those studies that explicitly used a cognitive formulation.

Generalized Anxiety Disorder: Empirical studies have demonstrated that cognitive therapy is an effective treatment for generalized anxiety disorder (GAD). One of the earliest controlled studies (Butler, Cullington, Hibbert, Klimes, and Gelder, 1987) compared patients within an anxiety management program to a waiting list control group. Findings indicated a large treatment effect size and highly significant improvement in anxiety and depression. These findings were later replicated upon administering the cognitive behavioral program to the wait-list group. Treatment gains based on an average of 8.7 sessions were maintained by both groups at a six-month follow-up. In the follow-up study, the relative contribution of cognitive and behavioral components of treatment was investigated.[31] A total of fifty-seven subjects were randomly assigned to a cognitive-behavioral treatment modeled on our cognitive therapy (CT), behavior therapy (BT), or a wait-list control group. Findings on these individually delivered treatments indicated a "clear advantage" for CT over BT based on outcome measures of anxiety, depression, and cognition. Interestingly, while subjects were lost from the BT group (16%), no attrition was observed for the CT group. The six-month follow-up data indicated maintenance of treatment gains.

Durham and Turvey had conducted a similar study in 1987. Their findings based on the random assignment of forty-one GAD patients to either CT or BT indicated no significant difference amongst the two groups post-treatment. However, at their six-month follow-up, CT patients either maintained treatment gains or even improved on a number of outcome measures, whereas BT patients reverted back to their pre-treatment status. In a later study, the value and cost effectiveness of cognitive therapy were evaluated in comparison to psychodynamic therapy.[32] Results indicated the superiority of cognitive therapy over analytic psychotherapy. Patients assigned to cognitive therapy also showed higher levels of clinically significant change as compared to the anxiety management group at their one-year follow-up.[33] Cognitive therapy patients were again found to show superior improvement. Furthermore, significant reductions in medication usage and more positive attitudes about treatment were also noteworthy among CT patients. An important long-term outcome study of CT based on eight- to fourteen-year follow-up data showed significantly lower levels of symptom severities and negative affect for those patients receiving cognitive therapy.[34]

In an earlier published study (Power, Jerrom, Simpson, Mitchell, and Swanson, 1989), 101 GAD patients were randomly assigned to one of five treatments: 1) diazepam, 2) pill placebo, 3) cognitive-behavior therapy, 4) diazepam plus cognitive-behavior therapy, and 5) placebo plus cognitive therapy.[35] Post-treatment and six-month follow-up data demonstrated the superiority of the cognitive therapy alone.

These findings were supported in a later published study (Power, Simpson, Swanson, Wallace, Feistner, and Sharp, 1990) that compared the relative effectiveness of cognitive therapy, diazepam, and pill placebo in thirty-one GAD patients.[36] Findings showed largest effect sizes for the cognitive therapy condition. These treatment gains were again maintained by CT patients who reported the lowest need for subsequent psychotropic and therapeutic interventions at their twelve-month follow-up.

Panic Disorder: Cognitive therapy of panic disorder (PD) is based on our model of treatment as well as Clark and Salkovskis's (1991) later adaptations.[37] The utility of cognitive interventions in the treatment of PD has been examined in several studies.[38] Overall, large effect sizes for cognitive therapy have been noted by Levitt, Hoffman, Grisham, and Barlow for panic frequency, fear of fear, and generalized anxiety.[39] Follow-up data of one to twelve months have revealed maintenance of treatment gains or even further improvement for patients receiving cognitive therapy.

The short- and long-term effects of focused cognitive therapy for panic disorder were investigated in a study by our group.[40] We randomly assigned thirty-three patients diagnosed with PD to either individual focused cognitive therapy (CT) or brief supportive psychotherapy. Findings indicated significantly greater reductions in panic symptoms and general anxiety for CT patients. Eight weeks of treatment resulted in 71% of panic-free patients within the cognitive therapy group as compared to 25% in the supportive psychotherapy group. One-year follow-up data were noteworthy in that

87% of the CT patients remained free of panic attacks. Similar findings (i.e., 79% panic free) were reported for the patients in supportive psychotherapy after they were crossed over to the cognitive therapy condition.

Cognitive therapy was later compared with other psychological and pharmacological treatments. Clark, et al., randomly assigned sixty-four patients with PD to cognitive therapy, applied relaxation, imipramine, or wait-list control.[41] After three months, cognitive therapy was superior to both imipramine and applied relaxation. Fifteen months out, cognitive treatment gains were still maintained and recognized as superior to both applied relaxation and imipramine. A briefer version of cognitive therapy has also proven to be effective in the treatment of panic disorder. Clark, et al. (1999) evaluated the efficacy of a full CT (FCT) protocol and brief CT (BCT) protocol against a wait-list control group.[42] Findings based on a total of forty-three patients indicated the superiority of cognitive therapy, whether offered in full or brief format, on all measures. Both treatments demonstrated very large and almost identical effect sizes (approximately 3.0). Treatment gains in both cognitive therapy conditions were maintained at their twelve-month follow-up.

Post-traumatic Stress Disorder (PTSD): Ehlers and Clark (2000) have provided a theory-driven patient-individualized therapy for PTSD based on the cognitive model. To date, cognitive therapy in the treatment of PTSD has been empirically validated in four studies (Ehlers, Clark, Hackmann, McManus, and Fennell, in press, Study 1 and Study 2; Ehlers, Clark, Hackmann, et al., 2003; Gillespie, Duffy, Hackmann, and Clark, 2002).[43] The overall reported pre-treatment-to-post-treatment effect sizes have been noticeably and consistently large, ranging from 2.5 to 2.82. Follow-up findings are encouraging in that they reflect the maintenance of these substantial treatment gains.

The most recent empirical findings on the utility of a cognitive treatment program for PTSD patients have been presented by Ehlers, Clark, Hackmann, McManus, and Fennell.[44] These authors had previously demonstrated highly significant improvements in PTSD, depression, and anxiety symptoms in a consecutive case series of twenty PTSD patients. Recently, they reported their findings based on a randomized controlled trial comparing cognitive therapy to a wait-list condition. Cognitive therapy resulted in significant reductions in PTSD symptoms, disability, depression, and anxiety that were maintained at six-month follow-up. Treatment outcome was related to changes in patients' dysfunctional post-traumatic cognitions as expected based on the cognitive model.

Additional support for a cognitive model of intervention was provided in yet another randomized controlled trial that focused on recent onset

PTSD in motor vehicle accident survivors.[45] PTSD patients were assigned to either cognitive therapy, a self-help CBT booklet, or repeated assessments. Cognitive therapy was found to be the most effective in reducing PTSD symptoms, disability, depression, and anxiety. During a nine-month follow-up, cognitive therapy patients maintained their gains and significantly fewer qualified for the diagnosis of PTSD.

The effectiveness of the cognitive model proposed by Ehlers and Clark (2000) was also empirically investigated by providing cognitive treatment to a consecutive series of ninety-one PTSD patients who had experienced the Omagh, Northern Ireland, car bombing incident in August 1998.[46] An average of eight cognitive therapy sessions provided by the trained Community Trauma and Recovery Team in Omagh resulted in significant improvements in PTSD which were comparable to findings provided in previous research trials.

Cognitive therapy of social phobia based on our work has received much attention within the past decade. D. M. Clark argues that a significant number of patients fail to benefit from existing treatment options.[47] For instance, Heimberg, et al., classified fewer than 60% of their treated patients with group CBT as treatment responders.[48] Understanding the cognitive factors underlying social phobia is important for treating patients who fail to respond to combined cognitive behavioral methods and for obtaining overall cognitive change.[49] Cognitive treatments based on this model have proven to be effective in case studies of resistant social phobic patients.[50]

D. M. Clark evaluated the effectiveness of this cognitive intervention in the treatment of fifteen consecutively referred cases of social phobia.[51] Treatment consisted of sixteen sessions and the pre-post effect sizes were large, indicating substantial overall improvement. Subsequently, D. M. Clark, et al., reported their findings on a randomized placebo-controlled trial of cognitive therapy versus fluoxetine in the treatment of social phobia.[52] Even though significant improvement was noted for all three treatment conditions, CT was superior at mid-treatment and post-treatment for all measures of social phobia. This superiority persisted at the twelve-month follow-up. Scholing and Emmelkamp randomly allocated seventy-three patients with social phobia to 1) exposure in vivo, 2) cognitive therapy followed by exposure in vivo, or 3) cognitive-behavioral treatment in which both components were integrated from the start.[53] Three-month follow-up data showed the greatest improvement for group treatment consisting of cognitive therapy followed by exposure in vivo. Interestingly, the integrated group showed the least progress.

Health Anxiety: Our cognitive theory of anxiety (1985) has contributed to the understanding and treatment of hypochondriasis, a persistently severe form of health anxiety.[54] Cognitive interventions of health anxiety aim to change the distorted patterns of thinking through discussion and collaboratively designed and implemented behavioral experiments (Barsky, Geringer, and Wool, 1988; Salkovskis, Warwick, and Deale, 2003).[55] Warwick, Clark, Cobb, and Salkovskis (1996) randomly allocated thirty-two patients to CT or to wait-list control. Significant improvements were noted for patients receiving the active treatment and these gains were maintained at their three-month follow-up. In another controlled trial (D. M. Clark, et al., 1998), CBT was compared with a stress-management package and a wait-list control group.[56] Significant gains on several key measures were obtained for the cognitive behavioral condition; patients maintained these gains at their one-year follow-up. Furthermore, Avia, et al. (1996), reported findings on a controlled trial of a group cognitive educational intervention where patients receiving the cognitive treatment showed a significant decrease in illness-related fears, somatic symptoms, and dysfunctional beliefs; long-term positive effects were noted as well at one-year follow-up.[57] Based on a randomized controlled study of 102 patients assigned to six sessions of CBT and eighty-five patients assigned to usual medical care, Barsky and Ahem (2004) reported clinically significant treatment effects.[58] Twelve-month follow-up data have indicated significantly lower levels of health-related anxiety and hypochondriacal beliefs for patients receiving cognitive behavioral interventions.

In summary, the theoretical framework provided in this volume has been supported by a substantial amount of literature. Moreover, further refinement and extension of the basic cognitive model have increased our understanding not only of Generalized Anxiety Disorder and Panic Disorder but also Post-traumatic Stress Disorder, Social Phobia, and Hypochondriasis. The clinical application of theory and strategies to each of these disorders demonstrates that these are the preferred psychotherapeutic approaches.

NOTES

1. Beck, A. T.; and Clark, D. A. 1997. "An information processing model of anxiety: Automatic and strategic processes." *Behavior Research and Therapy*, 35: 49–58.

2. Clark, D. M. 1986. "A cognitive model of panic." *Behaviour Research and Therapy*, 24: 461–470.

3. Beck, A. T. 1988. "Cognitive approaches to panic disorder: Theory and therapy." In S. Rachman and J. D. Maser,. eds., *Panic: Psychological Perspectives* (pp. 91–109). Hillsdale, NJ: Erlbaum. Wenzel, A.; Sharp, I. R.; Sokol, L.; and Beck, A. T. 2004. "An Investigation of Attentional Fixation in Panic Disorders." Manuscript submitted for publication.

4. MacLeod, C.; Mathews, A.; and Tata, P. 1986. "Attentional bias in emotional disorders." *Journal of Abnormal Psychology*, 95: 15–20. Mogg, K.; and Bradley, B. P. 2002. "Selective orienting of attention to masked threat faces in social anxiety." *Behaviour Research and Therapy*, 40: 1403–1414.

5. Mogg, K.; Bradley, B. P.; Williams, R.; and Mathews, A. 1993. "Subliminal processing of emotional information in anxiety and depression." *Journal of Abnormal Psychology*, 102: 304–311.

6. Amir, N.; Foa, E. B.; and Coles, M. E. 1998. "Automatic activation and strategic avoidance of threat-relevant information in social phobia." *Journal of Abnormal Psychology*, 107: 285–290.

7. Greenberg, M. S.; and Beck, A. T. 1989. "Depression versus anxiety: A test of the content-specificity hypothesis." *Journal of Abnormal Psychology*, 98: 9–13.

8. Coles, M. E.; and Heimberg, R. G. 2002. "Memory biases in the anxiety disorders: Current status." *Clinical Psychology Review*, 22: 587–627.

9. Mathews, A.; Mogg, K.; May, J.; and Eysenck, M. 1989. "Implicit and explicit memory bias in anxiety." *Journal of Abnormal Psychology*, 98: 236–240.

10. Coles, M. E.; and Heimberg, R. G. 2002. "Memory biases in the anxiety disorders: Current status." *Clinical Psychology Review*, 22: 587–627.

11. Ottaviani, R.; and Beck, A. T. 1987. "Cognitive aspects of panic disorder." *Journal of Anxiety Disorders*, 1:15–28.

12. Wells, A.; Clark, D. M.; and Ahmed, S. 1998. "How do I look with my mind's eye: Perspective taking in social phobic imagery." *Behaviour Research and Therapy*, 36: 631–634.

13. Hirsch, C. R.; Clark, D. M.; Mathews, A.; and Williams, R. 2003. "Self-images play a causal role in social phobia." *Behaviour Research and Therapy*, 41: 909–921.

14. Greenwald, A. G.; McGhee, D. E.; and Schwartz, J. L. K. 1998. "Measuring individual differences in implicit cognition: The Implicit Association Test." *Journal of Personality and Social Psychology*, 74: 1464–1480.

15. Teachman, B. A.; Gregg, A. P.; and Woody, S. R. 2001. "Implicit associations for fear-relevant stimuli among individuals with snake and spider fears." *Journal of Abnormal Psychology*, 110: 226–235.

16. Teachman, B. A.; and Woody, S. R. 2003. "Automatic processing in spider phobia: Implicit fear associations over the course of treatment." *Journal of Abnormal Psychology*, 112:100–109.

17. Hope, D. A.; Gansler, D. A.; and Heimberg, R. G. 1989. "Attentional focus and causal attributions in social phobia: Implications from social psychology." *Clinical Psychology Review*, 9: 49–60.

18. Woody, S. R. 1996. "Effects of focus of attention on social phobic anxiety and social performance." *Journal of Abnormal Psychology*, 105: 61–69.

19. Woody, S. R.; Chambless, D. L.; and Glass, C. R. 1997. "Self-focused attention in the treatment of social phobia." *Behaviour Research and Therapy*, 35: 117–129.

20. Shafran, R.; and Rachman, S. 2004. "Thought-action fusion: A review." *Journal of Behavior Therapy and Experimental Psychiatry*, 35: 87–107.

21. Clark, D.M. 1986. "A cognitive model of panic." *Behavior Research and Therapy*, 24: 461–470.

22. Wenzel, A.; Sharp, I. R.; Brown, G. K.; Greenberg, R.; and Beck, A. T. 2004. _Dysfunctional Beliefs in Panic Disorder: The Panic Beliefs Inventory._ Manuscript submitted for publication.

23. Wenzel, A.; Sharp, I. R.; Sokol, L.; and Beck, A. T. 2004 _An Investigation of Attentional Fixation in Panic Disorder._ Manuscript submitted for publication.

24. Beck, A. T. 1988. "Cognitive approaches to panic disorder: Theory and therapy." In S. Rachman and J. D. Maser, eds., _Panic: Psychological Perspectives_ (pp. 91–109). Hillsdale, NJ: Erlbaum.

25. Beck, A. T. 1988. "Cognitive approaches to panic disorder: Theory and therapy." In S. Rachman and J. D. Maser, eds., _Panic: Psychological Perspectives_ (p. 101). Hillsdale, NJ: Erlbaum.

26. Clark, D. M.; and Wells, A. 1995. "A cognitive model of social phobia." In R. G. Heimberg, M. Liebowitz, D. A. Hope, and F. Schneier, eds., _Social Phobia: Diagnosis, Assessment, and Treatment._ New York: Guilford.

27. Wells, A. 1995. "Meta-cognition and worry: A cognitive model of generalized anxiety disorder." _Behavioural and Cognitive Psychotherapy_, 23: 301–320.

28. Riskind, J. H.; Williams, N. L.; Gessner, T. L.; Chrosniak, L. D.; and Cortina, J. M. 2000. "The looming maladaptive style: Anxiety, danger, and schematic processing." _Journal of Personality and Social Psychology_, 79: 837–852.

29. Rachman, S. 2002. "A cognitive theory of compulsive checking." _Behaviour Research and Therapy_, 40: 624–639. Ehlers, A.; and Clark, D. M. 2000. "A cognitive model of posttraumatic stress disorder." _Behaviour Research and Therapy_, 38: 319–345.

30. Chambless, D. L.; and Gillis, M. M. 1993. "Cognitive therapy of anxiety disorders." _Journal of Consulting and Clinical Psychology_, 61: 248–260. Chambless, D. L., and Peterman, M. 2004. "Evidence on cognitive behavioral therapy for generalized anxiety disorder and panic disorder." In R. Leahey, ed., _Contemporary Cognitive Therapy._ New York: Guilford. Gould, R. A.; Otto, M. W.; Pollack, M. H.; and Yap, L. 1997. "Cognitive behavioral and pharmacological treatment of generalized anxiety disorder: A preliminary meta-analysis." _Behavior Therapy_, 28: 285–305.

31. Butler, G.; Fennell, M.; Robson, P.; and Gelder, M. 1991. "Comparison of behavior therapy and cognitive behavior therapy in the treatment of generalized anxiety disorder." _Journal of Consulting and Clinical Psychology_, 59: 167–175.

32. Durham, R. C.; Murphy, T.; Allan, T.; Richard, K.; Treliving, L. R.; and Fenton, G. W. 1994. "Cognitive therapy, analytic psychotherapy, and anxiety management training for generalized anxiety disorder." _British Journal of Psychiatry_, 165: 315–323.

33. Durham, R. C.; Fisher, P. L.; Treliving, L. R.; Hau, C. M.; Richard, K.; and Stewart, J. B. 1999. "One year follow-up of cognitive therapy, analytic psychotherapy and anxiety management training for generalized anxiety disorder: Symptom change, medication usage and attitudes to treatment." _Behavioural and Cognitive Psychotherapy_, 27: 29–35.

34. Durham, R. C.; Chambers, J. A.; MacDonald, R. R.; Power, K. G.; and Major, K. 2003. "Does cognitive-behavioural therapy influence the long-term outcome of generalized anxiety disorder? An 8–14 year follow-up of two clinical trials." _Psychological Medicine_, 33(3): 499–509.

35. Power, K. G.; Jerrom, D. W. A.; Simpson, R. J.; Mitchell, M. J.; and Swanson, V. 1989. "A controlled comparison of cognitive-behaviour therapy, diazepam and placebo in the management of generalized anxiety." *Behavioural Psychotherapy*, 17: 1–14.

36. Power, K. G.; Simpson, R. J.; Swanson, V.; Wallace, L. A.; Feistner, A. T. C.; and Sharp, D. 1990. "A controlled comparison of cognitive-behaviour therapy, diazepam, and placebo, alone and in combination, for the treatment of generalised anxiety disorder." *Journal of Anxiety Disorders*, 4: 267–292.

37. Salkovskis, P. M.; and Clark, D. M. 1991. "Cognitive therapy for panic attacks." *Journal of Cognitive Psychotherapy: Special Panic Disorders*, 5: 215–226.

38. Beck, A. T.; Sokol, L.; Clark, D. A.; Berchick, R.; and Wright, F. 1992. "A crossover study of focused cognitive therapy for panic disorder." *American Journal of Psychiatry*, 149(6): 778–783. Clark, D. M.; Salkovskis, P. M.; Hackmann, A.; Middleton, H.; Anastasiades, P.; and Gelder, M. G. 1994. "A comparison of cognitive therapy, applied relaxation and imipramine in the treatment of panic disorder." *British Journal of Psychiatry*, 164: 759–769. Clark, D. M.; Salkovskis, P. M.; Hackmann, A.; Wells, A.; Ludgate, J.; and Gelder, M. 1999. "Brief cognitive therapy for panic disorder: A randomized controlled trial." *Journal of Consulting and Clinical Psychology*, 67(4): 583–589. Margraf, J.; and Schneider, S. November 1991. "Outcome and Active Ingredients of Cognitive Behavioral Treatments for Panic Disorder." Paper presented at the meeting of the Association for Advancement of Behavior Therapy, New York. Newman, C. F.; Beck, J. S.; Beck, A. T.; and Tran, G. Q. November 1990. "Efficacy of Cognitive Therapy in Reducing Panic Attacks and Medication." Paper presented at the meeting of the Association for Advancement of Behavior Therapy, San Francisco. Sokol, L.; Beck, A. T.; Greenberg, R. L.; Wright, F. D.; and Berchick, R. J. 1989. "Cognitive therapy of panic disorder: A nonpharmacological alternative." *Journal of Nervous and Mental Disease*, 177: 711–716.

39. Levitt, J. T.; Hoffman, E. C.; Grisham, J. R.; and Barlow, D. H. 2001. "Empirically supported treatments for panic disorder." *Psychiatric Annals*, 31: 478–487.

40. Beck, A. T.; Sokol, L.; Clark, D. A.; Berchick, R.; and Wright, F. 1992. "A crossover study of focused cognitive therapy for panic disorder." *American Journal of Psychiatry*, 149(6): 778–783.

41. Clark, D. M.; Salkovskis, P. M.; Hackmann, A.; Middleton, H.; Anastasiades, P.; and Gelder, M. G. 1994. "A comparison of cognitive therapy, applied relaxation and imipramine in the treatment of panic disorder." *British Journal of Psychiatry*, 164: 759–769.

42. Clark, D. M.; Salkovskis, P. M.; Hackmann, A.; Wells, A.; Ludgate, J.; and Gelder, M. 1999. "Brief cognitive therapy for panic disorder: A randomized controlled trial." *Journal of Consulting and Clinical Psychology*, 67(4): 583–589.

43. Ehlers, A.; Clark, D. M.; Hackmann, A.; McManus, F.; Fennell, M. J. V.; Herbert, C.; et al. 2003. "A randomized controlled trial of cognitive therapy, a self-help booklet, and repeated assessment as early interventions for PTSD." *Archives of General Psychiatry*, 60: 1024–1032. Gillespie, K.; Duffy, M.; Hackmann, A.; and Clark, D. M. 2002. "Community based cognitive therapy in the treatment of posttraumatic

stress disorder following the Omagh bomb." *Behaviour Research and Therapy*, 40: 345–357.

44. Ehlers, A; Clark, D. M; Hackmann, A; McManus, F.; and Fennell, M. J. V. (in press). "Cognitive therapy for posttraumatic stress disorder: Development and evaluation." *Behaviour Research and Therapy*.

45. Ehlers, A.; Clark, D. M.; Hackmann, A.; McManus, F.; Fennell, M. J. V. ; Herbert, C.; et al. 2003. "A randomized controlled trial of cognitive therapy, a self-help booklet, and repeated assessment as early interventions for PTSD." *Archives of General Psychiatry*, 60: 1024–1032.

46. Ehlers, A., and Clark, D. M. 2000. "A cognitive model of posttraumatic stress disorder." *Behaviour Research and Therapy*, 38: 319–345. Gillespie, K.; Duffy, M.; Hackmann, A.; and Clark, D. M. 2002. "Community based cognitive therapy in the treatment of posttraumatic stress disorder following the Omagh bomb." *Behaviour Research and Therapy*, 40: 345–357.

47. Clark, D. M.; Ehlers, A.; McManus, F.; Hackmann, A.; Fennell, M.; Campbell, H.; Flower, T.; Davenport, C; and Louis, B. 2003. "Cognitive therapy versus fluoxetine in generalized social phobia: A randomized placebo-controlled trial." *Journal of Consulting and Clinical Psychology*, 71(6): 1058–1067.

48. Heimberg, R. G.; Liebowitz, M. R.; Hope, D. A.; Schneier, F. R.; Holt, C. S.; Welkowitz, L. A.; et al. 1998. "Cognitive behavioral group therapy vs. phenelzine therapy for social phobia: 12-week outcome." *Archives of General Psychiatry*, 55: 1133–1141.

49. Wells, A. 2000. "Modifying social anxiety: A cognitive approach." In R. W. Crozier, ed., *Shyness: Development, Consolidation and Change.* New York: Routledge.

50. Bates, A.; and Clark, D. M. 2002. "A new cognitive treatment for social phobia: A single-case study." In R. L. Leahy and D. E. Thomas, eds., *Clinical Advances in Cognitive Psychotherapy: Theory and Application.* New York: Springer Publishing. Bowers, W. A.; and Yates, W. R. 1992. "Cognitive therapy during discontinuation of alprazolam for social phobia." *Psychotherapy: Theory, Research, Practice, Training*, 29(2): 285–287.

51. Clark, D. M. 1999. "Anxiety disorders: Why they persist and how to treat them." *Behaviour Research and Therapy*, 37: S5–S27.

52. Clark, D. M.; Ehlers, A.; McManus, F.; Hackmann, A.; Fennell, M.; Campbell, H.; Flower, T.; Davenport, C.; and Louis, B. 2003. "Cognitive therapy versus fluoxetine in generalized social phobia: A randomized placebo-controlled trial." *Journal of Consulting and Clinical Psychology*, 71(6): 1058–1067.

53. Scholing, A.; and Emmelkamp, P. M. 1993 "Exposure with and without cognitive therapy for generalized social phobia: Effects of individual and group treatment." *Behaviour Research and Therapy*, 31(7): 667–681.

54. Salkovskis, P. M.; Warwick, H. M. C.; and Deale, A. C. 2003, "Cognitive-behavioral treatment for severe and persistent health anxiety (hypochondriasis)." *Brief Treatment and Crisis Intervention*, 3(3): 353–367.

55. Barsky, A . J.; Geringer, E.; and Wool, C. 1988. "A cognitive-educational treatment for hypochnodriasis." *General Hospital Psychiatry*, 10: 322–327.

56. Clark, D. M.; Salkovskis, P. M.; Hackmann, A.; Wells, A.; Fennell, M.; Ludgate, J.; et al. 1998. "Two psychological treatments for hypochondriasis: A randomized controlled trial." *British Journal of Psychiatry*, 173: 218–225.

57. Avia, M. D.; Ruiz, M.; Olivares, M. C.; Guisado, A. B.; Sanchez, A.; and Varela, A. 1996. "The meaning of psychological symptoms: Effectiveness of a group intervention with hypochondriacal patients." *Behaviour Research and Therapy*, 34:, 23–31.

58. Barsky, A. J.; and Ahem, D. K. 2004. "Cognitive behavior therapy for hypochondriasis: A randomized controlled trial." *Journal of the American Medical Association*, 292(12): 1464–1470.

Preface to the 1985 Edition

The phenomenon of anxiety has engaged the attention of writers for centuries. In recent years, a flood of publications has addressed this subject; and it has even provided the title for Leonard Bernstein's symphony, "The Age of Anxiety." The importance of anxiety in both normal and abnormal behavior is highlighted by the central role ascribed to it by various learning and psychoanalytic theories.

This volume is an attempt to understand anxiety from a somewhat different perspective. The main thesis is that a central process in adaptation is cognition, or information processing. When there is a disturbance in this central mechanism of cognition, there is a consequent disturbance in feeling and behavior. Moreover, our cognitive perspective posits that correction of a disturbance in thinking will relieve disturbances in feeling and behavior.

Attributing a central role to cognition or information processing raises several questions. How did an apparatus develop that could, on the one hand, so magnificently enable human beings to adapt to the perils of the environment, and, on the other hand, plunge them into untoward suffering in the form of anxiety, depression, and other psychological disorders? Further, how can presumed disturbances in information processing account for the variegated symptoms of the anxiety disorders? Finally, how can one go about reversing such disorders?

The aim of this book reflects a relatively recent change in the Zeitgeist of the behavioral sciences. From an exclusive emphasis on affect, motivation, and behavior, concern has shifted to the acquisition, sorting, interpretation, and storage of information. This change—the so-called cognitive revolution—has had an impact on such diverse disciplines as anthropology, social psychology, political science, clinical psychology and psychoanalysis.

This book is divided into two parts. The first part, by myself, Aaron T. Beck, elaborates the clinical picture of anxiety disorders and phobias and presents an explanatory model to account for the rich complexity of these phenomena. The second part, by Gary Emery, details the therapeutic principles, strategies, and tactics developed on the basis of the cognitive model of anxiety disorders and phobias.

A central theme of part I is the apparent perversity of systems that have evolved to protect the individual, yet become directed in such a way as to work against him. I attempt to show how anxiety symptoms are a manifestation of survival mechanisms directed by cognitive processes. The adaptive value of information processing can be observed beginning with relatively simple creatures such as the amoeba and the paramecium, which are programmed to make rapid decisions in order to adjust to changes in the milieu. In humans, an analogous process filters out relevant data, makes decisions, and implements adaptive behavior. It also plays a role in the generation of anxiety.

Part I asserts that innate or preprogrammed responses are as relevant to humans as to single-celled organisms. The centrality of preprogrammed behavior in nonhuman animals has been generally accepted. It may be a bit more difficult to accept the notion that, to a large degree, humans function in ways similar to other animals. Few of our psychological processes are conscious; most are involuntary. In no area is the operation of these nonvolitional processes more apparent than in anxiety disorders—in which, for no apparent reason, one may suddenly become mute, find one's mind going blank, and become rooted to the spot. In this section, I will attempt to unravel the mystery of such paradoxical reactions.

Part I takes an open-ended approach to the cause of anxiety. We do not conceive of cognitive factors as "causing" anxiety disorders. Although aberrant cognitive processing leads to a variety of unpleasant feelings and inhibitions, the triggering of this mechanism is produced by a variety of factors. In the future, the role of heredity, experience, and hormonal factors in activating these mechanisms will have to be delineated.

The first part of the book tries to explain how an apparatus that was developed for purposes of survival can produce so much distress. The first chapter lays the groundwork by defining terms and concepts, particularly the distinctions between fear and anxiety, realistic and unrealistic fears, and differences in mobilization for both present and future danger. Throughout, the adaptational function of anxiety is stressed.

The second chapter looks into the analysis of the symptoms as manifestations of the hyperactivity of certain vital systems. The operation of these systems is seen as occurring in a variety of patterns that serve different functions. Only when there is a substantial mismatch between a person's perception of the environment and its actual characteristics does a psychological disturbance occur.

The problem of the mismatch is detailed in chapter 3, which focuses on the relation between thinking, on the one hand, and affect and behavior, on the other. Chapter 3 delineates the crucial importance of cognitive processing in estimating danger and in activating primitive strategies for dealing with the danger; while chapter 4 develops the concept that a "new program"—or mode—is activated in anxiety disorders. The cognitive mode leaves its stamp on the way that much of the environmental input is processed. Thus, certain sets of "rules" are used to classify relatively innocuous events as dangerous; the rules tend to exaggerate the probability as well as the degree of damage in mildly threatening situations.

The core psychological problem in anxiety disorders—namely, a pervasive sense of vulnerability—is explored in chapter 5. Vulnerability is discussed first in terms of an individual's tendency to devalue his problem-solving ability as well as to exaggerate the degree of threat in a problematic situation. The dysfunctional behaviors are seen as basic functions or strategies used for self-protection. These self-protective patterns are likely to become mobilized in areas where the individual feels specifically vulnerable. These vulnerable areas involve public and private sectors and consist specifically of threats to a person's social bonding or sense of individuality, freedom, and identity.

The preceding chapters lay the theoretical groundwork for the understanding of generalized anxiety disorders discussed in chapter 6. The exploration of a patient's automatic thoughts and images reveals his specific fears and his own peculiar constructions of problematic situations. The differentiation of a generalized anxiety disorder from depression is discussed in terms of the anxious patient's more positive self-image, more optimistic outlook for the future, and more pleasant recollection of past experiences. Attention is paid to the tendency of the anxious patient to criticize himself for *specific* deficiencies and performance (behavioral self-blame), in contrast to the depressive who is more likely to attribute his problems to a global, structuralized deficiency (characterological self-blame). The relationship of panic disorders to generalized anxiety disorders is discussed in terms of the central feature of panic centering on the misreading of internal physiological sensations as indicating a serious threat to life or to psychological equilibrium.

Simple phobias are described in chapter 7, and the diverse meanings of each of the more frequent phobias are reviewed. The importance of the dual belief system—whereby an individual may believe that the phobic situation is not dangerous as long as he is distant from it, but may change that belief as he approaches the situation—is also discussed. The danger that the person attributes to the situation is often demonstrated by his visual images as well as his automatic thoughts.

Chapter 8 reviews the riddle of agoraphobia. This condition is seen as deriving from a combination of factors, including a person's fear of being in strange places, his tendency to interpret unpleasant or inexplicable internal sensations as a sign of severe pathology, his drive to escape to safe places when he is experiencing anxiety, and his dependence on a caregiver to help him cope with his problem.

The evaluation anxieties—including social anxieties, public-speaking anxiety, and test anxiety—are discussed in chapter 9. The common denominator of each of these problematic areas is the "danger" of having one's ability evaluated by others, and of thus risking the possibility of being stamped as inferior and inadequate. Attention is paid to fantasies of catastrophe connected with the possible consequences of substandard performance and concern about being sabotaged by internal inhibitions when thinking and speaking.

Part II outlines a treatment program based on the theoretical model for anxiety disorders developed in part I. Chapter 10 presents the working principles of cognitive therapy and introduces techniques that are elaborated in later chapters. Chapter 11 describes basic approaches to cognitive restructuring in the anxiety disorders. Chapter 12 presents techniques for addressing the imagery component in anxiety and for using imagery to alleviate a disorder. The affective and behavioral components of anxiety are addressed in chapters 13 and 14, respectively. A second level of cognitive restructuring, that of the patient's major concerns and underlying assumptions, is described in chapter 15.

The evolution of this book began in 1978 when, shortly after completing our *Cognitive Therapy of Depression,* Dr. Emery and I developed a treatment manual for anxiety following a format similar to that for the manual described in our book on depression. After completing the first version of the treatment manual for anxiety, we hastened to "test out" various strategies and techniques with patients at the Center for Cognitive Therapy in Philadelphia. We also received valuable feedback from the fellows at the center and from colleagues elsewhere. On the basis of this experience, we revised the manual through two additional versions. The final version of the treatment manual (Beck and Emery) was completed in 1979 and, since then, has been used by clinicians and researchers.

Beginning in 1979, Dr. Emery and I conferred regularly as we revised and expanded the manual. Each of us gravitated toward a different component of the writing, and these different areas of concentration culminated in the organization of the present volume. My own interest was primarily theoretical analysis while Dr. Emery, because of his ongoing clinical practice, was in a position to evaluate and refine the techniques of therapy. Although the final version of the book represents our collaboration, the first part bears the stamp of my thinking, whereas the second part clearly reflects Gary Emery's thought and experience. For this reason, each of us is designated author of his respective part.

Throughout the development and preparation of this book, Ruth L. Greenberg has been invaluable in making technical suggestions, preparing clinical anecdotes, providing additional text material, and giving us much-needed critical evaluation of the text itself.

Many others have contributed to the development and preparation of this volume. We especially want to thank all of the past fellows of the Center for Cognitive Therapy, who participated in weekly seminars during which were discussed many of the ideas that were eventually incorporated into the book. In addition to their contributions, I received substantial feedback on various aspects of the theoretical formulations from many of my colleagues. Among those who have contributed their understanding and wisdom, we can single out only a few, including David M. Clark, Barbara Fleming, Michael Mahoney, Brian Shaw, Elise Sutter, and John Rush. Some sections, for example the chapter on agoraphobia, reflect feedback from as many as twenty-five clinicians and behavioral scientists. They are too numerous to list, but we do wish to extend our appreciation to these contributors. We want to express special gratitude to Dr. Marjorie Weishaar, who read over the entire manuscript and provided many valuable suggestions.

We deeply appreciate the adept assistance of our editor at Basic Books, Jo Ann Miller, from the initial preparation of the manuscript to its final appearance in book form. Phoebe Hoss of Basic Books also provided valuable editorial support.

We would also like to express our gratitude to the various people who participated in the preparation of the typescript. Among them was Pat Day, who did the bulk of the typing for Dr. Emery. I received a great deal of assistance from Barbara Marinelli, Joan Doroba, and Jeanette Weiss. We are also grateful to Tina Inforzato, Julie Jacobs, and Susan Rosati for their help.

We acknowledge with appreciation receiving permission from the *Journal of Nervous and Mental Disease* and the Williams & Wilkins Company to publish, in slightly altered form, portions of Aaron Beck's 1970 article, "Role of Fantasies in Psychotherapy and Psychopathology," in chapter 13 of this volume. We are also grateful to the *British Journal of Psychiatry* for granting permission to publish, again in modified form, the tables which appear in chapter 9; the tables originally appeared in an article, "Social Phobia: A Comparative Clinical Study," by P. L. Amies, M. G. Gelder, and

P. M. Shaw, to whom we also wish to express thanks. Finally, the American Psychiatric Association has generously granted permission to reproduce sections of the third edition of its *Diagnostic and Statistical Manual of Mental Disorders* (1980).

About language: Although we have for the most part used masculine pronouns ("he," "his") when speaking in general terms about therapist or patient, we by no means consider either the one or the other as being of a single gender. We have retained the traditional usage because of its simplicity and flexibility.

AARON T. BECK, M.D.
February 1985

PART I

Theoretical and Clinical Aspects

BY

AARON T. BECK

Chapter 1

Turning Anxiety on Its Head:

An Overview

The Paradox of Anxiety

An accomplished violinist finds that his fingers become stiff as he starts to play in front of an audience.

A student taking an oral examination finds that her mind has gone blank and she is unable to talk.

A medical student participating in his first operation starts to faint.

Each of these mishaps is characteristic of the condition commonly labeled *anxiety*. One of the paradoxical features of acute anxiety (or fear reaction) is that a person seems to bring on unwittingly what he fears or detests the most. In fact, fear of an unpleasant event seems to enhance the probability of its actually happening.

To understand how the anxiety (or fear) reaction seems to produce just those things that an individual most abhors, reflect on this report by a college professor with fears of public speaking:

As I stand talking to the audience, I hope that my mind and voice will function properly, that I won't lose my balance, and everything else will function. But, then my heart starts to pound, I feel pressure build up in my chest as though I'm ready to explode, my tongue feels thick and heavy, my mind feels foggy and then goes blank. I can't remember what I have just said or what I am supposed to say. Then I start to choke. I can barely push the words out. My body is swaying; my hands tremble. I start to sweat and I am ready to topple off the platform. I feel terrified and I think that I will probably disgrace myself.

We see from this passage that, in a fear episode, practically every system of the body is affected: (1) the physiological system is manifested in sweating, increased heart rate, and dizziness; (2) the cognitive, in the anticipation that "I will probably disgrace myself"; (3) the motivational, in the wish to be as far from the traumatic situation as possible; (4) the affective or emotional, in the subjective feeling of terror; (5) the behavioral, in swaying and in inhibited speaking or thinking. In this example, the total psychobiological reaction is disturbing and involuntary and takes partial control of the individual until it has abated.

Nature has provided us with a nervous system that functions exquisitely under ordinary circumstances. Why should this system start to work against us in those very instances when we most want it to work effectively?

Part of the answer may be that, up to a point, the symptoms associated with anxiety are adaptive and pose a problem only under certain circumstances. Another explanation is that symptoms that may have been adaptive in our prehistoric ancestors are no longer so. Finally, our tendency to exaggerate the importance of certain situations—believing them to be a matter of life and death—overmobilizes our apparatus for dealing with threats and thus overrides normal functioning. It has been said that "evolution favors anxious genes." It is better to have "false positives" (false alarms) than "false negatives" (which miss the danger) in an ambiguous situation. One false negative—and you are eliminated from the gene pool. Thus, the cost of survival of the lineage may be a lifetime of discomfort.

To unravel the mystery of anxiety or fear reactions, a clinical example of acute anxiety will allow us to see what factors besides subjective anxiety may be present: A forty-year-old man had gone on a skiing trip near Denver and, while on the slopes, had begun to feel shortness of breath, profuse perspiration, faintness, and weakness. He also felt cold and had a feeling of instability. He had difficulty in focusing on any object and had waves of severe anxiety. Over all the symptoms hovered a sense of unreality. He was in such a state of collapse that he had to be taken from the slopes in a stretcher and rushed to a hospital. When no physical abnormalities were found, he was told he had an "acute anxiety attack."

What psychological disturbance could have been so strong as to produce a complete derangement of this man's physiological and psychological systems? The clue is found in his thoughts and imagery. Prior to the episode on the ski slope, he had the thought several times, "If I should have a heart attack up here, it would be almost impossible for me to get emergency care." Later when he started to have shortness of breath and other symptoms, he thought, "This must be a heart attack . . . this is what it's like to be dying." He then had an *image* of himself in a hospital bed, with an oxygen mask firmly placed on his face, intravenous infusions running through his arms, and doctors in white robes hovering over him. Each time he had this image, he experienced an acute increase in his symptoms. Thus, the missing piece in this puzzle is his *cognition*—his interpretation of normal physiological responses to exercise in a cold environment and a rarefied atmosphere as indicating a life-threatening disorder.

A more complete understanding of this man's misadventure must be sought in his total life situation. It appears that, since all of the tests showed there to be no organic disorder, the profound reaction occurred in the setting of some psychological predisposition. It is important to note that he had skied many times before on high mountains and had experienced symptoms that initially were similar to those described previously. When he was skiing in this air, he would start off with shortness of breath, which would often be accompanied by chest pain, particularly after he had been skiing for some time. He generally would feel cold and sweaty.

In this particular instance, however, his episode on the slopes was colored by a recent bereavement in his family. His brother, who was ten years older, had died several weeks previously from a heart attack. This man's thinking seemed to go something like this, "If it could happen to my brother, it could happen to me. . . . My brother got his heart attack after exercise and so could I." Hence, instead of making the most plausible explanation of his symptoms (as due to skiing in a cold, rarefied environment), he interpreted them as what he feared the most—namely, a fatal coronary attack.

When I saw the patient one week after the episode, he stated that he found his experience on the ski slope completely incomprehensible. To pinpoint precisely the nature of his thoughts, I asked him what went through his mind just before his full-blown attack. At first he had difficulty recovering the memory. Then he recalled having had a "flash" when he became aware of the chest symptoms: "This could be a heart attack—just like my brother's." Then he had an *image* of himself in an intensive care unit and another of himself receiving cardiac massage.

The crucial element in anxiety states, thus, is a cognitive process that may take the form of an automatic thought or image that appears rapidly, as if by reflex, after the initial stimulus (for example, shortness of breath), that seems plausible, and that is followed by a wave of anxiety. When the missing link is identified, then the "mysterious" arousal of anxiety can be understood. Of course, a specific thought or image is not always identifiable. In such cases it is possible, however, to infer that a cognitive set with a meaning relevant to danger has been activated.

Changing Concepts of Anxiety

Until recent years, anxiety disorders have been regarded as an expression of an emotion (anxiety) that has burst out of control. It seems probable that the emphasis on the emotional component may have come about because such feelings as anxiety and terror are the most dramatic features of this disorder. The other components, which may actually play a more important role in the genesis of this condition, are eclipsed by the subjective feelings. This emphasis on the feeling component has drawn the attention of psychiatrists and psychologists away from what may be the central feature of anxiety disorders—namely, a person's preoccupation with danger and his responses to it.

When we speak of "turning anxiety on its head," we mean looking at the role of a neglected part of the complex, viewing the phenomenon from the standpoint of the cognitive, or thinking, component—the "head," as it were. A patient's complaints generally center around feelings in the peripheral areas—sweaty palms, trembling of the hands, heart palpitations; and most research on anxiety has focused on systematically measuring these symptoms. Although it is true that patients generally do not volunteer much data about their thinking, particularly when they are in the throes of acute anxiety, we find, when we question a patient specifically, that his consciousness is saturated with thoughts and images of a threatening nature.

The anecdote of the skier with a pseudo heart attack illustrates an important feature of anxiety attacks: namely, that once the fear reaction has started, it tends to build on itself. Clinical observations suggest that the autonomic arousal produced in this way is interpreted by the patient as a sign of serious physical or mental derangement—an interpretation that leads to further arousal. This mechanism is observed in everyday life when the anxiety-prone person experiences a rapid heart rate after exercise or an arousing event. The skier had characteristically been hypervigilant in regard to physical symptoms. During the skiing episode, his normal physical response to moderate exercise alarmed him. The patient interpreted his physiological symptoms as signaling a medical emergency. The interpretation of a possible heart attack led to a fear of death, which triggered further physiological symptoms. Thus, a vicious cycle was established (see figure 1.1 and chapter 3, page 46.)

Distinguishing Anxiety, Fear, Phobias, and Panic

The definitions of *fear* and *anxiety* are often confounded, the words being used interchangeably for the same general concept, even though there are obvious advantages to using two distinct words to designate separate though related phenomena. In order better to understand the meanings of these terms, consider their dictionary definitions and derivations. The traditional meanings are more useful in clarifying the semantic and conceptual confusion than are some contemporary distinctions made by behavioral scientists.

The word *fear* comes from the Old English word *faer* (*Oxford English Dictionary*, 1933), which meant "sudden calamity or danger." It is currently defined as "an agitated foreboding often of some real or specific peril" (*Webster's Third International Dictionary*, 1981) and as "the possibility that something dreaded or unwanted may occur" (*Standard College Dictionary*, 1963). These definitions underscore several connotations of the word *fear;*

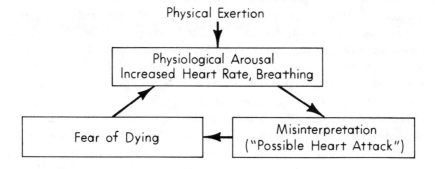

Figure 1.1
Vicious cycle: "Physical" threat.

it points to the possible occurrence of an "unwanted" or calamitous event; the event has not yet occurred (that is, it is in the future); and the individual is concerned (agitated foreboding) about the event. Fear, then refers to the *appraisal* that there is actual or potential danger in a given situation. It is a cognitive process as opposed to an emotional reaction.

Anxiety, on the other hand, is defined as a "tense emotional state" (Funk & Wagnalls, 1963) and is "often marked by such physical symptoms as tension, tremor, sweating, palpitation and increased pulse rate" *(Webster's Third International Dictionary,* 1981). The term *anxiety* comes from the Latin word *anxius,* and its usage dates back as early as 1525. The Latin term was defined as a condition of agitation and distress. The stem of *anxious—anx* —comes from another Latin word, *angere,* which means "to choke" or "to strangle." The word *anxius* probably referred to the choking sensation frequently experienced by anxious individuals (Lewis 1970).

Phobia refers to a specific kind of fear and is defined as "an exaggerated and often disabling fear" *(Webster's Third International Dictionary,* 1981). A phobia is also characterized by an intense desire to avoid the feared situation, and evokes anxiety when one is exposed to that situation. The word is derived from the Greek work *phobos* for "flight," which was in turn derived from the name of a Greek deity, Phobos, who was able to provoke fear (and panic) in his enemies. The Roman encyclopedist Celsus coined the term *hydrophobia* in the first century to describe a common symptom of rabies. Hippocrates wrote two of the earliest clinical descriptions of phobic men: a man who feared nightfall and also a cat phobic. The first nonmedical writing about phobias appeared in the thirteenth century when demonphobias and theophobias were described by philosophers. The term *phobia* was not introduced into psychiatric literature until the nineteenth century.

The clinical descriptions of phobias have not changed much since their earliest descriptions. Tully and Demosthenes had stage fright. Augustus Caesar could not sit in the dark. In *The Merchant of Venice,* Shakespeare described a cat phobic. Pascal, a mathematician, was said to suffer from what is known today as agoraphobia. C. Westphal (1871–72) wrote three clinical descriptions of agoraphobia. The clinical syndrome of agoraphobia has not changed radically since Westphal's writing.

Panic is defined as a "sudden overpowering fright . . . accompanied by increasing or frantic attempts to secure safety" *(Webster's Third International Dictionary,* 1981). The word, which was in use as early as 1603, derives from the name of the Greek deity Panikos, the god of woods and shepherds, who was regarded as the cause of panic among the Persians at Marathon and, by the Greeks, as the cause of any sudden, groundless fear.

ANXIETY AND FEAR

Anxiety may be distinguished from fear in that the former is an emotional process while fear is a cognitive one. Fear involves the intellectual appraisal of a threatening stimulus; anxiety involves the emotional response to that appraisal. When a person says he fears something, he is generally referring to a set of circumstances that are not present but may occur at some point in the future. At this point the fear is said to be "latent." When a person has anxiety he experiences a subjectively unpleasant emotional state characterized by unpleasant subjective feelings, such as tension or nervousness, and by physiological symptoms like heart palpitations, tremor, nausea, and dizziness. A fear is *activated* when a person is exposed, either physically or psychologically, to the stimulus situation he considers threatening. When the fear becomes activated, he experiences anxiety. Fear then, is the appraisal of danger; anxiety is the unpleasant feeling state evoked when fear is stimulated. In addition to anxiety, a variety of symptoms referable to the autonomic and the somatic nervous systems may be provoked concurrently.

PHOBIAS AND PANIC ATTACKS

A phobia refers to a specific object of fear. Initially, a person is afraid of a specific type of situation or event (for example, heights, closed spaces, or deep water). When in the situation, he is acutely afraid of the consequences (falling, suffocating, or drowning). When a phobia or fear is activated, the individual's reaction may range from mild anxiety to panic. The objects of phobias can range from small animals to natural occurrences such as thunderstorms or to events in the social arena, such as speaking in front of large groups or going to parties. The main quality of a phobia is that it involves the appraisal of a high degree of risk in a situation that is relatively safe.

An example will clarify the complex interrelations among these terms. A person with a fear of small animals perceives these animals to be dangerous. However, he does not experience anxiety until he finds himself exposed to a small animal or imagines himself in such a situation. The presence of, say, a mouse on the scene activates the fear, and the person may think, "The mouse may bite me and I might get rabies and die," or, "The mouse may bite me and I might faint and become embarrassed in front of all these people." The person who perceives this threat as overwhelming may have a panic attack. The concept of danger arises from the possible consequences of contact with the animal. Before a person has contact with the mouse, the fear is latent. Once in the presence of the mouse, the fear is activated; and all the unpleasant affective and physiological symptoms associated with panic attack are aroused.

Similarly, a person who is phobic of certain social situations such as attending parties or giving lectures is less afraid of the situations themselves than of possible consequences of being in them. The social phobic is afraid, for example, that, in a social situation, he will make a fool of himself or "go out of control" and embarrass himself. This person might feel jittery or shaky, sweat profusely, and experience any or all the uncomfortable affective and physiological symptoms of anxiety or panic.

Panic is an intense, acute state of anxiety associated with other dramatic physiological, motor, and cognitive symptoms. The physiological correlates of panic are an intensified version of those of anxiety—that is, rapid pulse, dizziness, cold and profuse sweating, and tremor. In addition, one has a sense of impending catastrophe, pervasive inhibitions, and an overwhelming desire to flee or get help.

"REALISTIC" AND "UNREALISTIC" FEARS

Making a distinction between affective response and cognitive process resolves semantic contradictions like "realistic" or "neurotic anxiety," "rational anxiety" or "irrational anxiety." It is illogical to qualify an emotion or a feeling state with adjectives ("rational" or "irrational," for example) that are usually applied to ideas or concepts. One can label a fear as being realistic or unrealistic, rational or irrational. A fear is realistic if based on a sensible assumption, logic and reasoning, and objective observation. It is unrealistic if based on fallacious assumptions and faulty reasoning and is contrary to observation. Anxiety, on the other hand, cannot be labeled realistic or unrealistic because it refers to an affective response not to a process of evaluating reality.

Freud made a distinction between realistic anxiety and neurotic anxiety (1915–17). He regarded realistic anxiety as "something very rational and intelligible" and "a reaction to the perception of external danger"—that is, of an injury which is expected and foreseen. He regarded anxiety as being "connected with the flight reflex" and as "a manifestation of the self-preservative instinct" (pp. 393–94). According to Freud, neurotic anxiety results from the perception of internal danger (1926). He proposed that neurotic anxiety is an affective reaction that occurs when unconscious impulses threaten to become conscious, and results from the fear of the consequences if the defense mechanisms fail and allow the demands of the id to push a person into impulsive instinctual action.

HOCH'S PARADOX

While a large proportion of writers concur with Freud's concept, some, like P. Hoch, have challenged the logic of his formulation. Hoch posed the question, "If anxiety is a signal that repressed instinctual forces have begun to erupt, why should the alarm burn down the house?" (1950, p. 108).

Hoch's paradox applies especially to cases in which the fear syndrome interferes with a person's ability to cope effectively with a dangerous situation, and thus greatly increases the danger. There are times, for instance, when a person freezes in the face of physical threat. Picture a young man driving a car on a crowded metropolitan street. He signals to make a left turn. As he enters the intersection, he hears the blaring of a car horn. He feels acute anxiety and automatically slams on the brakes. The car is hit from the right. In this example, the automatic defensive response interfered with his ability to execute an effective coping response. If he had accelerated rather than stopped the automobile, he would not have been hit. The freeze reaction, associated with anxiety, was clearly not adaptive in this situation.

The preceding example not only illustrates that fear can interfere with the execution of an effective coping response, but also demonstrates that subjective anxiety is not a necessary condition for the execution of the coping response. In fact, the driver of the car could have executed the appropriate response in this situation if his skillful behavior had not been disrupted by his primitive inhibitory response and the distraction of the anxiety. Similarly, an athlete can readily mobilize his resources in a split-second movement to make a net shot or catch a runner off base—without experiencing anxiety. The competitive situation is sufficient to activate the central nervous system rapidly. It therefore seems that anxiety is neither a sufficient nor a necessary condition for the activation of an instrumental coping response. It can even hinder the execution of an adaptive response to a threatening situation.

Future Danger and Present Danger

I have previously emphasized the essential future orientation of fear (Beck 1967). A particular noxious event may be about to happen—but it has not happened yet. Or, it may be happening, but the ultimate dire consequence has not yet occurred. A person's fear is activated as he gets closer to the threatening situation. Indeed, he may become fearful simply by talking or thinking about the dangerous situation—or by imagining it. Dwelling on the fear makes the threatening situation more salient and more imminent: that is, it brings a distant danger into the here-and-now.

There is often a notable change in a person's reactions between anticipation of confronting a danger and actually facing it. As one enters the "dangerous" situation, emergency patterns—such as flight, inhibition, or fainting—may be activated. A medical student became increasingly fearful and anxious as the date for a final examination approached. As she sat down and started to read the examination questions, there was an enormous leap in her degree of fearfulness. She thought, "I don't know how I can answer these questions." Her mind became "blank," and she could not focus on the questions. Her anxiety then built up so far that she could not tolerate it and felt impelled to flee from the room. Direct confrontation with the threat triggered an automatic escape mechanism.

The transition from anticipation of noxious physical trauma to its actual experience is illustrated by a young man who nervously awaited some dental work. When he was finally in the dentist's chair and the dentist was drilling his teeth, he had vivid visual images of the drilling penetrating his skull. He began to sweat profusely and started to faint. Or, another young man was very apprehensive about giving a public speech. When he was finally in the auditorium and facing the audience, he suddenly "choked up" and found it extremely difficult to utter a word.

In those examples, it is clear that immersion in the dangerous situation may provoke certain automatic behavior that was not evoked in usual life situations. In the case of the medical student taking an examination, there was not only a sharp increase in anxiety but also mental blocking and mobilization to escape. The dental phobic had a profound reaction of the parasympathetic nervous system (sweating and fainting). These examples suggest that the disabling and disturbing symptoms, such as blocking and fainting, represent survival mechanisms that were once useful, say, in prehistoric times for mitigating the extreme consequences of an attack. In actuality, these primitive reactions only accentuate the problem and, indeed, make the individual even more fearful of confronting the situation in the future—lest the primitive response be repeated.

The Function of Anxiety

ADAPTATIONAL ASPECTS

When we consider such reactions as anxiety, inhibition, blanking out, fainting, it is not at all clear what useful function they serve. However, when we regard these symptoms as having served a function in the evolution of our species, their presence begins to make sense. Terms such as *teleonomic* and *adaptational* are used to refer to behaviors that have had survival value in an evolutionary sense (Lorenz 1980). In the same regard, the term *adaptational* may also be applied to behavior that promotes the major goals of the organism—survival, growth, reproduction, maintenance, mastery.

Since there is continuous pressure to engage in self-enhancing behavior, the organism with its overall systems of checks and balances depends on the "fear reaction" as a check on overly expansive or careless patterns. Aggressive behavior relevant to exploration or competitiveness, for example, could, if unchecked, lead to injury or death. The individual has a set of such automatic regulators that deter him from advancing too far. An example of such an inhibitor is the "visual cliff reflex" (Marks 1969). It has been observed that many infant mammals, including humans, show an immobility response when they come to the edge of a ledge. This inhibition then serves as a restraint on further advance into the danger zone. Such a "regulator" often persists into adulthood and is manifested by a sense of dizziness and physical inhibition as one approaches the edge of a cliff.

When we consider the common fears of childhood—falling, being injured, drowning, suffocating, the dark, deep water, and so on—we can see that some of these at least may serve to deter the child from venturing into unfamiliar or dangerous places before he has the requisite abilities and skills (for example, depth perception, ability to swim). The interpersonal fears, such as fear of strangers or of separation from a caretaker, may be conceived of in similar terms. The growing child experiences gratification as he develops self-sufficiency. But, if unchecked, the child may wander into unknown areas that have as-yet-undefined potential dangers. Thus, most children have a set of engrained fears of being abandoned or of getting lost that are triggered before a child has traveled too far from the caretaker.

How are those teleonomic mechanisms expressed in stage fright, interpersonal anxiety, agoraphobia? The fear of negative evaluation seems to serve as a deterrent to behavior that will alienate other people. Ultimately, alienation of others could produce abandonment by the kin group or overt disapproval by others. Thus, the individual with stage fright is mobilized, on the one hand, to obtain gratification from being approved by the audience but, on the other, is apprehensive about the possibility of experiencing the pain of disapproval. The anticipated pain of disapproval is sufficient to trigger the "vulnerability mode," which—by its mechanisms of inhibition of speech and action—is designed to prevent "reckless" behavior (chapter 4). The person with agoraphobia, in contrast, has a complex set of fears revolving around the notion of an *internal* catastrophe, such as a heart attack, loss of control, or mental derangement. Because the individual believes he cannot cope with these dangers without the help of key figures, he feels more frightened when he is away from a potential caretaker.

In a sense, the fears operate as a warning of the individual's vulnerability to social sanctions (stage fright, social anxiety) and to physical dangers (panic attacks). It should be noted, however, that fears go in both directions: they serve to discourage not only hazardous, unduly aggressive behavior but also regressive, childish behavior. Thus, the individual who avoids situations of risk is fearful of being subjected to the taunts of his peers. The full play of the system of counterbalances is seen in stage fright, when a person is simultaneously inhibited from self-expression for fear of "appearing foolish" and frightened by the prospect of appearing inhibited and immature because of his fears.

ANXIETY AS A STRATEGY IN RESPONSE TO THREAT

Anxiety is a dramatic experience that generally overshadows other components of the threat response. Human beings are so designed as to experience an intensely unpleasant emotion (anxiety) in response to present danger and are strongly moved by the experience to take steps to reduce it and to prevent its recurrence. Furthermore, patients, clinicians, and theoreticians are inclined to highlight the unpleasant experience of anxiety as the central overriding element in pathological conditions such as panic attack. Anxiety, however, is not *the* pathological process in so-called anxiety disorders any more than pain or fever constitute the pathological process in an infection or injury. We should not allow nature's mechanism for dramatizing the feeling of anxiety to mislead us into believing that this most salient subjective experience plays the central role in the so-called anxiety disorders.

Anxiety acts as an attention getter. It draws attention away from other concerns or preoccupations and onto this unpleasant subjective experience. The experience is generally sufficiently unpleasant that the individual wants to reduce it. He does this by adopting a *shift in strategy:* for example, from advancing into an unsafe area to skirting around it; from standing in the path of an advancing vehicle to jumping out of the way. Also, by alerting the individual to the notion that he can be hurt, anxiety induces him to put the brakes on "imprudent" action or to initiate defensive behavior. Measures that are successful in reducing the danger will generally reduce the anxiety. If these measures do not reduce the danger, the anxiety generally persists.

The function of anxiety may be likened to that of pain. The experience of pain impels a person to do something in order to terminate or reduce the pain—by stopping whatever activity is producing an injury, by taking measures to repair the injury, and so on. Pain, however, is not the disease (it is not, say, appendicitis but may be a sign of it): and similarly, anxiety is not the cause of psychological disturbance. In the anxiety disorders, the unremitting generation of anxiety represents a persistent, ineffective mechanism designed to impel the organism to reduce the supposed danger that is activating the anxiety response. When, however, the problem is not an actual danger but a misperception or exaggeration of the danger, the experience of anxiety is inappropriate for initiating remedial action. If the danger is nonexistent or exaggerated, the individual has no way to head it off.

Thus, the main problem in the anxiety disorders is not in the generation of anxiety but in the overactive cognitive patterns (schemas) relevant to danger that are continually structuring external and/or internal experiences as a sign of danger (Beck 1971).

Survival Mechanisms

The phenomenon of anxiety represents but one of many separate but interrelated "strategies" for dealing with threat and thus should be analyzed within the total framework of an organism's responses to danger. In the broadest sense, these responses include not only those patterns generally associated with anxiety but also the class of hostile behaviors associated with anger. W. B. Cannon (1929) formulated the well-known paradigm of the "fight-flight reaction" to designate the characteristic physiological patterns of response to threat. The individual, however is equipped with a much broader range of specific protective mechanisms, each designed to deal with specific dangers. The automatic responses include protecting against the entry of noxious substances or ejecting them, defending against an external blow, inhibiting one's own actions, fainting, and reaching to others for help. A more complete term for the survival strategies would be the "fight-flight-freeze-faint reaction." Because these wide-ranging behaviors are primitive (in the sense that they may be observed in other primates) and involuntary, occur as if by reflex, and appear to be a basic line of defense against danger, I have labeled them "primal reactions."

REFLEXES

One class of automatic reactions consists of discrete reflexes designed to ward off or eject potentially harmful agents. These reflexes include eyeblink; gagging, coughing, bronchospasm; vomiting and diarrhea. A more complex set of reflexive behaviors is designed to defend against the possibility of trauma to the body as a whole. We are exposed to a variety of threats, such as being struck by inanimate objects (falling debris, missiles, and so on) and attacked by living creatures. The response to the threat of being hit by a moving object includes such actions as ducking, dodging, flinching, retracting, and stiffening.

DEFENSIVE PATTERNS

The most general external physical "attacks" that we encounter in everyday life actually occur in a medical or dental setting and often elicit maladaptive defensive behavior. Thus, procedures such as palpation of the abdomen generally produce an automatic tightening of the abdominal muscles. Similarly, dental work may elicit stiffening of the jaws or gagging. Many people show a curious response to injections and especially to procedures involving withdrawing blood: they experience a pronounced drop in blood pressure, profuse sweating, and faintness. This response, markedly present in blood phobias, can perhaps best be understood as an archaic mechanism designed to minimize blood loss (and possibly reduce mobility) when a person is subjected to a penetrating, unavoidable attack.

Other automatic protective reactions operate to curtail a person's progress into a danger zone. As pointed out previously, a person may automatically recoil or stiffen when he perceives himself to be at the edge of a cliff. In a related way, he will automatically grasp a stationary object if he senses he may be falling or drowning. Finally, he may automatically cry for help and grab another person for support when in danger of falling, drowning, or being attacked.

The defensive structure may also be analyzed in terms of the level of intentionality involved in a specific protective reaction. The instant response consists of the discrete reflexes involving the somatic nervous system: eyelid reflex, coughing, flinching, and freezing. Although these reflexive actions are carried out by "voluntary" muscles, they are automatic and involuntary. Their adaptative value depends on their speed and their ability to bypass the slower-acting volitional structures.

Another type of response, geared to less imperative dangers, is more gradual and involves the autonomic nervous system. This set of operations involves nausea, vomiting, diarrhea. These responses are more gradual in terms of their onset and build-up than are reflexes such as coughing and gagging, which are designed to deflect more vital threats—namely, to the airway. The more gradual gastrointestinal responses, in contrast, can provide adequate protection against the danger of absorption of noxious substances without requiring immediate action.

The most common type of primal response depends on the generation of unpleasant subjective sensations which prompt an intentional action designed to reduce a danger. The various behaviors instigated by anxiety fall into this category. Thus, the anxiety evoked when a person perceives that he is not in complete control of the vehicle he is driving may induce him to reduce his speed until he again feels in control. Similarly, the sense of faintness or dizziness evoked by being at the top of a tall ladder or on the edge of a cliff may induce one to get a better grip or to back off to a safer position.

Another type of "protective" reaction associated with anxiety is illustrated by panic attacks. This condition is generally characterized by a fear of impending internal disaster (heart attack, stroke, mental derangement), by a sense of having lost control over physical and mental functions, as well as by acute severe anxiety. The sense of being unable to think or act is a particularly disabling feature. Moreover, since the "danger" is internal, the individual does not have available resources to eliminate it and is swept by a sense of helplessness. But he can turn to a caretaker for help. Thus, some types of panic attack may be viewed as an alarm evoked to ward off an overwhelming danger and as a stimulus to escape from the situation and seek help. Other types of panic attack are also evoked by the fact of an "overwhelming" external threat. This condition is seen clinically when a phobic person is suddenly exposed to a phobic situation. For example, someone with claustrophobia may have a catastrophic reaction ("being suffocated") when put in a closed space. In these cases, the solution is simple: get out of the situation and avoid it in the future. Hence, the need for help is not as imperative as when a person feels threatened by an overwhelming *internal* derangement, as in the agoraphobic syndrome.

Chapter 2

Symptoms and Their
Significance

Systems and Symptoms

The anxiety disorders (as well as depression) can best be understood in terms of the functioning of the total organism rather than as a single-etiology disease, such as herpes or measles. The specific groups of symptoms associated with anxiety, for example, correspond to the functions of specific primal systems and subsystems (cognitive, affective, behavioral, and physiological), which are integrated into the master system—namely, the psychobiological or organismic totality. These component systems are not isolated from each other, and their operations are generally coordinated and integrated by the master system. The master system is designed to carry out certain objectives (such as self-preservation, feeding, or breeding), and the specific systems operate together to implement that "master plan." These objectives are labeled "adaptational" in that they are derived from evolutionary principles relevant to survival of a particular lineage in a given environment.

The operation of both the master system and the component systems varies according to demands at a particular time. Thus, specific primal responses to life-threatening situations (such as fight, flight, freeze, or faint) will differ from each other as well as from responses involved in feeding and breeding—even though the same system is employed. Emergencies involve total mobilization of all systems for action; whereas in feeding, certain subsystems are activated, and others deactivated. In flight, for instance, the motor apparatus and the sympathetic subsystems are highly activated, and the parasympathetic subsystem is largely deactivated; whereas in feeding, the parasympathetic is selectively activated, and the motor apparatus is selectively deactivated.

Under ordinary conditions there is smooth coordination of the various systems as the organism switches flexibly from one function to another depending on the demands of the situation and of the master program. The specific operations of the systems and the subsystems vary from one moment to the next in accordance with the operating programs.

Integrated responses generally make sense in terms of situational requirements and thus appear to be controlled by a reality-oriented program. Suppose we see a bear, a baby, and a mosquito. We do not hug the bear, swat the baby, or run away from the mosquito (see Leventhal 1982). The operation of our apparatus proceeds according to a comprehensible design, not mindlessly or at random but under the control of the perceptual-cognitive component. The cognitive system integrates input, selects an appropriate plan, and thus activates the rest of the apparatus. The cognitive apparatus draws on the eyes and ears and other sense organs to construct meaningful patterns at the perceptual level. We hear and see relationships rather than absolute sounds and light-waves. (In fact, we do not have receptors for all the stimuli in the environment and integrate only a small proportion of them.) The relationships or patterns likely to be most salient are those that are relevant to our "vital interests"—for example, survival and sex. Hence, in understanding anxiety disorders, we should think of the symptoms not as foreign experiences but as expressions of basic (primal) psychological functions.

In terms of our present focus, then, we can say that in the presence of a threat, the cognitive apparatus makes selective appraisals of the environmental configurations and the available coping resources, determines whether there is a clear and present danger, and sets in motion the sequence of affective, behavioral, and physiological subsystems. The affective component—in this case, anxiety—serves to speed up the reaction by enhancing the sense of urgency. The behavioral component consists of both activated action patterns and inhibitions. The physiological system includes the autonomic components that "service" somatic mobilization.

One of the problems in anxiety disorder and other disorders is that the flexible switch from one operation to another—for example, from flight to feeding—is impaired. For example, a person remains geared for defensive action long after a danger has passed. Furthermore, an anxious person overreacts or reacts inappropriately to fresh encounters. Thus, one may perceive maximal danger when it is only minimal or nonexistent. In other words, one has not slipped completely out of the "danger mode."

A good deal has been written about the lack of concordance of various measures of anxiety. The expectation that there is a single monolithic system for dealing with danger, and that the various systems should show an equivalent amount of activation, is based on a simplistic notion of the nature of the response to threat. It seems more likely that, in order to prepare to deal effectively with danger to life or limb, a person draws on each system. The composition of the operations shifts as the sequence progresses from sounding an alert, to defining the danger, to assessing and selecting appropriate coping strategies, to mobilizing the appropriate motor apparatus, and finally, to providing appropriate autonomic innervation to support the somatic mobilization. As feedback is integrated, the operation of the master system and the component systems continues to shift according to the demands of the situation.

In addition to the direct response to danger, certain homeostatic mechanisms are necessary to provide temperature control, to regulate vasomotor and cardiac functions, to adjust energy output and so on. Thus, to understand the response of the organism to threat, we need to have a comprehensive view of the individualized actions and interactions of the cognitive, affective, physiological, and behavioral subsystems to a given threat at a given time. We also have to recognize that the operations of each system may shift from one moment to the next.

The picture increases in complexity when we consider that different strategic operations (modes) may be activated concurrently. Thus, an individual confronted with a danger may have to decide between "Should I retreat from danger?" and "Am I capable of performing competently despite the danger?" For example, in public speaking, the primal mode may be "self-protection," whereas the person's conscious intentions may be concerned with adequate performance; consequently, the speaker may be caught between the operation of both sets.

The primal mechanism tends to operate as long as the person feels vulnerable to a present "danger," so he may struggle unsuccessfully to override or inactivate it. Thus, we can see the paradoxical phenomenon of the public speaker actively attempting to perform skillfully in the face of a threat (such as possible disparagement by the audience) and, at the same time, having his performance undermined by the action of the primal systems. While he is attempting to speak, for instance, his primal systems are geared to self-doubt (cognitive), stiffness and aphonia (behavioral inhibition), anxiety generation (affective), wish to escape (motivational), and rapid heart rate and breathing (physiological). In this situation, the basal mechanism is responding not to the person's particular wishes and goals but to the threat of negative evaluation and ineptness. There is reciprocal interaction between how effective the individual believes and expects himself to be and the degree of mobilization of the primal self-protection mode. Whereas the workings of the primal defense mode undermine the sense of efficacy, an increase in self-confidence tends to modify the sense of vulnerability and consequently the defensive systems. The symptoms of an anxiety disorder, thus, are an inappropriate anachronistic response based on an excessive estimate of the degree of danger in a given situation and on underestimation of the person's ability to perform adequately.

SYMPTOMS AND FUNCTIONS

The symptoms denoting an anxiety disorder may be divided into cognitive, affective, behavioral, and physiological, referring to four functional systems that are coordinated to produce adaptive responses to situations of danger. Anxiety disorders represent a malfunction of the system for activating and terminating a defensive response to a threat (prolonged anxiety)—a nonadaptive response that can be understood as inappropriate domination by a primal mechanism (such as flight, freeze, or collapse) over the more adaptive mode (such as social competency). The activation of the primal response to a threat such as possible rejection by an audience undermines more mature functioning (for example, speaking in public) and thus increases the actual threat. The symptoms are expressions of the excessive functioning of a person's systems, or of an interference with the function of a particular system.

Table 2.1 lists many of the "cognitive symptoms" associated with anxiety disorders. It will be apparent that many of these symptoms are intensified versions of normal functions—for example self-consciousness or hypervigilance. Other symptoms appear to be the result of inhibition of the normal functions (loss of concentration, blocking). Still other symptoms denote erosion of voluntary control over processes ordinarily under such control (loss of objectivity and reassessing).

The sensory-perceptual symptoms appear to be an offshoot of interference with normal cognitive function, possibly a result of cognitive strain (see Beck 1984a). Thus, when the integration of visual impressions with the cognitive schemas is unbalanced, and the individual experiences perceptual aberrations, which are readily recognized as such and have an "as if" quality: "Things *seem* to be different, but I know they aren't." Many agoraphobic patients report, for instance, that, after they have been looking at the broad fluorescent light in a supermarket, objects seem to be split

TABLE 2.1

Cognitive Symptoms in Anxiety Disorders

1. *Sensory—Perceptual*
   "Mind": hazy, cloudy, foggy, dazed
   Objects seem blurred/distant
   Environment seems different/unreal
   Feeling of unreality
   Self-conscious
   Hypervigilant

2. *Thinking Difficulties*
   Can't recall important things
   Confused
   Unable to control thinking
   Difficulty in concentration
   Distractibility
   Blocking
   Difficulty in reasoning
   Loss of objectivity and perspective

3. *Conceptual*
   Cognitive distortion
   Fear of losing control
   Fear of not being able to cope
   Fear of physical injury/death
   Fear of mental disorder
   Fear of negative evaluations
   Frightening visual images
   Repetitive fearful ideation

horizontally and the separate parts are dissociated. This type of symptom is significant not because of its severity or its interference with general function, but because it is unfamiliar and not immediately controllable, and thus suggests to the susceptible person that he may be "losing his mind." In fact, such perceptual distortions may occur at times in non-anxious people, who generally ignore them. The vulnerable individual, however, attributes pathological significance to symptoms, such as visual distortions or dissociations, and these fears may provoke a panic attack.

Self-consciousness is familiar to most people when they are the center of attention and feel apprehensive about it. However, in anxiety disorders, this symptom may be evoked even when the patient is not the center of attention.

Thinking difficulties may be produced by a variety of factors. Cognitive inhibition may interfere with recall and produce blocking. In addition, the focusing of attention on the notion of danger may automatically produce "tunnel vision" which blocks out extraneous (that is, not danger-related) ideation. Further, one's cognitive capacity may be so taxed by coping with the "danger" that little capacity remains to satisfy other demands on cognitive processing. The strained cognitive capacity may also be involved in the difficulties in reasoning and in maintaining objectivity toward the symptoms associated with anxiety.

The conceptual problems are related to the "usurpation" of the cognitive processes by the primal mode and reflect preoccupation with the sense of vulnerability and danger. The focus on fears, loss of control, and inability to cope are an expression of the cognitive set of "danger" and "vulnerability."

The affective symptoms are often the most dramatic in the anxiety disorders and are responsible for giving this syndrome its name. So much importance has been ascribed to these symptoms that whole theories have been built around them (for example, Hullian learning theory). In fact, two major schools (psychoanalysis and behavior therapy) attribute major importance to anxiety in the genesis of psychological disturbances. It is a matter of controversy whether other symptoms of the threat syndrome are simply manifestations of anxiety. It is our contention that anxiety is just one of several built-in mechanisms for coping with danger (chapter 1). The qualitative experiences of anxiety may differ from one situation to another and also over time: thus, a person may simply feel edgy at the prospect of taking an exam but may be terrified at the thought of asking the boss for a raise (see table 2.2).

The types of symptoms of anxiety will vary according to the nature of the problem. If it is immediate and severe, the person may experience panic. If the problem is chronic, he is more likely to experience uneasiness or a "wound-up" feeling.

The behavioral symptoms, as we will discuss later, generally reflect either the hyperactivity of the behavioral system or else its inhibition. Tonic immobility is an expression of the freeze reaction, whereas restless behavior and tremors represent the body's mobilization for action. The

TABLE 2.2

Typical Affective Adjectives

Edgy	Fearful
Impatient	Scared
Uneasy	Frightened
Nervous	Alarmed
Tense	Terrified
Wound-up	Jittery
Anxious	Jumpy

shaking and trembling may represent the preparation for survival behavior prior to the formulation of a clear-cut strategy (see table 2.3).

The physiological symptoms reflect a readiness of the total organism for self-protection. The sympathetic branch of the autonomic nervous system facilitates an active coping strategy. Thus, increased heart rate and blood pressure help a person to defend himself actively or to escape. The parasympathetic symptoms, in contrast, facilitate the strategy of collapse, ultimately an expression of the notion that the person is helpless and has no active coping strategies for dealing with a threat (see table 2.4). Some physiological symptoms result from behavioral reactions; for example, numbness and tingling sensations in the extremities and faintness may be caused by over-breathing (hyperventilation syndrome).

MAJOR REACTIONS: MOBILIZATION, INHIBITION, DEMOBILIZATION

The organism's response to threat can be discussed in terms of three major types of reaction. *Mobilization* prepares the individual for active defense. *Inhibition* (an expression of the freezing reaction) is designed to curtail "risky behavior" and to buy time to determine an appropriate strategy. *Demobilization* denotes de-activation of the motor apparatus and reflects the sense of helplessness in the face of an overwhelming threat.

1. *Mobilization* may be represented physiologically by activation of the systems for purposes of action. This pattern may be observed as follows in the various systems:
   a. *Cognitive:* The individual is hypervigilant for any cues relevant to danger. The threshold for unexpected or loud stimuli is lowered. The *content* of ideation deals with dangerous events past, present, and future and may take the form of repetitive automatic

TABLE 2.3

Behavioral Symptoms

Inhibition
Tonic immobility
Flight
Avoidance
Speech dysfluency
Impaired coordination
Restlessness
Postural collapse
Hyperventilation

TABLE 2.4

Symptoms According to Physiological Systems

Cardiovascular	
Palpitations	Faintness (P)
Heart racing	Actual fainting (P)
Increased blood pressure	Decreased blood pressure (P)
	Decreased pulse rate (P)

Respiratory	
Rapid breathing	Shallow breathing
Difficulty in getting air in	Lump in throat
Shortness of breath	Choking sensation
Pressure on chest	Spasm of bronchi (P)
Rapid breathing	Gasping

Neuromuscular	
Increased reflexes	Fidgeting
Startle reaction	Pacing
Eyelid twitching	Strained face
Insomnia	Unsteady
Spasm	Generalized weakness
Tremors	Wobbly legs
Rigidity	Clumsy motions

Gastrointestinal	
Abdominal pain (P)	Heartburn (P)
Loss of appetite	Abdominal discomfort
Revulsion toward food	Vomiting (P)
Nausea (P)	

Urinary Tract	
Pressure to urinate (P)	
Frequency of urination (P)	

Skin	
Face flushed	Generalized sweating
Face pale	"Hot and cold spells"
Localized sweating (palm region)	Itching

Note: (P) Represents parasympathetic symptom

thoughts. The person has frequent *visual images* with a content of personal adversity and is also likely to have nightmares.

b. *Affective.* The emotional symptoms may vary from edginess and tension to terror.

c. *Behavioral.* There is an increase in muscular activity even when sitting. This may be manifested by grimacing, by continuous movements of hands and often the rest of body, and by chain smoking, sighing, shaking, tremors, and pacing back and forth.

d. *Physiological.* The organ systems show increased sympathetic activity—for example, increased heart rate and blood pressure, and sweating.

2. *Inhibition* involves active interference with normal cognitive and behavioral functions.

a. *Cognitive.* There is selective blocking of various functions—especially when a function is being evaluated or challenged. There may be interference with recall of vital information (content of a speech, responses to a test, people's names, phone numbers). Reasoning, concentration, objectivity, perspective are impeded. The blocking and impediments may be varied over time as though a switch is being turned on and off. The "clouding of consciousness," "mental blurring," and sense of "passing out" may also be attributed to cognitive inhibition. This constriction of consciousness may intensify to the point that the patient believes that he is about to faint.

b. *Behavioral.* There is inhibition of spontaneous movements, especially of facial muscles, so that the person may present a blank face. Some rigidity of facial muscles is apparent. There is also general muscle rigidity, so that movements are jerky and clumsy and activity requiring skill, such as playing a musical instrument, is impeded. There is often a problem with phonation and with dysfluencies such as stuttering, choking on words, or even partial mutism.

3. *Demobilization.* The symptoms of collapse occur most obviously in an overreaction to blood and injury but may be apparent in other reactions. The main symptoms are weakness and faintness. The main parasympathetic symptoms—most prominent in the blood-injury phobias—are a lowering of the blood pressure and heart rate that may culminate in fainting.

FREE-FLOATING ANXIETY—FACT OR ARTIFACT?

A physician in the emergency room of a local hospital examines a patient. The patient's body is drenched with sweat, his breathing is rapid and shallow. He states that his heart is racing and that he can't catch his breath. His face is contorted with terror. He complains of severe abdominal pain and has some abdominal spasm. The physician considers the diagnosis of an acute appendicitis but finds no corroborative evidence. In view of a family history of a dissecting aortic aneurysm, she briefly considers that diagnosis. After she is certain no physical disease is causing the attack, she diagnoses "panic disorder" and notes in the patient's file that he experienced an acute anxiety attack characterized by "free-floating anxiety."

Observation of such patients as this, who have experienced anxiety in the absence of objective danger, has led to the notion of "free-floating anxiety." Behavioral, psychoanalytic, and biochemical theorists have fastened onto this presumed phenomenon and have advanced complex explanations to account for it. Behaviorists (for example, J. Wolpe [1969]) postulate that a patient will react to a neutral stimulus with acute anxiety if that stimulus has once been paired with an aversive or threatening stimulus. Freud (1915–17) initially proposed that free-floating anxiety results from the accumulation of sexual tension. His later view (1926) regarded anxiety as a reaction to the threat of unconscious impulses breaking into consciousness. A number of biochemical explanations also assume the validity of the "free-floating" concept. E. Kraepelin (1907) suggested that anxiety is a disorder of the nerves. More recently, proceeding from Kraepelin's work, other writers have proposed that anxiety represents an imbalance in the autonomic nervous system. F. N. Pitts, Jr. (1969) attributed anxiety to excessive lactic acid or deficient calcium. Further studies in this area (Levitt 1972) challenged this theory, but recent research has provided some support (Klein 1981).

Although these theories are dissimilar, they share a common theme: the explanations for the anxiety disorders lie outside of a person's thinking processes. One can reasonably raise the question: Is the phenomenon of free-floating anxiety—the centerpiece for the more widely accepted theories of anxiety disorders—a fact, or is it an artifact of the type of observation and analysis?

While the clinician or the researcher may believe that anxiety is totally dissociated from conscious fears, the person who is anxious does not necessarily agree and, when questioned, he expresses a strong sense of impending disaster. The previously described patient, interviewed by a psychiatrist in the emergency room, reported two main thoughts dominating his consciousness; first, that he had a severe organic crisis such as an appendicitis; secondly, that he was dying and would surely die if he did not get prompt attention. He also had vivid visual images of being operated on and also of being in a coffin. Apparently, he was suffering from intestinal spasm after overeating. He interpreted his abdominal symptoms as a sign of a life-threatening disorder and thus increased his anxiety. A relative of his had recently died from a dissecting aneurysm of the aorta.

Thus, the key to understanding anxiety is clarification of a patient's frame of reference and his cognitive distortions through eliciting his thoughts and images. The anxious patient selectively attends to stimuli that indicate possible danger and becomes oblivious to stimuli that indicate that there is no danger. He makes arbitrary inferences and overgeneralizes. He becomes preoccupied with his own anxiety symptoms and dwells on thoughts of dying or other catastrophes.

The anxious patient enters a subjective world which is not readily understandable to an outside observer. This person's fears are, to him, totally reasonable: While he is in the throes of anxiety, the danger is "real," and the risk of disaster seems high. As John Bowlby noted:

> Unless we know what is or has been going on in our patients' private environments we are in no position to decide there is no recognizable threat, or the threat is, by reasonable standards, quite out of proportion to the emotion it seemingly evokes.
>
> Clinical experience shows, indeed, that the more we know about natural fear and the more we learn about our patients' personal environments, the less do the fears from which they suffer seem to lack a reasonable basis, and the less does anxiety appear free floating. Were we therefore to confine our usage of the word anxiety to conditions in which threat is absent or judged inadequate, we might well find the word gone quietly out of use. (1970, p. 86)

The psychological core of acute anxiety attacks can center around fears of internal physical disaster (for example, heart attack, acute abdominal catastrophe, or cancer) or of mental disorder ("going crazy") or of social catastrophe (public disgrace). Sometimes a person cannot pinpoint the precise nature of an anticipated catastrophe but expects that some very noxious event is occurring or is about to occur.

The preceding example illustrates how an anxious person can attribute too much significance to physical sensations, interpret physical distress as a sign of physical disaster, and become anxious. The resulting increase in physical symptoms leads to an increase in anxiety. A vicious cycle is set up which can be broken if the patient can recognize the role faulty thinking plays in maintaining his or her anxiety.

The concept of free-floating anxiety as the classical line of distinction between anxiety neurosis and phobic neurosis has been challenged by research findings (Beck, Laude, and Bohnert 1974; Hibbert 1984). Specific fears expressed during an anxiety attack seem to account for the anxiety and for other symptoms experienced in both anxiety and phobic disorders. The fact that anxiety may be related to conscious fears is not surprising.

Any realistically hazardous situation, which an individual judges to be dangerous, may be expected to trigger anxiety. The difference between such an adaptive anxiety response and the response of the pathologically anxious patient is that the latter repeatedly misconstrues an innocuous situation as posing a threat or exaggerates the actual danger.

NORMAL VERSUS PATHOLOGICAL ANXIETY

When is anxiety "normal," and when can it be diagnosed as a symptom or a syndrome? Anxiety is generally considered a normal reaction if it is aroused by a "realistic" danger and if it dissipates when the danger is no longer present. If the degree of anxiety is greatly disproportionate to the risk and the severity of possible danger, and if it continues even though no objective danger exists, then the reaction is considered abnormal. Another way of making the judgment is by assessing the impact of the reaction on the individual's functioning. If he appears to be suffering a great deal, if there is some psychosomatic effect (for example, colitis or dermatitis), and if intellectual functioning or social/vocational adjustment is impaired, then there is justification for stating that a person has clinical or abnormal anxiety even though the symptoms do not fit into a clear-cut syndrome.

Drawing a precise line between normal and abnormal anxiety, however, is difficult and is governed to some degree by social norms. If a person, in keeping with the superstitions of his society, is chronically anxious because an enemy has put a curse on him, is he reacting abnormally? Do we label as pathologically anxious a novice parachutist who becomes panicky before his first jump?

It is often difficult to establish the boundary between a realistic fear and a phobia. Consider a person who develops symptoms of anxiety about taking a train to work and subsequently, avoiding trains, assumes the greater risk of driving on a freeway that has a high accident rate. Using social norms as a guide, we can state he has a phobia about (rather than a simple fear of) trains. The more severe the anxiety and avoidance compared with the actual risk, the easier it is to apply the label *phobia*. We can readily make the diagnosis when the content of the fear is far-fetched. Consider the young man who avoids all outdoor activities for fear of sudden electric storms, or the woman who avoids subways and buses for fear of suffocation. Also in this category is a woman who had a fear of eating chocolate and another with a fear and avoidance of eating vegetables (Rachman 1978).

Thinking Disorder in Clinical Anxiety

ATTENTION, CONCENTRATION, AND VIGILANCE

It is easy to observe that the anxious person is incapable of focusing on a specific object or subject for a sustained time. Furthermore, his diminished ability to concentrate and retrieve information from short-term memory may be attributed to an inability to focus on a given task (for example, taking a test or giving a speech).

The patient's attention, however, is not as erratic as it may seem; it is focused, although involuntarily, on the *concepts of danger or threat.* His attention is "bound" to stimuli perceived as threatening. The patient is hypervigilant, constantly scanning the environment for signs of impending disaster or personal harm. Such hypervigilance severely limits his ability to focus on specific tasks or to engage in reflective thinking. Because the patient "uses up" a large part of his cognitive capacity by scanning for threatening stimuli, the amount available for attending to other demands is severely restricted.

"ALARM SYSTEM" AND "AUTOMATIC THOUGHTS"

An anxiety disorder can be conceptualized metaphorically as a hypersensitive alarm system. The anxious patient is so sensitive to any stimuli that might be taken as indicating imminent disaster or harm that he is constantly warning himself, as it were, about the potential dangers. Because almost any stimulus can be perceived by him as dangerous and can "trip off" the alarm, the anxious patient experiences innumerable "false alarms," which keep him in a constant state of emotional stress and turmoil.

The preoccupation with danger is manifested by the perseverative, involuntary intrusion of automatic thoughts (in verbal or visual form) whose content involves possible physical or mental harm. These thoughts tend to occur repetitively and rapidly and seem completely plausible at the time of their occurrence. Many times a thought is so fleeting that the patient is aware only of the anxiety it has generated. He can be easily trained however, to perform an "instant replay" and recover the automatic thought preceding the affect. This thought is derived from the information-processing system that activates the affect.

LOSS OF OBJECTIVITY AND OF VOLUNTARY CONTROL

In addition to having repetitive thoughts about danger which set off false alarms, ability to "reason" with these thoughts is impaired. While the patient may agree that these fearful thoughts are illogical, his ability to evaluate them objectively (without help) is limited. The person behaves as though he believes in the validity of his misinterpretations, though he may suspect they are not totally realistic. Objectivity is similarly lost when a person attempts to test the reality of the visual images that may accompany or substitute for verbal cognition.

Another characteristic of anxious thinking is its involuntary nature. Automatic thoughts exert a continuous pressure even though a person has already determined that they are invalid and would like to be rid of them. The involuntary character of the anxious thinking and the other mechanisms (blocking, "choking") may lead the patient to think he is "losing his mind."

STIMULUS GENERALIZATION

The range of stimuli that can evoke anxiety in generalized anxiety disorder may increase until almost any stimulus is perceived as a danger. For example, a woman in an acute state of anxiety had the following experience: The sound of the siren of a fire engine evoked the thought, "My house may be on fire." An airplane flying overhead triggered a visual image of herself in an airplane crashing into another plane. After seeing the scene of an accident on television, she visualized herself bleeding or suffering.

The increased range of anxiety-evoking stimuli is especially evident in those who "relive" particular traumatic events, as does a person with a post-traumatic stress disorder. A war veteran, for example, might experience unpleasant visual imagery when exposed to any stimulus reminding him of his war experiences: the sound of an airplane overhead or a car backfiring, or any allusion to fighting made in conversation, could trigger a repetitive fantasy of frightening experiences he had in combat.

During a fantasy or a period when the individual re-experiences a traumatic event through visual imagery, the anxiety experienced may be as intense as it was during the event itself. For example, a man's brakes failed while he was backing up his automobile on an upper floor of a parking garage. The car broke through a guard rail, and the man remained in the car, teetering back and forth on the ledge for over an hour until he was rescued. Afterward, the man constantly re-experienced the traumatic event, with vivid fantasies of being in the car. The accompanying anxiety was as intense as that of the actual event.

CATASTROPHIZING

One type of faulty thinking which is characteristic of many anxious patients is "catastrophizing" (Ellis 1962). Such people tend to dwell on the worst possible outcome of any situation in which there is a possibility for an unpleasant outcome. The anxious person overemphasizes the probability of this catastrophic outcome and usually exaggerates the possible consequences of its occurrence. Examples of catastrophizing are: (1) A woman taking an airplane trip dwelled on the possibility of the plane's crashing and of her being killed. (2) A successful college student taking an examination was preoccupied with the possibility of his failing. He imagined that if he failed the test, he would flunk out of college and as a consequence would end up as a drifter. (3) A new college instructor was to give his first lecture to a large group of students. He was afraid that he might forget what he had to say, and would make a fool of himself and faint or start screaming in an insane way. The ultimate outcome would be a ruined career and a ruined life.

SELECTIVE ABSTRACTION AND LOSS OF PERSPECTIVE

A person with a psychological disorder tends to select, from his present and past experience, data consistent with the cognitive set characteristic of that disorder. Thus, an anxious patient will be hypersensitive to any aspects of a situation that are potentially harmful, but will not respond to its benign or positive aspects. Such a person is likely to be very aware of his difficulties in handling a problematic situation but not of his assets. Thus, he misses the broader picture, the total context, and has a biased view of the degree both of the danger he is in and of his own vulnerability.

DICHOTOMOUS THINKING

Another characteristic of the thinking of an anxious patient is the tendency—when there is any question of danger—to interpret events in dichotomous terms. Thus, unless a situation is unmistakably safe, the person is likely to appraise it as unsafe. He has no tolerance for uncertainty or ambiguity. The rustling of the venetian blinds indicates an intruder; the backfiring of an automobile sounds like the firing of a gun; shortness of breath means he may stop breathing entirely.

The anxious patient also tends to view possible dangers in absolute, extreme terms. The possibility of failing an exam becomes highly likely; a failure to recall somebody's name is a sign of probable mental deterioration; some friction with a spouse is interpreted as a probable break-up of the marriage. The tendency to think in absolute, extreme terms increases as one approaches the danger situation. On the way to an exam, the probability of doing poorly skyrockets. As an airplane takes off, the phobic expects it to crash. We should point out, however, that when the individual is away from the "danger," he is generally able to view it realistically.

LACK OF HABITUATION

After repeated exposure to moderately frightening stimuli, non-anxious people tend to adapt, or habituate, while highly anxious ones become more anxious. This statement is supported by both experimental data and clinical observation. M. Lader, M. G. Gelder, and I. Marks (1967) compared highly anxious with non-anxious subjects according to the degree to which each became sensitized or habituated to certain sequences of sounds. The researchers found that, while both groups initially showed an increase in perspiration (or skin conductance), the physiological responses of the non-anxious group diminished with time while those of the anxious group actually increased. This finding suggests that the anxiety level of the anxious subjects also increased.

Clinical observation also supports Lader's conclusion. We have noted that, with repeated exposure to a threatening situation, the average individual shows greater confidence and less anxiety, while the highly anxious person may become more anxious. A possible explanation for both the experimental and the clinical findings is that the non-anxious person is able to determine fairly rapidly that a given stimulus does not necessarily signal a threat. The anxious person, on the other hand, is unable to make the distinction between what is or is not safe.

Classification of Anxiety Disorders

The various anxiety disorders have been succinctly described in the *Diagnostic and Statistical Manual of Mental Disorders* or *DSM-III* (American Psychiatric Association 1980).

PANIC DISORDER

The essential features are recurrent panic (anxiety) attacks that occur at times unpredictably, though certain situations, e.g., driving a car, may become associated with a panic attack.

The panic attacks are manifested by the sudden onset of intense apprehension, fear, or terror, often associated with feelings of impending doom. The most common symptoms experienced during an attack are dyspnea; palpitations; chest pain or discomfort; choking or smothering sensations; dizziness, vertigo, or unsteady feelings; feelings of unreality (depersonalization or derealization); paresthesias; hot and cold flashes; sweating; faintness; trembling or shaking; and fear of dying, going crazy, or doing something uncontrolled during the attack. Attacks usually last minutes; more rarely, hours. . . .

. . . The individual often develops varying degrees of nervousness and apprehension between attacks. (P. 230)

GENERALIZED ANXIETY DISORDER

The essential feature is generalized, persistent anxiety of at least one month's duration without the specific symptoms that characterize Phobic Disorders . . . Panic Disorder . . . or Obsessive Compulsive Disorder. . . . The diagnosis is not made if the disturbance is due to another physical or mental disorder, such as hyperthyroidism or Major Depression.

Although the specific manifestations of the anxiety vary from individual to individual, generally there are signs of motor tension, autonomic hyperactivity, apprehensive expectation, and vigilance and scanning. . . .

. . . Mild depressive symptoms are common. (P. 232)

POST–TRAUMATIC STRESS DISORDER

The essential feature is the development of characteristic symptoms following a psychologically traumatic event that is generally outside the range of usual human experience.

The characteristic symptoms involve reexperiencing the traumatic event; numbing of responsiveness to, or reduced involvement with, the external world; and a variety of autonomic, dysphoric, or cognitive symptoms. . . .

. . . Symptoms of depression and anxiety are common, and in some instances may be sufficiently severe to be diagnosed as an Anxiety or Depressive Disorder." (Pp. 236–37)

ATYPICAL ANXIETY DISORDER

This category should be used when the individual appears to have an Anxiety Disorder that does not meet the criteria for any of the above specified conditions. (P. 239)

PHOBIC DISORDERS

The essential feature is persistent and irrational fear of a specific object, activity, or situation that results in a compelling desire to avoid the dreaded object, activity, or situation. . . . The fear is recognized by the individual as excessive or unreasonable in proportion to the actual dangerousness of the object, activity, or situation. (P. 225)

AGORAPHOBIA

The essential feature is a marked fear of being alone, or being in public places from which escape might be difficult or help not available in case of sudden incapacitation. Normal activities are increasingly constricted as the fears or avoidance behavior dominate the individual's life. The most common situations avoided involve being in crowds, such as on a busy street or in crowded stores, or being in tunnels, on bridges, on elevators, or on public transportation. Often these individuals insist that a family member or friend accompany them whenever they leave home. (P. 226)

SOCIAL PHOBIA

The essential feature is a persistent, irrational fear of, and compelling desire to avoid, situations in which the individual may be exposed to scrutiny by others. There is also fear that the individual may behave in a manner that will be humiliating or embarrassing. Marked anticipatory anxiety occurs if the individual is confronted with the necessity of entering into such a situation, and he or she therefore attempts to avoid it. The disturbance is a significant source of distress and is recognized by the individual as excessive or unreasonable. . . . Examples of Social Phobias are fears of speaking or performing in public, using public lavatories, eating in public, and writing in the presence of others. . . .
. . . Considerable unfocused or generalized anxiety may also be present. (P. 227)

SIMPLE PHOBIA

The essential feature is a persistent, irrational fear of, and compelling desire to avoid, an object or situation other than being alone or in public places away from home (Agoraphobia), or of humiliation or embarrassment in certain social situations (Social Phobia). Thus, this is a residual category of Phobic Disorder. This disturbance is a significant source of distress, and the individual recognizes that his or her fear is excessive or unreasonable. . . .
. . . The most common Simple Phobias in the general population, though not necessarily among those seeking treatment, involve animals, particularly dogs, snakes, insects, and mice. Other Simple Phobias are claustrophobia (fear of closed spaces) and acrophobia (fear of heights). (Pp. 228–29)

Chapter 3

The Cognitive Model of Threat Reactions

The Role of Context

In order to understand the cognitive processes involved in the production of the anxiety syndrome, let us examine them in the context of an individual exposed to an acute physical danger. Although this example is shorn of the complexities and the multiple subtle interactions involved in our usual anxiety-producing experiences, it has the advantage of delineating the precise mechanisms and operations involved. In attempting to clarify such reactions, we should keep in mind that the interpretation of danger will normally vary according to the context.

The importance of the precise nature of the circumstances in determining a person's cognitive response is indicated in the following illustration: A hunter about to cross paths with a lion in the wild may experience an immediate fear reaction. Place the lion behind bars and the situation is quite different. The lion may charge and roar violently without evoking anxiety in the onlookers. It is apparent that the appraisal of danger is bound to be different in the two situations: it integrates not only such factors as the proximity and the intent of the predator but also such protective factors as the cage.

PRIMARY APPRAISAL

The role of the context is further delineated when we examine an individual's construction of a potentially dangerous situation. The construction may be broken down into a series of steps: primary appraisal, secondary appraisal, and reappraisal (Lazarus 1966).

An individual's construction of a particular situation may be likened to taking a series of photographs or a motion picture, when one scans the relevant environment and then determines which aspect (if any) to focus on. Cognitive processing, like a photograph, reduces the number of dimensions in a situation (three dimensions are reduced to two in a photograph). Consequently, such processing sacrifices a great deal of information and introduces distortion into the "picture." Specific *settings* (lens, focus, speed) have an enormous influence on the final picture. Depending on the type of lens (wide-angle or telephoto), for example, breadth is sacrificed for detail, or vice versa. In addition, certain aspects are highlighted at the expense of others, the relative magnitudes and prominence of particular features are distorted, and there are varying degrees of loss of perspective. In addition, there may be blurring or loss of important detail due to the type of focus and the speed of the exposure; moreover, the use of filters further influences the salience and coloring of particular features.

The analogy suggests that specific characteristics of the receiving apparatus (the camera or the cognitive organization) have a decisive influence on what one sees. Moreover, taking a picture is not a passive process. The cameraman plays a crucial role in selecting particular "strategies"—sequencing, highlighting, focusing, framing, and so on. Similarly, in conceptualizing a particular event, the *cognitive set* influences the "picture" one sees: Whether the mental image or conception is broad, skewed, or narrow, clear or blurred, accurate or distorted depends on the cognitive setting. The existing cognitive set—that is, this composite of expectations, interests, and concerns—determines which aspects of a scene will be blown up, which glossed over, and which excluded. Furthermore, the individual's purpose in approaching a situation will influence the patterns he will look for and see.

The following discussion will focus on those cognitive processes that may lead to anxiety. These "first shots" of an event provide information that either reinforces or modifies a pre-existing cognitive set. An *initial impression* may be formed on the basis of scanty data and is important in that it indicates the general nature of a situation: specifically, whether it directly affects the person's *vital interests* (or domain).* It should be noted that the first impression is especially important because, unless modified or reversed, it sets the course of subsequent steps in one's conceptualization of and total response to a situation. The person who judges a situation

*A comprehensive consideration of the concept of the personal domain may be found in Beck 1976, pp. 54–57.

as profoundly affecting his vital interests shows what I call a "critical response." The critical response is evoked by a broad spectrum of situations ranging from possible disaster in the future to an immediate threat to life.

The type of critical response that best illustrates the psychological and biological response to threat is the "emergency response." This response is activated when a person perceives (correctly or incorrectly) that there is a clear and present danger to his domain—for example, an immediate threat to survival, individuality, functioning, or interpersonal attachment. The threats cover a wide range, including attack, depreciation, encroachment, thwarting, abandonment, rejection, or deprivation.

An essential feature of the emergency response is that it is *egocentric*. Through a sequence of cognitive processing, one conceptualizes a situation in terms of "How does it affect me?" If a person's immediate vital interests appear to be affected, then he selects data and molds them to provide a meaningful (that is, egocentric) answer to this question. The initial conceptualization tends to be global, absolute, and arbitrary. Thus, the cognitive system or subsystem that is activated is significantly different from that activated in stress-threatening or in neutral situations. The oversimplified conceptualization seems to reflect a less mature although more rapidly acting organization than the kind of conceptualization derived from reflective thinking. (This relatively primitive organization corresponds roughly to what Freud described as "primary process.") Data not clearly relevant to the specific content of the emergency interpretation are minimized or omitted in the conceptualization. On the other hand, many situations are classed erroneously as immediate threats because they may involve immediate vital interests. The tendency to include *possible* threats along with actual damage leads, as we have said, to many false alarms, which are generally turned off as a result of subsequent reappraisals. In anxiety disorders, however, the false alarms are not terminated by contradictory information. The reappraisal either does not occur or fails to incorporate data inconsistent with the dominant cognitive set, or mode (chapter 4).

For our present purpose, let us assume that the first impression of a situation indicates that it constitutes a threat to the domain. We label the initial impression of a situation "primary appraisal" (after Lazarus 1966). If the primary appraisal suggests that the situation is noxious, successive reappraisals are made to provide preliminary answers to a series of questions:

1. Does the noxious situation appear to be an immediate threat to vital interests?
2. Does it involve possible physical injury?

3. Does it involve possible psychological injury—for example, rejection or devaluation?
4. Does the threat involve violation of rules constructed to protect vital interests?

SECONDARY APPRAISAL

At the same time that he is evaluating the nature of the threat, the individual is assessing his resources for dealing with it. This process (labeled "secondary appraisal" by R. S. Lazarus) aims to assess the availability and effectiveness of an individual's internal resources for buffering or deflecting the potential damage resulting from a specific assault. His perceptions of the external resources available to him (for example, allies) are also factored into the formula determining probability of damage.

For example, a youngster confronted by a bully much larger than himself may anticipate that he will be badly beaten and that his resources (instrumental behaviors) for protecting himself are minimal. The risk of some damage is high, at least until the youngster has put a safe distance between himself and the bully.

It should be noted that primary and secondary appraisals are probably not separate processes but are often integrated into the same overall evaluation. The youngster, for instance, simultaneously assesses the potential harmfulness of the bully and his own coping ability and matches one against the other. The comparison of potential damage and potential resources comprises primary and secondary appraisal. Suppose that the next time he has a confrontation, he brings along his older brother, who is larger than the bully. The availability of this powerful external resource is a crucial part of the total context. In this new context, the confrontation is essentially nonthreatening. It will be noted later that the presence of a "caretaker" generally reduces the perceived threat in clinical conditions such as agoraphobia (cf. Chambless and Goldstein 1982).

The final construction of the noxious situation is based on a formula that takes into account the amount and the probabilities of damage inherent in the threat in relation to a person's capacity to deal with it. The balance between potential damage and coping resources determines the nature and intensity of one's emergency response. These assessments are not cool, conscious, deliberate computations but are generally very rapid and, to a large degree, automatic. The equation is based on highly personal evaluations that are susceptible to considerable variation and error. For example, two people with similar coping capacities might respond in a vastly different manner to the same emergency situation.

If a person judges the threat to be low relative to his coping mechanisms, he may choose to eliminate or deflect the threat by attacking the source ("fight"). If he judges the risk to be high relative to his coping resources, he is impelled to reduce the degree of threat through a variety of mechanisms such as escape ("flight"), self-inhibition ("freeze"), or collapse ("faint").

The cognitive processes involved in the emergency response may present a one-sided, exaggerated view of the stimulus situation—because of the exclusionary and categorical nature of a person's thinking at this primal level ("primary process"). These cognitive processes are instruments of basic functions involved in protection and survival and tend to be activated automatically as if by reflex.

ESTIMATE OF DANGER

How does a person decide that a particular situation is dangerous? What criteria does he use to estimate the severity of the danger? For the purpose of this explication, we will use the example of a physical threat. However, the same formula would apply to imponderable, complex situations involving social "dangers," such as threat of rejection, isolation, and humiliation.

The visual method of determining the degree of danger basically involves an appraisal of the entire context. One's initial impression of the situation involves a comparison of the properties of the threatening object with one's own capabilities and power. For example, the size of the threatening object compared to one's own size is an important factor. Thus, if you are out in the woods, you will be less concerned about meeting a bear cub than its full-sized parent. This type of comparison in decisions regarding "fight" or "flight" is observed at every level of the animal kingdom. The stickleback fish, upon encountering another stickleback, will attack if it is larger than the intruder and retreat if smaller. (Rule: "If bigger, attack; if smaller, retreat.")

In addition to comparisons regarding size and fierceness, the individual also makes an appraisal of his own resources—the availability of external aids (some kind of a weapon, other allies) and his power and abilities (skill at running, handling a weapon). As the situation develops, he makes a series of reappraisals which generally delineate it more clearly: he quickly gets a better notion of the danger and of his ability to cope with it.

The degree of mobilization (behavioral arousal) and of subjective anxiety is proportional to one's subjective estimate of danger—although the degree of arousal will vary widely among individuals exposed to the same threat. In the final analysis, the degree of estimated danger (that is, the *risk* of injury or death) and consequent fear reaction is proportional to the person's estimate both of the severity of the potential injury and of the probability of its occurring.

We should emphasize that the individual does not apply this formula in an intentional, reflective, logical way. Once set in motion, the rapid series of impressions and "computating" occur automatically. They are influenced by the interplay of predisposition, learning experiences, and memories; the composite formed by this interplay may range from reasonably accurate to highly inaccurate.

The fear of physical injury can be readily transposed to a psychosocial situation. Consider a graduate student taking oral exams. She responds to the danger of not performing well as a result of inadequate preparation, "hostile" examiners, and the symptoms associated with her sense of vulnerability—anxiety, blocking, choking up, faint feeling, and so on. Each of these threats can be counterbalanced by coping strategies: learning the material so well that she can recite it despite a fearful reaction; trying to "charm" the examiners; using relaxation techniques to alleviate muscular tension; focusing to neutralize her blocking; and performing special movements to counteract faintness.

HOSTILE RESPONSE

What circumstances are likely to elicit a "fight" (hostile) rather than a "fear" response? When exposed to a threat, the organism makes a rapid comparison of the threatening agent and its own counterharm resources. If the noxious agent is perceived as too formidable to attack, then the individual retreats or prepares to defend itself. If, however, the organism perceives itself as capable of defeating or scaring off the intruder, it will mobilize for hostile action. Mobilization may range from staring down the offender or screaming at it to physically attacking it. The affect associated with hostile behavior in humans is generally anger; effective neutralization of a noxious stimulus serves to reduce anger just as reducing danger relieves anxiety.

A key factor in the counterattack or hostile response is the presence of "self-confidence." Confidence in one's ability to cope directly with a threat may be bolstered by symbolic or actual assistance from other people. The schoolboy who returns with his older brother to confront the school bully can muster a bracing self-confidence.

We also observe the "fight" response when a person is trapped. In the context of being unable to escape or protect himself through immobility, he may fight as the last resort, with the goal of slowing down or deterring the adversary. In this case, however, his affect is anxiety, not anger.

The Nature of Cognitive Processing

The preceding formulation is compatible with theories of information processing advanced by other authors. As pointed out by John Bowlby (1981) and N. F. Dixon (1981), current studies of human perception show that before a person is aware of seeing or hearing a stimulus, the sensory inflow coming through his eyes or ears has already passed through many states of selection, interpretation, and appraisal—a process that excludes a large proportion of the original inflow. Bowlby explains that "the reason for this extensive exclusion is that since the channels responsible for the most advanced processing" are of limited capacity, they must be protected from overload. This ensures "that what is most relevant gets through and that only the less relevant is excluded" (1981, p. 13). He points out that, although this processing is done at extraordinary speed—almost all of it outside awareness—much of the inflow is carried to a very advanced stage of processing before being excluded.

In the ordinary course of a person's life, the criteria for selection of relevant information reflects an "adaptational principle" regarding what—in teleonomic terms—appears to be in his best interests at any one time. Thus, when a person is hungry, stimuli regarding food are given priority, whereas other information that might ordinarily be useful is excluded. Bowlby emphasizes the essential order of priorities within the cognitive organization. This order of priorities is manifested by the self-protection program's pre-emption of the cognitive processing when an organism perceives that it is threatened. Suppose a person is eating:

> Should danger threaten, priorities would quickly change so that inflow concerned with issues of danger and safety would take precedence and inflow concerned with food be temporarily excluded. This change in the criteria governing what inflow is to be accepted and what excluded is effected by evaluating systems central to the personality. (Bowlby 1981, p. 14)

The emergency response may be conceptualized in terms of cognitive processing: The construction of a situation is an active process that includes successive appraisals of a noxious situation, of one's internal (coping) and external resources, and of the risks, costs, and gains of a particular response. When a person regards his vital interests to be at stake, the cognitive process provides highly selective data processing and conceptualization. When an individual perceives acute danger, his cognitive-motor apparatus is mobilized to deal with it immediately.

THE RELATION OF BEHAVIORAL ACTIVATION AND INHIBITION TO MOTIVATION

The term *motivation* has been generally used to explain the internal stimulus to behavior. However, there have been so many uses of this term, that it has lost its definitional boundaries. Its domain has ranged from "basic needs" or "drives" such as hunger, thirst, sex, and the need to sleep to abstract notions such as unconscious hostility. Furthermore, while some reputed motivations are clearly conscious and intentional, others are outside awareness and involuntary.

Consider the person giving a speech in public who suddenly "freezes" and then feels faint. Although his overwhelming conscious desire (motivation) is to speak fluently, the internal process activating the blocking, blanking, and rigidity is powerful enough to override this desire. To apply the term *unconscious motivation* to the nonconscious instigation of involuntary behavior implies that in some way the person "wants" to freeze, block, and faint. This semantic usage is misleading since it implies that the processes leading to blocking are similar to those leading to effective speaking— except for differences in the level of consciousness. Conscious intentions, volitions, and the like appear to be of a totally different order from the processes activating the automatic primal defensive patterns; using the same concept or term, *motivation,* to apply to both types of process is misleading.

It would seem most parsimonious in theorizing about threat responses to consider the primal response (chapter 1) as a nonvolitional behavioral pattern activated by the perception of a threat. This pattern might or might not be consistent with the *conscious* motivation to reduce the threat. In the previous example, the defensive reaction (blocking, blanking, fainting) is obviously contrary to the conscious wish to speak fluently. The person is unable to fulfill his conscious desires because of the general inhibition. In the interest of semantic clarity, it would seem best to reserve the term *motivation* for conscious wishes, drives, urges, and the like. The term *primal response* is applied to the automatic, nonconscious, nonvolitional activation of a cognitive behavioral pattern and also to the inhibition of a cognitive or behavioral process. Thus, an example of behavioral activation in flight reaction and inhibition is illustrated by the freeze reaction and mental blocking.

DISTINGUISHING BETWEEN BEHAVIOR AND EMOTIONS

The popular concept of emotions—which is also reflected to some degree in psychoanalytic theory—revolves around the metaphor of these phenomena as a fluid or a reservoir. When the internal hydraulic system reaches a certain level, it builds up a pressure for overt expression. According to the same metaphor, the flow of certain emotions such as anxiety or anger into various organ systems can lead to a wide variety of ills ranging from headache to ulcerative colitis. Although it has been stated that the free and open expression of anger can relieve psychosomatic disorders, no school of thought seems to argue that the free expression of anxiety has similar ameliorative affects.

How do we know that a person is "expressing" his emotions? A person may stand in front of an audience with a "frightened" facial expression, shake uncontrollably, clench his fists until his muscles are white, and finally slump to the floor—and yet not experience anxiety. This scenario may be portrayed by a seasoned actor who is feeling no anxiety. In fact, as H. Leventhal points out, the observation that professional actors could show the characteristics attributed to an emotion without experiencing the emotion led William James to conclude that emotions are not central phenomena (Leventhal 1982).

For conceptual clarity, it is desirable to draw the line between emotion and behavior. While they often appear together, it is possible to exhibit "anxious" behavior without being anxious, and vice versa. How then do we differentiate anxiety and the behavior generally associated with it? As we have already pointed out, affect and behavior are best conceptualized as two separate but interrelated systems. It is possible to activate one system without the other. A person simulating an emotion consciously and intentionally portrays "anxious" *behavior.* He cannot, however, intentionally activate the *feeling* of anxiety unless he thinks of a dangerous situation—because the experience of anxiety is an involuntary response. The overt behavior is similar whether consciously contrived or spontaneous and accompanied by affect. In any event, we never *see* the emotion in another person. We see only the behavior, from which we may infer the emotion. The sequence from cognitive processing to behavioral mobilization and the arousal of anxiety is illustrated in figure 3.1. The experience of anxiety, while activated by the cognitive appraisals, also feeds back into the cognitive system and, consequently, enhances the decision to prepare for defensive action. The physiological arousal is not represented separately since it is an integral part of behavioral mobilization. We should point out that the physiological "signs" (increased heart rate and blood pressure; muscular tension) of mobilization precede overt action. The mobilization is not manifested overtly until the appropriate time and, in fact, may be inhibited and not manifested at any time.

THE VICIOUS CYCLE

The spiraling, or vicious cycle, in anxiety disorders can be delineated as we observe how a particular symptom may, in itself, pose a threat—either by impairing performance or by indicating to a suggestible person that it is a sign of a serious disorder. These secondary effects make the individual feel even more vulnerable. As the sense of danger increases, more primal responses are activated, and these in turn may present further handicaps and threats. Unfavorable feedback from others has a similar negative effect.

Take a public-speaking situation, for example. Suppose a person perceives a serious flaw in his performance. He may base this "perception" on noxious responses in the audience (such as slumbering, yawning, restlessness) or on observations of his own dysfluency, lack of proper inflection, rambling. Next he has a fear such as "I may not be able to hold their attention——They may look down on me because of my lapses——I may not be able to keep going." These ideas increase the sense of vulnerability and stir up anxiety and other defensive mechanisms. The anxiety itself leads to further dysfunction. First, the unpleasant emotional experience serves to distract the person from the task at hand just as would a sudden sharp pain. Secondly, he interprets his anxiety as a sign that he is not functioning well, that he does not have control over himself: that is, the intensity of his anxiety rather than any accurate assessment of his actual

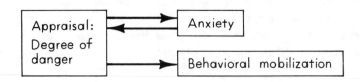

Figure 3.1
Relation of Appraisal to Components of Fear Syndrome

performance is taken as the index of dysfunction. He is in the grip of notions such as "This is a sign that I'm not making it."

As the individual's attention is diverted to his anxiety, there may, indeed, be an increase in his outward show of "nervousness" as well as increased difficulty in performance. This behavior may be observed by the audience, and the person may observe a negative response. ("They can tell I'm nervous. They believe I'm weak. They have a low opinion of me.") The result of this interaction is a precipitate drop in his confidence in being able to influence the audience and a feeling that his power is draining out of him. As he becomes increasingly "weak and powerless," he senses his greatest danger and his vulnerability to disapproval from the audience. He begins to believe that he cannot depend on his functional capacities to see him through this crisis.

If the speaker is receiving positive signals from the audience and therefore believes that he is performing well, he is less likely to feel threatened. He thinks, for instance, "At least I'm getting across somewhat to the audience," and "They seem receptive so I guess they are not going to attack me." Any interference with his voluntary control over his thinking and speech, over his posture, and over subjective sensations such as nervousness, will erode the basis of his self-confidence. However, symptoms such as swaying, a quivering voice, faint feelings, loss of fluency, rigid postural inhibition, all mean to him, "I'm not in control of my body." The sense of one's control slipping often means that "anything can happen," and leads to catastrophic thinking ("I have no control at all"). The loss of voluntary control is especially devastating to people who place a high premium on having control because of their autonomy. Diminution of control is also important to sociotropic people who find it essential to present an image of self-control in order to obtain the approval, and to ward off the disapproval or antagonism, of other people.

The relationship between cognition, affect, and behavior is illustrated in figure 3.2. The negative appraisal of the self, of the performance, and of the audience's response increases the anxiety, which further interferes with performance and reinforces the notion of deficiency.

Primal Responses to Threat

What happens to an organism (human or nonhuman) when it perceives that it is in danger? Depending upon the nature and the context of the

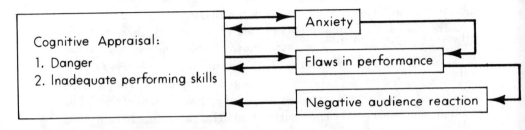

Figure 3.2

The Vicious Cycle, Incorporating Unpleasant Emotional Feedback (Anxiety),
Unpleasant Performance Feedback, and Unpleasant Audience Feedback

threat, the individual may show a variety of relatively stereotyped responses. Since these patterns appear to be "programmed" and are largely
automatic, I have applied the term "primal." They are more innate than
the learned or acquired responses that involve more skill and are under
voluntary control. Some of the common behavior patterns are:

1. *Fight:* If a person is trapped, fight takes the form of protective action:
   warding off a blow, attempting to deter further attack by using
   threatening display, or defensive fighting.
2. *Flight:* Generally the method chosen, if feasible, when the individual
   is about to be attacked; instigated largely by anxiety.
3. *Freeze:* Occurs prior to actual attack; provides time to appraise the
   situation before deciding on the type of strategy; also prepares the
   individual to absorb the impact of an attack. In humans, this response
   tends to occur automatically in the presence of danger and is manifested by general inhibition of voluntary actions such as movement or
   speech as well as cognitive processes. It also occurs to prevent hazardous actions, such as walking off a steep embankment.
4. *Faint:* Automatic, atonic reaction when the individual is helpless,
   overwhelmed, or exposed to mutilation or blood; and associated with
   "collapse reaction."
5. *Retraction:* Drawing back from a dangerous situation (height, attack).
6. *Duck, Dodge, Jump:* Evading missiles or falling objects.
7. *Clutching, Clinging:* Grasping to maintain balance, prevent falling,
   drowning, and so on.
8. *Reflexes:* Eyeblink, gagging, coughing.
9. *Calling for Help:* A spontaneous distress call.

THE ANERGIC AND THE ENERGIC SYSTEMS

Two major behavioral systems are activated—either separately or to-gether—in response to threat: the energic, tonic system; and the anergic, atonic system. These systems have been described by E. Gellhorn (1968) as the "ergotropic" and the "trophotropic" systems; they include, respec-tively, the activation of the sympathetic and the parasympathetic branches of the autonomic nervous system.

Both types of response include a complete psychobiological reaction comprising the cognitive, motor, and physiological systems and, in hu-mans at least, an affective component (anxiety). The tonic, energic system prepares the individual for active coping with a danger (fight, flight) (see Fowles 1982). The atonic, anergic system is triggered when active coping is inappropriate or counterproductive (faint).

Let us analyze the case of Mr. A, who is going to have a surgical opera-tion. Upon entering the hospital, he becomes aware of rapid pulse, sweat-ing, general tension throughout his body, perhaps also of some clenching of his fists. When seen by the physician, he is told he is too tense to be examined and that he must relax. However, he keeps blinking during his eye examination and gags and chokes during his throat examination.

Why is Mr. A so inappropriately tense and defensive? The reason seems to be that, in an anachronistic sense, the reaction is appropriate. The person facing imminent attack in the wild is well served by becoming thus mobil-ized for fight, defense, or flight. The defensive response is activated on the basis of a primitive survival mechanism and not of contemporary reality; hence, it could be called "adaptational" although it is not "adaptive" in the present context.

This type of defensive reaction consists essentially of reflexes (gag, cough, eyeblink, nausea) designed to prevent foreign substances from invading airway, gastrointestinal tract, or eye. These reflexes are significant clinically in that they can be triggered by the *anticipation* of gagging, chok-ing, nausea, and so on. Furthermore, these reflexes can be triggered in some people in an interpersonal context, in response to some noxious interac-tion.

CHANGES IN COGNITIVE CONTENT AND PHYSIOLOGICAL REACTIONS

Now let us take an example where an individual experiences a situation as devastating. Mr. A is wheeled into the operating room, strapped onto the cot, and surrounded by surgeons, nurses, and so on. At this point, the threat is overwhelming: he perspires profusely, his pulse slows down, his blood pressure drops, and he starts to feel faint. His state is that of behavioral and physiological collapse.

An interesting contrast may be found in the cognitive content of the two types of response. When first entering the hospital, the cognitive content revolves around the notion of "Do something. Protect yourself. Get out of here." When he is overwhelmed by the "threat" in the operating room, the cognitive content revolves around the notion "There is nothing you can do, you're helpless."

It should be borne in mind that the sympathetic and parasympathetic reactions are each part of a larger systemic reaction. The autonomic reactions are peripheral manifestations of a central process that activates, in addition, the subjective feeling of anxiety and the increase or decrease in muscular tone. The autonomic manifestations are important clinically because they account for some of the distressing characteristics of the anxiety attack (for example, change in heart rate, change in blood pressure and pulse, and faint feelings). The activation of the sympathetic branch appears to provide the appropriate support for the active coping response (all of these except fainting and falling).

The tonic, energic system may be inactivated when an active response is inappropriate or counterproductive (in an adaptational sense). For example, in the case of an acute coronary occlusion, further activity on the part of the victim may actually increase the threat to life. Similarly, a person goes into the state of shock when there is bleeding or severe pain or injury. The degree of shock is frequently disproportionate to the actual loss of blood. In these instances, the atonic-parasympathetic reaction is a kind of reflex designed to minimize the adverse consequences of the injury. Thus, the atonic, anergic reaction represents a *passive* "coping response."

The atonic-parasympathetic reaction can occur when a person believes (incorrectly) that he may be on the verge of dying. For example, a patient with a chronic gastritis experienced acute pains due to an inflammatory reaction in the stomach, but he interpreted it to be the signs of a heart attack. The thought that he could be having a fatal heart attack apparently triggered a parasympathetic reaction. The patient began to feel "woozy," he started to sweat all over, and he found that his pulse was slow and "thready." In this particular case, the apparent drop in blood pressure and consequent faint feeling convinced the patient that he was indeed dying and consequently aggravated the vicious cycle. A similar reaction has been described in an individual who believed an assailant was about to fire a gun pointed at his head. Although this "vasovagal" (parasympathetic) reaction may serve an adaptive function when there is an actual injury or acute internal disturbance, it is obviously not adaptive when it occurs in the presence of an "imaginary" or incorrectly attributed physical disorder.

The vasovagal reaction has been described in cases of acute, severe pain and among people who have had even a minute quantity of blood withdrawn from them, who have observed the drawing of blood from other people, or who have observed mutilation of themselves or others. In the case of a serious loss of blood, the drop of blood pressure would help prevent or cut down on the volume of blood lost and adjust the blood pressure to the amount of blood remaining. This response is obviously maladaptive when there is no actual bleeding. Faintness at the sight of blood is a familiar reaction among medical students and student nurses and is well documented in blood phobias (Marks 1981).

Thus, the tonic, energic system provides a wide array of active coping responses (fighting, freezing, jumping) to deal with different types of threat. The cognitive content is: "Do something." The atonic, anergic system provides a stereotyped immobility response (fainting) when active coping would increase the danger (symbolic or actual). The cognitive content is: "I'm helpless. There's nothing I can do." The atonic response, in particular, seems to be anachronistic and counterproductive for most situations where it is evoked.

THE RELATION OF ANXIETY TO OTHER DEFENSIVE RESPONSES

A variety of mechanisms are used to "protect" a person against threat. Because appearances of these responses to threat are often temporally associated with anxiety, writers are inclined to consider them "somatic manifestations of anxiety." However, they are alternative responses or "strategies," not expressions of anxiety. Examples of these non-anxiety responses are increased muscular tension, faint feelings, dysfluencies, and concentration difficulties. These alternative mechanisms do not depend on a conscious decision in order to operate, but become operative without any conscious decision. In fact, they are often triggered despite powerful wishes for them not to occur.

Since anxiety is a conscious experience, it plays a role in the application of conscious (as opposed to automatic) strategies. It stimulates the conscious formulation and implementation of counterharm strategies. Thus, it impels an individual to decide on a course of action that will reduce danger, but does not instigate automatic reflex maneuvers—for example, inhibition of speech, tonic immobility (freezing), coughing, and gagging.

Similarly, reactions such as ducking, flinching, or jumping out of the way of a moving object do not require anxiety in order to be evoked: that is, these maneuvers can occur automatically without anxiety, or one may unintentionally initiate them in order to reduce anxiety.

Since the experience of anxiety takes time to be recognized and to provide an impetus to a defensive strategy, it does not lend itself to providing instant protection as well as the reflexive behaviors do. These differences suggest the operation of several systems in response to emergency.

The *inhibitory system* is designed for instant reaction. The reflexive behaviors are usually associated with such descriptive terms as "clutching up," "freezing," and "blocking." These patterns do not have to be triggered by anxiety and, indeed, may occur when anxiety is low.

The *anxiety-reduction system* is designed for slower reaction and incorporates more complete information processing and selection of strategies. The motor activity of this system is essentially voluntary: that is, it is under conscious direction and control. Although mobilization for action does not depend on the generation of anxiety in order to occur, it is often instigated and enhanced by the experience of anxiety.

The reflexive behaviors are the first line of defense against danger. Since the cognitive-behavioral pattern must operate rapidly in response to possible danger and tends to be overly reactive in perceiving possible threats, there will be a fairly high proportion of false positives ("false alarms"). The anxiety-reduction system serves as an alternate strategy. It is useful in providing more time for information processing than is available in automatic reflexive behaviors, since the anxiety-contingent strategies require more time to develop than do those of the purely reflexive system. The time elapsed between the perception of threat and the selection of an appropriate strategy allows for more thorough data collection, evaluation, and decision making. The presence of anxiety is particularly important in motivating a person to mobilize his resources for defense. Without the spur of anxiety, he might be too fatigued or preoccupied with other matters to mobilize for prompt action.

Both the reflexive system and the anxiety-contingent system are triggered at the same time. Since the anxiety system takes longer to "go into action," it provides a follow-up to the reflexive actions in the form of a selection of an appropriate strategy. Thus, the automatic, reflexive system uses a highly restricted repertoire of stereotyped behavior, whereas the anxiety-reduction system is much broader and consciously draws on a variety of flexible strategies.

The anxiety-contingent strategy consists of (1) generation of the affect followed by (2) forced attention to the dangerous situation, and then (3) the institution of an appropriate strategy to reduce the danger. Subjective anxiety plays a crucial role when one is exposed to a danger requiring a higher level of cognitive activity and skill (that is, other than simply freezing, falling, or retracting.) Following the initial reflexive response, which buys time until a more suitable strategy may be instituted, anxiety may induce a person to make an adaptive instrumental response to reduce the danger (find a weapon, call for help, maneuver around the danger).

Chapter 4

Cognitive Structures
and Anxiogenic Rules

Cognitive Schemas

We have seen in the previous chapter that a person's responses to a "threat" situation depend on his rapid analysis both of the harmful components of the situation and of his counterharm resources. In going from situation to situation, however, he does not have to analyze anew each time the nature of the threat and the availability of his coping skills. He needs to make appraisals with some regularity so that, upon entering a new situation, past experience can warn him what to expect and provide data on how to cope. In other words, a person is prepared to focus on important aspects of a situation and to apply the appropriate "formulas" to their analysis. This advance preparation involves the activation of "cognitive structures" *(schemas)* that orient the individual to a situation and help him to select relevant details from the environment and to recall relevant data. At times a person may be overprepared, so that he "sees" what he expects to see instead of what is actually present in the situation.

The role of the cognitive organization in information processing has been described previously (Beck 1967; 1976). According to this conception, the organization is composed of assemblies or constellations of structural elements—namely, cognitive schemas. The schemas are the basic structural components of cognitive organization. These schemas are further organized into cognitive constellations, which are grouped into the subsystems, the modes. The cognitive set is the *expression* of the controlling cognitive constellation and provides a composite picture of a specific situation. When specific schemas or a constellation of schemas is activated, their content directly influences the content of a person's perceptions, interpretations, associations, and memories at a given time. The cognitive schemas are used to label, classify, interpret, evaluate, and assign meanings to objects and events. The range of a given schema may be relatively narrow, as in labeling a concrete object such as a shoe. On the other hand, the content may be broad and abstract, as when it incorporates concepts such as "personal rights" and "self-esteem." The schema embodies various sets of rules and formulas for defining objects: for example, schemas differentiate a shoe from a slipper or a sock. A more complex schema contains a variety of rules, beliefs and assumptions—for example, the schema for designating an object as "dangerous."

Schemas are organized into clusters—the cognitive constellation—for dealing with the diverse aspects of life situations. The term *cognitive constellation* (Beck 1984a) refers to the structural counterpart of what has been traditionally labeled the "cognitive set." The term *cognitive constellation* has the advantage over the term *set* in that the former embodies the notion of relatively enduring structures whereas the concept of set implies a transient state. For the sake of maintaining continuity with traditional terminology, however, I will favor the use of the term *set* in its conventional sense, with the additional qualification that it denotes a constellation of schemas that has been activated.

The term *cognitive set* is a hallowed name in psychology. It is defined by H. B. and A. C. English (1958) as a temporary but often recurrent condition of a person that (1) orients him toward certain environmental stimuli or events rather than toward others, selectively sensitizing him for apprehending them; and (2) facilitates certain activities or responses rather than others. In terms of our present formulation, the term denotes the operation of the schemas or the cognitive constellation activated in relation to a specific class of situations—such as taking a test, asking for a raise, jumping from a cliff. When a particular constellation (set) is hypervalent, for example, the individual may experience tunnel vision, which blocks out information not relevant to the content of the constellation. In psychopathology, this exclusivity may be carried to an extreme. The anxious or panicky person can see only danger in a situation but none of the safety factors; the depressive, only his negative but none of his positive attributes.

When a threat is perceived the relevant cognitive schemas are activated; these are used to evaluate and assign a meaning to the event. The specific schemas that are activated are relevant to the specific characteristics and context of the threatening event. There occur a series of adjustments to "fit" appropriate schemas to a specific threat. One's final interpretation is the result of interaction between the event and the schemas.

The content of the constellation of schemas (or set) determines the broad range of affective responses and behavioral mobilization. Content concerned with vulnerability and danger activates a behavioral pattern relevant to flight, freezing, or collapse, and the feeling of anxiety. When the content of a set centers around "invulnerability" in the context of a noxious situation, the behavioral response is directed to attacking the offender, and the associated affect is anger. The expectation of receiving desired interpersonal "supplies" (such as expressions of affection) may stimulate feelings of elation and the desire to be closer to the other person. In contrast, a cognitive set relevant to perceived disapproval triggers sadness, and, often, the desire to avoid the other person.

The cognitive set comprises *specific* concepts, assumptions, overlays, and rules that are applied to a given situation at a given time. The *mode,* as we shall see, constitutes a broad sector of the cognitive organization and imposes a general bias that influences the type of set a person selects as he moves from one situation to another.

THE FUNCTION OF COGNITIVE SET

Cognitive sets are essential for drawing meaningful information from a particular situation. They allow us to extract relevant data, pick out relationships, and form patterns from the environment which would otherwise appear to be either bland and relatively homogeneous or else a confused array of stimuli, each competing for attention. Once evoked, a cognitive set rapidly processes incoming data. The power of a cognitive set is increased by its exclusionary capacity: it blocks out dissonant or irrelevant information. Thus, the coast watchers in England in the Second World War were able to spot enemy planes in a fraction of a second and to exclude any other, extraneous data. Nonetheless, ambiguous stimuli are counted as "positive sighting," so that sets tend to be overly inclusive as well as exclusionary.

A cognitive set is adaptive in the sense that it enables a person to obtain the greatest amount of information relevant to his present concern and to process it in the shortest time. A defensive or vigilant cognitive set is evoked when a person is in enemy territory, and is particularly sensitive to any information of an adverse nature. Because of this sensitivity, he will have many false alarms or false positives (perceive danger excessively) but fewer false negatives (label unsafe stimuli as safe) than if he were in an unthreatening cognitive set. The continuous activation of this "danger" or "defensive" set in friendly or neutral circumstances is generally an expression of psychopathology. Such persistence is an expression of the operation of a broader component of the cognitive organization—namely the mode.

At times, a cognitive set is under voluntary control and can be activated or switched at will. A student who decides to study can readily turn on the appropriate set. However, during an examination, the "test-taking set" may be activated involuntarily and may consist of automatic magnification of the difficulties of the test and automatic derogation of the student's own ability. The set—composed of assumptions such as "I don't have any mathematical ability" or, "Tests are constructed to reveal my ignorance" —will be reflected in automatic thoughts such as "I don't know how to answer this question." When the test is over, the student regains control over his set and may have thoughts such as "I can tackle difficult problems." The automatic activation of a fearful set is similar to conditions in anxiety disorders—except that, in those disorders, when confrontation is over, the individual is not able to switch to a different set (because of the hyperactivity of the "danger mode").

THE CONTINUOUS CYCLE

In order to complete the formulation of cognitive-affective-behavioral processes, we should postulate a feedback loop from the behavioral and affective schemas to the cognitive schemas: for example, proprioceptive and other sensory data are fed back to the cognitive schemas and enhance, modify, or diminish that activity (see figure 3.2).

In this formulation the central role of the cognitive structures is extended to include not only activation of the other structures but also control and modulation of them. Whether an impulse will be expressed in overt behavior is dependent on the controlling cognitive set. The movement from cognition to action is triggered by an "instruction." For example, a young man, faced with a possibly embarrassing encounter with a former girl friend who is approaching him, expects that he will feel uncomfortable and, consequently, starts to walk in another direction. However, as he considers the consequences of his attempt to "flee," he realizes that the young woman will regard this as a sign of weakness. He makes a conscious decision not to flee, inhibits further evasive movement, and waits for his girlfriend to reach him.

Translated into structural terms, the activation of the cognitive set ("This will be embarrassing") leads to a decision to flee and, consequently, mobilization of the motor apparatus. The consideration of the consequences of flight leads to a reversal of strategy and a new instruction—namely, one to control or inhibit action. Such instructions are generally tacit and present the connecting link between cognition and behavior. The result of this cognitive-motor sequence is that the individual is mobilized for flight but is prevented by internal controls from carrying it out; the inhibiting instructions arrest but do not deactivate the mobilization, which persists and is discernible in taut muscles, rapid heart beat, sweating. The inhibition described is but one aspect of a system of controls whose functions range from sensitive modulation of movement to blanket inhibition.

We should note that although anxiety is aroused, its role is to prod the individual to take remedial action, but it is not part of the mobilization for action. The cognitive appraisal of danger stimulates anxiety; the unpleasant quality of anxiety then impels the formulation of a strategy to reduce the danger, which, theoretically, should reduce anxiety. However, anxiety persists until a person perceives that he is no longer in danger of being shamed or depreciated. In more technical terms, anxiety is maintained until there is some modification of the set—the "all clear" signal, as it were. This modification may result not only from an appraisal that the danger has passed but also from a change in the person's dominant conceptualizations through cognitive restructuring. In this case, a change in cognitive focus from anticipation of disapproval to the notion "I don't care what she thinks" or, "She is probably glad to see me" may be sufficient to switch off the anxiety and the mobilization for flight.

Suppose the young man becomes increasingly anxious at the prospect of a confrontation and does decide to walk in the other direction. This sequence may be described as "disinhibition": the controls over flight are lifted.

In essence, then, depending on the specific content of a cognitive set, the behavioral disposition may be toward flight, freezing, or fainting. The associated affect is the same for each disposition—namely, anxiety. These behavioral and affective patterns can be regarded as organized into structures, with primacy assigned to the controlling cognitive constellation (set) which activates and controls the behavioral inclinations and the affective response. The feedback loop carries information regarding the internal state (for example, anxiety) and performance. This information is cognitively processed and leads to a modification in instructions and in the controlling cognitive set.

The Modes

Under ordinary conditions, the activation of the cognitive-behavioral-affective configuration facilitates adaptation and problem solving. This basic mechanism also is responsible for producing the wide range of normal emotions as well as normal behavior. Under certain circumstances, however, problems may arise when the primitive, egocentric cognitive system is activated and remains hyperactive (Beck 1967, pp. 281–90). This prolonged activation occurs when a person perceives that his vital interests (for example, survival, health, bonding, or status) are at stake.

If the resultant behavioral and affective mobilization is sufficiently intense or prolonged, then a variety of symptoms associated with anxiety disorder appear: distress, tremors, inhibitions, muscular tension, and frequently disturbance of biological functions such as appetite and sleep. Such a condition may result from prolonged or intense activation of the "danger" schemas, as in post-traumatic stress disorder; from continued exposure to a fear-evoking situation, such as an intimidating superior; or from an overriding belief that any body sensation may be a sign of a fatal illness. This condition is described in greater detail in chapter 6, on generalized anxiety disorders.

Discussion of the prolonged activation of the schemas leads directly to consideration of the operation of a sector of the cognitive organization—the modes. Under ordinary circumstances, the cognitive set varies in response to changes in the nature of the stimulus situation. If the content persists over diverse situations, the set is reflecting the bias of a superordinate organizing principle labeled the "mode." The mode is a subsystem of the cognitive organization and is designed to consummate certain adaptational principles relevant to survival, maintenance, breeding, self-enhancement, and so on. Thus, we have a depressive mode, a narcissistic mode, a hostility mode, a fear (or danger) mode, an erotic mode, and so on.

The specific set operative in a specific situation is dependent on the customary linkage between a specific set of schemas and that type of situation. However, the type of schemas or set that is evoked may be determined by a dominant mode that may be active at the time. For example, in the example of the student taking a test, as he enters the classroom he will have his typical cognitive set relevant to the specific situation—namely, the fear of having his incompetence or ignorance exposed. However, if the dominant mode is depressogenic, his approach to the test will reflect such notions as "What's the use of trying——I'm going to fail anyhow——I can't understand this." If the dominant mode is hostile, his set will reflect such notions as "They have a lot of nerve pulling this test on us——It's an unfair test." This mode is operative across a variety of situations, although the situational characteristics of the set change. Thus, the sets of someone who is "stuck" in the hostile mode will vary somewhat from situation to situation (from classroom to sports, to social contacts, to family interactions), but they will all have a common thread or theme—namely, the sense that one is being encroached on, abused, treated unfairly.

SYNDROMES AND MODES

The various syndromes may be conceptualized in terms of the domination of certain modes: in depression, the self-constricting mode is hypervalent; in anxiety, the vulnerability or danger mode; in paranoid cases, the hostility mode; and in mania, the self-enhancing mode.

The activity of the modes is reflected in the typical thinking disorder characteristic of anxiety, depression, and the other related disorders. Because of the biased selection and processing of data, a person makes such conceptual errors as misinterpretation, overgeneralization, and exaggeration. Such selective bias may be found throughout his cognitive processing from perception to recall. The bias results from the activation of schemas relevant to the content of a mode and from the deactivation of schemas inconsistent with it. Thus, in anxiety disorders, the schemas utilized for processing dangerous information are hypervalent, while those relevant to safe information are relatively inactive. Similarly in depression, schemas for processing unpleasant information are more active than those used for pleasant data. Some preliminary experimental data support this notion. M. L. Gilson (1983) found that depressed patients showed a perceptual bias toward unpleasant images presented in a binocularscope, whereas nondepressed subjects selectively perceived pleasant pictures.

ASSUMPTIONS, RULES, AND FORMULAS

In a previous work, I pointed out that a person has a system of rules or a code according to which he deciphers and evaluates his experiences and regulates his own behavior and that of others (Beck 1976). These rules operate without one's being aware of them. He selectively screens, sorts, and integrates the flow of stimuli and forms conclusions without articulating to himself the rules and concepts that dictate his interpretations. Groups of rules and concepts are organized around certain broad themes and correspond to what I have just described as mode. Specific rules and formulas are embodied in the schemas. The rules applied to a given situation provide the framework for the cognitive set, which organizes the specific content of a particular situation.

The rules or assumptions lead to and may be inferred by a clinician from the behavior of the individual. Cognitive schemas, which are a configuration in the mental apparatus, are activated by an isomorphic configuration in the environment and, in turn, trigger appropriate behavioral patterns. In the case of non-human mammals, it seems probable that some imagery is elicited prior to the behavior that it guides. Other vertebrates and invertebrates seem to have an analogous circuitry or "program" to regulate behavior.

It has been established, for example, that certain birds (such as the bunting) fixate on the northern constellations to guide them in their northward migrations (Alcock 1979). It seems probable that they have some cognitive configuration that matches certain patterns of stars and not others. Even a small portion of the northern sky which matches this configuration is a sufficient guide. Also, a set of rules dictates direction of flight; for example, "North in the spring, south in the autumn."

Some aspects of human behavior may be guided by analogous structured configuration, and humans are thus capable of responding quickly to a life-threatening situation with a programmed cognitive-behavioral response. For example, a person who sees approaching a *form* that looks like a tiger may complete the "gestalt" and visualize an actual, threatening animal such as a tiger. He then becomes prepared for emergency action such as fight, flight, or freeze. In human adults, it is possible in many cases to establish the existence of images preceding an experience of anxiety. In the study I conducted with R. Laude and M. Bohnert (1974), we demonstrated that people have images of a dangerous content when they are exposed to certain situations that are relevant to their conscious fears (see also Sewitch and Kirsch 1984).

Some rules seem to have a basic matrix that is innate but is developed on the basis of experience. These rules do not necessarily operate in a verbal form. For example, an infant's avoidance response to strangers does not have words connected with it; it seems likely that the cognitive processing of the stimuli is based on images (visual, kinesthetic, auditory). Later, the introduction of words as a result of social interaction provides the basis for learning self-control. Thus, verbal forms become powerful "persuaders," vehicles for conveying to the child formulas, injunctions, and prohibitions of the social organization.

Many of the rules that evolved over the millennia have practical value in adult humans but are likely to be too imperative and absolute for easy adjustment. In other words, some of the rules may have been functional in the wild but are dysfunctional in our present highly structured, comparatively "safe" environment. Many of these rigid rules appear to be a component of the primal program designed for rapid response to danger. These rules seem to be organized into the basic matrix of the cognitive organization and thus are not readily susceptible to modification.

RULES IN PROBLEMATIC SITUATIONS

The operation of cognitive-behavioral machinery is often flawed, particularly in complex, ambiguous problematic situations. For example, interaction with significant other people is often impaired because the patient applies the wrong rules. In a situation in which he is being evaluated or has a conflict of interest, a person may utilize an inappropriate code and then infer incorrect *meanings* from other people's behavior: their underlying attitudes toward him, their present intentions, their probable future conduct toward him. For example, a college student is corrected by her graduate student boyfriend. She wonders: "Is he trying to help me or does it mean that I've irritated him? Does it indicate that he believes I'm stupid? Is he likely to be disgusted and want to end the relationship?"

With this wide range of possible inferences from a particular interaction, is it surprising that many of us are hypersensitive to even a whiff of criticism? In this case, the woman applied a series of negatively oriented rules to decipher her boyfriend's intent. As a result, she became a "quivering mass of protoplasm," not knowing whether he would reject her.

The rules are similar to what M. Polanyi (1964) has called "tacit assumptions." A person may not be aware of these assumptions any more than he is aware of the rules of grammar when he is speaking. Yet these assumptions have a considerable influence on how he reacts to situations. Derivative from the assumptions are "conditional statements" or "conditional formulas," which are evoked according to the nature of a particular situation ("special case") and are then applied to it. The silent assumptions may not be conscious, but the rules, formulas, and equations become progressively more conscious as one moves from the general and abstract to the specific and concrete. Further, in psychiatric disorders, these rules are more obvious and more rigid, and less adaptive, than in normal functioning.

The following are examples of rules elicited from patients with "social problems" or generalized anxiety disorder. In discussing fears with them, we found that they tended to show the following assumptions (and applied them generally across a wide variety of situations):

1. "Any strange situation should be regarded as dangerous."
2. "A situation or a person is unsafe until proven to be safe."
3. "It is always best to assume the worst."
4. "My security and safety depend on anticipating and preparing myself at all times for any possible danger."
5. "I cannot entrust my safety to someone else. I have to ensure my own security."
6. "In unfamiliar situations, I must be wary and keep my mouth shut."
7. "My survival depends on my always being competent and strong."
8. "Strangers despise weakness."
9. "They will attack at a sign of weakness."
10. "If I am attacked, it will show that I appeared weak and socially inept."

In the light of these assumptions, the following responses could be expected when one of these patients is faced with the problem, say, of approaching a group of strangers to ask directions:

First, he will operate on the *assumption:* Strangers have strict rules and dislike intrusions on their privacy.

The *special case* is: If I approach those people to ask directions, they will be annoyed and will retaliate. Since I won't know the probability or intensity of their negative reaction, it is safer to overestimate it than to underestimate it.

The *conclusion* is: I had better not interrupt their conversation. (Furthermore, if our subject decides to overrule the conclusion, he is likely to feel anxious.)

The *self-instruction* is: Keep your mouth shut. (The instructions result in inhibitions.)

The consequence of these automatic assumptions, directives, and rules is that when the patient decides that he really needs to ask a question, he finds that he is inhibited and has trouble getting it out. We, thus, find another set of rules:

11. "Don't bother other people."
12. "When in doubt, keep my mouth shut."

These are part of the socialization rules that will be discussed in chapter 6. If they are broken, a person feels vulnerable.

Let us assume that the patient decides to overcome the resistance presented by the rule about keeping his mouth shut. As a result of this inhibition, he feels anxious and stumbles. Aware that his stumbling and nervousness are apparent to formidable strangers, he is concerned that he probably appears incompetent and weak and that they will therefore depreciate him. Thus, a new nest of assumptions and rules is uncovered, which are expressed as follows:

13. "If I show weakness to strangers, they will jump on me."
14. "Stumbling and nervousness are a sign of weakness that bring out the critical impulses in other people."
15. "If they retaliate, it is a sign that I did something wrong, and there is something wrong with me for having stepped out of line."

Hence, any adverse reaction validates the avoidance rule. Moreover, this person is bound by another contradictory rule.

16. "If I don't assert myself, I'm a weakling."

With this nest of assumptions, a person is likely to fear close encounters with strangers. In approaching a stranger, he finds himself in a "no win" situation: if he expresses himself fully, he runs the risk of antagonizing the stranger; if he remains quiet, he feels weak and self-critical for not asserting himself.

Thus, we can see that the assumptions and rules fall into at least three categories:

1. Generalized warnings: "Strangers are dangerous."
2. Specific warnings: "If I approach them, they will hurt me."
3. Inhibiting imperative: "Stay away from them."

In a formal evaluation situation, a similar interplay of cognitive structures may be found. Let us assume this patient is taking an oral exam. The following conditional rules enter into this case:

1. "If I fail the exam, I will never be able to face my friends or family."
2. "Because of this, it is imperative that I pass the exam."
3. "If I appear too knowledgeable, they will think I am cocky, and will be offended."
4. "If I don't seem to be knowledgeable enough, they will certainly flunk me."
5. "If I stumble, they will think that I really don't know the subject, and will count that against me."

6. "If I show any lapse of memory, they'll interpret it as lack of information."
7. "If I show my nervousness, they will think me too immature and
incompetent to get my doctorate."

The person who attempts to attain a specific goal such as the demonstration of specialized knowledge of a subject is beset by such a series of
obstructing rules that it is surprising he can function at all!

RULES IN ANXIETY DISORDERS

Each of the psychiatric disorders has its own set of rules. In anxiety
disorders, the rules concern the concept of danger and vulnerability and
the patient's estimate of his capacity for coping with the danger and for
compensating for his vulnerability. The *conclusions* derived from the application of the rules take the form of predictions such as "I am in immediate
danger of dying"; "I am not capable of dealing with this danger"; or, "I may
lose my job." The specific rules triggering these conclusions are applied (or
misapplied) to specific events: "My rapid heart beat means I'm having a
heart attack, and I may die if I don't get help"; or, "If I make a mistake,
my boss will fire me."

In anxiety disorders, the rules are generally conditional: "If a specific
event occurs, it may have adverse results." Thus, when the event occurs,
it still may have an innocuous outcome. In contrast, the rules in depression
are absolute and unconditional: "My present weakness means I will always
be a failure."

The rules are also conditional in phobias and apply to situations that the
patient is successfully able to avoid: "If I go into a closet, I might suffocate"; or, "If I go to an unfamiliar area, I may get lost." In these cases, the
patient also operates under the rule "I won't be able to cope with the
situation myself." Although these rules assume an unfortunate consequence to be highly probable, the patient is often fortified by an assumption such as "If a trusted person is with me, he can save me." Hence, many
phobic people can enter a frightening situation if a "caretaker" is available.

A sequence of questions is generally necessary to elicit the rule.

ANXIOUS PATIENT: I think I am dying.
THERAPIST: What makes you think so?
PATIENT: My heart is beating hard. Things seem blurred. I can't catch my
breath . . . I am sweating all over.

THERAPIST: Why does that mean you are dying?

PATIENT: Because this is what it is like to die.

THERAPIST: How do you know?

PATIENT: [*After some reflection*] I guess I don't know, but I *think* these are signs of dying. [Beck 1976, p. 99]

The patient's rule is that this pattern of symptoms, which are characteristic of anxiety, may equal *imminent death.* In actuality, however, the signs (palpitations, difficulty in focusing, shortness of breath) are typical signs of panic attack if they are not associated with typical signs of organic damage. The patient's ideation and symptoms become involved in a vicious cycle. Thoughts of dying lead to aggravation of the symptoms, which in turn are interpreted as signs of imminent death.

The thinking disorder characteristic of anxiety disorders may be analyzed in terms of the operation of the rules. Since the content of the primal rules tends to be extreme and very broad, patients are precipitated into making exaggerated, overgeneralized, inflexible conclusions. In normal states, a flexible set of rules operates. However, when an individual's specific fears are activated by the incursion of a specific stimulus, the more primitive rules tend to displace the more mature concepts. Moreover, if the patient accepts their validity, there is an increasing expansion of the primitive rules.

A host of rules may be extracted from a person's reactions to a wide variety of problematic situations. Some of the rules involved in evaluation anxiety will be found in chapter 9, and those involved in simple phobias, in chapter 7.

Chapter 5

Vulnerability:
The Core of Anxiety Disorders

Peter Byarus gives instance (as I have said [else-where]): *and put case* (saith he) *in one that walks upon a plank; if it lie on the ground, he can safely do it, but if the same plank be laid over some deep water, instead of a bridge, he is vehemently moved, and 'tis nothing but his imagination,* the idea of falling being impressed upon him, *to which his other members and faculties obey.*

—ROBERT BURTON
The Anatomy of Melancholy (1621)

The Concept of Vulnerability

How can we account for the fact that a particular skill that is taken for granted, and is applied smoothly and automatically under ordinary circumstances—for example, walking, talking, swimming, driving, playing an instrument—can suddenly be disrupted in the face of a threat, especially when the skill is most needed? A clue to understanding this paradoxical reaction may be found in one's cognitive-affective state when one feels threatened—namely, the sense of vulnerability.

In this context, vulnerability may be defined as a person's perception of himself as subject to internal or external dangers over which his control is lacking or is insufficient to afford him a sense of safety. In clinical syndromes, the sense of vulnerability is magnified by certain dysfunctional cognitive processes. A patient underestimates the positive aspects of his personal resources (minimization). He is inclined to focus primarily on his weaknesses (selective abstraction). He sees each flaw as a gaping hole (magnification); or each mistake as a harbinger of disaster, each slip as a potential slide into oblivion (catastrophizing). Because of his tendency to overgeneralize from each slip, he feels increasingly vulnerable after a particular mistake. For example, a person speaking in public who makes an error may become preoccupied with the audience's evaluation of it and visualize a permanent blot on his reputation. More than that, he may be primed to expect more errors, building up to a crescendo of public humiliation.

Even large successes in the past may have no permanent effect because the "vulnerable" person believes that he can always slip in the future, and that the consequences of the slip will be far more drastic than any success could be. He apparently has greater access to negative memories of previous performances than to positive ones. His selective recall appears to be a function of the "vulnerability" mode. In a state of vulnerability, he is more likely to be influenced by past events suggesting flaws and dangers than to factors relevant to success. For instance, a "vulnerable" athlete who is having some difficulty in a contest tends to have an image of himself performing below his usual standard—an image based either on specific "inadequate" performances in the past or on a fantasy of how he will appear if he fails.

Formal thinking processes are also impaired. A person finds it difficult to be objective about his negative self-appraisals, even if he tries. Furthermore, his ability to gain an overall perspective of his immediate difficulties is undermined. He sees an error in absolute terms and finds it difficult to view it in the total context that includes successes. It is as though only failure counts; success does not offset it.

There is usually consistency between cognitive and somatic manifestations of vulnerability. The individual who lacks confidence may have a cognitive set of helplessness and tends to feel passive, weak, and "mushy." Alternatively, he may perceive himself as under attack and may experience tension or muscle spasm.

Looking at cognitive processes at a more global level, we can recognize that a person's self-confidence is diminished. We define self-confidence as the individual's positive appraisal of his assets and resources in order to master problems and deal with threats. A positive appraisal gives a person a sense of self-efficacy (Bandura 1977)—the expectation of success in the tasks he undertakes. There is a positive subjective feeling: the individual feels strong. This feeling may reflect a certain degree of tension in his jaw and the muscles of his back and abdomen, which may give positive proprioceptive feedback. He is poised, ready to attack the problem.

THE ROLE OF SKILL DEFICITS

A person feels vulnerable if he believes he lacks the important skills necessary to cope with a particular threat. Many difficulties may turn into threats if he realizes that he does not have the minimal skills for attacking a problem with serious ramifications. For instance, a person who is unfamiliar with a particular foreign language will face the problem of communicating with other people when visiting that country, where his inability makes him vulnerable to a host of possible dangers. For example, he can find it very difficult to obtain help if he gets lost or becomes ill.

On the other hand, increasing a person's skills can counteract the danger he associates with certain activities. An individual who learns to swim, drive a car, ride a bike, climb a tree, jump over creeks, and so on, reduces his vulnerability in several spheres of action. Moreover, with increasing experience, he can count on his skills to prevent a serious accident—for example, falling or drowning. Similarly, the acquisition of interpersonal skills (for example, initiating conversations, asking for directions, asserting his rights) provides a basis for negotiating the pitfalls of social interaction. His acknowledgment that he has the basic skills for dealing with problems presented by his impersonal and personal environment can balance his self-doubts and sense of weakness and leads to realistic self-confidence.

SELF-DOUBT

A person reacts with self-confidence or a sense of vulnerability depending on his appraisal of his ability to cope with a threatening situation. When coping seems inadequate, the following sequence occurs: (1) He goes into a threatening situation. (2) He appraises the situation in terms of the degree of danger and his own resources in terms of dealing adequately with the threat. (3) The perception of danger and of insufficient coping skills triggers the vulnerability mode. (4) Once the mode is activated, incoming data are processed in terms of the individual's weaknesses rather than of his strengths. The focus shifts from the individual's skills to his weaknesses. A sense of uncertainty may pervade each of his acts. The "nervous" tennis player, for instance, may think, "What if I can't hit the ball?" The frightened public speaker will think, "What if I can't remember my next line?"

In the vulnerable mode, the person tends to downgrade his own abilities. Since the immediate theme is weakness rather than strength, ineptness rather than skill, he will be more tentative in confronting challenges than when he is in the self-confident mode. Furthermore, the obstacles created by his continuous self-questioning and uncertainty require much more intellectual effort to overcome. The person thinks, "Can I do it?" He then may make negative predictions: "I won't be able to speak well"; or, "My anxiety could get out of control." His attempts to focus on carrying out goal-oriented behavior or to evaluate the positive aspects of his psychological state have to go against the stream of negative ideation.

THE ROLE OF CONTEXT AND EXPERIENCE

Self-confidence is based on a belief that one's abilities will allow one to reach a goal and protect the self against the debilitating consequences of failure and negative evaluation by others. As long as a person has a firm belief in his competency, he is protected from the sabotage of uncertainty, self-questioning, and concern about failure. In the social sector, the belief in his competence can be shaken by exposure to the possibility of criticism and humiliation. Thus, an individual who has absolute confidence in his ability to perform in private (speaking, playing an instrument) may find that this confidence erodes in front of a group. Technically, we can say that the self-confidence set is replaced by a vulnerability set. The change in *context* from private to public is responsible for changing the set, the individual's belief in his own competence, and often the quality of his performance. The vulnerability mode may have some merit in protecting the immature child lacking in social skills from exposing himself to ridicule, but its persistence after the person has acquired competence is generally counterproductive.

The notion of self-confidence and competence can be further clarified if we examine the difference between a veteran soldier and a fresh recruit. The "green" soldier exposed to combat may well be swamped by a sense of vulnerability: his cognitive focus is on the dangerous aspect of a combat situation and on his own deficiencies. He finds it difficult to concentrate on the details of his assignment—for example, a scouting mission. Moreover, when confronted with an unexpected danger, his available life-preservative mechanisms are limited to the primal responses—flee, freeze, collapse—which he must overcome if he is to function at all. The experienced soldier, in contrast, has a confident task-oriented set, concerned with maximizing the probabilities of surviving, mastering the challenge, utilizing his skills. When confronted with an unexpected danger, he is already programmed to respond appropriately, presumably because previous exposure and practice in adaptive responses have forestalled the activation of the primal response. Moreover, his confidence precludes activation of the vulnerability set which predisposes one to the primal responses.

In everyday life, it is possible to be task-oriented when questions of evaluation by other people are not involved. Thus, a person can carry on a conversation with a family member, write a letter, take a walk, or drive to work without questioning his own ability. However, change the context to speaking in front of a group, taking an examination, walking on a high narrow platform, or driving in an auto race, and self-questioning emerges. The individual no longer has confidence in his ability to articulate, write fluently, keep his balance, or steer adequately. This loss of confidence may be understood as resulting from activation of the vulnerability set.

Why is the experienced professional or veteran able to respond to his specialized emergencies without the activation of this vulnerability set and the associated primal, reflexive behavior? His cognitive set in situations that other people would regard as threatening is essentially directed toward problem solving rather than toward protecting himself or escaping. His "reflexes" are just as rapid as the primal reflexive behavior. He is able to function freely at a high level because his belief in his competence is strong enough to forestall the activation of the vulnerability mode. Further, he limits his focus to the job to be done. Thus, the experienced surgeon carrying out a difficult operation is so completely invested in the task and procedures that questions regarding his competence do not arise; he does not consider the consequences of failure because it is not part of his perspective. He responds to emergencies during an operation by rapidly applying his skills. Should his confidence be reduced, however, he may then be vulnerable to the primal defensive mechanisms (for example, inhibition) that can override the operation of his skillful behavior.

The problem of retaining confidence is related to several factors: (1) the strength of the belief in one's own competence militates against vulnerability; (2) the change in context from non-evaluative to evaluative may increase the sense of vulnerability; and (3) the introduction of questions regarding the consequences of failure or regarding possible injury or death changes the set from being problem-oriented to being danger-oriented.

Adopting a confident attitude involves focusing on the positives in a situation, minimizing the dangers, and often assuming that one has greater control than one actually has. This set usually maximizes the probability of success and neutralizes the vulnerability set. However, a change in context—for example, from non-evaluative to evaluative—activates the vulnerability set. The trained professional, the seasoned veteran can, nonetheless, enter into an evaluative or a dangerous situation without its activating his vulnerability set. His mastery or self-confidence set is strong enough to withstand the pressures to activate the primal reflexive system relevant to survival.

INTERFERENCE WITH EFFECTIVE PERFORMANCE

The foregoing discussion should make clear how a person's perception of a lack of competence in dealing with a particular threat can cause him to be tentative or to withdraw from it. It may be somewhat less apparent that the impairment is not simply related to an absence of skill but results from an *active interference* with functioning. Thus, an individual who is exposed to a danger (if, for example, he undertakes a dangerous task or is unexpectedly attacked) and believes that he lacks the ability to deal with it, finds internal obstacles inhibiting his performance (blocking of speech, rigidity of muscles, mind going blank). Even more significant is that, although a person may be well skilled in a particular activity, the *anticipation* of possible incompetence and subsequent injury may act to block the operation of that skill.

We now have to examine how the perception or the misperception of inadequate coping resources leads to crippling inhibitions. The key factor in maintaining stability in a presumably risky activity seems to be whether one has confidence that one can proceed without incurring an unacceptable risk. A person who seriously questions his ability to perform adequately or safely begins to experience inhibitions and anxiety. The danger signals are triggered, and inhibitory pressures build up to discourage further movement into the "danger zone." Anxiety in this instance is an unpleasant signal to stop forward progress. If the person stops or retreats, his anxiety decreases. If he advances, it increases. If he makes a conscious decision to proceed, he may be able to override the primal inhibitory reaction.

The role of the reflex inhibitory system may be viewed as an archaic safety or precautionary mechanism (chapter 1), which is brought into play when there is a clear and present physical or interpersonal danger. The role of the inhibition is to curb or slow down action that can jeopardize safety.

As long as a person is confident of being able to negotiate the task, the mechanism remains inoperative. As soon as confidence wanes, the mechanism is activated.

Thus, there is a tug of war between advance, stop, go slow, pull back. If the individual proceeds skillfully (maintains his balance, jumps over obstacles and ravines, avoids edges of cliffs), he may remain cool. As soon as he sees an unexpected trouble spot and is not certain whether or how he can handle it, he is likely to experience physical as well as psychological restraint. Although the automatic inhibition may check impulsive risk taking, it makes movements more clumsy and in this way jeopardizes his safety. In any event, there may be continual alternation between confident mobility and fearful immobility.

It is important to note how actual automatic actions are tied in with cognitive appraisals. If the attitude is "The coast is clear," or "I can handle this," the behavior progresses—unimpeded by internal restraints. If the person views the potential danger as problematic, he is automatically held back by cautionary mechanisms—restraints and inhibitions.

The same type of cautionary mechanism is called into play in interpersonal social situations. A public speaker, for instance, may start off confidently. He notices that some members of the audience look disdainful or bored—an observation that raises the possibility of negative evaluation and leads to the fear that he may be harshly criticized. His concern about negative evaluation then activates the inhibitory mechanism. The rationale would seem to be: "Stop talking—until you are sure how you'll handle this." While this mechanism might have had some survival value in the wild, it is difficult to see its merit in social situations in contemporary life.

CATASTROPHIC PREDICTIONS AND VICIOUS CYCLES

An individual's confidence that a particular skill is adequate to prevent an injurious occurrence is not necessarily stable but may fluctuate according to the degree of anticipated danger in the situation. For example, even innumerable successful experiences of highly competent performance do not necessarily make confidence unshakable—because there is always a possibility of a slip-up. Many entertainers and actors acknowledge "stage jitters" before going on stage despite numerous successful performances (Zimbardo 1977).

In order to understand how a threatening situation can reduce self-confidence and consequently undermine functional behavior, let us consider the following situation: None of us would have any difficulty in walking across a narrow plank on the ground. Elevate the plank, say, to a height of a thousand feet, and most of us will hesitate, our muscles will become tense, and we will worry that a false step will make us fall. We may feel faint or dizzy, sense that we are losing our balance, and walk in a wavering lock-step fashion. The key factor in this highly dysfunctional reaction seems to be the sharp realization that the consequences of inept performance will be disastrous. Thus, a particular action that would ordinarily be carried out automatically and competently is disrupted by a concern for safety and, paradoxically, leads to a reaction that may undermine the individual's safety—a vicious cycle.

Another major cognitive pattern concerns "catastrophic predictions." The threatened person tends to interpret in the worst possible way any sign of weakness, mistake, negative feedback, and so on, and thus aggravates the problem. Moreover, even when doing well, he anticipates that he may slip and fall. Such catastrophic predictions exacerbate reflex inhibitions and lead to tentativeness, stiffness, and ineptness. This interference with skillful behavior, of course, increases the sense of vulnerability and thereby sets up another vicious cycle.

The "Function" of Dysfunctional Behaviors

PHYSICAL DANGER

Why does the fear of physical or psychological injury lead to a decline in performance which increases the danger of such injury? The dysfunctional behavior cannot be attributed simply to lack of skill because observation shows that the dysfunction consists of *active interference* with functional behavior. We often find, for instance, that a person has been reasonably skillful when not in a threatening situation. The answer seems to be that the demand for survival and protection against injury triggers a primal survival mechanism that is geared to terminate "risk-taking" behavior. If while foraging for food or exploring, a primitive man is confronted with a sudden danger (say, an ambush), all of his systems switch to a different mode: exploratory behavior is turned off, and defensive behavior is activated. His forward motion is interrupted; he experiences anxiety that will intensify should he attempt to override his inhibitions and proceed into the danger zone. The inhibitory mechanism, oriented toward self-protection, is triggered like a reflex and opposes his conscious intention to go forward. The unpleasantness of the anxiety and the increased effort required because of his inhibitions may force him to abandon his plan to proceed. This mode is *designed* to produce a sense of insecurity and to interfere with any action that brings the person closer to a "dangerous" confrontation.

The triggering of the self-protection mechanism is determined by a person's estimation of the amount of damage that will result if he performs inadequately (for example, whether he might sustain a slight injury or be killed), and of the probability of his performing inadequately. There is an interesting relationship between the estimated magnitude of damage and the expectation of poor performance: that is, the more drastic the consequences of poor performance, the more poorly an individual expects to perform. Thus, the average person would have no doubt that he could easily walk across a plank at an elevation of one foot but would have serious doubts at one hundred feet. A researcher might not have qualms about discussing his scientific ideas with several close friends but would lose confidence in his ability to present them before a large audience which had the power of severely damaging his reputation.

This "watch your step" phenomenon—that is, the greater the potential damage, the greater the call for caution—seems to operate through the cognitive and somatic systems. The cognitive system ensures caution by evoking a series of self-doubts, negative evaluations, and negative predictions. The somatic manifestations often consist of feelings of wobbliness, faintness, and weakness and the sense that one is losing one's balance.

The notion of decreased confidence with increased danger can be tested experimentally. People in the hypothetical situation can be asked to walk across a plank at various elevations above the ground. We predict there will be a progressive decline in self-confidence ratings at progressively greater heights. Moreover, an individual at a greater distance from the ground would walk more stiffly and awkwardly than his counterpart at a lower level.

This stiffness is a primal reaction designed to impede any action that would lead to a fall: "brakes" are applied, as it were, with each step. Of course, as an individual attempts to brave his fears and proceed along the plank, the stiffness, designed to protect him, may actually be dangerous.

The person's reaction to a threat may best be understood in terms of global concepts such as self-confidence. This construct refers to a constellation of attitudes involving a person's positive estimation of his instrumental capabilities and his belief in the efficacy of exercising them. Low self-confidence implies that the individual has a low rating of his instrumental capacity and a negative expectation of success.

The issue of self-confidence raises several questions: (1) What factors lower (or raise) self-confidence? (2) How does lowered self-confidence translate into impeded performance? What psychological and physical mechanisms lead to poor performance? (3) What function is served by lowered self-confidence and the resulting deterioration of performance?

Of the factors affecting self-confidence in the presence of a threat to life or limb, I have already suggested the severity and probability of possible physical injury. Thus, the prospect of a severe fall will reduce confidence more than will the prospect of a minor injury. On the other hand, the presence of a railing that one can grasp if one starts to slip will increase self-confidence. This safety feature provides a back-up system should a person stumble or lose his balance. Similarly, a safety net to break his fall may increase his confidence in his ability to maintain balance.

In other words, the presence of some insurance against serious injury makes a person more confident of his performance and thus reduces the probability of his falling due to his ineptness. We see analogous features in the way an individual tries to reduce social threats by eliciting favorable feedback from other people. If he can elicit a smile from others in an unfamiliar social situation, for example, he feels more confident and can operate with greater finesse and fluency. Moreover, the greater an individual's preparation for and previous experience with such situations, the greater his confidence will be.

The self-protection mechanism is manifested by restricted mobility, inhibition of performance (writing, speaking, walking), inflexibility, and cautiousness. These behavioral components are involuntary expressions of the primal defensive system. The belief that one will not (or may not) perform adequately in a situation of threat, and thus will not be able to fend off danger through one's standard operation procedures, automatically activates "extraordinary" precautions.

PSYCHOSOCIAL DANGER

A person's fear of making irreversible or fatal slips may be just as intense when speaking before a large audience as when walking along a high bridge. It seems that the same apparatus (inhibition, instability) that prevents a person from venturing into physical danger also deters him from exposing himself to psychosocial danger (say, public display of incompetence). Ironically the inhibition, instability, and blocking in a social situation, by impeding skilled performance, increase the very danger they are designed to protect the individual against.

In addition to physical immobilization, of course, the social dangers evoke mechanisms to inhibit fluency and spontaneity. In a wide variety of activities, ranging from taking an arithmetic test to telling a joke in public, the common denominator of the social dangers seems to be the possible revelation of a weakness or an impropriety to other people. This fear of displaying a weakness and of being devalued as a result is markedly present in "social phobias" and "performance anxiety" and is a frequent component of generalized anxiety disorders.

A person's reactions to a psychosocial threat may be illustrated by the example of "stage fright." The greater the magnitude of the potential "disaster" (incoherence, fainting, massive rejection), the greater the lowering of self-confidence. If a person considers that he has a vital interest at stake, and suspects that he may perform poorly and be harshly judged, he is more susceptible to lowering of his confidence, to feelings of vulnerability and anxiety, and to impeded performance. If he has a high stake in performing well, he has more to "lose" from a poor performance than does a person with no investment in his performance. Thus, the situation poses a threat if the individual's self-esteem is tied up with his performance. Interestingly, when students are told that a test does not count, they are substantially less subject to self-monitoring, self-criticism, negative predictions, blocking, tension, and so on and perform at least as well as when a test does count (see Sarason 1972).

The keynote of the self-protection pattern seems to be: "I cannot cope with this danger, so I must be cautious and guard against any slips." The cognitive constellation (set) consists of rules and formulas that serve to enhance the perception of danger (increased vigilance for internal signs of weakness and external signs of threat). As a result, the individual is increasingly aware of his thinking and behavior. In public speaking, this enhanced focus on himself is accompanied by magnified awareness of the audience's scrutiny—the phenomenon of self-consciousness (Buss 1980). In monitoring his performance, he is exquisitely sensitive to any slips. Because of the dangers of inept performance, the demand for perfect performance increases. Any slip is regarded as potentially "fatal." Certain contextual factors enhance the sense of threat: a large audience, which magnifies the potential disgrace; a formalized setting, which restricts the range of "acceptable" behavior; and the absence of supportive feedback, which accentuates one's sense of being isolated and disapproved of.

Thus, decreased self-confidence and impaired performance (in confronting either physical or psychosocial danger) result from the self-protective operation designed to prevent the person from advancing into unsafe areas and to minimize the injury if he is already in such a situation. This organization automatically, and often inappropriately, produces dysfunctional inhibition.

The Domains of Vulnerability

SECTORS OF THE DOMAIN

We can now examine the various spheres of a person's life to understand how the notion of vulnerability can pervade his important objectives, attachments, and relationships. The important spheres are conceptualized in terms of sectors of the domain. A person's major objectives may be conceptualized in terms of two major dimensions of personality—sociality and individuality (Beck 1984*b*; Beck, Epstein, Harrison, and Emery, 1983).

Sociality encompasses those strivings and goals that are necessarily dependent, for their satisfaction, on close relationships with other people. This construct includes the various personal relations that an individual regards as vital to his survival or gratification. Included in this construct, therefore, is dependency, which is manifested in the desire for help or support (1) in carrying out the functions necessary for survival, (2) in relieving discomfort or pain, and (3) in carrying out goals, solving problems, achieving mastery. The other aspect of sociality involves behavior that is expressly intended to bring gratification through possible interaction with other people. Such interaction includes intimacy, sharing, understanding, approval, affection, and so on.

Individuality is an expression of values, goals, and attitudes that are relevant to advancing the person's sense of identity, mastery, and independence. These functions include the person's (1) self-definition and protection of the boundaries of his domain, (2) the establishment of his status, rights, and privileges, (3) mastery of the functioning of the body and development of skills, and (4) acquisition of power and control over interpersonal and impersonal aspects of the environment. This construct encompasses a person's investment in developing his own capacities and interests. Other people are not the primary focus, although they may serve as a practical vehicle or standard for attaining individual goals. The earmarks of this construct are self-assertion, self-control, self-enhancement, and self-reliance. This construct is associated with notions such as "maturation drive," "differentiation," and "separation" (Rank 1932).

THREATS TO THE DOMAIN

Any threat—whether it be symbolic, hypothetical, or real—to an individual's domain is regarded as a threat to his "vital interests," which may range from his position in the social hierarchy to his ability to control his emotions. Any event that impinges on the domain is endowed with special meaning in terms of gain or loss or of threat. Consequently, such an event can trigger pleasure or pain, anger or anxiety.

The domain may be divided into two main categories according to the type of investment. Goals or strivings that are directed primarily toward other people are classified under sociality. Goals or strivings that are primarily invested in the individual himself are classified under individuality. Each of these categories is subdivided according to the areas in which these strivings and goals are manifested. In concise terms, these represent public relations or private relations. Thus, we have four subcatagories: sociality, public and private; individuality, public and private (see table 5.1).

1. The sphere of sociality, public sector, deals with a person's strivings in reference to his social group. These strivings include group belonging, support, approval, and physical closeness. The person is inclined to transcend his own individualistic strivings to mold himself into the group process (group spirit). He subordinates his own interest to the group interest.

2. In the private sector, sociality is expressed in the desire for gratifying interactions with another person: intimacy, unconditional acceptance, nurturance, help, affection, empathy, and understanding.

3. Individuality is similarly expressed in both sectors. It is most easily delineated in the private sector, where it is expressed in terms of strivings for autonomy, self-sufficiency, optimum functioning of mind and body, maintenance of health, and, ultimately, survival. The individual's private investment in himself is a concept we call "psychobiological integrity," and involves objectives of freedom, effectiveness, mastery, and health. Thus, the key words in this sphere are independence, competence, and self-control.

TABLE 5.1

Threats to Vital Interests in the Domain

Sphere	Sociality	Individuality
Public Sector	Disapproval Exclusion Separation Isolation	Defeat Depreciation Default Thwarting
Private Sector	Deprivation Disapproval Rejection Desertion	Disability Dysfunction Disease Death

4. In the public sector, the individual strivings are expressed in terms of utilizing other people as instruments for carrying out individual desires and as standards by which a person can measure his success in fulfilling his social role. Thus, he uses comparisons and competition with other people to help him measure his own efficacy or success. Specific areas in which a person expresses individual goals include school, vocation, and family. Consequently, his strivings for mastery, control, and achievement will be manifested in his social role as student, worker, or member of the family. For example, in the context of individualistic striving, the parental role is important to him not so much for gratification from interaction with his children as in its meaning in terms of his own goals, such as achievement and personal maturity. Within the social organization, the individual seeks to establish his identity, to preserve and protect his position in the hierarchy, to assert his rights, to compete for more recognition, and to resist merging with the group or subordinating his interest to the group.

THREATS TO SOCIALITY

We can now examine the various subcatagories in terms of their relevance to the concept of vulnerability. The threats to sociality in the *public* sector, are concerned with the possible loss of the social gratifiers such as group identification, group acceptance, and conviviality. The ultimate threat is exclusion and isolation. Isolation means complete separation from the group. In the *private* sector, a person is vulnerable to the varying types of loss or negative interaction with a significant other, which include deprivation, disapproval, rejection, and desertion.

THREATS TO INDIVIDUALITY

In the *public sector,* a person is vulnerable to threats to identity, to success in competition, to recognition of rights and achievements, and to maintenance of position in hierarchy. The form of the threat is generally concerned with devaluation: depreciation, defeat, domination. A person's pride is specifically vulnerable to threats of defeat, loss of status, or thwarting. The injuries to pride are often expressed in terms of "shame" (see chapter 9).

In the *private sector* ("psychobiological integrity"), individual goals are threatened by events that pose the possibility of disability, dysfunction, disease, or death. The notion of disability presents a specific threat to a person's highly valued mobility, functional integration, and achievement orientation. Dysfunction (for example, "loss of control over emotions") represents a threat to his idealized concept of self-mastery. Fear of loss of control is frequently based on a dichotomous concept: some slippage of control over thought processes or behavior may represent (to the individual) the onset of total collapse and thus generate considerable anxiety, as in the panic disorders. Similarly, the prospects of disease or death threaten the overall sense of identity and personal significance.

SPECIFIC FEARS

The specific fears that people complain of may be understood if we attempt to "assign" them to specific spheres and sectors. Fears of group disapproval or exclusion, for example, generally represent sociotropic investment in public acceptance; whereas fears of abandonment (intentional or unintentional) or of rejection by a significant other represent a sense of vulnerability in the private sector. Actual strains in a relationship can evoke fears of a complete rupture. Concerns of being thwarted by other people represent individualistic fears in the public arena: a person is fearful of any actions by other people that could conceivably interfere with his expansive goals or lead to a loss of status or defeat. Fears of possible encroachment on the person's sense of identity, functioning, or health are individualistic concerns. Thus, a person may overreact to experiences that make him susceptible to disease or loss of control or diminish his psychological functioning.

Chapter 6

Generalized Anxiety Disorder and Panic Disorder

Incidence

The statistics regarding the incidence and the prevalence of anxiety disorders vary considerably. According to some reports, those with anxiety disorders form a significant proportion (6 percent to 27 percent) of all psychiatric patients (Marks and Lader 1973). I. Marks and M. Lader found a good deal of agreement among five population studies conducted in the United States, the United Kingdom, and Sweden between 1943 and 1946. They reported a prevalence rate of from 2 to 4.7 per 100 population and found that the condition was more prevalent in women, particularly between the ages of sixteen and forty. S. Agras, D. Sylvester, and D. Oliveau (1969) reported annual community rates of phobia in the range of 7 to 8 per 100. C. G. Costello (1982) reported very high annual rates of phobias of all types in women (19.4 percent). In a 1975 survey in New Haven, M. M. Weissman, J. K. Myers, and P. S. Harding (1978) reported the rate of anxiety disorders of all types as 4.3 percent with a substantial overlap within the anxiety disorders group. Over 80 percent of the people with generalized anxiety disorder had had panic disorder and/or phobia at some time in their lives. Thirty percent of those with phobias reported having had panic disorders.

General View of the Etiology of Anxiety Disorders

It is probably counterproductive to speak of "The Cause" of the anxiety disorders, as there is a wide variety of possible *predisposing factors.* These include: (1) hereditary predisposition, (2) physical diseases leading to persistent neurochemical abnormalities (hyperthyroidism) or producing continual fears of impending disaster (mitral valve prolapse), (3) developmental traumas leading to specific vulnerabilities, (4) inadequate personal experiences or identifications to provide appropriate coping mechanisms, (5) counterproductive cognitive patterns, unrealistic goals, unreasonable values, assumptions, or imperatives learned from significant others.

Similarly, there is a vast array of possible *precipitating factors.* Some examples of these are: (1) physical disease and/or toxic substances, (2) severe external stress (for example, a series of exposures to physical or psychological danger), (3) chronic insidious external stress (for example, continuous, subtle disapproval from significant others), (4) specific external stress impinging on specific emotional vulnerability (for example, the imposition of strict military discipline on an autonomous individual).

A particular case of anxiety disorder may have any combination of the preceding factors. One case, for instance, may show an extreme amount of genetic predisposition with minimal environmental stress; another, no hereditary factors but an unusual degree of environmental danger. The "cause" of these psychological disorders may be found to reside in no specific factor but is best viewed as a composite of many interacting factors —genetic, developmental, environmental, and psychological.

BIOLOGICAL STUDIES

Some preliminary evidence of a familial pattern in anxiety disorders is presented in a number of articles. R. R. Crowe et al. (1983) found a high incidence of anxiety disorders of all types among the relatives of patients with panic disorder. Another study by S. Torgersen (1983) studied monozygotic and dyzygotic twins with anxiety disorders. He concluded that, for generalized anxiety disorder, genetic factors were not evident. However, they did appear to influence the development of other anxiety disorders, especially panic disorder and agoraphobia with panic attacks. Thus, there seems to be evidence that panic disorder is related to genetic mechanisms, but the role of hereditary in generalized anxiety disorder still needs to be clarified.

In a series of studies, a group of investigators have presented evidence that panic disorder can be induced by biochemical infusions and can be relieved through pharmacotherapy. F. N. Pitts, Jr., and J. N. McClure, Jr., (1967) reported the precipitation of anxiety after an infusion of sodium lactate. H. J. Grosz and B. B. Farmer (1972) challenged their conclusions on the following grounds: (1) Unless exercised, anxiety neurotics do not as a rule have elevated blood-lactate levels even when acutely anxious. Although they may bring about some elevation in the blood-lactate level by hyperventilating, normal subjects can do so too. (2) Anxiety neurosis is not typically present in patients with lactic acidaemia—that is, with very marked and chronic blood-lactate elevations. (3) With neither the sodium lactate nor the sodium bicarbonate infusion is the onset of symptoms associated with significant blood-lactate elevations.

Since that time new reports tend to lend some support to the findings of Pitts and McClure. Panic attacks have been precipitated through the infusion of sodium lactate (Appleby, Klein, Sachar, and Levitt 1981). Similarly, Klein and his associates found that the administration of imipramine as well as other "antidepressants" serves to ameliorate this disorder (Gorman, Levy, Liebowitz, McGrath, Appleby, Dillon, Davies and Klein 1983). These findings, which are being subjected to further clarification at other centers, may cast some light on the biochemical mechanisms in this disorder. However in view of the strong evidence of cognitive and other psychological factors in this disorder as well as behavioral methods for relieving it, it seems premature to make a commitment to an exclusive organic etiology.

PRECIPITATING PSYCHOLOGICAL FACTORS

1. *Increased demands:* A variety of factors appear to be involved in the precipitation of generalized anxiety disorder (GAD). These seem to involve an increased threat to important values and a depletion of coping resources. An individual typically has greater expectations, increased responsibilities, and an overall increase in energy output. The result is that he becomes more concerned about failure. If he strongly believes that his intrinsic value is based on his level of performance, the threat of failure is aggravated. Examples are the new type of demand imposed on a parent after the birth of a child. Similarly, a job promotion that increases responsibilities, expectations, and work load can precipitate this disorder.

2. *Increased amount of threat in a life situation:* A person's circumstances may change in a way that poses a serious threat to him. For example, an ambitious young physician moved into a new position under the supervi-

sion of a hostile chief. He felt continuously "under the gun" and believed that at any time he could commit a catastrophic error that would cost him his job. Similarly, a new mother was faced with an infant that was susceptible to various infections. The mother became increasingly concerned that she would not take proper care of the child (for example, the child might suffocate if the mother did not hear her cry).

3. *Stressful events that undermine confidence:* A person may have a number of moderate reversals or a major reversal that makes him believe that he may not be able to achieve an important objective. For example, a young lawyer failed an examination to qualify for admission to the bar. He was faced with the immediate problem of not being accepted by the firm that had hired him. At the same time, his girlfriend had informed him that she did not love him. The overall impact was to make him fear that he could never be happy on his job and, even worse, that he would never be able to have a loving wife and a family. Each of these notions contributed to a chronic state of anxiety. His two major sources of satisfaction were threatened.

INTERACTION OF PRECIPITATING FACTORS WITH PREVIOUS PROBLEMS

In cases of GAD, we often see that the problems reported by the patient did not start with the precipitating events but actually extended far back into the developmental period. The precipitating stressors are potent only insofar as they strike at a person's specific vulnerabilities. The mother who was chronically anxious after the birth of her child had experienced long-standing "feelings" of inadequacy. However, the problem now was: Her inadequacy could risk the baby's life and thus became a source of danger. A person faced with the threat of failure in his career now thinks seriously for the first time, "I may not be successful in my career and thus I can never be happy." The young lawyer had always believed that he lacked personal charm, but now he was faced with the problem that he might never find an acceptable mate who would accept him.

DO COGNITIONS CAUSE ANXIETY DISORDERS?

Many statements have been made in the literature and elsewhere to the effect that cognitions cause depression or anxiety disorders. We believe that this conception is misleading. We consider that the primary pathology or dysfunction during a depression or an anxiety disorder is in the cognitive apparatus. However, that is quite different from the notion that cognition *causes* these syndromes—a notion that is just as illogical as an assertion that hallucinations cause schizophrenia.

What, then, is the relationship between cognition and anxiety disorders? We propose that an upset in the regulatory functions of the cognitive system leads one indiscriminately to interpret environmental events as dangers. Ordinarily there is a reasonable balance among the modes (chapter 4) relevant to danger, threat, enhancement, and loss, so that when one of them has been hypervalent for a prolonged period, an opposing mode is activated. Thus, during a period of elation, an individual becomes sensitized to negative feedback, and the self-deflation mode may be activated by a disappointing experience. Similarly, hostility is generally counterbalanced by anxiety. These cognitive appraisals of a situation influence affect and behavior. Although the usual appraisals probably do not deviate drastically from reality, it sometimes happens that one mode becomes so dominant—say, the self-enhancement mode—that the integration of corrective feedback is blocked. Thus, for a time, experiences are overinterpreted exclusively in self-inflating ways. This imbalance is generally corrected eventually, and the individual does not remain in a state of elation and inactivity. However, in psychopathology, there seems to be interference with the turn-off of the dominant mode, which progresses to a level of hyperactivity for a prolonged period. The results are systematically biased interpretations of positive information (in mania) and of danger (in anxiety disorders) and consequent excessive mobilization of the somatic and the autonomic nervous systems. This overmobilization itself can produce secondary symptoms, such as gastrointestinal dysfunctions.

What factors are responsible for the failure of the hyperactive cognitive system to "turn off"? It is possible that fatigue may interfere with the action of the rational cognitive system to exert a corrective influence by producing more realistic interpretations. However, why the opponent mode remains relatively inactive and thus cannot contribute to a more balanced view of reality is obscure at this time. It could be speculated that certain neurochemical disturbances either stimulate an overactivity of the danger schemas and prevent their habituation to danger, or else interfere with the activation of the "security" mode.

In essence, far from being a cause of anxiety disorders, cognitive processes constitute a major mechanism by which the organism adapts itself to the environment. When a variety of factors interfere with the organism's smooth operation, it becomes the mechanism through which anxiety disorders or other disorders are produced.

Generalized Anxiety Disorder

SYMPTOMATOLOGY

The symptoms in anxiety disorders reflect overactivity of the cognitive, affective, and behavioral systems. The affective and somatic symptoms are found in table 6.1; the cognitive-behavioral symptoms in table 6.2. The most common symptom—inability to relax—found in 96.6 percent of 100 cases, appears to represent an overmobilization of all the systems and incorporates anxious feelings and mind racing. The rest of the affective-somatic symptoms reflect anxious affect (frightened, terrified), motoric mobilization (tense, jumpy), and activation of the sympathetic nervous system (hands perspiring, heart racing) or of the parasympathetic system (sweating all over, difficulty catching breath, urgent desire to urinate, nausea, diarrhea, or faint feeling). There are also signs of the "collapse" of the motor systems (feeling wobbly and weak all over).

The most common symptom of cognitive impairment is difficulty in concentration (86.2 percent). The high frequency of confusion, mind blur-

TABLE 6.1

Frequency of Affective and Somatic Symptoms in Generalized Anxiety Disorder

Symptom	Frequency (%)
Unable to relax	96.6
Tense	86.2
Frightened	79.3
Jumpy	72.4
Unsteady	62.1
Weakness all over	58.6
Only hands perspiring	51.7
Terrified	51.7
Heart racing	48.3
Face flushed	48.3
Wobbly	44.8
Sweating all over	37.9
Difficulty catching breath	34.5
Urgent desire to urinate	34.5
Nausea	31.0
Diarrhea	31.0
Faint or dizzy feeling	27.6
Face is pale	24.1
Feeling of choking	13.8
Actual fainting	3.4

ring, and inability to control thinking indicates that "cognitive impairment" is an important aspect of GAD. The most common symptom referable to the theme of danger is the fear of losing control which occurs in 75.9 percent and thus is an unexpectedly important feature of GAD. The fear of being rejected (72.4 percent) is almost as common.

Difficulty in communicating (for example, blocking, broken sentences) occurs in a significant proportion of the cases and thus must be considered a salient feature. Similarly, certain symptoms of uncontrolled motor activity (trembling, shaking, swaying) constitute a significant minority. In sum, the symptomatology taken as a whole suggests a composite of the activity of the various systems.

TYPES OF GENERALIZED ANXIETY DISORDER

There are two general types of cognitive content in generalized anxiety disorder. In the first, there has been a traumatic event, involving actual injury or threat of injury or a threat to an interpersonal relationship. The most dramatic expression of this type of disorder is the "combat neurosis" characterized by perseverative ideation relevant to catastrophic events in battle. A similar reaction is seen in less dramatic ways in civilian life and may be precipitated by a frightening event such as a surgical operation or observing injury to another person. These traumatic reactions are found

TABLE 6.2

Frequency of Cognitive and Behavioral Symptoms in
Generalized Anxiety Disorder

Symptom	Frequency (%)
Difficulty in concentration	86.2
Fear of losing control	75.9
Fear of being rejected	72.4
Inability to control thinking	72.4
Confusion	69.0
Mind blurred	65.5
Inability to recall important things	55.2
Sentences broken or disconnected	44.8
Blocking in speech	44.8
Fear of being attacked	34.5
Fear of dying	34.5
Hands trembling	31.0
Body swaying	31.0
Body shaking	27.0
Stuttering	24.1

most commonly in acute anxiety states. The second form of generalized anxiety disorder seems to be an extension—and aggravation—of fears that a person has experienced during his early development, and takes a more chronic form.

Acute Anxiety State. The acute anxiety syndrome occurs in situations that are considered to constitute a serious threat to an individual's physical or psychological survival. This syndrome is generally associated with actually being *in* the danger situation or having images of the danger that are so vivid that the individual believes, at least partly, that his life is threatened. The acute anxiety syndrome consists of total mobilization for immediate action. There is an activation of reflexive behavior (for example, flight, freeze), of the subjective experience of anxiety, and of the autonomic nervous system (palpitations, rapid breathing, profuse perspiration). Because of the intense somatic and affective feelings, this state can escalate into panic attacks.

When the danger is not perceived as immediate, anxiety and partial motor and autonomic mobilization may occur. At this point, the mobilization involves primarily sympathetic innervation. As the individual enters the danger situation, there may be a switch from preparation for action to generalized inhibition (interference with spontaneous activity and fluency of thought and speech). Moreover, certain susceptible people (blood or injury phobics) will experience a switch from mobilization of the sympathetic system to an atonic (weak, wobbly), parasympathetic (faint or actual fainting) reaction.

The acute syndrome will be discussed in terms of the type of traumatic event that precipitated it: namely, events producing a serious threat to life or limb (mutilation), and events presenting a serious danger to a crucial interpersonal relationship.

Traumatic Event Involving Physical Danger. The first major class of generalized anxiety disorders could be labeled "traumatic anxiety disorders." This condition has been included in the DSM category of "posttraumatic stress disorder." In this disorder, the major problem generally involves a perceived threat to the individual's health or life. In our experience, we have found that a frightening incident, such as a surgical operation or an accident, may have such a powerful impact on a person that he is not able to assimilate the experience; it remains in the background of his thinking, easily activated by any relevant stimulus. The features of the experience—for example, its life-threatening nature and the patient's helplessness—undermine his belief that he can cope with such a situation, and thus he cannot dismiss the fantasy. Many cases of acute anxiety—lasting a few days to a few weeks before a person sought help—had an acute onset following an experience that was directly or indirectly threatening.

Autonomous Images.   A bus driver, for example, had repeated fantasies of getting into an accident while driving his bus. Each fantasy had generated anxiety, which had become so intense that he had taken a leave of absence from his job. This disorder occurred following his observing a fatal bus accident. Even after he left his job, his anxiety continued. Another patient, whose acute anxiety followed an automobile accident, continually "relived" the accident in fantasy. A third patient, after learning that her best friend had cancer, began to have continual images of dying of cancer and experienced continuous anxiety. In each of these cases, the images appeared to be producing the unpleasant anxiety.

Autonomous or "uncontrolled" images are activated in these cases and tend to persist without the patient's being able to stop them (Beck 1970). We have found that the fantasies in these acute syndromes have the following features: First, they are not under volitional control. A person experiences them despite his attempts to stop them. They may be evoked regularly by relevant stimuli, such as hearing about someone else having an accident or a fatal illness. However, they often occur without any particular external stimulus. Once an image has started, the person cannot "turn it off." It continues or repeats itself until he is distracted or goes to sleep. Secondly, the person who is having the image experiences it as though the traumatic episode were actually occurring *in the present:* that is, he cannot discriminate between the image and present reality. It is as though the past has encroached on the present. Finally, the terror and anxiety wax and wane predictably according to the sequence of events in the fantasy.

The core problem in the traumatic neuroses may be explained as follows: The normal person is able to determine fairly rapidly whether a stimulus is a signal of a real danger. As he is able to label the stimulus an insignificant sound or scene rather than a danger signal, his anxiety dissolves. In contrast, the anxious patient does not discriminate between safe and unsafe and continues to label the sound as a danger signal. His thinking is dominated by a concept of danger. Once a stimulus has been tagged as a danger signal, the association between the stimulus and the concept "danger" becomes fixed.

Traumatic Psychosocial Event.   This disorder usually starts with an identifiable precipitating "cause," such as a traumatic event (say, a threatened break-up of a relationship), a sudden increase in demands and expectations (say, the birth of a child or a new, more demanding job), or an increase in the threatening components in a situation. The effect of the event is to jeopardize certain valued functions, such as maintaining a relationship or performing adequately at home or at work.

The *automatic response* to these threats is the mobilization for self-protection leading to a kind of spastic interference with one's goal-oriented performance. A person's arms are tight, and he is clumsy in performing vital functions. He is taut and tongue-tied in the presence of the person who may reject or depreciate him, such as his lover or boss. When not in the threatening situation, the person fears what might happen in the next confrontation. He has images of being abandoned or fired or making a fatal mistake. He not only has continuous anticipatory anxiety but, after a "test" of his abilities or desirability, fears that he may have alienated his lover or made a serious error on the job which will lead to disaster.

Another consequence of the acute anxiety reaction is the development of a range of physical symptoms, such as headache, gastrointestinal disturbances, chest pain, palpitations. These physical symptoms, in turn, trigger fears of a serious physical disorder and catch the individual in the web of increasing fears, leading to increased symptoms which reinforce the sense of vulnerability and undermine efficacy. The vicious cycle helps to explain why the anxiety state escalates instead of subsides.

Chronic Anxiety Disorder. Anticipatory anxiety is most important in chronic anxiety disorder, as in the following examples: (1) A college student worried and felt anxious throughout a school year because he believed he would perform poorly (according to his own standards). He was apprehensive when he was studying; before going to class; after class; before, during, and after exams—in short, all the time. (2) A young psychiatrist was concerned whenever he heard the telephone ring that he might hear a patient of his had relapsed or committed suicide. At other times, he feared that he was not treating his patients adequately, that his patients and supervisor might disapprove of his performance, and that his patients might get worse. (3) A newspaper reporter had chronic anxiety in her work situation: she feared that the people she interviewed would consider her an inept interviewer, that her editor would reject the typed copy, and that the readers would disapprove of the printed story. When working in the newsroom, she was concerned that the other staff people were judging every move she made.

In all of these cases, the anxiety seemed to be an extension of problems the patients had experienced throughout most of their lives. It appeared that the most common feature of these chronically anxious patients was the continuation into adulthood of fears originating in the developmental period.

The areas relevant to developmental fears can be condensed into (1) the problems revolving around relations with other people (sociality), and (2) those relevant to identity, mastery, autonomy, and health (individuality). An individual's survival, satisfactions, and attainment of goals are to some degree dependent on the support of other people and to some degree on his own competence in eliciting the support of others, in protecting himself from various dangers, and in implementing his goals. The psychosocial fears, thus, revolve around the threat of losing caregivers and consequently being vulnerable to injury or death, or the threat of performing ineptly outside the family and being subjected to ridicule or rejection. In addition, a person fears that his lack of competence will prevent him from mastering problematic situations and reaching his goals. In the developmental period, many of the potential sources of fear are relatively quiescent because the child has the protection and support of his kin group. As he gets older, he is propelled into confronting some of these "dangerous" situations on his own and is expected to draw on his own repertoire of gradually developing skills to deal with them.

When the development of new skills has not yet caught up with new demands, the individual may be fearful of failure, public show of incompetence, and ridicule. In addition to the concerns about not being able to satisfy the expectations for mature behavior, he may continue to be vulnerable to any threats to his closeness to and dependency on key figures —and thus is subject to fears of abandonment and rejection. Besides his fears about establishing autonomy and mastering problems, the individual fears that his own sense of individuality and freedom may be taken away because of external domination and restriction.

Curiously, the fears of behaving incompetently may persist long after a person has developed a broad range of competence. The development of skills does not necessarily expunge the sense of incompetence or fear of failure. A late adolescent who has developed an ability to initiate conversations, make requests, and present his ideas publicly may still have strong residual fears of appearing foolish and awkward. Thus, a person at this stage of development has three related sets of problems: fear of being incompetent; fear of appearing incompetent; and fear of loss of support of key figures. These fears are central in the development of many cases of anxiety disorder and social phobia.

In addition to the fears related to competence in dealing with problems are fears of externally imposed mishaps, such as accidents or illness. These adverse events are not only uncontrollable but to varying degrees require outside assistance in order for their effects to be mitigated. Within the family or school situation, help is automatically available to staunch bleeding, make diagnoses, and summon medical care. The price of increasing autonomy, however, is the decreased access to this kind of help. People who develop fears of having some overwhelming physical, mental, or behavioral derangement, thus, maintain their "need" for access to a caregiver and are threatened by situations that limit this access. The coupling of fear of disaster with fear of distancing from a caregiver is dramatized in agoraphobia but is present to a lesser degree in many anxiety states.

It appears that a person is influenced by two opposing modes: self-confidence, based on a demonstrated degree of success in managing challenges; and vulnerability, derived from earlier periods of actual lack of competence. When a person's self-confidence—or "self-efficacy estimates" (Bandura 1982)—is firmly established, his self-doubts and uncertainties may be temporarily quiescent. When the vulnerability or insecurity mode is activated, however, he may strongly question the basis of his self-confidence. The insecurity imposes severe strictures on his attempt to confront threats, challenges, and demands. These strictures are expressed in the form of crippling inhibitions, painful anxiety, and generalized patterns of avoidance, all of which impair functioning and lead to further fear of incompetent performance and consequent failure and depreciation.

A generalized anxiety disorder may derive from a reactivation or extension of developmental fears regarding a person's capability of mastering problems and his acceptability to other people. Thus, we often see the precipitation of the disorder when a person's life has shifted in the direction of increased demands and expectations; when there is a decrease in the amount of support from significant others; or when he undergoes experiences that sharply undermine self-confidence and sense of acceptability.

In this sense, generalized anxiety disorder may be distinguished from social phobia. In the former, there is generally a reduction in self-confidence from a previous level. In the case of social phobia, the individual has not yet mastered the skills demanded by social interaction. For example, he may have a sense of incompetence in approaching strangers, in interacting socially with members of the opposite sex, or in negotiating with authorities. However, he is still comfortable in familiar situations and, with further psychological maturation, shows progressive improvement in social skills and self-confidence.

The crucial feature of the social performance of the individual with a generalized anxiety disorder is that he is impaired not simply by a relative deficiency of skills and low self-confidence but by an active *inhibition* of the skills he has already acquired, and thus he becomes more vulnerable to being insulted, ridiculed, and taken advantage of in the vicious cycle we have already described (pages 73–74).

SPECIFIC FEARS

The widely accepted concept of generalized anxiety disorder as a disturbance in which the source of the anxiety is unknown creates an unfortunate tautology. Since, by definition, the patient is unaware of the source of anxiety, the clinical investigator or therapist is unlikely to make a thorough exploration of the patient's phenomenal field. The patient's spontaneous explanations are likely to be discounted as rationalization rather than as pertinent data (Marks 1981). Although generalized anxiety disorder has conventionally been conceived of as diffuse and not related to specific situations, the investigator or therapist is able to pinpoint situations that appear to generate or exacerbate anxiety. Moreover, by factoring into the analysis one's anxiety *prior* to entering a problematic situation (anticipatory anxiety) and *after* leaving it (retrospective anxiety), an investigator is able to provide at least a partial explanation of one's anxiety episodes.

Using a "cognitive analysis," the therapist may establish even more precisely that the anxiety is not "diffuse" but is related to specific fears. Some of the fears are like discrete phobias in that they are attached to specific situations. Generalized anxiety states differ from phobias in that the former fears cut across a heterogeneous group of situations. Moreover, these fears may be active even when the person is not in a "threatening" situation. They can be understood in terms of ultimate "consequences," such as dying or being rejected or attacked. Some cross-situational fears are concerned with psychosocial traumas. Other fears are more pervasive and are related to the possibilities of losing control, not being able to cope, failing, or having a potentially fatal disease (such as heart disease). In some cases, especially following a brush with disaster or an actual trauma, there is a pressure of ideation related to the trauma; hence, the person may have frequent thoughts of being traumatized (dying, falling, getting mutilated, suffocating, drowning). These traumas are similar to those classified as "post-traumatic stress disorders," but the anxiety states do not qualify for that diagnosis since they are not stresses "outside the range of usual human experience."

"Social anxiety" or "interpersonal anxiety" appear to be the cornerstone of most cases of generalized anxiety disorder, as shown in systematic studies by A. T. Beck, R. Laude, and M. Bohnert (1974); by N. A. Fox and Beck (1983); and by G. A. Hibbert (1984). These individuals are apprehensive of any interaction where they would risk being dominated, devalued, rejected, or abandoned. Thus, whether at work, play, or home, they are continually experiencing fears and, consequently, anxiety. Before a job interview, for example, the GAD patient is anxious about how he *will* perform; during the interview, he feels anxious about how he *is* performing and about the outcome; and afterward, he feels anxious about how he *did* perform—specifically, about the possible negative consequences of inadequate performance.

Beck, Laude, and Bohnert (1974) found that their patients with GAD showed ideation (images and automatic thoughts) revolving around at least one of the following general fears: physical injury, illness, or death; mental illness; psychological impairment or loss of control; failure and inability to cope; and rejection, depreciation, domination. It is significant that the majority of the patients (70 percent) had fears in at least three of these areas. Patients without panic attacks focused on psychosocial rather than physical fears. Almost all patients with panic attacks had fears of physical or mental damage. Hibbert (1984) found that most of his GADs without panic had a central fear of not being able to cope with other people, whereas those with panic attacks had fears of a physical disaster.

The nature of the fears in GAD may be delineated by comparing them with the fears in phobias. The anxiety-producing situations in GAD are situations in which avoidance is not feasible. One of the major problems in GAD (especially in panic disorder) revolves around the persistence and escalation of distressing internal sensations which lead to a fear of loss of control or of some serious pathological process. These are "dangers" that *should be attended to* rather than avoided. If a person is bleeding or believes he is having a heart attack, it might save his life to feel helpless and to call for help.

Another source of danger lies in the domain of interpersonal relationships. If an individual is uncertain about his interpersonal skills in a threatening situation, it might be advantageous for him to experience anxiety as a spur to develop or polish these skills. An immature person who lacks social skills, and keeps getting rebuffed in social situations because of his ineptitude, eventually will be isolated from the social group and may become depressed. His anxiety, thus, deters him from actions that will elicit social reprisal and may increase the pressure to develop more adaptive behavior.

In essence, then, anxiety (along with several of the other negative affects, such as shame) is a powerful spur to socialization and maturity. It also helps to deter the individual from getting into dangerous situations that he should avoid (raging fires, shaky tree limbs, collapsible tunnels, deep water) and discourages rash behavior in social situations. A person's anxiety may be reduced to some extent in social situations by the development and application of social competences. (This factor may be the reason that training in social skills is often so effective in generalized anxiety.) As an alternative to self-development, the immature individual may take the option of leaning on a more skillful relative or companion for promoting his interests in social situations and, consequently, maintain juvenile dependency.

The fears of the GAD patient, thus, may be understood in terms of the excessive impact of the exposure to socialization. A major dread of these patients is that of being depreciated, ridiculed, or rejected. Generally, the trigger for such expectations is their perception of "inept behavior." Thus, a person who behaves immaturely is subject to epithets such as "You're a baby, grow up!" The fear of such a sanction stirs anxiety and stimulates him to monitor and control his behavior. If he feels like crying, for example, he inhibits its expression. Anxiety may lead further to overmonitoring and inhibition and thus can produce awkward behavior for which the patient may be criticized. Consequently, more anxiety is generated.

Another major fear, especially in panic attacks, is that of loss of control. This fear also tells us something about the rigidity of a person's standards: namely, that he considers the maintenance of control to be imperative and the prospect of loss of control to be a catastrophe. In a study of the fears of GAD patients at the Center for Cognitive Therapy, we found that about 75 percent reported fear of loss of control as a major fear.

Fear of failure and of being unable to cope with the demands and expectations imposed by oneself or others is a theme that runs—subtly— through the ideation of most cases of GAD. One factor activating this fear is the "paralysis" of function in acute confrontations: that is, inhibition of spontaneous movement and interference with speaking, thinking, and recall. A person fears confrontations because of the possibility that his apparatus for effective communication will shut down and leave him vulnerable and helpless. In addition, the generalized concept of himself as not being sufficiently skilled or competent to meet his goals haunts him whenever he undertakes an important task or attempts to solve a difficult problem.

Proximal Fears and Ultimate Fears. To a large extent human beings are programmed to fear potentially harmful places and events. A specific fear can be formulated in terms of three different levels or points: fear of a specific place, situation, or object or event; fear of having an unpleasant affect or sensation (anxiety, panic, shame, physical pain, choking, and so on); and fear of the *outcome* or consequences of being in that particular place or of having that unpleasant sensation or feeling. The first two fears are labeled "proximal" in the sense that they represent the frightening place or object and the symptom (anxiety) activated as a person approaches it; thus, the patient has a fear of the situation and a fear of the anticipated anxiety and other symptoms.

These three "types" of fear are obviously components or aspects of the same process and have a logical relationship. For example, a young woman, notified that her boss wants to see her, initially feels anxious at the thought of entering his office (the "situation"). She shudders at this unpleasant experience (the "affect") and would like to terminate it. Then she fears that her anxiety will get worse and that she will be very uncomfortable. Finally, she is afraid of a specific outcome once she is in the situation: namely, that she will be fired (the "consequence"). In this case, the fear of the situation and of her anticipated symptoms may be labeled the "proximal fear"; and the fear of being fired, the "ultimate fear."

The three facets may be analyzed in terms of their function in the survival mechanism. The most pragmatic way to prevent dangerous encounters is to label as "dangerous" a concrete, identifiable object or place associated with a possible harmful encounter. For example, children are often afraid of the dark or of strange places. However, the actual danger, if any, is not the object or the place itself but what might occur *in* the situation (for example, one might be attacked by ghosts or strangers). The aversive place is tangible and thus easily identified. A person is programmed to perceive it as the danger and experiences anxiety as he approaches it. He may not "know" why it is dangerous. The global meaning of "dangerous" is sufficient to produce the anxiety and avoidance behavior.

The next level of fear is attached to the anticipation of anxiety. Just as one avoids exposing oneself to the risk of physical damage because of the fear of physical pain, so one avoids exposure to psychological trauma because of the fear of anxiety. The agoraphobic person may say, "I know that there is nothing unsafe about public places, but I also know I am afraid that I'll be very uncomfortable if I go there" (in this sense, the fear is "realistic": that person probably will feel discomfort if he goes there).

The final, ultimate level has to do with the anticipation of harmful consequences if one is in the dangerous situation. Thus, a person may decide against engaging in a hazardous activity because he determines the risk of being harmed is too great. He does not need anxiety to deter him;

the knowledge of the danger is sufficient. For the anxiety patient, the precise nature of the ultimate fear may not be apparent until he is actually in the situation. Thus, a person may feel tense on entering a classroom. Once there, he will recognize that his fear centers on the idea that he will look foolish when he is asked to perform.

The specific nature of the proximal fears may be understood in terms of the automatic protective (primal) functions of the organism. The early global fear is relatively primitive in that it is attached strictly to the physical, topographic classification of a dangerous situation. This focus on the physical features has the advantages of eliminating judgment from the fear reaction. The rule regarding the "dangerous" place is simple, unequivocal, and absolute; there is generally no need for delay or confusion in applying it. On the other hand, the breadth and rigidity of the classification make it overly inclusive; and consequently, the individual is likely to experience a number of false alarms. The warning system appears to be most effective if the concept of danger is shifted from a noxious event that *might* occur, were the individual in contact with the place or object, to the object itself. By attaching the label of danger to the concrete object, he is alerted to danger at the earliest point. Thus, the experience of anxiety and avoidance motivation impel him to *prevent* the danger from becoming actualized. Once he is in the situation, however, the automatic mechanisms are directed to escape, freezing, or seeking help.

The role of cognitive therapy, as we will point out, is to test whether a particular situation labeled dangerous is actually dangerous. Thus, through questioning the degree of danger, evaluating danger-laden automatic thoughts, and experimental exposure, the patient is enabled to detach and "extinguish" the fears that have been erroneously attached to a given situation or object.

Systematic Studies of Automatic Thoughts and Images.   A detailed analysis of the content of the ideation of thirty-two GAD patients (Beck, Laude, and Bohnert 1974) indicated that each patient anticipated being harmed physically or psychologically, or both. In acute-severe conditions, a patient's ideation revolved around the fear of a physical disaster or of some social, interpersonal catastrophe, or both. In more chronic and less severe conditions, this feared event or trauma was of a less "severe" nature—anticipation of being criticized or rejected or of failing.

The cognitions that occurred just before the onset or exacerbation of anxiety had the common theme of imminent danger. They were experienced as discrete thoughts, such as "I am having a heart attack," or "I will look foolish." In the more severe cases, the patient attached a high degree of probability to the occurrence of the feared event. Even in the less severe cases, the automatic thought of danger seemed plausible to the patient and the likelihood of being hurt seemed high. Despite a history of repeated disconfirmations, the expectation of danger recurred when a patient was exposed to the typical "dangerous" situation.

Of the thirty-two patients, thirty reported having experienced conscious images of an unpleasant or a disastrous experience. These visual experiences had the same content as the verbal cognitions. When asked to experience the fantasies during the interview, the patients were able to visualize the unpleasant event and felt anxious as the visualized scenario developed. Specific features of thoughts and images reported by a given patient often clearly related to unique aspects of his conceptual configurations and to his past experience. Therefore, these personal variations often shed the most light on the relation between the patient's mode of integrating his experiences and the arousal of anxiety.

For instance, eight of the thirty patients had recurrent, anxiety-associated ideation about dying. However, the nature of the feared event, the situations associated with anticipation of death, and the expected consequences of the anticipated catastrophe differed substantially. One woman patient, for instance, feared sudden death by heart attack or suffocation. This fear developed after two experiences, involving fainting associated with chest pain and dyspnea, that she had misinterpreted as heart attacks—an erroneous conclusion that was reinforced by the apparent concern of the doctors observing her in the hospital. However, no evidence of any disease was found.

Another woman was specifically fearful of dying from a slowly deteriorating illness, associated with chronic pain, wasting, and deformity. A close friend of hers had been afflicted with chronic, progressive neurological illness; and at the time our GAD patient experienced unexplained pains and paresthesia, which disappeared several years before her examination in the study. She interpreted almost every unusual sensation in any part of her body as indication of a progressive disease. These ideas ultimately culminated in her experiencing a severe anxiety attack.

A third patient, who had been raped by an armed man while alone at night, believed that the terrifying emotions aroused in her then were sufficient to permanently damage her mind. Being alone in her apartment or walking alone in the city activated fantasies of being attacked. It is important to recognize that the crucial object of her fear was not the danger of being raped again *per se,* but rather the disastrous consequences that she assumed would result from the terror she would feel. She believed it was likely that she would be at least momentarily paralyzed and might die from the terror.

A fourth patient was chiefly concerned with the consequences of dying suddenly and unexpectedly. From a strong orthodox Catholic background, she feared an afterlife of eternal punishment if she was not prepared for death. She had been warned several times during an impressionable period of early childhood that if she was lazy or sinful in her life, she might die in her sleep, unprepared and without warning, and wake up in hell. Subsequently, she believed that she was particularly vulnerable to some unpredictable event that could cause her death.

All of the other patients who were afraid of death traced their fears to actual life experiences that had frightened them. One woman, who was afraid of having a heart attack, had witnessed her mother doubled up with pain from attacks of angina, one of which culminated in her death. Another patient had a severe choking episode while receiving anesthesia during an operation and was continually haunted by the fear of choking to death. Still another patient had a severe allergic reaction to penicillin and was afraid of having a sudden fatal reaction at any time.

Fear of rejection was a prelude to anxiety in ten patients. The particular characteristics and consequences of the anticipated rejection, however, varied considerably among the individual cases. One patient had the specific fear that her behavior would be regarded as peculiar, foreign, and distasteful by her social peers, and that she would therefore be systematically and irreversibly excluded from her peer group. She anticipated that rejection would extend to total ostracism, and that she would lead a life of unbearable loneliness.

Another patient who anticipated catastrophic consequences of rejection leading to complete ostracism, however, feared that she would be found fundamentally lacking in wit and intellectual ability and would therefore not fit into her peer group. It is perhaps significant that these two patients also had fears of being physically attacked by other people.

The fear of rejection experienced by another patient was associated with imagery of collective exclusion by a social group, but the anticipated rejection was limited to certain specific situations—namely, large groups and interaction with men—and was not seen as complete ostracism extending to all social contexts. In six patients, the recurrent thematic content of anxiety-associated thoughts and imagery was disgrace and humiliation because of inept performance in specific situations. The patients anticipated rejection resulting from unfavorable comparison with other people in specific contexts, usually related to work, school, or social situations. However, they had no expectation of being completely ostracized by an entire class of people or of being excluded in all social interaction.

A more recent study by Fox and Beck (1983) of GAD patients demonstrated a similar relationship between the occurrence of automatic thought relevant to danger and the anxiety experienced. The theme of physical or psychological vulnerability was present in all cases. The themes relevant to psychosocial dangers centered in notions of deficient coping abilities; in fears of being observed, depreciated and isolated; and finally in fears of failure.

Similar themes were reported by Hibbert in his 1984 study of GAD patients. Those *with* panic attacks had fears centering on physical danger. Hibbert found that those patients *without* panic attacks primarily had fears of not coping with psychological problems.

These studies clearly demonstrate the presence of a cognitive component in anxiety neurosis. The specific cognitions that occurred both in verbal form and in visual images centered on the theme of personal danger. These specific cognitions were reported as consistently as the affective and physiological components of the anxiety syndrome.

The most regular sequence observed weekly in the self-reports of those patients who received psychotherapy was that the anticipation of danger generally preceded the onset or the exacerbation of anxiety. As the patient's belief in the probability of harm was reduced by information or clarification from the therapist, by increased attention to reality testing, and by improved discrimination between fantasy and fact, his subjective distress gradually dissipated.

SELF-CONCEPT IN GENERALIZED ANXIETY DISORDER

The general definition of the self-concept in the literature varies from a cluster of beliefs regarding the effectiveness of a highly specialized skill in a particular confrontation to a generalized global view of the self, such as a weakling or an inadequate personality—unable to cope with ordinary life demands, expectations, and problems—or a superman or genius.

For the severely anxious patient, most life situations pose a threat because "inadequate" performance makes him feel constantly vulnerable to negative evaluation and rejection. The notion of vulnerability may progress into the concept of hopeless ineffectuality, which leads to ideas of quitting, of abandoning normal goals and the prospect of getting normal rewards. At this point, the self-concept has moved from anxious to depressive.

The notion of the self-concept in GAD can be illustrated by an analysis of the reactions to situations of immediate interpersonal confrontation, such as (1) confrontation with an authority (for example, teacher, boss); (2) confrontation with the group (for example, public speaking); (3) subjection to immediate evaluation of ability (for example, test taking, athletic competition); (4) subjection to social evaluation (for example, asking for a date); or (4) confrontation with a stranger (for example, a sales clerk).

Each of the preceding confrontations involves important facets of an individual's life—namely, his perceived competence in dealing with problematic situations and his ability to obtain respect and acceptance of his individuality, his rights as a person. The individual is being judged (or at least believes that he is) in evaluative terms. Even if he is not being judged by others, he may judge his performance severely since he believes he has a great deal to lose. A lowered self-confidence results in susceptibility to anxiety or in an actual persistent low level of anxiety. With this background anxiety, further lowering of efficacy by factors such as fatigue negates the sense of control over thinking and performing. In addition, an acute confrontation may produce inhibitions of speech and action and thus further limit effectiveness and reduce self-confidence.

The GAD patient is different from the depressive in that he can see the positive aspects of his personality and also can separate the consequences of inadequate behavior from the durable concept of himself. He can regard himself as having a behavioral deficit without a characterological deficit. Thus, he can think and say, "I made a fool of myself"—a statement indicating that he did not consider himself a fool *before* the performance, and that he does not regard being a fool intrinsic to his personality or as a durable characteristic. The depressive, on the other hand, would view inept performance as a manifestation of an inadequate personality.

The self-image of the anxious person may fluctuate according to the degree of risk he perceives in a situation. Thus, he may view himself as competent and effective in an unthreatening situation but switch to an image of himself as childlike, small, and inept when confronted with threatening situations such as confrontation with authority.

This observation—which could be labeled the "shrinking phenomenon" —suggests that such a person has at least two images of the self: one, competent, mature, and confident; the other, incompetent, immature, and insecure. It is conceivable that these conflicting self-concepts have motivational properties and lead to behavior that is consistent with them. Further, it is possible that they serve some adaptive function, the negative concept serving as a check against excessive, prolonged ventures into precarious activities. In any event, the negative image of being weak, tongue-tied, immobile may appear at the time a person reacts to a threat with inhibitions.

SELF-CRITICISM IN ANXIETY AND DEPRESSION

Another aspect of the negative concept is self-criticism. It is apparent that, even in specific threat situations such as taking tests or preparing reports, anxious people are likely to criticize themselves for not having prepared better, for not concentrating well, and for not doing as well as other students or workers. As we have said, the anxious person is unlike the depressive, who criticizes himself in more global terms, in that he criticizes specific lacks in preparation performance and ability. In fact, the criticisms produce anxiety—as though the individual were simply warning himself about the dire consequences of his deficiencies.

The differences between the two groups may be summarized in terms of the target of criticism: The anxious person tends to reproach himself for specific flaws ("behavioral self-blame"), such as not preparing adequately, not spending time optimally, or misunderstanding a question. The depressive blames himself for global deficits ("characterological self-blame"), such as being stupid, lazy, or generally inadequate (Beck 1976; Peterson and Seligman 1984).

THE DIFFERENCES BETWEEN ANXIETY AND DEPRESSION

There is a significant overlap between anxiety and depression in that patients with GAD often are depressed and depressed patients often are anxious. Moreover, even "pure" cases of each disorder show roughly similar characteristics in terms of depreciated self-concept (as pointed out earlier), negative predictions, and negative bias in appraising current experiences. The differences between the two groups, however, are revealing and illuminate the specific nature of each disorder:

1. In depression, negative appraisals are pervasive, global, and exclusive; in anxiety, they are selective and specific, do not encompass all aspects of functioning, and do not exclude consideration of positive factors.

2. The anxious patient sees some prospects for the future; he has not voluntarily given up. The depressed patient sees the future as blank; he believes he has already lost an "essential" relationship or been defeated, and he has given up voluntarily.

3. The anxious person does not regard his defects or mistakes as irrevocable, as indicating rottenness in the central core of his personality, or as justifying self-loathing. The depressed patient sees his mistakes as meaning that he is defective "through and through" and is beyond redemption.

4.   The anxious patient is tentative, uncertain in his negative evaluations; the depressed person is absolute. The differences between the two syndromes will be highlighted in the examination of their specific dimensions.

5.   The anxious patient anticipates possible damage to his relations with others, to his goals and objectives, to his ability to cope with problems and perform adequately, and to his health or survival. The depressed patient *regrets* that he has lost sources of gratification, that he has been deprived of significant other people, that he has been defeated in his objectives, that he is already diseased, and that he is incapable of doing anything to change his adversities or improve his performance.

6.   The depressed individual has a global view that nothing will turn out right for him; and for this, he feels regretful and sad. However, when faced with a specific confrontation—say, with a boss or an audience—he reacts the way a GAD patient might—with anxiety. The anxious patient predicts only that certain specific events may go badly—for example, confrontations.

The cognitive-motivational-behavioral difference between generalized anxiety disorder and the affective disorders may be discussed in terms of specific psychological functions or dimensions:

Avoidance. The depressive has given up on routine tasks—for example, making phone calls, answering letters, balancing his checkbook, getting out of bed, tending to chores, going out for a walk, preparing meals.

The anxiety patient, as we have said, avoids only those specific tasks that endanger his vital interests and present some probability of confrontation or failure or of not being able to cope (public appearances, calling a person for a social engagement, or asking for a raise). If in such a situation the possibility of the danger is lessened, the patient gains confidence in being able to cope with it and is less likely to avoid the situation; indeed, he might be motivated to enter it. In this case, the anxious patient is much more sensitive to fluctuations in a negative confrontation and adjusts his approach-avoidance behavior to them.

Motivation and Energy. Depressives "lack" the energy to carry out tasks. They experience a decathexis of the motivational-motor apparatus, which is manifested by a *loss of will power* and by *psychomotor retardation.*

The anxiety patient often has the energy to undertake a project (study for an examination, enter a contest) but may be inhibited (countercathexis). He has a subjective sense of some internal force that automatically opposes or offers *resistance to his wishes* and that also may be manifested in active inhibition of action and of effective mental activity. Some patients have described this as a kind of rigid motor paralysis (all the muscles of the body become taut) and mental paralysis. If the inhibition is lifted, then one has abundant energy to carry out the task. For example, a young man felt a rigid inhibition when he prepared himself to call a girl for a date (difficulty in talking, blank mind). When he was informed that she was very eager to hear from him and wanted to go out with him, the inhibition disappeared; he was able to carry on a long, animated conversation with her. He could not have done this had he been depressed.

The depressive has given up on whole categories of objectives and so sees no use in trying. The anxious patient would like to pursue these objectives but feels straitjacketed by a sense of vulnerability, by a fear of being hurt, and by automatic reflexive inhibitions.

Expectation of Failure. The depressed patient expects failure. He feels regret—as though the failure has already occurred—even though he has not yet undertaken a task. When he contemplates his activities for the day, he thinks, "I won't be able to do it——I won't know what to say——I won't accomplish anything today." He feels sad and discouraged. In more severe cases, the patient has already decided that the burden of a task is too great, and that he will not even make an effort. Thus, even in the early morning, he has "written off" the day as a failure.

The anxiety patient is actively afraid of failure and the consequences of failure, but he views the event as still in the future. A student, for example, may think, "If I don't finish the paper, I will flunk out." He may even believe that he will probably flunk, but he has not taken the expected failure as a *fait accompli.* Nonetheless, since he does consider the consequences of flunking a source of future pain, he experiences anxiety (not sadness, because the failure has not yet occurred).

We should note that the anxiety patient is not concerned about failure unless a vital interest is concerned. For example, a generally anxious medical student decided to take the Law School Admissions Test just to see how well he would do and also to fulfill a bet. Although he had always been anxious about taking medical exams in the past, he had no anxiety about failing the law exam since he had nothing at stake in regard to his needs or expectations of himself. His motivation to do well, however, was high because a good score represented a source of satisfaction. In contrast, a depressed college student, interested in law, wanted to avoid taking the examination. He could see no point in subjecting himself to failure, as he believed that he was totally incapable of performing the task.

Self-Concept. The differences in self-concept have already been discussed in the section on that topic (pages 101–2). In brief, the anxious patient focuses on specific areas of vulnerability in his repertoire of skills, coping mechanisms, and strategies for solving problems; his uncertainties are related in that any of these areas of uncertainty *can* show weakness under conditions of stress or confrontation. The depressed patient is generally unrealistic in his sweeping negative generalizations about himself.

It should also be noted that the anxious patient sees the consequences (disgracing himself) of his failure as occurring *after* the possible failure and therefore as something to worry about and possibly fear. The depressed patient, on the other hand, sees the consequences as starting *right now,* since he has already "incorporated" the failure and is passing judgment on himself for "having failed." Whether he takes the exam is irrelevant to him: either way he is a failure.

Automatic Thoughts. Automatic thoughts that are followed by anxiety are different from those followed by sadness and reflect the differences in ideational content between depression and anxiety disorders. In a systematic study, outpatients were asked to check typical thoughts in specific situations and to indicate the associated feeling. The following automatic thoughts occurred frequently on entering a social situation and were associated with anxiety but not with sadness:

"I will make a fool of myself."
"I won't know what to say."
"People will laugh at me."

Automatic thoughts followed by sadness included:

"I'm a social failure."
"I'll never be as good as other people are."

Anxiety-producing thoughts when the patient works on a project were as follows:

"What if I fail?"
"Other things might get in the way."
"I won't have enough time to do a good job."
"I'm falling behind."

Typical thoughts associated with sadness were:

"I'll never be as capable as I should be."
"I'm not as capable as I used to be."

In the category of physical health, anxiety was found to be associated with the possibility of a specific injury or illness ("What if I get sick and become an invalid?"), and sadness, with a sweeping generalization ("I am a defective human being").

Panic Disorder

DESCRIPTION

Charles Darwin wrote the following vivid description of the somatic and behavioral characteristics of acute terror in animals:

> With all or almost all animals, even with birds, Terror causes the body to tremble. The skin becomes pale, sweat breaks out, and the hair bristles. The secretions of the alimentary canal and of the kidneys are increased, and they are involuntarily voided, owing to the relaxation of the sphincter muscles, as is known to be the case with man, and as I have seen with cattle, dogs, cats, and monkeys. The breathing is hurried. The heart beats quickly, wildly, and violently; but whether it pumps the blood more efficiently through the body may be doubted, for the surface seems bloodless and the strength of the muscles soon fails. . . . The mental faculties are much disturbed. Utter prostration soon follows, and even fainting. A terrified canary-bird has been seen not only to tremble and to turn white about the base of the bill, but to faint; and I once caught a robin in a room, which fainted so completely, that for a time I thought it dead. [1872, p. 77]

Darwin went on to develop the concept that fear, derived from innumerable injuries in the course of evolution, prepares the animal for possible injury and automatically mobilizes the body for defense.

Compare Darwin's description with the verbatim description of a panic attack experienced by a young woman, and note the similar symptoms— shallow breathing, rapid heart rate, profuse sweating, faintness, difficulty in thinking:

> My breathing starts getting very shallow. I feel I'm going to stop breathing. The air feels like it gets thinner. I feel the air is not coming up through my nose. I take short rapid breaths. *Then I see an image of myself gasping for air and remember what happened in the hospital.* I think that I will start gasping. I get very dizzy and disoriented. I cannot sit or stand still. I start pacing. Then I start shaking and sweating. I feel I'm losing my mind and I will flip out and hurt myself or someone else. My heart starts beating fast and I start getting pains in my chest. My chest tightens up. I become very frightened. I get afraid that these feelings will not go away. Then I get really upset. I feel no one will be able to help me. I get very frightened I will die. I want to run to some place safe but I don't know where.

The patient's description of her panic disorder illustrates the misery of this most dramatic of psychiatric disorders. D. V. Sheehan (1982) reports that panic disorder occurs in 2 percent to 5 percent of the general population and in 10 percent to 14 percent of patients in a cardiology practice. In its most severe form, the panic attack is manifested by a variety of intense, unpleasant, strange experiences, as follow:

1. Such reactions are generally qualitatively different from previous experience. Some patients compare the strangeness of the experience to adverse reactions to drugs or to having a nightmare. External familiar objects seem peculiar, distorted, or unreal. The patient's *internal* experiences seem strange and peculiar. He may experience loss of normal sensations in his extremities or in the interior of his body. He may experience peculiar sensations or numbness (paresthesia) in his limbs. His body may feel very heavy or weightless.

2. Perhaps the most frightening aspect of the panic attack is the *slippage of controls* that the individual has always taken for granted. He has to struggle to retain or regain voluntary control over focusing, concentration, attention, and action. At times, the difficulty in focusing extends into a sense that he is losing consciousness, but actual loss of consciousness is rare. He has difficulty framing his thoughts or pursuing a consistent logical line of thinking or reasoning. His awareness of his surroundings is altered, and he may feel remote or detached from events. Paradoxically, however, he may be exquisitely sensitive to certain stimuli, especially those of a frightening nature: another person's voice may seem to boom and resonate (Beck 1976, p. 78).

3. He often feels *confused and disoriented.* Even though he may correctly identify who he is and where he is, he feels unsure that "this is really me." The extreme form of this disturbance has been labeled a "catastrophic reaction." The uncanny experiences may be described in terms such as "I don't feel that I'm really here——I feel different——Things look different." The quality of the eerie experience is captured by expressions such as "I feel I am ready to pass out"; "I feel I'm losing my grip"; "I'm going out of my mind"; "I'm coming apart"; "I'm dying"; "I'm going crazy"; or, "I'm having a stroke." Although patients often interpret "weird feelings" as a sign of insanity, they are specific signs of acute neurotic reactions rather than of psychosis.

4. Of course, the striking characteristic of the panic attack is the feeling of being engulfed by uncontrollable anxiety. This feeling has been described as "unendurable pain" and "the worst experience I could imagine." Another essential feature of the panic attack is the automatic suppression of reasoning powers. The individual may be aware that the panic attack may be a "false alarm," and he may even be able to recall previous panic

attacks that turned out to be innocuous. However, he cannot bring this reasoning to bear against the onslaught of symptoms and frightening ideas. He cannot get out of his mind the overwhelming notion that "this time it is the real thing. *I really am dying (losing control, choking, going crazy)."*

5. In addition, the patient has a variety of symptoms associated with parasympathetic or cholinergic activation and motor "collapse": faintness and pervasive weakness. These symptoms are usually more frightening than the more familiar palpitations and generalized sweating associated with acute anxiety. Further, a number of symptoms, such as peculiar sensations in the extremities and a sense of losing consciousness, may be a consequence of rapid shallow breathing or gasping (hyperventilation syndrome).

Although panic attacks have been described as "spontaneous," we have found that patients who are trained to monitor their anxiety can identify "inexplicable" physiological sensations (such as faintness or "palpitations") followed by frightening automatic thoughts as a prelude to an attack. Also, patients have specific fears during an attack. From their standpoint, the danger is real and plausible. What do we learn if we ask a patient, "What are you afraid of during an attack?" At first, his attention may be so fixated on his anxiety, his peculiar feeling states, and his loss of control that he may find it difficult to focus on the question. With a minimum of introspection, however, it is possible for him to respond. Often—but not always—he is overwhelmed by thoughts that he is dying. The fear of dying may be activated by his unexpected physical sensation for which he has no benign explanation. He interprets the physical distress as a sign of a devastating physical disorder and becomes more anxious and symptomatic; and a chain reaction is set up.

MEANING OF PANIC ATTACKS

Panic attacks seem to signify helplessness in the face of serious danger. The sense of helplessness appears to be the result of an internal mechanism that leads a person to believe that he is trapped in a dangerous situation or is overwhelmed by an internal derangement. The fear of his own vulnerability interacts with psychological and affective responses to produce a vicious cycle. With the onset of the symptomatology, the person has a sequence of responses.

For example, a patient experienced abdominal distress after a dietary indiscretion. His various systems were activated in the following sequence:

1. *Cognitive:* "Something terrible could be happening."
2. *Physiological:* Activation of autonomic nervous system—rapid heart beat, faintness, more abdominal sensations ("butterflies"), sweating.
   Affective: Anxiety.
   "Mental": Blocking, distraction, confusion.
3. *Cognitive:* "Something terrible is happening. I can't control my thinking, feeling, behavior. This could be a sign that I am dying (going insane, losing control, and so on)."
4. The *cognitive* elaboration escalates: "This must be pretty bad if I can't stop the feelings. This means it can go all the way (say, death, insanity, homicide). If I don't get help, I'm a goner."

The cognitive-affective-physiological mechanism almost appears to be *designed* to produce (1) the belief that he is endangered by internal disturbance that he cannot control, (2) the fear that the derangement will progress to an ultimate disaster, and (3) the belief that he should turn to a caregiver for help.

The specific fear engendered by this mechanism varies from person to person but seems to be relevant to the particular sensations:

Symptoms of abdominal or chest pain plus faintness = heart attack.
Peculiar sensations in limbs, freezing, tremor, weakness of muscles = stroke.
Changes in mental functioning (difficulty in focusing, fogginess, depersonalization, and so on) = incipient insanity or cerebral accident.
Faintness = passing out in public and being disgraced or loss of consciousness leading to coma and death.
Difficulty catching breath = "I will stop breathing and will die."
Generalized sense of loss of control over internal sensations = uncontrollable or bizarre behavior; insanity; homicidal or other antisocial acts; suicide; flagrant sex "misbehavior."

The crucial devastating symptom is the inability to control one's mental, physical, and affective symptoms. When the anxiety becomes so intense that the person believes he cannot control it by himself and that it will not subside spontaneously, he starts to catastrophize: "This cannot be simply an emotional upset. I'm having a heart attack (stroke, ruptured intestine)"; "I'm going crazy (lapsing into a coma)"; or, "I will be driven to bizarre behavior (suicide, destructive acts, sexual acting out)."

In the case of the "simple phobias" (fear of animals, heights, closed spaces), escape from the phobic situation offers relief. However, if escape is not possible, then the individual may have a panic attack similar to the one just described. In agoraphobia, the individual is trapped and, consequently, "needs" help in order to be rescued. In order to avoid having panic, he either takes a guardian with him or makes certain that he has ready access to the guardian.

The importance of loss of control is supported by the following observations: First, it has been reported that panic attacks associated with performance anxiety can be controlled by drugs that block the peripheral action of the sympathetic nervous system (beta adrenergic blocker). These drugs reduce tachycardia and tremors (but not the other symptoms of panic). Thus, the individual recognizes that there is a limit to the escalation of the symptoms, that they are being controlled (by the drug), and he no longer fears the "disastrous" consequences of not being able to perform. The "beta blockers" do not have any effect on generalized anxiety (Sheehan 1982). When a patient's problem is primarily premonitory (anticipatory) anxiety, drugs to prevent escalation of symptoms are not called for since the problem at this stage does not center around such escalation. Valium has an effect on generalized anxiety but not on panic attacks: as it acts primarily on the subjective experiences of anxiety but not on the behavioral or physiological reactions, it does not put a "stopper" on the acute symptoms of the emergency reaction (tachycardia, faintness, freezing).

FUNCTIONAL ANALYSIS OF PANIC ATTACKS

The acute primal mechanisms take over in these conditions. These mechanisms are not under volitional control but are, in fact, contravolitional. Depending on the particular situation, a person's primal physical reaction will be freezing (to cope with ambiguous danger), tonic or atonic immobility (to prevent falling), gagging and coughing (to prevent obstruction of the airway), ducking or jumping (to avoid a moving object). These reflexes are programmed to *prevent* death or injury but actually may increase vulnerability because they are automatic and stereotyped, are triggered by psychological as well as physical danger, and actually undermine coping. These reflexes are not an expression of anxiety. Indeed by interfering with skillful performance, they may increase anxiety. These primal mechanisms may have some survival value in children—prior to their developing more mature coping skills. Their persistence into adulthood may be a behavioral manifestation of the phenomena of neoteny (or juvenilization).

Panic attacks differ qualitatively as well as quantitatively from the feeling of anxiety generally experienced in GAD. Not only are affective and cognitive symptoms more intense, but the person experiences additional symptoms, such as change in perceptions of the self and the outside world (depersonalization and derealization) and an inhibition of cognitive functions relevant to reasoning, recall, and perspective-taking. The loss of the ability to reason is often the most prominent symptom, exceeding in intensity the subjective anxiety and physiological symptoms. The parasympathetic response involving fainting or actual fainting and involuntary defecation and urination suggests a more profound reaction than that involving the more familiar experience of anxiety. These qualitative differences suggest that the emergency response involving panic may denote the activation of a *different program* from that involved in the usual anxiety reaction. This program may be designed to deal with emergency situations in which the usual defensive strategies are inadequate. Although the "panic program" may be different from the other programs, it should be regarded as one component of the broader system. However, the alarm (panic) response should be investigated in terms of its own peculiar cognitive, behavioral, and neurophysiological correlates. The fact that panic attacks seem to be ameliorated by the administration of "antidepressive" drugs such as imipramine but not by "antianxiety" drugs such as benzodiazepam (Klein, Rabkin, and Gorman, in press) supports the notion of a separate organization.

PRECIPITATION OF PANIC ATTACKS

Although the attacks are often described as "spontaneous," we have found that some experience seems to activate a person's "alarm system" involving cognitive-affective and physiological components. The antecedent experience often consists of some change in a person's physiological status. He may, for example, feel faint after getting up quickly from a chair, get a flushed feeling when going from an air-conditioned room into a hot street, or experience rapid heart beat or shortness of breath from running up a flight of stairs. He interprets these normal physiological changes as signs of serious internal disorders. Of great importance is the fact that his ability to "reason" with himself regarding the gravity of these symptoms is impaired by fatigue, cognitive strain, use of drugs, and so on; and the vicious cycle is set up.

Not all cases of panic disorder involve the threat of internal derangement. Some cases center on terror of an overwhelming external psychosocial threat. For example, a patient who was a social worker had completed a difficult session with a client earlier in the day. As she reflected over her interview, she began to experience the following (in her own words): "intense anxiety . . . mounting nausea, feel hot, sweating, sense of removal from immediate reality, which makes me reluctant to drive home and is connected to a sense of doom, of foreshortening, of the future being cut off. Afterward, feel cold."

Automatic thoughts: "I messed it up. Her husband will make off with their car and money and leave her [the client] destitute. I'll have brought about exactly what she fears. . . . Her life will be ruined. She'll sue me and ruin my career. I'll lose my house—will have to pay court costs and a settlement. Martin [her fiancé] will be stuck with me, a failure, and question his love. I'll be barred from the profession. I'll be found out as an incompetent. I'll never have the marriage and professional status I want." She also had the following image: "Myself in Martin's apartment, alone. I have no job, no respect, nothing to do. His child despises me."

The waves of panic became so strong that she ran to the nearby office of Jim, a colleague. After talking to him, she was able to reason with herself, and her panic promptly subsided. Her rational response was: "People don't, and generally can't, do things like make off with the money in the way I envision. If they do, there are legal remedies for the wife. I would not be responsible for his behavior, in any case. According to Jim, I handled the client correctly. He also says that I have a distorted notion of what it takes to be sued for malpractice, and that I have blown this affair way out of proportion. Finally, I didn't create the situation, the couple did, over a period of twenty years."

The social worker's reaction illustrates what may be the essential ingredient of panic attacks, namely, the loss of ability to reason regarding the problem, whether it is physical or interpersonal.

The 1974 study by Beck, Laude and Bohnert (pages 98–100) included two groups of patients with generalized anxiety. The first, a psychotherapy group, had twelve patients. The second, patients seen on admission to the outpatient clinic at the Hospital of the University of Pennsylvania, consisted of twenty patients. Panic attacks were described in all but two patients in each sample—that is, twenty-eight out of thirty-two patients. The acute anxiety attacks were *superimposed on the base level of anxiety.* The acute panic attacks came on rapidly, caused severe distress, and were often totally disabling. They lasted from several minutes to a few hours, and their frequency for a given patient varied considerably from daily to once a month.

There is considerable clinical evidence that psychological factors can precipitate panic attacks. M. Raskin, H. V. Peeke, W. Dickman, and H. Pinsker (1982) described ten patients who experienced panic attacks following separations. Typically, the first series of panic attacks occurred shortly after each patient had left home; a subsequent attack occurred after the loss or possible loss of a "loved one." A variation of this theme was reported by a patient whose original panic attacks followed the death of her fiancé. Subsequent attacks occurred whenever she became sufficiently involved with a man to make him emotionally important to her; her attacks abated when she gave up the attachment. A somewhat analogous conflict occurred in the case of three male patients who reported a specific sequence of events leading to their initial panic attacks. Each had been ridiculed or abused frequently by his father throughout childhood and adolescence. The first panic attack for each occurred in late adolescence immediately following an act of open rebellion against his father. Some subsequent panic attacks followed conflicts with authority figures.

The conflicts leading to the panic attacks seem to represent threats to an individual's dependency or autonomy. For example, a patient in our clinic who experienced attacks only when deeply involved in a relationship would feel that she was losing her independence. The patients who experience attacks after rebellion against an authority figure may feel upset by the threat to their support system or may fear retaliation. In any event, a variety of fears stirred up by specific life situations impinging on the patient's vulnerabilities may provide the ingredients necessary to precipitate an attack

Chapter 7

Simple Phobias

Definition of Phobia

The term *phobia* derives from the Greek *phobos* meaning "flight," "panic-fear," "terror," and from the deity Phobos who could provoke fear and terror in one's enemies (chapter 1). The Greeks made fear masks by putting the image of Phobos on weapons such as shields, and examples of these appear on vase paintings. The term *phobia* was not used on its own until 1801, and during the next seventy years, it slowly gained acceptance in the sense it has today: namely, a persistent excessive fear attached to an object or a situation that objectively is not a significant source of danger (Marks 1969).

A phobia is a specific kind of fear. A standard dictionary of psychological terms defines it as "Nearly always, excessive fear of some particular type of object or situation; fear that is persistent and without sound grounds, or without grounds accepted as reasonable by the sufferer" (English and English 1958). A standard desk dictionary defines phobia as simply "An exaggerated, often disabling fear" (*Webster's Third International Dictionary*, 1981).

The first characteristic is observed when an individual is forced to face an object or a situation about which he is phobic. He usually (but not necessarily) experiences an unpleasant degree of anxiety. He may experience the symptoms of a person in a medical emergency: pounding heart, racing pulse, dizziness, nausea, and faintness. His mouth may become dry, and he may start to sweat profusely. The second characteristic is a powerful wish to escape or avoid contact with the object or situation of fear. When able, the phobic person avoids the feared situation and thus restricts his life activities. If he is unable to avoid the situation, he either overcomes the phobia or develops chronic anxiety. The third characteristic is the ability to recognize, when not in the phobic situation, that the fears are exaggerated but, despite such realization, the inability to eliminate the fears or reduce the avoidance.

An important clue to understanding phobias is the finding that the object or the situation feared by the phobic person may also be feared by non-phobic people. One of the key qualities that makes a fear into a phobia is the magnification of the amount of risk in a feared situation and the degree of harm that will come from being in that situation. Because of the greater hazard the phobic person imputes to situation or object, he experiences much greater anxiety than the non-phobic individual in the fear situation, as well as a greater desire to avoid it. This observation prompts a more comprehensive definition of phobia than that suggested by either dictionary definition: "A fear of an object or a situation that by social consensus and the person's own appraisal when detached from the situation is disproportionate to the probability and the degree of harm inherent in that situation." The phobic experiences disproportionate anxiety in such situations and tends to avoid them and, in doing so, substantively restricts his life.

While this definition might appear to clarify the distinction between the phobic person and the person with a generalized anxiety disorder, the distinction is not always clear. Some people are phobic about more than one object or situation. The person with multiple phobias may find it difficult to avoid all feared situations. Because he must, at least sometimes, face situations where he has unrealistic fears, he experiences anticipatory anxiety. This anxiety is indistinguishable in quality from the anxiety experienced by people with generalized anxiety disorder who are "afraid of everything" but who may find it impossible to avoid every stimulus they perceive as noxious. Thus, individuals with multiple phobia are at times difficult to distinguish from individuals who have GAD.

DIFFERENTIATING PHOBIAS FROM FEARS

In clinical practice, the phobias are usually so well defined that it is rarely difficult to distinguish them from "normal fears." A phobic patient generally seeks help either because he realizes that he suffers in situations that do not trouble other people or because he can no longer tolerate the restriction on his life occasioned by avoiding such situations. Many phobics seek treatment because they have developed painful symptoms as the result of new circumstances in their lives that force them into situations they had been able to avoid in the past. For example, a medical student with a fear of the sight of blood may experience an anxiety attack when required to witness a surgical procedure.

Many people who are phobic about certain situations are completely comfortable in situations that produce severe anxiety in others. One patient, for instance, who had a great dread of being crawled over by cockroaches and other small insects, was always calm in public speaking, relished meeting new people, and was fearless in various athletic events. He felt extremely anxious whenever he was alone in his apartment at night because of his fear of being attacked by insects. As a result of this phobia, he sought professional help.

THE REFRACTORINESS OF PHOBIAS

Another distinguishing characteristic of phobias is that recognition or education through experience of the unreasonableness of a fear does not modify it. As pointed out by I. M. Marks (1969), the English author Robert Burton made shrewd comments, in his *Anatomy of Melancholy* in 1621, on the role of will power in overcoming phobias, and his advice could well be heeded by relatives and physicians of phobic patients today. Burton observed that phobias are not the result of insufficient will power but are due to causes outside the control of the patient: "Counsel can do little good; you may as well bid him that is sick of an ague not to be adry, or him that is wounded not to feel pain" (1927, p. 359).

The phobic individual is usually better able to appraise realistically the actual danger of his feared situation from a distance. As he approaches his feared situation, his appraisal becomes less realistic due to cognitive distortions. Often the reason for the development of a phobia is unclear.

CONTENT OF FEARS AND PHOBIAS

The kinds of objects and situations people fear have changed during the course of history, yet the characteristics of phobias and phobic individuals have not (Marks 1969). With technological advances, new phobias, like fear of exposure to radiation, have emerged while other fears, like demonphobia or satanophobia (fear of Satan) which were rampant in the sixteenth century, have largely disappeared. Some rather strange phobias have been reported: one patient feared eating vegetables, and another, eating chocolate (Rachman 1978).

It is interesting that in general the distribution of objects feared by phobic individuals follows the distribution of fears in the non-phobic population. In a study reported by R. P. Snaith (1968), the kinds of fear reported by phobic patients were primarily accentuations of fears experienced by numerous "normal" people in the general population. Snaith found that aside from agoraphobia, the most common fears reported were of thunderstorms, animals, illness, psychosocial trauma, and danger. These fears were loosely paralleled by his control group of normal people.

Burton noted that people with fears of particular objects and places can provide explanations for their fears—namely, the feared consequences:

> Montanus speaks of one that durst not walk alone from home, for fear he should *swoon, or die*. A second fears every man he meets *will rob him*, quarrel with him, or kill him. A third dares not venture to walk alone, for fear he should meet the Devil, a thief, *be sick*. . . . Another dares not go over a bridge, come near a pool, rock, steep hill, lie in a chamber where cross beams are, for fear he be tempted to *hang, drown, or precipitate himself*. If he be in a silent auditory, as at a sermon, he is afraid he shall *speak aloud at unawares, some thing undecent, unfit to be said*. If he be locked in a close room, he is afraid of being *stifled for want of air*. [1927, pp. 328–29; italics added]

Thus, when the specific content of a fear is elicited, that fear becomes more readily understandable.

The consequences feared by the phobic individual are usually both subjectively and objectively frightening—within his frame of reference—even though, to an observer, the feared object or situation may seem relatively harmless. For example, an adolescent young woman avoided eating solid foods. Her parents and family doctor chided her for her behavior. When, however, they attempted to find out what she feared about eating these foods, they discovered that she feared choking to death. She reported that a few weeks earlier she had choked on a large piece of meat, was unable to catch her breath, and at that time believed she would choke to death. Subsequently, she became particularly sensitive to stories of people choking to death and developed a phobia of eating solid foods. Once the feared consequences were unraveled, it was no longer necessary to search for tortuous explanations of the phobia. The source of this adolescent's anxiety was not a fear of eating solid food *per se* but a fear of choking as a *result* of eating solid food.

Classification

Many attempts have been made to classify and categorize phobias. Historically, they were classified by the name of the object of fear. Scholars coined at least 107 different names for types of phobia based on the specific phobic stimulus (Terhune 1949). Some of the more exotic names include ailurophobia (cats), anthophobia (flowers), astraphobia (lightning), brontophobia (thunder), and ophidiophobia (snakes). With so many objects and situations that can be excessively or inappropriately feared (and avoided), there have been a number of attempts to categorize types of phobias.

The notion of conceptual continuity in phobias is supported by case histories of "spreading phobias," in which a person's initial fear of a specific concrete situation extends to similar situations that are linked to it according to the type of danger that he could encounter. For example, a laborer was struck by a truck while painting a white line on a road, and subsequently developed a phobia of working on the road. The phobia then spread to a fear of riding a motorcycle or bicycle on a road (Kraft and Al-Issa 1965a). The same authors (1965b) described the case of a girl who witnessed the removal of the charred bodies of two children from a burning house. Subsequently, she developed a fear of washing in warm water, eating hot foods, or drinking hot water. The phobia spread to touching an electric hot plate in the "on" or "off" position.

It is important to note that, in these two cases, the phobia spread to objects or situations linked to the traumatic situation by a *similarity in the type of danger*—namely, being struck by a vehicle or being burned. The phobias did not spread to white lines, roads, or trucks, in the first case, or to houses or children. In other words, the phobias extended not to objects or situations present during the trauma (as one might expect on the basis of classical conditioning) but rather to situations that could produce the same type of damage. These examples illustrate that, in spreading phobias, the linkage is the similarity in consequences or danger rather than in objects or cast of characters.

A recent factor analytic study of the fears of 194 psychiatric patients at the Center for Cognitive Therapy found that the phobias fell into three major groups. The first factor was concerned with "social rejection" and included being criticized, speaking to people in authority, having a request refused, and appearing unattractive. The second factor appeared to have an agoraphobic content—namely, fear of traveling alone, heights, bridges, and crowds in theaters. The third factor was concerned with being cut or observing bleeding. These findings indicate that a person who fears height is likely also to fear tunnels but not necessarily being ignored. This study supports the notion that fears have as common denominator a similar type of injury (for example physical versus psychological) rather than similar superficial attributes of the feared object.

TRAUMATIC PHOBIAS

What specifically causes a phobia to develop? A good deal of evidence supports the notion that adult phobias develop as a result either of a traumatic experience—like that of the young woman who choked on a piece of meat—or of fixation on a fear of early childhood which a person has not outgrown.

The group of traumatic phobias develop as a result of an unpleasant or injurious experience. Other dramatic examples of this type of phobia include people with shell shock or those who develop driving phobias after being involved in an automobile accident. A person may develop a disabling phobia as a result of continued *exposure* to objective danger. For example, a pilot experienced in combat flying might develop severe symptoms of anxiety prior to taking off on a relatively safe mission; or a veteran bridge worker might develop incapacitating anxiety as he approaches a bridge.

Individuals with traumatic phobias are usually able to date the onset of the phobia from a specific traumatic event. For example, someone might date his fear of dogs to a time he was bitten by a dog, or trace a fear of heights to a time hé fell down a flight of stairs, or a fear of injections to a severe drug reaction.

FIXATION PHOBIAS

Fixation phobias include early intense fears, common in childhood, which the patient, unlike most adults, has not outgrown. The main quality of these phobias is that the person's maturation in respect to the feared event was arrested or "fixated" at an early stage in his development.

The kinds of object or situation on which people fixate tend to involve the danger of some kind of physical injury or death. Typical examples of these fears are fears of water, thunderstorms, doctors, and blood. In a study by A. T. Jersild, F. V. Markey, and C. L. Jersild (1933), 398 children between the ages of five and twelve were interviewed to determine the frequency of certain types of fear. The results showed that 19.2 percent of the fears were of supernatural agents like ghosts, witches, corpses, or mysterious events; 14.6 percent were fears of being alone, in dark or strange places, or being lost; 13.7 percent were fears of being attacked either by other human beings or animals; and 12.8 percent were of bodily injury, illness, falling, traffic accidents, surgical operations, or pain. In general, studies have shown that while the fears of younger children are generally concerned with physical harm, the fears of older children are concerned with psychosocial harm (Miller et al. 1972; Angelino and Shedd 1953; Berecz 1968).

The question remains why some individuals become fixated on their fears while most children outgrow these same fears. One possibility is that phobic individuals learn to avoid the feared object or situation by observing their parents' avoidance behavior, and that these fears and avoidance behavior are then reinforced by their parents. Another explanation is that particularly unpleasant events related to the feared object or situation occurred while the normal childhood fear was active, and thus led to avoidance behavior which was either reinforced by parents or became reinforcing in and of itself. The child might not have had to master the fear because he was successfully able to avoid the feared situation. With each subsequent avoidance, the phobia became more deeply entrenched. Finally, it is possible that some phobias have a biological basis in that an individual is genetically "prepared" (or predisposed) to respond with anxiety in situations that were dangerous during the evolution of the species (Seligman 1971).

SPECIFIC PHOBIAS

The number of objects or situations feared by phobic individuals can be unlimited. It is useful to consider the clinical picture of some of the phobias most prevalent today. The specific consequences that the individual fears when in a phobic situation give useful information—even more useful perhaps than the name of the object of fear alone. Agoraphobia—the phobic disturbance most common in clinical populations—is reserved for separate consideration in chapter 8.

Acrophobia, or Fear of Heights. A common phobia is acrophobia, or fear of heights. Acrophobics are afraid to be on high floors of buildings or on the tops of hills or mountains. Many of these phobics also fear being close to the edge of bridges or subway tracks. The fear of the acrophobic is usually concerned with the possibility of falling and being severely injured. Some acrophobics fear they may have a perverse uncontrollable urge to jump and may even feel as though some *external force is drawing them to the edge* of the high place. An acrophobic may have visual fantasies of falling and even experience bodily sensations of falling despite being firmly situated on solid ground. The sensations of falling or sliding are forms of *somatic imaging,* as a result of which acrophobics report feelings of dizziness.

Fears of balconies, staircases, and escalators are related to acrophobia.

These phobics usually feel faint or dizzy and, consequently, fear they will fall. Some fear that they will jump and injure or kill themselves. These fears are often active even though the person is protected by a guardrail or is situated far enough from the ledge to preclude the possibility of falling.

Elevator Phobia.   People who fear riding in elevators are frequently seen in clinical practice. While on the surface this does not appear to be a particularly dramatic phobia, it can seriously hamper a person's way of life. Those with this phobia are forced to make decisions about where to live or work on the basis of whether it is necessary to take an elevator to get there. Given the preponderance of high-rise office buildings and apartments in most metropolitan areas, this fear can change the entire course of a person's vocational and personal life.

The most common fear of the elevator phobic is that the cables will break and the elevator will crash. He usually believes there is some safe distance above ground and is willing to travel this distance by elevator (usually either the second or third floor). Once this level or height has been passed, the elevator phobic becomes extremely anxious. Some elevator phobics are afraid to travel even above ground level; and others, that the elevator will get stuck between floors, and that the doors will not open and they will be trapped. Others fear they may starve or suffocate to death. People whose fear of elevators involves the fear that they will be deprived of air generally fear other closed spaces like crowds and tunnels which also seem to threaten air deprivation. The fear of being trapped in an elevator often occurs in agoraphobia.

Some elevator phobics have a combination of physical and social fears regarding elevators. In addition to fearing an elevator will crash or get stuck, the elevator phobic may fear "going crazy" or fainting with subsequent embarrassment. Needless to say, this fear arises only if there are other people in the elevator.

Phobia of Closed Spaces (Claustrophobia).   Some people who fear being in tunnels, closets, or other closed spaces worry that they will suffocate due to insufficient air. They may also fear the tunnel will cave in and they will be buried alive or be killed by the falling structure. When they travel through tunnels, they may experience somatic imaging and feel shortness of breath as though their chests were constricted.

Airplane Phobia   Many people react with violent anxiety before and during an airplane trip and may even avoid such a trip at all costs—even when it is essential for their health. Some fear they will suffocate in the airplane due to deprivation of air as a result of interference with the plane's air supply. Others are afraid that their tension will build and they will lose control of themselves. More commonly, however, the airplane phobic fears the plane will crash and that he will be killed.

Other people who fear air travel are concerned about loss of control in social situations. They may be afraid they will vomit or faint in the airplane and subsequently suffer humiliation. Finally, a significant proportion of airplane phobias are related to agoraphobia, where there is a combination of the fear of being trapped in a closed space and the fear of being separated from a caretaker when one might have a serious disorder such as a heart attack.

Blood Phobia. The powerful physiological reactions of susceptible individuals to exposure to blood, injury, or illness pose a problem whose solution may clarify a great deal about the origin and structure of phobias. Susceptible individuals do not report that they are "afraid" of the sight of blood or injury; rather, they get a squeamish sensation when they see blood or injury in themselves or others and have a tendency to recoil. If they close their eyes, their upset is substantially less. Moreover, the type of behavioral-physiological response in this class of phobias differs from that of other phobias. Once the reaction is triggered, it is largely a "collapse type" with parasympathetic dominance and generalized muscular weakness. On only rare occasions is the person actually in any danger of injury or death. The profound reaction may occur simply on hearing a description of mutilation, witnessing a film about injury, or having an image of someone bleeding. Finally, many of these phobics show similar collapse-parasympathetic responses in reaction to other "threatening situations"— for example public speaking. The common denominator across these situations seems to be passivity and a sense of helplessness in the face of possible injury.

The physiological responses in blood phobics have been well described by L. G. Öst, U. Sterner, and I. L. Lindahl (1984). On exposure to a film of physical injury, they show a diphasic response. The initial response before exposure to the stimulus is an increase in heart rate and blood pressure. Just prior to and during the film, there is a sharp drop in heart rate and blood pressure. About one fourth of the blood phobics in this study lost consciousness or were on the verge of doing so.

Various writers (Engel 1962; Graham 1961; Marks 1969) regard this type of response as an innate reaction to threat. It is possible to speculate about the phylogenetic value of a reaction so profound that it essentially immobilizes an individual. One hypothesis is that the purpose is to take a person out of action. If he is indeed bleeding, then an autonomic response would help to conserve the blood supply and would inhibit him from engaging in further activity that might increase blood loss.

The Meanings of Phobias

It is important to recognize that, in any phobia, there are consequences the individual may fear when forced to face the phobic situation. Phobics who fear the same object or situation frequently fear different consequences as a result of being in that situation.

The different meanings attached to the same type of phobia were illustrated by I. Stevenson and J. D. Hain (1967) in a study of barbershop phobias. The investigators identified a number of different fears among people who shared a phobia of barbershops. One patient feared *public scrutiny* and was afraid of being embarrassed or feeling humiliated in a public place. His basic fear was present in other situations as well as in the barbershop—for example, when attending church or in school auditoriums and other public places. As a result of his fear, this man would run out of the barbershop just before his turn in the chair.

Another patient with the same phobia could not bear *being confined* in the barber's chair. He became extremely anxious during the waiting period involved in a trip to the barber. In addition to his fear of sitting in the barber's chair, he was fearful in traffic jams and in other situations where he was "unable to get away." The essence of this man's fear was that he feared situations in which he felt like a prisoner, unable to escape. A third patient, also a with barbershop phobia, feared *mutilation* as a result of the sharp tools used by the barber.

Thus, it can be seen that the same object or situation can arouse fear in individuals for a variety of reasons. In any phobia, numerous idiosyncratic meanings can be attributed to the object or situation of fear. The clinician needs to learn not only about the object or situation that the phobic patient fears but also about the consequences that patient fears will occur when he is forced to face his phobic situation. In general, phobias tend to focus on themes of physical harm, natural disaster, or social embarrassment.

MULTIPLE PHOBIAS: CONCEPTUAL CONTINUITY

Many phobic individuals fear more than one object or situation. On the surface, the different phobic stimuli do not appear to be related to one another. Probing beneath the surface, however, the clinician can usually find a central theme or common denominator: The patient generally fears the occurrence of the same or similar consequences in apparently dissimilar situations.

One woman, for example, feared flying in an airplane, lying on the beach on a hot day, standing still in crowded places, riding in a car or an open car on a windy day, elevators, tunnels, and hills. Questioning the woman to find out what she specifically feared about each of these situations made it possible to determine the relationship between her apparently unrelated fears. This woman's phobias centered around a fear of the deprivation of air: she feared she would suffocate in all these situations, and she avoided being in them. She was afraid to drive in an open car on a windy day because she had heard that the wind can be strong enough to blow the air out of your mouth. She feared lying on the beach because she had heard people say a day was so hot it was impossible to breathe. She was afraid to be on the top of hills because she had heard of people having difficulty breathing in the rarefied atmosphere on the top of hills and mountains.

B. W. Feather (1971) reported another case of multiple phobias connected by a common theme: this man feared going through swinging doors, driving his car, and disclosing business secrets. Additionally, he had an elaborate ritual regarding taking pills. The common denominator of his fears, which was discerned through questioning him about the consequences he feared in the above situations, was that he feared he might harm someone, either directly or indirectly. For example, he feared he might run over a pedestrian in his car and that by going through a swinging door he might hit and kill someone. He feared that by disclosing information about his business he might indirectly cause an airplane crash. Finally, he feared he might misplace or lose his pills, which might then be taken by someone else and result in harming that individual.

Another case with multiple phobias reported by Feather was a physician who feared airplane travel; sitting in a large audience at meetings, concerts, and lectures; speaking before large groups; and attending cocktail parties. While these were apparently disparate situations, it was relatively easy to discover the link between this man's fears by *questioning specifically what he feared* would occur in all of them. Upon probing, the therapist discovered that the physician feared losing control and harming other people in all these situations.

He was afraid of traveling in an airplane because he feared he would go berserk, lose control of himself, or strike out at other passengers. At public gatherings, he feared he would jump up, wave his arms, and shout obscenities at the audience. He had a recurring fantasy of sitting in the second row at a concert and completely disrupting the performance by vomiting over the person seated in front of him, or of stepping on people's feet as he left his seat. He feared he would distract the entire audience from the music.

His fear of speaking at professional meetings was related to a fear of demolishing someone else's theory. His anxiety at cocktail parties was related to the thought that he might spill a drink and also by the thought that he might impulsively tell people that they were stupid.

A woman with multiple phobias feared answering the telephone, reading aloud in front of others, making a bank deposit, telling stories at social gatherings, ordering food in restaurants, and proofreading typed papers for another secretary in the office. By questioning this woman, the therapist discovered that she was afraid of having difficulty with her speech in all these situations; and that through her difficulty, she risked humiliation and rejection by other people.

Because the meaning of a phobic object can vary from individual to individual, and a variety of fears within an individual can center around a common, though not always obvious, theme, it is important not to make a priori judgments regarding the ideational content of phobias. The clinician needs to assess the idiosyncratic meaning the phobic individual attaches to objects or situations of fear.

Relation of Fears to Phobias

Sometimes it is difficult to distinguish between a realistic fear and a phobia. There are several reasons for this problem. First, there are realistic dangers in the outside world that are avoided by non-phobic as well as phobic individuals: People are killed continually in automobile crashes, fires, explosions, and by disease. There are situations in which avoidance is the best policy: for example, it is obviously prudent to avoid blasting areas, people with infectious diseases, and crime-ridden streets late at night. Furthermore, there is usually some, though minimal, risk in situations feared by phobic individuals. It is easy to diagnose a phobia when the content of a fear is farfetched but less so when the fear seems to be reasonable. For example, it is fairly obvious that a person who avoids all outdoor activities for fear of being killed in a sudden electric storm, or who avoids subways and buses for fear of suffocation, has a phobia. It is less clear that a person who avoids walking to the store or riding in a subway late at night may have a phobia. Ascertaining the *reason* for avoiding the situation frequently provides the essential information—for example, an unreasonable fear of losing control or getting lost as opposed to a realistic fear of being mugged.

Some people seem able to buffer or to extinguish fears in situations that are obviously dangerous. Many people are engaged in occupations that are hazardous yet do not appear to experience anxiety. Police, firefighters, drivers of gasoline trucks, and professional soldiers all engage in activities associated with objective risk; yet these people neither experience the anxiety nor manifest the avoidance commonly seen in phobic individuals. Thus, there seems to be a spectrum extending from phobias at one end to realistic fears to "counterphobic" behavior at the other end.

SELF-CONFIDENCE VERSUS VULNERABILITY

Why do some people lack fears that would be considered objectively realistic in relatively dangerous situations? The answer seems to be that people who are repeatedly placed, or who work, in threatening situations are able to adapt to the frightening stimuli and subsequently experience less fear.

Experimental studies show that sport parachutists have reduced anxiety as they become more experienced (Epstein 1972; Rachman 1978). Novice jumpers showed increasing reactivity right to the moment of a jump, while experienced parachutists showed an initial rise in reactivity but then a sharp drop shortly before the jump. It appears that, after repeated exposure to danger, an *adaptive mechanism develops,* providing for an initial increase in activation which gives an early sign of danger; this is then inhibited from becoming disruptive at the crucial moment of the jump (Marks 1969). Similarly, seasoned troops experience less anxiety in a combat zone than do fresh recruits. Perhaps through repeated exposure to dangerous situations, these individuals believe that their worst fears about the consequences of these situations will not be realized. Moreover, they generally develop techniques for damping down the anxiety; for example, focusing on the task to be done. Subsequently, they experience less anxiety in "high-risk" situations.

DUAL BELIEF SYSTEMS

While the distinction between realistic fear and phobia is sometimes unclear to the outside observer, it is even less clear to the person who has the phobia. The phobic person seems to hold simultaneously two sets of contradictory beliefs about the probability of the occurrence of harm when in the situations he fears. When removed from the feared situation, he believes the situation is relatively harmless: the fear he experiences is proportional to the amount of objective risk in that situation. As he approaches the phobic situation, he becomes increasingly anxious and perceives the situation to be increasingly dangerous. The increasing "danger value" he imputes to the feared object or situation increases until the idea of threat completely dominates his appraisal of the situation. By that time, cognitive distortions, visual imagery, and somatic imagery combine to magnify the actual danger. His belief switches from the concept "it is harmless" to "it is dangerous."

The notion that phobic individuals can have contradictory beliefs about a feared situation—"dual belief system"—has been ignored in much of the technical literature on phobias. Much of this literature asserts that the phobic knows there is no danger in the situation he fears. For example, P. Friedman (1959) states that a phobia is a fear "which becomes attached to objects or situations which objectively are not a source of danger—or more precisely, are known by the individual not to be a source of danger." The assertion that the phobic individual *knows* that there is no objective danger in the feared situation is misleading because the objects and situations feared by phobic individuals—for example, crossing bridges, going into water over one's head, traveling through tunnels, or riding elevators— frequently involve some objective danger.

The observation that the phobic individual's estimation of the probability of harm increases as he approaches the situation has been tested many times. At a distance from a phobic situation, for example, an individual may state the probability of harm in that situation is almost zero. As he approaches the situation, the "odds" generally change: they may increase from zero to 10 percent to 50 percent, and finally to 100 percent once the person is actually in the feared situation.

Take the case of an airplane phobic who, when not planning a flight in the near future, estimated the chance of a plane crash as 1:100,000 or even 1:1,000,000. As soon as he was planning to make a trip by air, his estimated probabilities of a crash would increase dramatically. As the time for the flight approached, the likelihood of a crash progressively increased. By the time the airplane started to take off, he would figure the chances as 50:50. If the trip was bumpy, the odds would switch over to 100:1 in favor of a crash.

Many patients, accompanied into their feared situations, experience the sensation of whatever they fear would occur in such a situation. For example, when a woman with a fear of heights was accompanied to the top of a hill, she started to feel dizzy, began to sway, and "felt" a force pulling her over to the edge. On the fortieth floor of a skyscraper, she "felt" the floor tilt to a steep angle. Or, a woman with a fear of water started to have a visual image of herself drowning when accompanied on a trip to the beach. Or, a man who was concerned about having a heart attack when away from medical help, felt pains in his chest when accompanied into such a situation.

It seems then, that not only do the estimated probabilities of harm increase as phobic individuals approach their feared situations but that the phobic may also actually begin to experience, in fantasy, the catastrophic consequences he fears.

VISUAL IMAGES

Other types of phobias are related to the stimulation of visual fantasies. For example, a man avoided a section of the city in which he had had an automobile accident. Upon questioning the patient, the psychiatrist learned that whenever the man approached that geographical area he experienced a flashback of the accident and, as a result, experienced acute anxiety. In another case, a woman who had a water phobia recoiled at any stimulus that reminded her of being in the water, because such a stimulus gave her vivid fantasies of drowning. Here again, the anxiety experienced by the individual when in, or thinking about being in, the situation was different from his objective appraisal of the situation.

The visual images seem to play a role in "warning" a person of the consequences of being in a particular risky situation. Thus, depending on the nature of the stimulus, one may see oneself as drowning, getting hit by a car, or suffocating.

IDENTIFICATION WITH "VICTIM"

Sometimes there is no obvious risk in a situation feared by a phobic. For example, as we have said, some individuals experience violent anxiety at the sight of another person bleeding or undergoing a surgical operation. This is especially common among hospital professionals such as doctors or nurses. Since they are anxious in situations that are not objectively dangerous, their fears are somewhat enigmatic.

The puzzle seems to be solved if one tries to visualize the situation as it is perceived by the phobic individual, who experiences a high degree of identification with the victim. Usually, if questioned, the phobic is able to recall either visual or sensory imaging or some thought that indicates that he is reacting to the event as if he were the victim himself. Some examples of this phenomenon include: (1) a medical student, while watching an operation, had a visual image of himself on the operating table; (2) an intern, while performing a sternal puncture on a patient, felt pain in his own breastbone; and (3) a nurse felt dizzy and faint while observing a bleeding patient, and thought, "I wonder what it would be like if I were bleeding." While the blood-injury phobic may objectively recognize that he is not in danger, he still experiences intense anxiety when observing the feared situation.

Evolution, Rules, and Phobias

To clarify the nature of fears and phobias, we must analyze them in terms of a broad framework of the organism's response to threat. How does one make a "decision" to flee, freeze, or collapse in a given situation? Obviously, there needs to be an initial perception of an external stimulus and then an appraisal of this object as a threat. Depending on the nature of the threatening object *and* the total context, the organism becomes mobilized for protective action. It should be noted, however, that the decision to act or not to act has to be made on the basis of a predetermined scheme. There is scant time in case of an immediate danger to sort out all the aspects of a situation and to mull over the alternative strategies. The mechanisms for selecting the relevant data and determining the course of action depend on the utilization of rules (see Beck 1976, pp. 95–101).

The rules for promoting immediate survival are couched in a form that is unambiguous, inclusive, and absolute; it is not probabilistic or relative. These rules are invariant: they imply "always" or "never." Generally, the initial appraisal is made on the basis of a "part-object," such as a pair of eyes, or of a shape, such as the profile of a hawk in flight (Marks 1969).

The relevance of this formulation to the problem of fears and phobias is as follows: We assume that many of the fears are innate and serve a protective function in the earlier years of human development. There is evidence, for instance, that the fears of strangers, of unfamiliar situations, and of heights are built into the genetically determined psychological apparatus and become expressed at an appropriate time in the development of the child. These fears would be based on a rule (although not couched in actual words) such as "All strangers are dangerous" or "Going to the edge of a high place is dangerous." The rules are overly absolute and overly inclusive but serve a general protective function until the child is mature enough to operate according to a less absolute system.

Since the rules are preverbal, they are probably experienced in a visual/ kinesthetic configuration. When the sensory input matches this internal configuration, it triggers anxiety, avoidance, and physiological responses.

Many phobic patients have highly specific visual images when exposed to their phobic situation. It seems probable that these visualizations of catastrophic consequences serve to mobilize the individual for self-protection (Beck and Rush 1975).

Apparently a crucial element in passing from an immature fear to a more realistic pattern consists of learning either directly or vicariously that the primitive rule is too absolute and overly general, that the fear is unrealistic most of the time (but not always). Mature development, thus, consists of prying off the exaggerated consequences attributed to a particular state or activity and substituting a more appropriate rule. The absolute rule regarding strangers would be completely altered to take into account the circumstances, the threatening or nonthreatening appearance of a stranger, and the relative power of the individual and the stranger.

But these early rules or immature fears are not completely expunged. We not infrequently observe that, under conditions of considerable strain or illness, the erstwhile fears begin to be reactivated. Thus, an individual with prolonged sleep deprivation may begin to experience fears that he thought had disappeared with his childhood—fears of noises, strangers, speaking in public, and so on. Furthermore, a severe depression may often reactivate a wide array of phobias in a person. In addition, some fears appear to persist throughout life—for example, a person's fright at seeing a mutilated limb. The retention of such fears and phobias is suggestive of an evolutionary phenomenon known as "neoteny" (Montague 1981). Other fears remain latent until they are triggered by a generalized phobia, such as agoraphobia (see chapter 8).

These observations suggest certain features in the development of phobias. First, many phobias seem to derive from a primitive structure, whose content may be specific—small animals, high ledges, close spaces. This innate predisposition to develop fears has been labeled "prepotency" by I. M. Marks (1969) and "preparedness" by M. E. P. Seligman (1971). A problem in the notion of prepotency is that many objects that are the focus of a phobia do not occur in nature and thus could not have been selected by any known evolutionary process. The best explanation of these fears of man-made objects (knives, automobiles, airplanes) is that the fear is centered not on the specific object but on the *general concept*—namely, the danger of being stabbed by a sharp object, of being struck by a moving object, and of falling from a high place. It is not difficult to see that these phobias could be derived from innate fears of being mutilated or injured. This concept is thus applied, generally through learning, to the specific objects (knives) or events (car crashing).

Secondly, the content of many phobias seems to be encased in the original childhood form—for example, "All heights are always danger-ous." This feature of the phobia suggests that the usual deactivation of this rule has not occurred. We may assume that this rule persists either because it was overly potent by reasons of heredity or because it was "overlearned" (or both); for example, a person may have experienced a serious fall, which consequently tended to reinforce the rule in its original form—in other words, a fixation phobia (see pages 120–21).

The question naturally arises that, if the fears and phobias are derived in some way from primitive inherited structures, what can be their survival value? At first glance, it appears that many fears or phobias may seem to interfere with survival—for example, avoiding medical care because of a phobia of physicians, or "freezing" when one has to go across a narrow bridge to escape from enemies. Moreover, some phobias certainly produce discomfort and interfere with a person's life even though they may not threaten survival—for example, agoraphobia, fear of bridges, fear of public speaking. On further analysis, it may be proposed that these fears proba-bly had some survival value in the wild, and that in the earlier evolution of our species, the overgeneralized fears aided survival. In other words, it was better to make a mistake of the false positive type (that is, see a danger when it does not exist) than of a false negative (not seeing the danger). In this sense, the adage "Evolution favors anxious genes" seems to hold. The more common and distressing fears, including those encompassed under the notion of evaluation fears (test anxiety, social anxiety, public-speaking fear) may be more difficult to understand within an evolutionary frame-work. It may be that these fears are a byproduct of cultural heritage and socialization and are grafted into the basic survival apparatus for dealing with threats of abandonment and one's consequent vulnerability to preda-tors, the elements, or starvation.

Chapter 8

The Agoraphobic Syndrome

The Riddle of Agoraphobia

Certain features of agoraphobia seem to defy common sense or reason. Why should a woman who has progressed into her twenties, ostensibly with a minimum of psychological problems, suddenly develop a fear of going into public places, riding in cars, buses, trains, and elevators? Why should this person who is competent in many ways jeopardize a job or marriage or refuse to leave the house? Why should a woman who has engaged in numerous activities on her own in the past become so dependent that she will not travel without a companion?

These questions sorely vex those theorists who try to make sense of psychiatric disorders. In recent years, the problem of agoraphobia has attracted considerable attention as indicated by the large number of volumes that address this subject (for example, Chambless and Goldstein 1982; Dupont 1982; Emmelkamp 1982; Guidano and Liotti 1983; Klein and Rabkin 1981; Marks 1969; Mathew, Gelder, and Johnston 1981; Mavissakalian and Barlow 1981; and Thorpe and Burns 1983). The broad attack from the clinical, the behavioral, and the pharmacological vantage points may yield some answers to this riddle.

The Development of Agoraphobia

PREDISPOSITION AND PRECIPITATION

Why do agoraphobic symptoms tend to appear after the age of twenty (especially since most phobias originate in childhood)? It is suggested that these patients have an agoraphobic disposition that is not expressed until a change of circumstances activates it. For example, M. R. Liebowitz and D. F. Klein (1982) postulate that these individuals have a lowered threshold for panic attacks associated with separation, and thus are vulnerable to "episodic autonomic discharge." It is also proposed that these people have had a lifelong concern about their health or ability to manage emotional upheavals, but have managed to maintain their equilibrium as long as they had available one or more protective figures (parents, siblings, peer group). Many of these persons have a history of separation anxiety dating back to early childhood (Gittelman 1983). Thus, a prolonged stay away from home (for example, attending a distant college) could remove this prop and make one subject to agoraphobia. Similarly, a disruption of marital adjustment (Guidano and Liotti 1982; Mathew, Gelder, and Johnston 1981; Chambless and Goldstein 1982) jeopardizes the availability of a supportive person. The general circumstance that seems to be prevalent among most agoraphobics is the increasing expectation that the individual take on the demands of adulthood or parenthood and at the same time function more independently. Birth of a child, loss of a caregiver through separation or death, increased demands at home or at work, all may precipitate agoraphobic symptoms. The increased responsibilities represent threats to the patient since she believes that if she performs inadequately there may be disastrous consequences. Thus, her self-confidence may be threatened by the increased expectations and/or by a removal of a social support.

In a typical scenario, the individual perceives herself as being suppressed by another person on whom she depends for support. She has a large investment in her own sense of self-control and competence, shaky though it is; but the domination by another person tends to erode her confidence in her ability to function adequately on an independent basis. Since the new demands and responsibilities are viewed as crucial, she is likely to revert to an earlier stage of dependency. She becomes more threatened by external and internal problems and relies increasingly on her supporter to help her to cope with these dangers.

ONSET OF SYMPTOMATOLOGY

The future agoraphobic commonly begins to perceive a variety of possible dangers in the "outside world": for example, losing control of the car, getting lost in traffic, getting caught in a revolving door, being bowled over by a crowd. (These dangers resemble the relatively realistic fears of young children.) These fears both accumulate and expand, so that eventually almost every stage in the process of going out to a store or other place away from home becomes a serious confrontation. The result is that the individual perceives herself as increasingly vulnerable as she goes through each of these steps:

1. She perceives an unlimited number of opportunities to be immobilized, humiliated, crushed, suffocated, or attacked (in crowds, elevators, buses, tunnels, streets). She has no reliable defense against these external "dangers."
2. Automatic reflexive reactions produce symptoms suggestive of a serious internal disturbance—heart attack, stroke, fainting spell, attack of insanity. The woman has no way of warding off these "internal" attacks.
3. The patient experiences a sense of "malfunctioning" and decrement of competence. She believes that she cannot keep the car on the road, maintain her equilibrium while standing still, communicate orally to other people without blocking or stuttering, and so on.
4. The loss of control over reactions to threat reinforces the notion that she is a victim of internal and external forces over which she has no control.
5. This loss of a sense of competence plus fears of the "internal disturbance" lead the patient to seek assistance from a caregiver.
6. The intense anxiety in the threatening situation (department store, supermarket) may escalate into a panic attack. In any event, the strong anxiety triggers a strong wish to flee from the situation and return to a safe haven (generally home).
7. Home, or an equivalent haven, represents safety from the external danger. The patient experiences a strong resistence to venturing out again and generally feels anxious if she does leave the house.
8. The multiple inhibitions, submissive tendencies, and negative appraisals of self undermine self-confidence and thus lead to disequilibrium in relationships, further sense of inadequacy, and ultimately the sense of being trapped and dominated by other people.

Panic

Some authorities believe that agoraphobia results from a sudden panic attack away from home (Klein 1981). The panic attack severely undermines the patient's confidence that she can handle trips of this nature, and restricts her travels to places within easy access of home and to companions whom she can trust to help her if an attack should occur. Prior to entering a situation in which an attack has occurred, the patient may be primarily afraid of having the attack. But when she starts to feel intense anxiety, she is no longer afraid of the panic *per se* but of fainting, dying, losing control, or going crazy (Doctor, Gaer, and Wright 1983).

Not all cases of agoraphobia start with a panic attack. In fact, the *Diagnostic and Statistical Manual of Mental Disorders* (American Psychiatric Association 1980, p. 226) lists agoraphobia *without* panic attacks as a distinct diagnosis. The facts that many people may experience agoraphobia long before their first panic attack, and that many never have a panic attack, raise some question about the role of the attack as a necessary condition for the development and maintenance of agoraphobia. Moreover, many patients who have had panic attacks state that their primary fear, prior to entering the phobic situation, is of having a heart attack or of losing control rather than simply of having another panic attack. In addition, some patients who have overcome their avoidance of the phobic situation may continue to have panic attacks without relapsing into their former avoidance (Marks 1981).

ATTRIBUTION OF CAUSALITY IN PANIC ATTACKS

In many cases, the progression to a panic attack starts with a period of "tension" stemming from life problems that are novel to the patient (new demands or risks at home or at work) and for which she has no available coping strategies (Doctor, Gaer, and Wright 1983). The unsolved problems lead to a sense of helplessness and various somatic and psychological symptoms.

The origin and nature of these symptoms are mysterious to the patient: she has difficulty explaining them to herself. Rather than correlate her increased levels of tension with specific stressors or fears, she is likely to regard her symptoms as an expression of an inexplicable and dangerous internal process over which she has no control. She may have a strong "disease" orientation that leads her to think of explanations in terms of a serious pathological process (Guidano and Liotti 1983).

At some point in the progression of a specific panic attack, symptoms intensify beyond the person's capacity to discount them or to function effectively. Her interpretation of sudden uncontrollable symptoms as signs of impending physical or mental disaster then accelerates the process until a full-blown panic occurs.

Symptoms include dizziness, abdominal pain, lack of control over thinking, involuntary trembling, paresthesias, depersonalization; some of these sensations may be attributable to hyperventilation, which may begin or increase during an attack. As the symptoms start to mount, she begins to see them as signals of *immediate* danger such as: (1) mental and physical collapse; (2) heart attack or stroke; (3) loss of control of "emotions" (screaming, crying, weeping); (4) loss of control over behavior (hurting someone, attempting suicide, acting out sexually); (5) going crazy; and (6) other adversities (choking, epileptic fits, spontaneous termination of breathing).

The interpretation of symptoms as a threat to life, mental health, or ability to function leads to their intensification (increasing autonomic arousal, subjective anxiety, generalized weakness). The fact that the patient is unable to arrest the progression of symptoms confirms her belief in their extreme gravity. She not only makes negative interpretations of her symptoms but predicts the worst possible consequences (see table 8.1).

Evidence from a recent study suggests that imagery plays a role in the psychopathology of agoraphobia. Of eight patients interviewed, seven reported experiencing distressing images prior to entering a public place, while four reported also having such images in public places. The imagery involved fainting, collapsing, being humiliated or assaulted, having serious accidents, and other themes of illness, disability, and disgrace.

It should be noted that the panic attacks associated with agoraphobia are indistinguishable from those associated with generalized anxiety disorder. Consequently, as expected, we find the predominant symptoms just prior to the onset of the attack to be the same in both disorders. Some patients can train themselves to head off a full-blown attack through techniques such as distraction or cognitive restructuring—that is, through viewing the symptoms as an emotional reaction, not as a sign of catastrophe.

TABLE 8.1

Feared Consequences of Systems

Interpretation of Symptoms	Consequence
Having a heart attack, stroke	Death
Passing out	Hospitalization
Losing control over thinking	Go crazy
Losing control over "emotions" (scream, cry)	Public disgrace
Losing control over impulses	Kill somebody/self
Unable to catch breath	Death

COGNITIVE SET: VULNERABILITY

As the agoraphobic person approaches the phobic situation, she "locks into" a vulnerability set: an anticipation that some affliction is about to befall her. She is concerned about the possibility of a sudden, paroxysmal, uncontrollable internal disturbance. *Before* entering the situation, she does not regard this state of disturbance as being indicative of serious physical, behavioral, or mental disorder. When *in* the situation, however, she believes she may be developing a serious affliction.

What is the "cause" of the state of arousal in the first place? It appears to be based on the individual's concept that (when alone) she is vulnerable to a sudden serious medical, mental, or emotional disorder. She believes this disorder can be remedied if she has quick, unobstructed access to a place of safety, such as her home, a physician, or a hospital. Thus, relatively minor somatic sensations suggesting an affliction can be dismissed or ignored if she has access to assistance.

If she is distanced or blocked from such assistance, she may not be able to ignore these minor or major somatic symptoms that she regards as indicating some internal threat. The interpretation of the somatic symptoms (which may be manifested by chest or abdominal pain, choking sensations, faint feelings, or generalized muscular weakness) as a sign of an impending disaster increases her fear of a serious mishap. The increased fear leads to anxiety and its concomitants, which may further enhance the somatic symptoms (chest or abdominal pain, difficulty in breathing, faintness, and so on). A vicious cycle is set up. Finally, her difficulty in thinking prevents her from using her reasoning powers to negate the exaggerated fears.

A patient entering the agoraphobic situation, then, is operating on these principles:

1. "An overwhelming disturbance can occur at any time."
2. "There is nothing I can do to ward off or mitigate this occurrence."
3. "If I have access to a helpful expert (such as a physician) or a helper (friend or family member), I can avert or reduce the dire consequences."
4. "Any particular sensation (for example, chest or abdominal pain) may be a sign of this devastating process."
5. "If the process is not stymied, it can accelerate to the ultimate disaster (for example, death from suffocation)."

Why do specific locations or situations appear to trigger the attacks? One factor seems to be that they block easy access to home or to a helping figure. Crowded stores interfere with mobility. Riding on a train, a superhighway, over a bridge, or in a tunnel blocks access to emergency help. Similarly, being blocked from the exit in a crowded restaurant or theater impedes escape to a safe haven and access to help. The key word in these situations is "trapped."

The other possibly more important factor is that each of these situations is perceived as dangerous in itself. Thus, the person traveling to a specific "agoraphobic" situation such as an enclosed shopping mall or a department store encounters a host of potential dangers en route. She may drive the car off the road or hit a pedestrian, lose her way, get struck by a car while crossing the street, or get mugged while entering a subway station. Furthermore, subways and tunnels can cave in, bridges collapse, buses crash, and elevators get stuck.

The "dangers" when she has entered the agoraphobic situation are less obvious. Crowded stores interfere with free movement to the specific departments and counters as well as limit possibilities for flight and access to help. The crowded floors may produce a sense of being hemmed in and a feeling of being smothered, which may lead the patient to hyperventilate and, thus, experience certain symptoms (lightheadedness, tingling) associated with a panic attack. On the other hand, the cavernous spaces, the broad expanse of large windows, unfamiliar angles, converging geometrical lines may trigger anxietylike symptoms associated with depth perception—the so-called "opticokinetic reflex" (Marks 1969). This reaction, present only in some agoraphobic patients, is observed most clearly in large domed buildings, such as auditoriums, and in public squares (as originally noted by C. Westphal [1871–72]). Thus, the patient with hypersensitivity to external boundaries is caught between the fear of being constricted by inadequate room for movement, on the one hand, and of being engulfed by unlimited space, on the other. In addition to the problem of too much or too little space, she may fear that she will trip and fall off the escalator, jump down the stairwell, or topple out the large windows on the upper floors of the department store.

The agoraphobic is typically concerned with free movement and access to help. Paradoxically, however, one of her characteristic behavioral reactions involves immobility (Doctor 1982) and faintness (Thorpe and Burns 1983). The patient feels weak and helpless and fears she may faint. When it occurs, this parasympathetic-immobility response makes the phobic situation even more threatening because the behavioral response further interferes with freedom of action. In most cases, however, the urge to escape is so strong that it overrides these feelings of weakness.

Mobility has meaning that goes beyond providing a mechanism for escape and an antidote to faintness and weakness. Agoraphobic individuals place a premium on mobility for its own sake—freedom, self-determination, individuality. Any limitation by animate or inanimate objects makes one feel trapped, stuck, immobilized. These patients at times have fantasies of complete freedom—for example, flying in the air (Guidano and Liotti 1983). Some agoraphobic women report "involuntary" fantasies of flagrant sexual escapades, for which they are arrested. We may hypothesize that the fear of loss of control, so prominent in agoraphobic patients, is due, in part, to recognition of an impulse to break loose from conventional rules of behavior—by yelling, acting crazy, doing destructive acts.

The agoraphobic's conflict, then, seems to revolve around issues of dependency, autonomy, and control. On the one hand, since she believes she cannot deal with the dangers in the outside world by herself, she is impelled to obtain help from a "caretaker." On the other hand, seeking succor may lead to surrender of sovereignty to another person. Because she "needs" the other person, she has less claim to freedom, to exercising individuality, and to asserting right.

Not infrequently agoraphobics are caught in a complex marital interaction. They want to receive support from the mate and to be free and autonomous (Guidano and Liotti 1983). The sticky relationship tends to have several effects. First, their expression of autonomy is inhibited because it might alienate the spouse and, thus, threaten the patient's ability to rely on the spouse for help. Further, the spouse might use his position as caretaker to dominate his agoraphobic wife, to promote his own objectives, and to depreciate her. The result of this unequal relationship is to reduce her self-confidence and make her more dependent. Secondly, the patient's submissive strategies not only make her feel less potent but stir up a sense of impotent defiance. She then is caught in a conflict between wanting to please the caretaker and to kick over the traces.

In a study comparing the responses to the Sociotropy Autonomy Scale (Beck 1983) of thirty-nine agoraphobics with those of sixteen cases of generalized anxiety disorder, thirty-six depressives, and seventy-two normals, it was found that the agoraphobic patient has a greater investment in mobility and self-direction, and sensitivity to being restrained or controlled, than the other psychiatric patients and normal controls. These tendencies are manifested by extreme scores on the following attitudes:

1. "It is very important that I be free to get up and go whenever I want to."
2. "I feel confined when I have to sit through a long meeting."
3. "I get fidgety when sitting around talking and would prefer to get up and do something."
4. "I prefer to make my own plans—so I am not controlled by others."
5. "It bothers me when people try to direct my behavior and activities."

There appear to be varying combinations of attitudes and traits that make one vulnerable to the development of this disorder. Among these are: an emphasis on self-determination and a related hypersensitivity to control or interference; a tendency to react to threat with weakness and a desire to flee; a lack of security when away from home; a pattern of interpreting somatic symptoms as a sign of an immediate physical or psychological disruption; and a strategy of depending on a caregiver for reassurance and medical assistance. Interestingly, the agoraphobic person's reluctance to be too close to the caregiver, lest she be dominated, or too far, lest she encounter a situation where she needs help, is paralleled by her sensitivity to spatial configurations. She avoids spaces that are too narrow (crowds, closets, elevators) and too expansive (supermarkets, shopping centers, flat meadowland, amphitheaters).

The development of agoraphobia is illustrated in the following typical case, a composite of some cases we have observed: A woman with a high degree of investment in her autonomy finds herself caught in a sticky marital relationship. She depends on her husband to help her out emotionally and in a practical way, but in return has to adapt herself to being dominated. With the birth of her first child, she begins to question her ability to carry out the necessary functions for her child's proper nurturance, protection, and care. The continued domination by her husband makes her question even more her competence, her ability to cope with external problems and internal conflicts, and her ability to control herself. She begins to have fears that she might do something that would harm the child. With the rising anxiety she feels even less confident in carrying out her "domestic duties." She is not fully cognizant of her resentment toward her husband but is aware of tension which she attributes to some kind of physical disorder.

She now finds that when she leaves the house, she begins to doubt her ability to drive the car. When driving to the shopping center, for instance, she has continual fears about driving—specifically, that she may not negotiate turns properly and will go off the road or run into oncoming traffic; that she might lose her way; that she won't be able to park her car in the lot; that she won't be able to find her car when she comes back; that she may run out of gas.

When she enters the department store, she is afraid of getting caught in the revolving door, of losing her balance on the escalator, of not being able to find the right counter, of not being able to select the items she wants, or of not being able to assert herself with the sales clerk. The fluorescent lights bother her and seem to make objects appear disconnected and produce a general sense of disorientation. When she takes the elevator to the next landing, she feels faint and is afraid she may fall down. As she looks out the tall window at the landing, she is afraid that she may fall out the window, even though it is waist high. She decides to take the elevator down but is afraid that it may get stuck on the way. When she reaches the ground floor again, she feels crowded by the people scurrying around and begins to feel more and more breathless; she hyperventilates in order to get more air and then begins to feel "pins and needles" in her extremities.

At this point, the woman interprets her shortness of breath, her weakness, and the peculiar feeling in her extremities as signaling some terrible devastating disorder. She thinks that she may be dying right now. She is inhibited from asking anybody for help because she feels that they will be distant and nonresponsive, and she is vaguely aware that her symptomatology may be only a "false alarm." She manages to call her husband and, with his reassurance, is able to get home. Thereafter, whenever she leaves the house she thinks seriously about keeping some kind of line open for reaching her husband in case something bad happens. In addition, she becomes more fearful of each of the dangers that she confronts while driving to supermarket or shopping center. As the anxiety builds, she becomes worried once again that she may be having some kind of internal catastrophe and is then even more anxious, and finally she hurries back home in order to "save my life."

This composite example can illustrate how the agoraphobic individual is caught in a vise between her expectation of self-sufficiency and her "need" for help. As her self-sufficiency is thwarted, her dependency increases. Concomitantly, she becomes increasingly fearful of being dominated by her husband.

Dependency

The following case illustrates the *lifelong* pattern of separation fears and dependency that develop into agoraphobia: A thirty-year-old woman had always had problems in being away from home. She had difficulties in going to school and then to summer camp. She was always propped up by her mother who was very managerial but at the same time indulgent and concerned about the patient's welfare. The mother had a high degree of hypochondriasis herself and intended to interpret any sign of disorder in her child as a possible disease. She had a chest full of medicine of various types and, whenever the child was symptomatic, would administer one of these medications to her. The child would then experience relief.

This woman thus entered adult life with the following notions: (1) "I am a frail individual and need to be close to medical help at all times." (2) "I can manage successfully if I have a strong person to lean on."

This woman managed to navigate successfully until her husband was called into the service. At that point she got a job for the first time but experienced an enormous amount of fear and anxiety over her performance. With the increase of anxiety, she experienced her first panic attack. From then on, it becomes increasingly more difficult for her to go to the office, and she finally became completely housebound.

One of the enigmas of the agoraphobic syndrome is the phobic's desperate need for a trusted person when she enters the "danger zone." If access to this caretaker is available, the agoraphobic feels less threatened by the external situation and by the anxiety symptoms. A good part of this dependency may be attributed to the nature of the anxiety or panic attack. The facts that the attack is inexplicable, that the agoraphobic person feels incapable of turning it off, and that the capacity for objectivity and reasoning is impaired impel her to look for help for her physical or mental survival. Contact with a helper brings relief because it promises to provide access to prompt treatment if the agoraphobic patient is, indeed, on the verge of mental or physical collapse. Furthermore, the caretaker can help to evaluate the seriousness of the disorder and provide distraction. The role of the caretaker in reality testing is illustrated in the following interchange:

PATIENT: I'm choking. I can't breathe. I feel that I'm dying.
SPOUSE: Relax. Take some deep breaths. . . . What's happening now?
PATIENT: I'm breathing O.K. I guess I'm not dying.

A Synthesis

Systematic research about the personality, the conflicts, and the environmental problems of the agoraphobic is still relatively scanty, but the following propositions based on clinical observations may be advanced:

1. The agoraphobia-prone individual has latent fears of situations that might have constituted potential dangers during early childhood but that are not dangerous for adults. These include crowded stores or open spaces (where a child could get lost), closed spaces (suffocation), stationary or moving stairs (losing balance), windows (falling out). Susceptibility to these fears is increased when the person has become involved in stressful situations, which tax her capacity for modulating her emotional reactions and for testing her exaggerated fears against reality. Thus, the development of agoraphobia may be based on the activation and summation of these latent fears.

2. With the background of reduced internal and external resources, the specific fear of being away from a safe haven may become activated by a traumatic experience, such as being involved in an accident while driving in town, or witnessing someone having a heart attack in public. The agoraphobic may then start to fear having an accident while driving or having a heart attack away from medical help. The fear may focus on the specific circumstances and activity associated with the traumatic event. Thus, she may become afraid of—and avoid—driving in a car in the city and climbing stairs in a department store. As long as she avoids the traumatic circumstance, she is not threatened. In some cases, this "traumatic" experience may trigger a considerable anxiety attack, and the agoraphobic may through association begin to regard the type of location or of activity (for example, an intersection or driveway) as dangerous. As her sense of vulnerability increases, the safety zone, centered on her home, gradually shrinks, and the dangerous zone expands. If driving in town is unsafe, then driving in the country becomes unsafe. Situations that would ordinarily cause mild discomfort (for example, elevators, heights, crowds) can now activate full-blown anxiety and subsequently panic.

3. The panic attack is essentially a primitive response consisting largely of anxiety, faintness, dizziness, generalized weakness, and difficulty in thinking. The development of a panic attack in the agoraphobic patient follows the same sequence as in the patient with panic disorder. The patient experiences some physiological change as the result of physical or psychological stress, hyperventilation, sudden change in position, or anticipation of danger. The physiological changes are attributed to a serious internal disorder which the patient presumes will escalate into some disastrous consequence. The patient's ability to reason is inhibited and consequently he cannot view his symptoms objectively.

4. The fear of disaster coupled with the sense of physical and mental paralysis induces the agoraphobic to seek help from a caretaker. The care-

taker serves to provide access to professional help (if necessary), to help the patient to reality-test her fear, and to help to distract her from fixation on her fears.

Any distancing from, or blockage of access to, home or the caretaker can in itself induce fear and an overpowering wish to return home. The consequent restrictions on traveling are especially demoralizing to the agoraphobic, who tends to place a high premium on mobility and freedom from domination. Ultimately, the demoralization can lead to depression.

If the patient has had a panic attack in a particular place, the fear of having another attack is added to (and may overshadow) the fear activated by that place.

5. Thus, a number of circumstances can be interpreted by the agoraphobic as danger signals: (1) entry into a situation where a panic attack occurred or that resembles such a situation; (2) entry into a situation for which she has a latent phobia; (3) experience of a dramatic "internal" state that signals danger; (4) separation from a caretaker or from home.

6. The agoraphobic patient is hypersensitive to specific spatial configurations: too narrow spaces and too expansive spaces. The sensitivity to narrow boundaries and expansive boundaries is paralleled in personal relations—namely, the fear of being too close to, and the fear of being too far away from, a caretaker.

Chapter 9

The Evaluation Anxieties

The Essence of Evaluation Anxieties

BEFORE THE FALL

A person entering a socially threatening situation is like someone walking a tightrope. He feels *vulnerable* to a serious mishap if his performance is not *adequate*. For *safety's* sake, he must conform to a rigid set of *rules* regarding appropriate actions and movements. The greater his *confidence* in his skill, the less likely is he to make a potentially fatal *misstep*. If he has a *failure* of nerve, his *performance* may be sabotaged by primitive reflex reactions— freezing, motor *inhibition*. Thus, this exercise is a test of his *ability* and *maturity*. Smooth performance reaffirms his *image* of himself and maintains his *status*. Failure would shatter this image. Finally, every action is *observed* by a crowd of *evaluators* and appraised as clumsy or skillful, and he is *judged* according to his confidence and competence. The italicized words in this anecdote represent crucial aspects of the psychology of evaluative anxiety that will be described in this chapter.

The potential fall of the performer is paralleled by the "fall from grace" anticipated by an anxious person in the myriad of evaluative situations of everyday life. As in the case of the tightrope walker, *errors, missteps, inappropriate actions represent only a fraction of his overt behavior, but the damage is to the entire person*—or so he fears.

Common Features of Evaluative Threats

There are certain commonalities among the various situations in which an individual may experience "evaluation anxiety." The kinds of situation may be grouped as follows: (1) social situations—initiating or maintaining a person-to-person relationship; participating in a social gathering (for example, a party); (2) a school or vocational situation—performance evaluated by teacher, supervisor, or peer group; taking a test or examination; confrontation with a superior over a conflict of interest; athletic competition; (3) transactions in the "outside world" while shopping or traveling, with salespersons, waiters or waitresses, taxidrivers, strangers.

A complex web of factors in these situations may aggravate or mitigate fears. These factors involve the question of evaluation and vulnerability and include the following: (1) the relative status of the individual and the evaluator in the area of power or social desirability; (2) the individual's skill in presenting an attractive or effective "front"; (3) his confidence in his ability to perform adequately in a given threat situation; (4) his appraisal of the degree of threat, of the severity of potential damage and the probability of its occurring; (5) the threshold of certain automatic "defenses" (verbal inhibition, blockage of recall, suppression of spontaneity) that can undermine individual performance; (6) the rigidity and attainability of the "rules" relevant to acceptable performance, behavior, and appearance; (7) the anticipated punitiveness of the evaluator for nonadherence to rules or substandard performance, and so on.

VULNERABILITY

The individual who is anxious on entering into an evaluative situation has a network of implicit questions:

1. "To what degree is this a *test* of my competence or acceptability? How much do I have to prove myself to me or others?"
2. "What is my status relative to that of my evaluators?" If the individual feels parity with or superior to the evaluator, then the rules are less narrow and more flexible and the prospective "punishment" for failure is less important.
3. "How important is it to establish a position of strength about relative power status (as in dealing with service personnel) or a position of acceptability in dealing with social evaluators (as in blind dates or speaking before an audience)?"
4. "What is the attitude of the evaluator? Is he accepting and empathetic or rejecting and aloof? Are his judgments likely to be objective or harsh and punitive?"
5. "To what degree can I count on my skills (such as verbal fluency) to carry me through the difficult evaluation?"

6. "What is the likelihood of my being undermined by distracting anxiety and inhibitions?"

STATUS AND RANKING ORDER

A good part of the pressure to perform well is related to relative position on a vertical scale of power or social desirability. In a situation of confrontation with authority (teacher, supervisor, service personnel), the individual's perception of relative power determines his self-confidence and performance. If a person presents an appearance of self-confidence and competence, he reduces his "inferiority" on the power scale. If he perceives that he is lower, he is more likely to be less confident and less competent and thus will be vulnerable to being reduced in power even more. The dominance-submission dimension is generally also involved. The more dominant the individual perceives an evaluator to be, the more his own submissive tendencies are likely to be mobilized. Service personnel (physicians, cab drivers, receptionists, cashiers) are invested with authority and dominance by virtue of their position, which they can use to intimidate the individual.

In the case of a social confrontation in which a person wants to make a good impression, he is under pressure to maximize his social assets—attractiveness, dress, fluency, maturity, poise, grace. A high "score" on these assets may (depending on the values of the evaluator) make the person more desirable and thus ensure success in other encounters. A low "score" sets him up to be rejected.

A person may want to shun this type of confrontation because "failure" is painful. Moreover, avoidance leaves open the question of whether he is inferior, whereas a failure "confirms" his inferiority. Thus, social fearfulness is expressed in part by the experience of painful anxiety and the desire to reduce or avert the anxiety by avoiding or withdrawing from the aversive situation.

SELF-CONFIDENCE

Confidence in one's ability to perform adequately in the confrontation is related to the perceived magnitude of one's expectations, their difficulty, and the anticipated punishment for inadequate performance.

A disparity in the individual's sense of his power or desirability in relation to that of the evaluator increases the magnitude of the task, because the criteria for acceptable performance are higher, and therefore the demands on him are greater. When he perceives himself in a "one down" position, a person is less certain that he can fulfill these demands; and thus his global confidence in his competence is reduced. Moreover, if he antici- pates a drastic "punishment" for inadequate performance (loss of job, suspension from school, termination of a relationship), his self-confidence may be further undermined. Other factors being constant, there is a recip- rocal relationship between self-confidence and sense of vulnerability. As one goes up, the other goes down.

RULES AND FORMULAS

In an obviously evaluative situation (for example, test taking, public speaking, making a date), there is a pressure to conform to arbitrary, rigid rules in order to avoid "punishment." The individual fears that he may not be sufficiently facile, fluent, and unflappable and thus experiences anxiety and other symptoms that militate against his attaining his goal. Deviations from these rules during performance raise negative evaluations and self- doubts, such as "I look timid, frightened," "What I say sounds stupid," "I'm so awkward," or, "Will I foul it up?"

In public speaking, he believes he must adhere to stringent rules regard- ing the volume and tone of his voice, his articulateness and speed of speaking, his fluency and control of speech. The individual, thus, may fear that any departure from the rules may make him susceptible to disapproval and devaluation. In a social situation, deviation from the established can- ons may bring rejection.

In other types of interpersonal transaction (asking for information, re- questing a raise), a breach of the rules may evoke hostility and overt devaluation. In such encounters, the individual is faced with such rules as "You shouldn't impose on people." Thus, if he makes a legitimate request or asserts his rights in a reasonable way, he may fear that "This seems like an imposition."

AUTOMATIC PROTECTIVE REACTIONS

Automatic Inhibition. Reflex reactions in a dangerous situation have been discussed previously. Many people are susceptible to automatic inhibitory reactions that impede flow of speech, thinking, and recall. The "function" of these reactions under more primitive circumstances may have been to protect the individual from taking action that would provoke attack. Today this function is anachronistic and actually leads to dysfunction. Consequently, it is likely to evoke just the kind of attack that the individ- ual would like to avoid. There does not appear to be any volitional component in this freezing reaction. It is mobilized completely contrary to a person's intentions and wishes.

Anxiety.   Anxiety seems to be the product of a different system than is reflex inhibition. The function of anxiety seems to be to spur the person to take some action to reduce the danger. Then, he may be motivated to avoid going into a threatening situation or, if in the situation, to escape or minimize the danger by being inconspicuous (for example, not speaking up in class). It is obvious that, far from providing safety, the safety or protective patterns (inhibition blocking and anxiety-avoidance-escape) have a negative effect on performance. In fact, the anticipation of these reactions is in itself often sufficient to arouse anxiety and, then, to impair performance.

Faint.   People in evaluative situations not infrequently feel faint and often fear that they will lose consciousness. This type of response is obviously highly inappropriate in an evaluative situation and may be a throwback to a primitive fear of being physically injured—as is the blood-injury phobia.

Social Phobias and Social Anxieties

Social phobias and social anxieties are concerned with one's exaggerated fear of being the focus of attention and devaluation by another person or persons. According to the third edition of the *Diagnostic and Statistical Manual of Mental Disorders*, the essential feature of social phobia is "a persistent irrational fear of, and compelling desire to avoid, a situation in which the individual is exposed to possible scrutiny by others" (American Psychiatric Association 1980, p. 228). The present definition is probably too broad in that it would encompass a huge proportion of the population as well as a significant number of patients now appropriately diagnosed as having a generalized anxiety disorder. In contrast to the definition of social phobia, the official definition of agoraphobia does specify that "normal activities are increasingly constricted as the fears or avoidance behavior dominate the individual's life" (p. 226). This restrictive criterion applied to the definition of social phobia would be more in keeping with the general concept of phobia. Moreover, *DSM-III* includes as examples of social phobias "fears of speaking or performing in public, using public lavatories, eating in public, and writing in the presence of others" (p. 227). Certainly the fear of speaking in public should not be included since a very high proportion of the general population has this fear. If the more restrictive definition is used, a relatively small percentage of people with social anxiety actually would be considered social phobics.

Paradoxes of Social Anxiety

Unlike the phobias described in the previous chapters, a major feature of the social anxieties is that the actual fear (anticipation of being nervous and inhibited), prior to entering a situation, appears plausible and indeed seems to have a reasonable probability of being realized. Although a person with a phobia of heights, bridges, or elevators runs a minimal risk of falling or suffocating, an individual who is afraid of becoming tongue-tied when trying to carry on a conversation with a "blind date," or that his mind will go blank during an examination or interview, can reasonably expect these events to occur. The most interesting feature is that actually having the fear seems to bring on the undesirable consequence. A vicious cycle is created whereby the anticipation of an absolute, extreme, irreversible outcome tends to make a person more fearful, defensive, and inhibited when entering the situation. On the other hand, the person who does not experience the fear of inept performance in a particular situation is substantially less likely to respond ineptly.

An important aspect of social anxiety in which the fears are grossly inaccurate is the individual's expectation that his inept performance in a social situation will be a fatal blow to his social aspirations. The expectation that one's life will be ruined by a specific rejection or failure is rarely borne out by experience. The content and the probability of such dire consequences are grossly exaggerated. Even when the extreme outcome does not occur after a particular unsettling experience, the individual, nonetheless, expects the bad thing to happen "next time."

THE FEAR OF BEING EVALUATED

The central fear in the so-called social anxieties is that of negative evaluation by another person or persons—a fear that separates the social and the performance anxieties from agoraphobia. In the latter syndrome, a person may be afraid of wide-open squares, fields, or beaches where there are no people as well as closed-in groups or crowds of people. In agoraphobia, the fear of social disapproval appears to be secondary to the fear of losing control, fainting, going crazy, and so on. In contrast, in the social anxieties the central fear is of being the center of attention, of having one's "weaknesses" exposed, and consequently of being judged adversely by one or more people.

There is a symbolic confrontation in the social anxieties whether the individual is calling a stranger on the telephone, trying to initiate a conversation in a social setting, or performing before a group. When the socially anxious person is engaged in a one-to-one encounter with another person or group of people, he believes that he is being scrutinized, tested, and judged. Under observation are his performance, fluency of speech, self-assurance, and freedom from anxiety.

Unlike the agoraphobic, who is hypersensitive to internal signals suggestive of impending mental or physical collapse, the social phobic is hypersensitive to signals from other people regarding his acceptability. If he is receiving positive responses, he interprets them as a sign that he is making a good impression, and he feels less vulnerable and more self-confident. On the other hand, if he receives and integrates negative responses, he feels more vulnerable and less confident.

The physiological responses of the socially anxious individual may be similar to that of the agoraphobic person but are not as pronounced. As we shall discuss, he may feel the same type of sympathetic symptoms (rapid pulse rate, sweating) or parasympathetic symptoms (faintness, drop in blood pressure) as the agoraphobic; however, these evoke the fear that he will not perform adequately (which may be accurate), whereas the agoraphobic has the fear of an internal disaster (practically never accurate). It should be noted that some patients with public-speaking anxiety do, indeed, fear panic attacks, and some actually have a panic attack; but they are in the minority.

THE PRIMAL "DEFENSES"

The single factor that seems to be the most crippling to the socially anxious person is not the subjective experience of anxiety *per se*, although this indeed proves a handicap, but the various inhibitions, specifically those that interfere with his performance. Thus, the various types of inhibition—such as interference with verbal fluency, thinking, recall, and remote memory—are the most disabling factors in this disorder and, once they are involved in the vicious cycle, perpetuate the fear of going into the phobic situation.

These paradoxical responses to a threat, rather than priming the individual for more effective performance, actually impair his performance. The explanation seems to be, as we have said, that a primitive defensive system is mobilized as the individual goes into the social situation. This system, reminiscent of "freezing" and "atonic immobility" (Gallup 1980), prepares the individual to cope with a *physical* assault but does not, of course, prepare him to perform effectively and maturely. Furthermore, the nature of this primitive innate response pattern is *designed* to produce immobility and muteness. Thus, paradoxically the defense against a challenge to speak up and actively participate in a particular situation triggers just the opposite of the demands.

Differentiating Social Phobia from Agoraphobia

In a landmark article, P. L. Amies, M. G. Gelder, and P. M. Shaw (1983) brought out in a systematic way a number of features that differentiate these two syndromes and consequently help to clarify the understanding of each. Eighty-seven people with symptoms of social phobia were compared with fifty-seven people with the symptoms of agoraphobia to determine whether the symptoms were part of distinct syndromes (the authors used the nonrestrictive diagnosis of social phobia according to *DSM-III* [1980]). The pattern of phobic situations was different in these two groups, as was the pattern of autonomic symptoms. Symptoms that could be observed by others were more frequent among the social phobics, whereas "fainting" was more frequent among the agoraphobics.

SITUATIONS THAT PROVOKE THE PHOBIC SYMPTOMS

The social phobics reported more severe anxiety in being introduced, in meeting people in authority, in using the telephone; whereas the agoraphobics reported more severe anxiety in being alone or in unfamiliar places, in crossing streets, and in public transport. The list of phobic situations is presented in table 9.1.

In reviewing the situations that differentiate these two types of phobia, it becomes clear that the social phobic is concerned specifically about interpersonal situations, and that the center of the concern is being scrutinized by other people. The agoraphobic, in contrast, is concerned about being alone in unfamiliar or challenging places that present many kinds of stimulation and represent varying degrees of distancing or blocking from his home base (security). The social phobic, then, seems to encompass the notion of a *child being subjected to evaluation* by adults, whereas the agoraphobic

TABLE 9.1

Comparison of Major Fears in Agoraphobia and Social Phobias

More Severe When Main Complaint Is Social Phobia	*More Severe When Main Complaint Is Agoraphobia*
Being introduced	Being alone
Meeting people in authority	Unfamiliar places
Using the telephone	Crossing streets
Visitors to home	Public transport
Being watched doing something	Department stores
Being teased	Crowds
Eating at home with acquaintances	Open spaces
Eating at home with family	Small shops
Writing in front of others	Mice, rats, bats
Speaking in public	Snakes
	Flying insects
	Deep water
	Airplanes
	Blood, wounds

Source: Adapted from P. L. Amies, M.G. Gelder, and P.M. Shaw, "Social Phobia: A Comparative Clinical Study," *British Journal of Psychiatry* 142 (1983): 176.

seems to resemble the *child who has been placed in a strange place* for the first time. In the case of the social phobic, the other person or persons are involved in *paying attention* to the "child"; whereas in the case of the agoraphobic, the other people *ignore* him even to the point of not caring whether something disastrous happens to him.

In the Amies, Gelder, and Shaw (1983) study, the notion of being attacked is supported by the finding that the agoraphobic group is much more likely than the social phobic group to experience fears of small animals (mice, rats, bats), snakes, deep water, airplanes, injections, and so on. The typical agoraphobic's clustering of these fears suggests that this group is basically afraid of some kind of physical damage or attack.

SOMATIC SYMPTOMS

Certain somatic symptoms tend to be far more pronounced in the agoraphobic than in the social phobic. As noted in table 9.2, the agoraphobic is more likely to have typical "collapse" symptoms: weakness in the limbs, difficulty breathing, dizziness/faintness, and actual fainting episodes. This differentiation suggests that, in the agoraphobic, a different primal defensive response has been mobilized. This system—the parasympathetic—is generally associated with blood phobias but evidently also plays a role in agoraphobia.

TABLE 9.2

Comparison of Major Symptoms in Social Phobia and Agoraphobia

Item	Social Phobia (%)	Agoraphobia (%)	p Less Than
Blushing	51	21	.001
Twitching of muscles	37	21	(.07)
Weakness in limbs	41	77	.001
Difficulty in breathing	30	60	.001
Dizziness/faintness	39	68	.01
Actual fainting episode	10	25	.05
Buzzing/ringing in ears	13	30	.05
Palpitations	79	77	NS*
Tense muscles	64	67	NS
Dry throat/mouth	61	65	NS
Sinking feeling in stomach	63	54	NS
Feeling sick	40	40	NS
Trembling	75	75	NS

SOURCE: Adapted from P. L. Amies, M. G. Gelder, and P. M. Shaw, "Social Phobia: A Comparative Clinical Study," *British Journal of Psychiatry* 142 (1983): 176.
*NS = Nonsignificant.

The Phenomena of Social Anxiety

In a clinical study, K. A. Nichols (1974) discusses the features of social anxiety in thirty-five cases observed over a three-year period. The following clinical observations were drawn from different phases of therapy work, and each item was observed in at least 50 percent of cases:

1. The *perception* of disapproving or critical regard by others.
2. The *expectation* of disapproving or critical regard by others.
3. A strong tendency to perceive and respond to criticism from others which is nonexistent.
4. A feeling of being less capable and less powerful than others—low self-esteem.
5. Having rigid ideas of appropriate social behavior, and not being able to vary behavior in order to deal with difficulties.
6. Negative fantasy/imagination which produces anticipatory anxiety.
7. Heightened awareness and fear of being evaluated and judged by others.
8. A sense of being watched.
9. A discrimination and fear of situations from which sudden withdrawal would be unexpected and likely to attract attention.

10. A sense of being trapped/confined in such situations (that is, being socially closed).
11. An exaggerated interpretation of the sensory feedback related to tension or embarrassment.
12. Detection of bodily sensations within social situations.
13. A fear of being seen to be "ill" or losing control (that is, the physical signs of panic).
14. The experience of a progressive build-up of the discomfort.
15. The unpredictability of the anxiety response; the time available for prior fantasy and mood of the day seemed to be important determinants.

Nichols suggests that the incidence of social anxiety is related to some specific phase in development. He offers the late teens as a possible starting point. Finally, he adds that, in the development of social anxiety, the role of personality traits and their associated cognitive aspects becomes important.

SHAME AND "SOCIAL IMAGE"

The experience of shame is important in discussions of social anxiety because the socially anxious person is fearful of being shamed in many situations. Shame is an affect related to a person's conception of his public image at the time that he is being observed or believes he is being observed. His notion of his social image may be accurate or inaccurate; but if he *believes* that his image has been tainted, and he cares about the observer's opinion of him, then he is likely to feel shame. It should be noted that the possibility of being thought of as weak, inferior, or inept may be just as threatening as actually being talked about in these terms. In other words, what others think of him is the crucial ingredient of shame induction— irrespective of whether they communicate this opinion.

The key factor in the activation of shame is *exposure* to observation by one or more persons. This affect is triggered when a person realizes that he has been observed violating specific social norms, expectations, or demands, especially in relationship to appropriate appearance and behavior. His "deviant" appearance or behavior are judged (he assumes) to be reflections of his weakness, inferiority, ineptness, character flaw, or immaturity. The public sanctions for lack of conformity, by and large, take the form of making the individual feel inferior, depreciated, and immature. The actual social consequences may consist of covert depreciation or open expressions of disapproval, ranging from mild mimicking to overt ridicule.

It should be noted that if a person manages to conceal his "substandard" behavior or engages in a shameful activity in private, then he does not feel shame.

A person who feels shame sees himself as relatively helpless in attempting to counteract his depreciated public image. He believes he is subject to painful group reprisals, such as public humiliation and ridicule, and is *powerless* to ward off these attacks. The social opinion is absolute, finalistic, irrevocable. It is futile for him to try to modify or appeal the group verdict, and he must accede to the right of the members of the group to amuse themselves at his expense. Any protestations only increase their enjoyment of his embarrassment. The individual acknowledges his "inept" behavior by statements such as "I made a public display of myself," and hangs his head or attempts to hide to avoid their gaze.

In his mind, the antidote for shame is to vanish from the shameful situation. A person will say, for example, "I should like to fade away," or, "I felt like merging into the woodwork." In contrast, anxiety is generally accompanied by the inclination to flee or by passive immobility.

Public relations deal in the currency of public appraisal, such as admiration or devaluation. A specific social group emphasizes surface values (peculiar to that group)—acceptable appearance, smooth performance, appropriate manners and dress, maturity—and gives public rewards (admiration, respect, special privileges). A person who deviates from the group norm may receive "punishment" through disdain, ridicule, isolation. We should emphasize that, if the opinion of members of the group is irrelevant or immaterial to him, he does not feel shame.

When we talk about the public image at a particular time, we do not imply that the "unacceptable" behavior is necessarily observed by a group. The interaction may be with another person with whom there is no personal relationship but who is a representative of the social group: that is, a stranger on the street, a telephone operator. Along the same lines, it appears that strangers can enforce shame more readily than can one's intimates. Thus, it may be practically impossible for parents to shame a child for his infractions of their domestic rules. Yet the child can be exquisitely sensitive to shame induced by strangers or by his own peer group for minimal deviation from group norms.

Shame is a form of *social influence*. Other people attempt to produce shame in us so as to control our behavior now and in the future. Typically, a person is exposed to a situation that produces shame. Although this may be the first experience in which he links this type of situation with this unpleasant affect, the memory is stored, and it influences the ways he approaches similar situations in the future. In a sense, a particular rule is set up by the individual: "If I behave in such a way, then I will be ridiculed and feel shame." It is the affect of shame that puts "teeth" into the rule. The individual thus is inclined to follow the rule and avoid the shame that would result from its violation.

Anxiety and shame differ in many ways. For one thing, anxiety generally occurs before one enters a stressful or threatening situation and may continue during the situation. But it is relieved when the situation is over. The feeling of shame starts during the "exposure" to the shameful experience and may continue for a time after the experience has ended.

FEAR OF LOSS OF LOVE OR ABANDONMENT

In intimate relationships, the demands are more "personal" than in "public relationships" and have to do with satisfying the specific needs and expectations of a particular person rather than with preserving an image. The expectations generally center on intangible qualities such as consideration, understanding, and caring. If a person does not meet those expectations of the significant other person, the sanctions take the form of withdrawal of affection or rejection. The affect derived from this sort of sanction is sadness. The qualities valued in intimate relations (kindness, empathy, warmth) are more often associated with "character traits," whereas those admired by the group are related to appearance and performance. In intimate relationships, a person is less likely to be concerned about group norms and, to a certain extent, can drop his façade. The concern in the intimate relationship is usually with unconditional and total acceptance without having to preserve appearances.

Fears of loss of love or abandonment may at times become entangled with the same concerns about performance as do the other evaluation anxieties. In these cases, the individual fears that he will not live up to the expectations or demands of a loved one. He may then slide into the same rut as the socially anxious person: (1) a sense of vulnerability because the other person has the power to terminate the relationship. He may come to fear that nothing he can do is good enough; (2) a sense of being continually judged and possibly disapproved of; (3) a defensive inhibition, so that his actual behavior becomes stilted and artificial; (4) "catastrophizing" about the consequences of rejection. For example, a woman was in a continuous state of "high anxiety" over the possibility of being rejected by her lover. She believed that he was judging "everything" about her—how she dressed, spoke, prepared meals, arranged their social life. She worried that a single misstep would induce him to break the relationship. She sought continual reassurance that he was not displeased with her. Ultimately, he did leave her—not because of any deficiencies in her performance but because he could not tolerate her incessant requests for reassurance.

PUBLIC-SPEAKING ANXIETY

The various disabilities and symptoms involved in severe public-speaking anxiety encapsulate the various facets of evaluation anxiety: vulnerability to being the center of scrutiny or to being judged harshly, negative predictions, reduced self-confidence, sense of incompetence, being handicapped by involuntary inhibition, impaired control of thoughts and speech, adherence to stringent rules, expectation of "punishment" for breaking the rules.

On Being Able to Function. The first hope of a person who attempts to speak in public is to be able to "function." The speaker must be able to maintain an upright position, keep his balance, open his mouth, and speak intelligibly. If he cannot do this, it means that "he has no control over the functioning of his mind and body"—a devastating blow to his self-confidence. Since control over "mind and body" is ultimately essential for survival, the undermining of his functioning by the primal mechanisms represents a symbolic threat. Specific symptoms such as swaying, a quavering voice, faint feelings, loss of fluency, rigid postural control, all mean to him, "I can't control myself——I can't perform adequately——Anything can happen to me." The sense of being victimized by internal processes is similar to the experience of the agoraphobic, except that it does not imply the presence of a life-threatening or disintegrating disorder.

This demonstration of lack of control is perceived (or so the speaker believes) by the audience. The person then experiences not only the fear of being unable to function but also the greater fear that this lack of functioning will be judged by the audience as an indication of his "sickness, nervousness, immaturity, neurosis, inadequacy."

Role of Anxiety. Although the subjective aspects of anxiety are difficult to describe, they seem to be universally experienced in response to a sense of threat in the evaluative situation. The physiological symptoms are initially of the sympathetic type: increase in blood pressure and pulse and perspiration. These symptoms, however are not infrequently followed by a faint, dizzy, or wobbly feeling (parasympathetic). The faint feeling is sometimes a result of the drop in blood pressure and may be related to the pooling of blood in the lower extremities. Similarly, dry mouth and/or sweating are autonomic reactions.

Anxiety itself serves as a "stimulus" to further negative conceptualizations. First, the unpleasant experience itself serves to distract the person from the task at hand just as would a sudden sharp pain. Secondly, he interprets anxiety as a dramatic sign that he is not functioning well (and *will not* function well). The anxiety itself, rather than any focused systematic assessment of his capability, is taken as the index of dysfunction. He has a concept such as "This is a sign that I'm not making it." Next, his global self-confidence is eroded. As the individual's attention is diverted to his anxiety, and as his cognitive-motor apparatus is diverted to danger, there is likely to be an increase in his overt "nervousness" as well as increased difficulty in performance.

Performance Feedback. The typical individual with public-speaking anxiety uses feedback from the audience to tell him whether he is effective. If the response is negative, then his functioning is likely to suffer. If he decides that the audience considers him inadequate, this judgment may activate his notions of inadequacy and trigger nonadaptive "protective" responses. He may become disabled, impaired, possibly even mute. In actuality, he could function if he *believed* that he was capable of functioning in these circumstances. The negative response from the audience makes him believe that he cannot function at a good level, and thus starts the vicious cycle.

The dysfunctional attitudes "interact," are often accentuated by a negative response from the audience, and lead to a barrage of negative thoughts ("They can tell I'm nervous. They believe I'm weak. They're downgrading me"). As a result, the individual subjectively experiences a decrease in his sense of being able to influence the audience, and he feels his power draining out of him. As he becomes increasingly "weak and powerless," he senses great danger and feels vulnerable to attack or disapproval from the audience. The net effect is a catastrophic drop in his confidence in being able to depend on his functional capacities to see him through this crisis.

Cognitive Set during Speech. A person's cognitive set prior to presenting a speech includes a wide variety of negative attitudes and evokes unpleasant cognitions. The overall set is one of perceiving the audience itself as threatening, ready to pounce on any misstep. His view of their expectations is that he must speak clearly and articulately, that his content must be appropriate and interesting, that his manner must be free and confident, but not too casual or informal. He believes that any deviation from these rules will evoke a critical response. His self-perception is that he will be naked, exposed, and inadequate; and, furthermore, that he will suffer crippling inhibitions and painful anxiety which will impair his performance and open him to criticism or ridicule. This set is manifested in automatic thoughts such as "I won't be able to do it"; "They will be disappointed in me"; or, "I will make a fool of myself."

At the onset of the speech, the cognitive set consists of self-monitoring and evaluation of the audience response. This set is represented by negative evaluations and dire predictions: "I look silly"; "I'm not expressing myself well"; "I'll forget what I want to say"; "I sound childish"; "I won't be able to go on"; "I'll be forced to stop"; "I'll be disgraced." The interpretation of the audience response is based on selective focus and is expressed in such thoughts as "They're bored"; "They think I look pathetic"; "They wish this was over."

The cognitive set thus primes the person to meet a danger. The public speaker is prepared to deal with an adversary whom he perceives as more powerful than himself and who is poised to attack or to abandon him. The speaker feels vulnerable and exposed and does not perceive that he has effective weapons to ward off the anticipated attack. Hence a primitive defensive response is evoked—rigidity, inhibition of articulation. The problem is that the audience is not an enemy out to attack him, and that, consequently, the defensive protection does not protect him at all. In fact, it cripples his functioning and sets him up for what he wishes desperately to avoid: reduced control over his cognitive and physical functioning and his appearing to the audience to be weak and incompetent.

TEST ANXIETY

Test anxiety can be taken as an illustration of the processes involved in the anticipation of a specific confrontation with an evaluative situation—apprehension regarding available resources for dealing with the "danger" —and in mobilization of primitive "defenses" against the threat. Let us take the case of a good student who is anxiety-prone. Several months before the exam, he is confident that he will do well, and is probably reasonably realistic in appraising his ability to be adequately prepared. He may even overestimate his chances for success ("self-serving bias").

At some point, as the date of the exam approaches, the possibility of not doing well enters into his thinking about the exam. As the exam assumes the character of a serious threat, his orientation to the test starts to point toward the consequences of failure—a blow to his self-esteem, an obstacle to future plans, a personal defeat, a disgrace in the eyes of his friends, disappointment to his family.

Focusing on the prospect of his performance being evaluated, in addition to the possibility of failure and its consequences, affects his self-confidence. As the notion of threat takes hold, there is an automatic shift in his cognitive organization to a "vulnerability set." The student's attention is drawn to his various possible weaknesses—omissions in his coverage of the material, deficiencies in comprehension, difficulties in collating and expressing what he has learned. These flaws are given progressively greater salience and tend to overshadow his positive achievements and abilities. In fact, he may seriously question what he has learned and his ability to cover the additional material necessary for the test. Raising such questions casts doubt on how successfully he will perform on the test.

As the threat of doing poorly (by his standards) increases, his anxiety increases and may propel him to greater efforts to cover the material. As he studies, each difficulty, delay, or obstacle becomes a threat in itself and elicits a warning such as "You'll never be prepared in time."

Now let us suppose that the day of the exam has arrived. The vulnerability set is dominant. The student is concerned about his own weaknesses and the probability of examination questions or demands that may attack unknown gaps in his knowledge or comprehension. As the student looks at the exam, his cognitive set influences him to see the demands as enormous and his own resources as minimal. If the questions are realistically difficult, then the discrepancy between the demands and his own resources may be great. This discrepancy is translated into a threat: "I may not be able to handle this. I may blow it."

At this point one of the most disabling—and intriguing—phenomena associated with text anxiety may occur. His mind goes "blank," he has difficulty gaining access to material with which he is thoroughly familiar, and his reasoning ability seems to be paralyzed. The blocking is a component of test anxiety as well as of other evaluation anxieties that is difficult to explain. One possible explanation is that the individual perceives the task as overwhelming his available resources: for example, the questions may seem far beyond his comprehension or knowledge or ability. The perception (or misperception) that the test is overwhelming may have the same effect on him as when a task is indeed overwhelming. It can be postulated that, when confronted with a demand that overtaxes its capacity, the cognitive apparatus shuts down part of its capacity just as an electric company under analogous circumstances automatically shuts off part of its capacity. Another possible explanation of the massive inhibition of recall, reasoning, and verbal expression may be that the primitive inhibitory reflexes are activated in this confrontation to serve the anachronistic function of diverting all attention to the danger.

The cognitive component is obvious in cases of progressive test anxiety. While the student continues to grapple with the questions or instructions, he tends to exaggerate flaws in his knowledge and understanding and in his responses. Each flaw takes on the form of a danger and increases the prospect of a failure.

Most students, of course, seem able to mobilize their resources when confronted with an actual test; and once they begin writing, their thoughts begin to flow, and the vulnerability set is damped down. The seriously text-anxious subject, however, is unable to turn down or turn off the vulnerability set. He continues to operate at two levels: one deals with actual questions on the exam; and the other, with continual warnings, predictions, and self-evaluations. Notions such as "You're stupid," "You'll never finish in time," "You can't understand," place a great tax on his cognitive capacity and thus reduce efficiency and performance (Sarason and Stoops 1978). Some students pass from the defensive phase (body rigid, fists clenched) to the helpless phase (feeling faint, limp, and so on) —a response that suggests a parasympathetic reaction. Others may respond with a panic attack—overwhelming anxiety and uncontrollable desire to escape—and, indeed, may abruptly leave and not return.

A Synthesis

To the *sensitive subject,* being evaluated (for example, taking an examination, speaking in public, or going out on a date) is akin to being subjected to a painful probing. It may be likened to a dentist's probing teeth for an area of decay or a cavity. The evaluative situation is viewed as a confrontation or challenge that puts the subject on the defensive. He assumes that it is incumbent on him to prove himself to the evaluators and to *conceal* his presumed defects, ineptness, ignorance; whereas it is their role to *reveal* his ignorance, stupidity, and ineptness. Because he views the other persons (audience, graders of the test, dates) as looking for weaknesses, he assumes that they will pounce on every slip, flaw, or sign of nervousness and downgrade him for it. Thus, he stiffens after each misstep and imagines the immediate negative reaction of the evaluators and the long-range negative effects.

Since he regards himself as vulnerable, the reaction of the subject is self-protective: he automatically retracts into his shell so as to conceal any soft parts. In actuality, this retraction is expressed in the form of inhibition. Unfortunately for him, the inhibition not only conceals weaknesses (since it prevents him from saying or writing anything "stupid") but also interferes with effective presentation of the self. Consequently, the subject is undone by the very primal (reflex) mechanism designed to protect him.

The premonitory fears lead to stiffness *before* an encounter. The subject braces himself to absorb the impact of the aggressive scrutiny of the evaluators. This type of inhibition, however, interferes with spontaneous self-expression. Thus, at the onset of an encounter, his mind goes blank, he stutters, and he cannot focus on what he has to say or write. Moreover, he perceives the examination questions as being more difficult than they are, the audience as more unfriendly, and the date as more disdainful. He also underestimates his coping capacity. "Breaking the ice" consists of lifting the inhibition through action, by discovering that he does not need to retract and can allow free play of his personality or skill without reprisal.

PART II

Cognitive Therapy: Techniques and Applications

BY

GARY EMERY

Chapter 10

Principles of Cognitive Therapy

Cognitive therapy is more than a sum of techniques; it is a system of psychotherapy. The strategies and techniques are embedded within a therapeutic approach based on ten principles discussed in this chapter.*

1. Cognitive therapy is based on the cognitive model of emotional disorders.
2. Cognitive therapy is brief and time-limited.
3. A sound therapeutic relationship is a necessary condition for effective cognitive therapy.
4. Therapy is a collaborative effort between therapist and patient.
5. Cognitive therapy uses primarily the Socratic method.
6. Cognitive therapy is structured and directive.
7. Cognitive therapy is problem-oriented.
8. Cognitive therapy is based on an educational model.
9. The theory and techniques of cognitive therapy rely on the inductive method.
10. Homework is a central feature of cognitive therapy.

*For further explanation of these principles, see Beck (1976) and Beck et al. (1979).

Principle 1: Cognitive Therapy Is Based on the Cognitive Model of Emotional Disorders

The cognitive model of anxiety is used as a basis for intervention and is explicitly given as the rationale for treatment. Therapists who feel stymied in approaching a patient can refer to the model to develop strategies. For instance, the therapist encountering a patient who says, "I have ample justification for feeling anxious," asks, "Are there distortions in the patient's formulation?" The therapist will bear in mind that the patient's cognitive distortion may lie in his immediate appraisal of the situation, in his perception of long-term consequences, or in other associations. The cognitive model is of particular help when the therapist is faced with novel forms of anxiety.

The therapist needs to be versed in the cognitive model of anxiety, grasping the differences between cognition, emotion, behavior, and physiological responses. He must be able to communicate clearly that anxiety is maintained by mistaken or dysfunctional appraisal of a situation. The therapist gives this explanation of anxiety in the first session and reiterates it throughout therapy. This explanation is often therapeutic.

Patients are confused and troubled about their anxiety. Many have picked up ideas that add to the mystery and threat of their disturbance. Some believe that anxiety is a precursor to psychosis; others, that it is something they are voluntarily doing to themselves. The cognitive model has credibility for most patients. For a patient to see anxiety as a result of exaggerated, *automatic* thinking is often a relief.

People want to make sense of their emotions and find it helpful to perceive their emotional problems as falling into four general categories: *anxiety, anger, depression,* and *pleasure.* A patient's numerous complaints can usually be placed in one of the categories. For example, a complaint about jealousy, loneliness, shame, guilt, shyness, procrastination, lying, rumination, or indecisiveness may well be a problem of anxiety management.

At the first interview, one patient said he was having trouble with his fellow workers, in sleeping, in making decisions, with women, and in telling the truth. After listening to the details, the therapist realized that the patient's problem was how to manage anxiety, primarily, and anger, secondarily. This reduction of his problems was helpful to the patient in and of itself.

Once a patient sees that his problem is related to anxiety management, he is ready to accept a cognitive explanation of anxiety. Once the patient has grasped the idea that his misconstruing of his experiences has led to his anxiety, he may be encouraged to develop a mental set of catching and correcting his thinking and his anxiety.

DIDACTIC PRESENTATION

Inevitably, an anxious patient has misconceptions about anxiety, and helping him to correct these is one of the first tasks of therapy. The patient often believes his anxiety is abnormal, and frequently believes he may lose contact with reality. Because anxiety symptoms exaggerate fears, the therapist needs to spend more time discussing a patient's particular symptom cluster. The therapist can give the patients audio tapes that present an overview of cognitive therapy of anxiety.*

After an evaluation of a patient's problem, the therapist structures the initial interview around the presenting complaints. He explains the symptoms of anxiety to the patient in detail to decrease the patient's excessive concern with them. To effectively re-educate the patient, the therapist must possess a solid understanding of the symptoms of anxiety.

The specific symptoms vary for each person, presumably as a result of variations in physical predisposition or modeled family rules (for example, a family may signal anxiety through stomach troubles). The therapist has to look for uncommon signs of anxiety: during anxiety attacks, one anxious patient, for example, had a sense that lights were flashing.

The therapist can help to relieve a patient's distress by discussing the symptoms as being a natural bodily reaction to threat. Many patients respond well to an explanation of the fight-flight-freeze response. Similarly, many find helpful a discussion of sympathetic versus parasympathetic symptoms. One patient who suffered from speech anxiety and generalized anxiety found helpful the information that the freezing she felt while speaking in public was due to her parasympathetic nervous system. She said, "Just understanding what I'm feeling helps me cope with it."

The therapist can help to normalize much of the mystery attached to a symptom. Many patients also find helpful an evolutionary explanation of anxiety. Their symptoms and responses can be framed as mechanisms whose original adaptive usefulness is no longer called for.

The therapist should check that medical reasons for the patient's symptoms have been ruled out. One patient had symptoms that appeared to be anxiety attacks. His physical examination, however, revealed that he had a gall bladder disease. Once this was treated, the symptoms disappeared.

---

*G. Emery,"Overcoming Anxiety." This tape series is available through BMA Audio Cassettes, 200 Park Avenue South, New York, NY 10003.

Along the same lines, an anxious patient may have symptoms that are caused by a physical illness but that he misinterprets as anxiety. A patient with occasional periods of anxiety mislabeled as anxiety symptoms what were actually those of a viral infection. Instead of thinking, "I'm getting sick. I'd better go to bed," he thought, "I'm getting anxious," and this in turn created real anxiety. Once he discovered he really had the flu, his anxiety diminished.

INTRODUCING COGNITIVE THERAPY

In the first session, the therapist gives a brief explanation of the cognitive model and describes the course of treatment. He stresses that the success of therapy depends on the patient's ability to examine his own thoughts. If a patient has trouble understanding, the therapist rephrases his explanations. Questions from sophisticated patients should be answered early to allay any doubts. The therapist might state, "We have found that patients receiving this treatment do not require drugs, and there are some good reasons for not using drugs."

To explain anxiety, the therapist may find it helpful to draw diagrams and use the blackboard, as concepts alone are often difficult for an anxious patient to grasp. The therapist can use examples to show that the way a person appraises a situation determines feelings and how this appraisal is related to earlier learning experiences. For example, a man who has never before seen a particular poisonous plant will not be afraid of it; only after he has learned to associate it with danger will he become afraid.

LEVELS OF FEAR

The therapist can point out that what the patient really fears are his feelings and sensations. The therapist needs to describe the two levels of fear. The first is fear of the primary danger: fear of a dreaded disease, such as cancer or a heart attack; fear of accidents; fear of public humiliation; fear of suffocation; fear of drowning; and so on. The second level is fear of the symptoms of anxiety. Inability to overcome the first level of fear exaggerates the second level and leads to a panic cycle. The two levels of fear correspond roughly to the first two levels described in chapter 6.

While a patient cannot always immediately overcome the first level of fear, he can stop frightening himself over the anxiety itself. At the first session, the therapist gives the patient some concrete ways of handling the second level of fear (these methods will be detailed in chapter 13).

Principle 2: Cognitive Therapy Is Brief and Time-Limited

The typical course of cognitive therapy for anxiety is from five to twenty sessions. Specific performance anxieties or mild anxiety states may be alleviated in a few sessions. With moderate and severe cases of anxiety, treatment will take approximately twenty sessions, extended over several months. In the early stages of treatment, a patient may be seen twice a week to maintain improvement between sessions. The patient may also make telephone contacts between sessions to report on progress. Occasionally a patient will need to be seen more than twenty times. This longer treatment should be extended over a period of time, with "booster" sessions becoming less frequent.

Long-term therapy for anxiety is unnecessary and is, in many cases, undesirable. Brief therapy discourages the patient's dependency on the therapist (which is prevalent in anxiety disorders) and encourages the patient's self-sufficiency. Frequent reassurance from the therapist prevents the patient from thinking for himself. When the patient sees that therapy is short-term, he often begins to realize that anxiety is a problem that the therapist believes can be overcome quickly. Specifying a certain number of sessions puts the patient in a task-oriented frame for "getting down to business."

Because cognitive therapy is brief, the pace of therapy is relatively brisk. A minimum amount of time is spent acquiring background information, searching for original causes of anxiety, or engaging in conversation with the patient. Therapy is task-oriented and focuses on problem-solving—so much so that therapists trained in other systems often object to its fast pace. Time is a limited resource: each intervention has to have a purpose and a rationale. The therapist "rushes slowly"; he covers important material, but he moves quickly.

The following are some general strategies for keeping treatment brief:

1. *Keep it simple.* The abundance of psychological and psychiatric theories about emotional disorders enhance the human tendency to complicate problems. It is easy to complicate patients' problems and difficult to simplify them. A good rule to keep in mind is: "No matter how complicated a patient's problem may be, a therapist has it in his power to make it even more complicated." Complicating the conceptualization and treatment process prolongs treatment and often makes it less effective.

2. *Make treatment specific and concrete.* The more abstract the conceptualization and intervention, the longer the treatment. Keeping the language

relatively free of abstraction moves therapy along. Instead of referring to the four basic emotions as "anxiety, depression, anger, and euphoria," the therapist can call them "scared, sad, mad, and glad" and should aim for the lowest level of abstraction.

3. *Stress homework.* Homework gives a patient the best chance of getting better fast, and it is the therapist who conveys to him its importance. (Homework will be discussed later in the chapter.)

4. *Make ongoing assessments.* Most of the information that the therapist needs to make proper interventions will be obtained throughout the treatment. In the majority of anxiety cases, elaborate assessment is unnecessary.

5. *Stay task-relevant.* The therapist can easily go off on a tangent with an anxious patient, who usually wants to avoid discussing feared material. Discussing religious, spiritual, or philosophical beliefs, if not pertinent to a patient's main concern, prolongs therapy. If the patient insists on such discussions, the therapist can point out how it distracts from the main business of therapy.

6. *Use time-management procedures.* The therapist needs to look for ways to use therapy time effectively. Among effective methods are setting and sticking to an agenda for each session, providing written handouts and audio tapes on standard material, or using posters to illustrate strategies and techniques.

7. *Develop a brief-intervention mental set.* The therapist, by assuming that a patient can learn to manage his anxiety quickly, can create a self-fulfilling prophecy. The therapist should keep in mind that research indicates that long-term treatment is no more effective than short-term treatment.

8. *Stay focused on manageable problems.* Because cognitive therapy is time-limited, many of a patient's problems will remain unsolved at the end of treatment. By the time treatment ends, the patient will have enough psychological tools to approach and solve problems on his own, knowing that the therapist is available for booster sessions if necessary.

The length and timing of the sessions are kept flexible. Generally, a session is one hour; however, longer sessions are often helpful. One therapeutic strategy is for the therapist to provoke anxiety in the patient during the session and then show the patient how to bring the anxiety down. With some patients, this procedure may take two hours. Or, the therapist may find it helpful to have a patient come a half-hour before the session so as to have time to reflect on what he wants to discuss in the session. This is helpful for patients who come unprepared or have trouble getting into the flow of therapy. A number of patients have reported that this preview period helps to tune them in to the thoughts and attitudes behind their anxiety.

Similarly, while it is usual to see patients once a week, it is often beneficial to vary this schedule. A few patients, because of geographical constraints, come each day for one, two, or three weeks. Back-to-back sessions have certain benefits, including supervised daily practice in managing anxiety and accelerated learning of coping strategies and techniques.

With some patients it is beneficial to contract for a specific number of sessions in order to alleviate fears that the therapist wants to keep them in treatment indefinitely. Such a contract also gives a patient the message that the therapist believes that his anxiety problem is manageable. Contracting for a specific number of sessions also can prevent early termination. Early termination is usually due to a patient's failure to obtain relief from his anxiety or to his desire to leave because his severe anxiety is gone. In either case, the therapist can point out that the number of sessions was specified in the beginning to allow time for the techniques to work and for the exploration and modification of the attitudes that have predisposed the patient to anxiety.

Principle 3: A Sound Therapeutic Relationship Is a Necessary Condition for Effective Cognitive Therapy

The anxious patient is so bombarded with frightening thoughts that he is often unable to view his problem in other ways. An effective way to reduce his anxiety is to create a warm therapeutic relationship based on trust and acceptance. Without this, the techniques and procedures of cognitive therapy are unlikely to work.

The patient must talk openly about his fears for the therapeutic process to occur. Patients often avoid talking about their fears. One patient explained, "If I talk about going crazy, this will bring it on. It's so frightening I don't want to chance it." A major part of treatment consists of encouraging the patient to face frightening situations so as to be able to view them realistically; and talking about them is one way of achieving this aim.

Patients who have learned to manage their anxiety often attribute a large part of their success to the therapeutic relationship. As standard practice, we ask patients after treatment what they found helpful. Some common responses are:

"The concern and warmth of my therapist."
"Feeling free to talk about things that I've been reluctant to talk to others about."

Novice therapists learning to use cognitive methods seldom give high priority to the establishment of a good therapeutic relationship. For effective cognitive therapy, the therapist has to build rapport through such methods as sincerity, accurate empathy (correctly understanding what the patient is saying and conveying this understanding to him), and the expression of nonpossessive warmth. Cognitive therapy takes a middle ground on the use of these approaches. The therapist avoids overpowering a patient with humanity or sincerity.

Cognitive therapy has built-in features that enhance rapport. By focusing on a patient's way of viewing the world (inquiring about thoughts and images and reporting them back to the patient), the therapist conveys accurate empathy. Rapid relief from some anxiety symptoms also builds rapport. The cognitive therapist is continually asking for feedback from the patient. Distortions about therapy or the therapist are brought to the surface before they severely damage the relationship.

The therapist has to be acutely aware that the anxious patient often misinterprets and misunderstands the therapist's intention. In one session, the therapist used humor and the "so what if?" technique (that is, he hypothesized the worst possibility)—an approach that appeared helpful to the patient. At the end of the session, the therapist asked a standard feedback question, "Was there anything about the session that bothered you?" The patient responded, "You seemed to be making fun of me and taking my concerns lightly." This feedback enabled the therapist to correct these misperceptions immediately.

A therapist has to match his therapeutic stance to the general style of each patient. A serious, conservative patient would require a different approach than would a patient who preferred informality. Along the same lines, it is helpful for the therapist to look at a patient's style in terms of *autonomy* and *dependency* (Emery and Lesher 1982).

For the patients low in both dimensions, forming a working relationship is rarely a problem: the person can tolerate both intimacy and working on his own. Such a patient functions well with people and comes in for specific anxiety problems. Rarely does a problem in the relationship develop.

The therapist has to be warmer and stress the feelings of a patient who is not particularly autonomous but is highly dependent. Such a patient is more relationship-oriented and often wants to be the favorite patient.

Therapist self-disclosure is helpful with him and serves to bond therapist and patient. The latter is hypersensitive to lack of empathy on the therapist's part and can easily become overly dependent upon him. With such a patient, the therapist can work well by thinking aloud and sharing some of his ideas as they come up: "It seems like your problem is leaving social gatherings. Now what do you think we can do about this?"

The patient who is highly autonomous and not very dependent reacts in many ways opposite to the previous patient. The use of the pronoun *we* is counterproductive. He bristles when someone says, "How are *we* feeling today?" or, "How can *we* solve this problem?" He may feel that the therapist's attempts at empathy are intrusive and patronizing. Self-disclosure can easily go awry and be misinterpreted. The therapist should repeatedly ask this patient to take the lead in solving his problems.

Unlike the style of *we* used with the previous patient, the emphasis is on the pronoun *you:* "You seem to have problems. Have you thought about how you're going to find your way out?"

Most of the relationship problems in therapy come from the patient who is both autonomous and dependent. The individual wants intimacy but has trouble tolerating it, because he fears being rejected, controlled, or humiliated by the therapist. He frequently gives the therapist mixed messages. One patient told her therapist that she wanted him to disclose more about himself; when he did, she said he talked too much about himself. With this group of patients, the therapist has to have greater tolerance, acceptance, and flexibility. He can react in the particular mode (autonomy, dependency) each patient is operating in at a particular moment.

Principle 4: Therapy Is a Collaborative Effort Between Therapist and Patient

The cognitive therapist implies that there is a team approach to the solution of a patient's problem: that is, a therapeutic alliance where the patient supplies raw data (reports on thoughts and behavior relating to anxiety) while the therapist provides structure and expertise in how to solve problems. The emphasis is on working on problems rather than on correcting defects or changing personality. The therapist fosters the attitude "Two heads are better than one" in approaching personal difficulties. When the patient is so entangled in symptoms that he is unable to join in problem solving, the therapist may have to assume a leading role. As therapy progresses, the patient is encouraged to take a more active stance.

With whom does the therapist strive to collaborate? To join forces with the patient's anxious self may be to engage in "neurotic agreement": "Yes, you really can't handle this." The patient's unanxious self often is not present in therapy and, when it is, is often overconfident: "I just won't let myself get anxious."

Deikman's (1982) construct of the "observing self" helps to answer this question. He distinguishes between the thinking self, the emotional self, and the functional or acting self. He considers a fourth domain, the observing self, to be a phenomenon strikingly different from the other three.

The observing self is the part of a person that is aware; it is the most personal of all and comes before thoughts, feelings, and actions, because it experiences these functions. Deikman says, "No matter what takes place, no matter what we experience, nothing is as central as the self that observes. In the face of this phenomenon, Descartes's starting point, 'I think; therefore, I am,' must yield to the more basic position, 'I am aware; therefore, I am' " (p. 94).

The observing self is the one part of a person that does not change throughout life. It is featureless, like a mirror, and makes no value judgments. The patient cannot observe his observing self; he can only experience it. The more pronounced one's observing self (awareness), the greater the range of choices one can make.

The collaborative nature of the therapeutic interaction can be strengthened through the following methods:

1. *Develop the relationship on a reciprocal basis.* Neither therapist nor patient takes a superior role. The therapist can ask a patient to listen to tape recordings of a session to see if the latter can learn more from the session or provide the therapist with useful feedback. Here the therapist asks the patient's observing self to help his, the therapist's, observing self.

2. *Avoid hidden agendas.* All procedures are open and clearly explained to a patient. Treatment manuals or sections of them are often given to a patient as suggested reading so that he can become more aware of treatment strategies.

Although some techniques may appear paradoxical (for example, if someone is afraid of anxiety, he is asked to experience it), cognitive therapy avoids paradoxical techniques in the usual sense. The therapist does not prescribe symptoms or use restraint-from-change procedures unless in a straightforward way with the rationale clearly spelled out. We have, for example, had patients purposefully try to make themselves more anxious as a way to counteract their anxiety. This is presented as a coping technique that the patient can choose to use, and is not a strategy the therapist is covertly using to combat the patient's anxiety.

3. *Design homework collaboratively.* Homework assignments, as well as the agenda for each session, are the result of a joint effort between therapist and patient. The patient discusses whether he thinks the homework will work and ways it can be modified.

4. *Admit mistakes.* Therapists can enhance the collaborative effort by admitting the mistakes they make in therapy. A therapist who says something inappropriate, or greatly misses the mark, immediately admits it. The therapist nearly always serves as a model. A coping model (self-observation plus self-correction) is usually more effective than a mastery model.

5. *Maintain a collaborative environment.* The therapist's demeanor and the arrangement of the office can enhance or detract from a collaborative relationship. Patients often report that they are talked down to in such situations. In many therapy offices, the patient sits in a chair that is four or five inches shorter than the therapist's.

By listening to tapes of the sessions, the therapist can check and see whether he has achieved a collaborative spirit. A therapist can, without realizing it, easily develop a patronizing and condescending attitude toward the patient.

Principle 5: Cognitive Therapy Uses Primarily the Socratic Method

The cognitive therapist strives to use *the question* as a lead as often as possible. This general rule applies unless there are time restraints—in which case a therapist has to provide direct information to reach closure.

While direct suggestions and explanations may help to correct a person's anxiety-producing thoughts, they are less powerful than the Socratic method. Questions induce the patient (1) to become aware of what his thoughts are, (2) to examine them for cognitive distortions, (3) to substitute more balanced thoughts, and (4) to make plans to develop new thought patterns.

Good questions can establish structure, develop collaboration, clarify the patient's statements, awaken the patient's interest, build the therapeutic relationship, provide the therapist with essential information, open up the patient's previously closed system of logic, develop his motivation to try out new behavior, help him to think in a new way about his problem, and enhance the patient's observing self.

The therapist is modeling coping strategies by asking questions that expand a patient's constricted thinking. Often a patient reports that when confronted by a new anxiety-producing situation he will start by asking himself the same questions he heard from the therapist: "Where is the evidence?" "Where is the logic?" "What do I have to lose?" "What do I have to gain?" "What would be the worst thing that could happen?" "What can I learn from this experience?"

Principle 6: Cognitive Therapy Is Structured and Directive

The anxious person is often confused and unsure of himself; his mind races; he is overwhelmed by fearful thoughts and images and he is unsure whether he is going crazy. In short, he is in a state of disorder. Cognitive therapy, by giving the person a highly structured format for approaching his problems, provides some order. Structure both reassures patients and promotes learning. The therapist needs to vary the degree of structure according to a patient's response and feedback as well as to a patient's personality and the requirements of different phases of treatment. The socially dependent person usually requires more structure, and the autonomous person less.

Standard procedures are used to structure therapy. When the therapist deviates from them, the quality of the therapy usually suffers.

1. *Set an agenda for each session.* The therapist and patient develop an agenda for each session. The therapist asks what specific problems the patient would like to address in the session. The therapist then adds items that he would like to discuss and any left over from the previous session's agenda. Homework from the last session is always the first and last item on the agenda (early in the session the patient reports on homework assigned in previous sessions; later, new homework is assigned).

The therapist should make an effort to identify any hidden issues. If he suspects any, he can ask, "Is there anything else you want to talk about? Anything you may be reluctant to bring up?" Often the first words the patient says are related to his main concerns. Setting the agenda takes anywhere from five to fifteen minutes.

The therapist may have to spend considerable time mapping out the terrain. The therapist reports what he believes is the current concern until there is a good fit between what the patient means and what the therapist understands the patient to mean. In a typical hour's session, only two or three issues can be dealt with effectively.

The aim is equal participation by therapist and patient in discussing agenda items. Silence usually makes the patient more anxious. Although the therapist may initially do most of the talking, the aim is for therapist and patient to share therapy time equally. An imbalance is a sign that the therapy needs to be restructured. Generally the problem is that therapist and patient have been unable to target a problem that both believe is important.

2. *Focus on specific targets.* A treatment plan is developed for each patient. The first stage focuses on providing the patient with symptom relief. The second focuses on teaching the patient how to recognize distorted automatic thoughts. The third focus is on training the patient how to respond to his distorted thoughts with logic, reason, and empirical testing. In the fourth stage, the patient identifies and modifies his long-held dysfunctional assumptions underlying his major concerns.

Anxious patients tend to go off on tangents; the therapist can model task-oriented behavior by keeping the discussion on the problem at hand. The therapist has to set the appropriate tempo for therapy. If the pace is too fast, the patient may miss much of what is being discussed; and if too slow, he may lose confidence in the therapy.

The therapist reduces the patient's problems to a common ground or to an earlier causal link. If a person is afraid of strangers, his boss, and his parents, the common denominator may be fear of rejection. Such reduction makes problems more manageable. One woman had a fear of elevators that prevented her from looking for a job, and her joblessness caused even more difficulties for her. Dealing with the first problem, elevator phobia, solved her other problems. Another patient had many fears of starting a new job ("People won't like me——I won't be able to do the job——I don't think I'll like the people"), all of which could be traced back to the basic fear that her bosses would discover she had exaggerated on her job application.

The difficulties that a therapist most frequently encounters in setting the agenda are: (1) setting vague or incomplete agendas; (2) not using therapy time effectively by setting priorities, so that, for example, too much time is spent on a minor issue; (3) not getting the patient's full input about what to put on the agenda; (4) misunderstanding the explicit and implied concerns of the patient.

Sometimes a patient may prefer (for sound therapeutic reasons) to use a session simply to talk about his problems—rather than to solve them. At other times, a patient may present compelling reasons for spending the session "emoting" or evoking sympathy from the therapist. In a rare case, the patient may prefer simply to engage in "small talk," and might benefit from it.

After a period of discussion, the therapist needs to make a summary statement of his understanding of the patient's verbal communication—a statement that he prefaces with remarks such as "What you seem to be saying is——" or, "Does the problem seem to be——?" The therapist should encourage the patient to correct any misstatements in this summary (unless the patient is an obsessive, meticulous qualifier, in which case the therapist should be satisfied simply to get across the general idea). The therapist also needs to give periodic capsule summaries of his own verbal communication: Many anxious patients are relieved simply by hearing the therapist outline their problems within a structured discussion.

The therapist should ask for feedback regarding the session. Particularly in the initial and early ones, the therapist needs to assess the patient's reactions to the session so far. For instance, halfway through, the therapist may inquire, "Do I seem to be on the right track?" He should also elicit reactions to the session before it ends. If asked, the patient who has problems with the therapy will usually mention them.

Some patients are reluctant to bring up negative reactions to the therapist. If the therapist suspects this to be the case, he can provide the patient with a therapy feedback form to complete in the waiting room after leaving the therapist's office.

The best policy is for the therapist to stick to standard simple techniques during the session and to give relatively simple homework assignments. The therapist will find it helpful occasionally to take time off between sessions to rate his own behavior on the preceding points.

Principle 7: Cognitive Therapy Is Problem-Oriented

The initial focus of cognitive therapy is on solving present problems, largely because the patient can supply more accurate data on current concerns and is in a position where he can resolve the problems. Later therapy can help the patient restructure material from the past and make plans for his future. The patient is expected and encouraged to identify current problems to be worked on; the therapist may need to help translate the patient's vague complaints into specific problems. Together, therapist and patient work to identify and correct maladaptive thoughts and behavior that are maintaining a problem and blocking its solution.

The therapist should avoid problems where closure cannot be reached during the session. Without some closure, discussion often can increase a patient's distress. Toward the end of one session, a therapist touched on the patient's fear of being promiscuous. As there was not enough time to cover this topic in depth, the patient was extremely anxious about it until the next session.

At times a patient will lose his symptoms of anxiety quickly and believe he has solved the problem. Here the therapist should encourage the patient to stay in treatment for several more sessions to see whether his symptoms are permanently gone; this time can be used to explore the underlying beliefs that predispose the patient to anxiety, and to help him design his future. The therapist may also ask about potential anxiety-producing situations the patient may wish to work on.

In applying the problem-solving format, the therapist needs to go through a four-step process: first, to *conceptualize* the patient's problem; second and third, to *choose a strategy* and *a tactic or technique* to implement that strategy; finally, to *assess the effectiveness* of the tactic.

CONCEPTUALIZATION

When one asks novice cognitive therapists how they would handle a specific clinical problem such as procrastination, they usually can give a variety of techniques, which might include graded task assignment, participatory modeling, relabeling the problem, and so forth. A few might suggest strategies such as "Work on patient's perfectionism." Rarely does the novice address the most important step—*conceptualization.*

Conceptualizing a patient's problem involves placing it in context. The reason an autonomous person procrastinates is usually different from the reason a socially dependent person procrastinates. The nature of a task and the way it is assigned may be factors. The autonomous patient may have a reactive response ("No one can tell me what to do"), while the socially dependent patient may be fearing rejection ("I can't let others down by doing a poor job").

In conceptualizing the patient's problem, the therapist has to elicit from the patient what the problem *means* to him. The passive-aggressive person may be procrastinating because he believes this is the way to avoid being controlled by others. The anxious patient, the depressed patient, the angry patient, and the manic patient will all have different reasons. Procrastination may indicate a shift of priorities that the patient has not fully accepted; or it may be due to a secondary gain such as a way to get attention or a rationalization ("I could be a great painter, but I don't have the self-discipline").

The point is that there are many reasons a patient may be procrastinating. Therapist and patient need to conceptualize the problem jointly before an adequate strategy can be chosen. Conceptualization, strategy selection, and technique implementation influence and feed each other. Usually this process is an evolving one of conceptualization and reconceptualization with corresponding strategy shifts.

GENERAL STRATEGIES

Cognitive therapy becomes aimless and erratic unless it is directed by a therapist with a clear strategy or plan in mind. A strategy is an organizing principle of human behavior; and embedded within a particular strategy are tactics or techniques, which are less important and of less magnitude. A tactic is concrete and specific; a strategy, general.

The trial-and-error method is used as a check on strategy and tactics rather than as a guiding force in therapy. The therapist chooses tactics he believes will most further the goals of the strategy. For example, one patient's problem was conceptualized as fear of being controlled. One strategy used in therapy was for the patient to "gain control by giving up control." Some of the tactics used were: (1) relaxation (rationale: "Letting go control of your muscles causes you to feel more in control"); (2) acceptance of anxiety (rationale: "Not trying to fight and control your anxiety makes you feel more in control"); (3) agreeing quickly to others' requests (rationale: "Choosing to let others be in control puts you in control"); (4) accepting others as they are (rationale: "Trying to control others makes you feel out of control").

The art of cognitive therapy is to know which strategy to use when. The experienced cognitive therapist is concerned more with conceptualization and strategy than with tactics and techniques. Strategy allows the therapist to know where he is going in therapy rather than to rely haphazardly on techniques. In training we have found three types of therapists: those who direct the therapy, those who react to what the patient says, and those who do not seem to know what is going on. The goal is to become the first type.

The therapist needs to keep in mind that the object of therapy is to help a patient manage his anxiety as soon as possible, as the time, energy, and money put into therapy can deplete his resources. The ends often determine the means. If the aim of therapy is to get a patient to trust himself and to trust the world as fast as possible, the means become clearer.

The cognitive therapist uses a variety of standard strategies as well as designing a particular strategy for a particular patient. The following are some common strategies in cognitive therapy:

1. *"Simplify, simplify, simplify."* The strategy of simplifying is used throughout therapy. One patient had six years of psychoanalytically oriented therapy, which gave her much insight but little help in managing her anxiety. Although she knew this, she still had a tendency to overcomplicate her problems. Throughout therapy, the strategy of simplification was used. One of her most effective anxiety-reducing tactics was the simple self-instruction, "When anxious, take constructive action."

Some related strategies are: "Specific is better than vague," and, "Concrete is better than abstract." Many therapists and patients have a tendency to become lost in tangential and overly abstract discussions that are rarely helpful to the patient. The strategy of simplifying helps to counter this tendency.

2. *"No time like the present."* In general, the therapist can design a strategy that allows a problem to be worked on in the session. This strategy also involves having a patient approach, in the here-and-now, problems that he has been avoiding. A speech-anxious patient can outline the speech in the session or practice giving a few minutes of it. It is always better to elicit and restructure a patient's cognitions when they are "hot"; that is, thoughts that the patient is having in the session. Talking about the past or the future is rarely as productive as focusing on the present.

The therapist can have a patient do a variety of tasks in the session that are related to the patient's problem, and can, for this purpose, use props. For example, I have an exercise bike in my office with electronic digital readings. The anxious patient can be asked to cycle for a mile without being told how the digital readings work. If the patient is unable to figure out how they work, I ask him to think aloud and see how his anxious thoughts impede his ability to work out the problem. One patient's thoughts were, "I've never done this before. How does he expect me to know? I'm stupid, I hate this."

By correcting such thoughts, the patient can focus on the task. The therapist thus can allow a patient to experience mastery, to see how, by focusing on a task, he can complete it. Actually cycling for a mile allows patient and therapist to become aware of what the former is thinking while engaged in a task. There is an almost unlimited number of tasks that can be introduced during therapy. H. L. Weinberg (1973) has developed and uses over two hundred similar tasks.

3. *"You don't know unless you try."* A general strategy is to encourage the patient to err on the side of inclusion. One standard lead—"What will you learn if you go versus what will you learn if you don't go?"—can be applied to a variety of situations. One patient, who wanted to avoid a wedding where he might run into an old girlfriend, erred on the side of

inclusion and went. There he found that he no longer was emotionally overwhelmed by seeing her.

4. *"When you're off track, take the opposite tack."* If the therapist is not able to help the patient modify a situation for whatever reason, a useful strategy is to reverse and help the person accept the situation. For example, a therapist who was making little progress in helping a patient modify his expectations of getting cancer, reversed his approach: "Okay, let's say you're going to get cancer. What will you do then?" Another way of stating this strategy is: "If you can't beat them, join them."

5. *"Patient persistence."* A general strategy with the anxious patient is to persist in helping him overcome his fears. The patient often needs this persistence to learn new ways of thinking and acting. The therapist, by not getting frustrated and giving up, is modeling the important strategy of patience. Such patience is particularly necessary in dealing with the obsessively anxious patient and with the mistrusting patient.

6. *"Divide and conquer."* The therapist focuses on the components of the patient's anxiety that have the least resistance and tells the patient that his anxiety is made up of three parts: his thinking, his feeling, and his actions. The most sensible approach is to work on the parts that are most modifiable: If the patient has a behavioral problem, therapy focuses on thoughts and feelings; if he has a thinking problem, therapy focuses on feelings and behavior. Because anxiety is primarily a feeling problem, therapy focuses on thoughts and behavior.

7. *"Do the unexpected."* Cognitive therapy often emphasizes encouraging a patient to do the unexpected, to surprise himself, to step out of character. This strategy is presented as one of the best ways to defeat the anxiety. Many patients, when given the homework "surprise yourself" will return with a number of examples of occasions when they have taken specific risks and surprised themselves.

8. *"Go with the flow."* The specific tactic to use with a patient depends on the strength and intensity of his anxiety. Do not encourage a patient to approach frightening situations all at once. Find out which part of the patient's anxiety formulation is weakest and attack that part. When the patient is highly defended against learning new material, an indirect approach may have to be used, by providing information and using stories and metaphors. Rush and Watkins (1981) have described some other indirect methods of correcting cognitive distortions. For example, a patient was ashamed of going to therapy. Without directly talking about therapy, the therapist talked about the importance of education and of bettering oneself. This approach seemed to alleviate the patient's concerns, while the direct approach did not work.

In some cases, conceptualization, choice of strategy, and tactic are developed early in treatment; in other cases, these three evolve over a period of time. In these examples the conceptualization of the patient led to a strategy and a specific tactic.

Case A: A fifty-seven-year-old man experiencing acute anxiety. History of only one other severe attack occuring twenty years earlier.

Conceptualization: No major psychological problem. Anxiety being maintained by feedback loop (anxiety over anxiety) and misinformation about anxiety ("I'm going to have a nervous breakdown").

Strategy: Nothing succeeds like success.

Tactic: Get patient anxious during session, and show ways to alleviate symptoms.

Case B: A thirty-year-old highly verbal man.

Conceptualization: Tendency to overintellectualize, overanalyze problems.

Strategy: The simpler the better.

Tactic: Graded task assignment to approach feared situation.

Case C: A twenty-three-year-old male with many obsessive rules.

Conceptualization: Fear of being imperfect.

Strategy: When you're off track, take the opposite tack.

Tactic: Anti-shame exercises. When he makes mistakes, he tells others about them.

Case D: A thirty-three-year-old woman with chronic problems.

Conceptualization: Well defended, oversensitive to criticism.

Strategy: Practice art of indirect approach.

Technique: Self-disclose ways you, the therapist, handle criticism; think aloud during therapy.

Case E: A forty-five-year-old successful businessman.

Conceptualization: Highly autonomous person who likes challenges.

Strategy: Use patient's strengths.

Tactic: Have patient approach areas he most wants to avoid as a personal challenge.

Case F: A twenty-nine-year-old woman with long-term problems.

Conceptualization: Low self-confidence.

Strategy: No time like the present.

Tactic: Role reversal, with patient playing role of therapist during the session.

Case G: A seventy-year-old man who has previously been in long-term therapy.

Conceptualization: Wants intellectual stimulation as well as relief.

Strategy: Support patient's choices.

Tactic: Use teaching stories and other forms of intellectual stimulation to get points across.

<u>Case H:</u> A forty-eight-year-old woman.

Conceptualization: All-or-none thinking.

Strategy: If you can't beat 'em, join 'em.

Tactic: Stress that there's *absolutely no way* that she can get rid of all of her anxiety, but she can learn to control most of her anxiety.

<u>Case J:</u> A forty-four-year-old professor.

Conceptualization: Logical, rational preferences.

Strategy: Attack weakest point.

Tactic: Use logic to show where patient is being irrational.

Principle 8: Cognitive Therapy Is Based on an Educational Model

A premise of cognitive therapy is that one develops anxiety not because of unconscious motivations but because one has learned inappropriate ways of handling life experiences. This premise suggests that with practice one can learn more effective ways of leading one's life.

One of the therapist's functions is to educate. J. Singer has expressed a similar view of psychotherapy: "In some ways the psychotherapist can be viewed as a teacher, as well as a technician. This does not mean that he gives formal lectures, for even good teachers know that they are not always the best method of influencing their pupils" (1974, p. 23). It is helpful for the therapist to view himself as a teacher of anxiety-management skills.

Cognitive therapy, in addition to providing corrective experiences for a patient, incorporates didactic techniques such as providing information, assigning reading, listening to audio tapes, written homework, and suggesting that the patient attend a lecture.

LEARNING TO LEARN

Implicit in the educational approach is the concept of *learning to learn*. The goal of therapy is to teach the patient not only a series of coping techniques but how to profit from his experiences. The learning process is expected to continue after therapy ends, through practice, experimentation, and improved information-gathering methods.

Learning to learn addresses what has been called the "neurotic paradox" (Raimy 1975): a person fails to profit from experience and repeats the same mistakes. This is a central problem in all forms of therapy because of the human tendency to repeat the same self-destructive patterns. Raimy says, "A defensive misconception protects the individual from having to recognize an alternative misconception which is more threatening than the defensive misconception" (1975, p. 14). One patient, for example, anxious about failing, considered himself "too laid back" to take on challenges—a more acceptable reason than the thought that he was inadequate.

Guidano and Liotti (1983) believe that people have a "metaphysical hard core" of basic assumptions surrounded by a "protective belt" that defends the hard-core belief. People use a variety of methods to reconfirm their basic assumptions about themselves. These methods include the types and ways problems are formulated ("How can I get people to accept me?"), repetitious problem solutions ("I'll have to impress them"), and self-fulfilling prophecies ("I always choose men who reject me"). Patients manipulate environmental situations until they create a situation that is in consonance with their self-image. They reduce their domain to fit their images.

The problem becomes severe when one's attitude toward oneself becomes fixed. Guidano and Liotti note that a rigid attitude about oneself prevents restructuring and gets in the way of dealing effectively with the world. One's behavior becomes stereotyped and repetitious. A large part of the problem is that a person is unaware of having a closed mind.

The Patient's Reluctance to Be Taught by Therapy. The patient has to consent to learn before therapy can develop. The reluctant patient may argue with the therapist or tune out what the therapist says. When the therapist spots this problem, he needs to address it. The therapist can ask the patient if he has ever been in a class where he made up his mind that he was not going to let the teacher teach him anything. And then ask the patient to compare this experience with a class where the patient gave the teacher permission to teach him.

Part of this problem is related to the amount of trust a patient has in his therapist. The first therapeutic order of business may be to develop trust in the patient by setting up a system for feedback from him and by continually erring on the side of honesty with him. The second step is to ask the patient how he can benefit by allowing himself to learn.

Slow Learners. Patients vary in their capability to learn how to learn, and some patients may be more ready than others. After many years of frustration, a businessman was ready to give up his dysfunctional beliefs. He had believed that the way to get ahead is to push others out of the way—a belief that led to a series of failures, resulting in anxiety and depression episodes. Although it took him years to reach this point, he did want to rearrange his values and was willing to let the therapist teach him.

Another group of people are socially and emotionally slow learners. Even though they are adults, they respond much like adolescents. Their major problem frequently is social anxiety, and they have little experience in dating and other interpersonal behavior.

With such patients, the therapist needs to focus on learning to learn, before tackling the first order of primary learning to correct distortions. The patient's second order of abstraction is less resistant and has less anxiety associated with it, and he has a greater sense of choice in this area. For example, one thirty-five-year-old man lived with his mother and had had only a few dates in his life. He needed to learn ways to deal with the opposite sex; however, the therapist focused first on learning how to learn. The patient had to go to places where he could meet women, but with the goal of learning as much about his reactions as possible. He first had to find out how he was preventing himself from learning from his experiences.

The therapist needs to help the patient learn how to remove or transcend the blocks that have prevented him from learning from his experiences.

Principle 9: The Theory and Techniques of Cognitive Therapy Rely on the Inductive Method

The development of the cognitive model was based on inductive reasoning and empirical research; in the same vein, patients are trained in a scientific way of thinking about their problems. Patients are taught to consider beliefs as hypotheses, to pay attention to *all* available facts, and to revise hypotheses according to incoming data. They are also taught to conduct experiments to test their hypotheses. The emphasis throughout therapy is on the patient's "getting the facts."

The inductive method is also manifest in the way a therapist processes information about a patient. Therapists are trained to formulate hypotheses and to test and revise these hypotheses according to therapy-generated data. For example, a patient may report feeling discomfort when meeting people of the opposite sex. The therapist may hypothesize that the problem is a deficit in social skills or confusion over sexual preference. In either case, the hypotheses is tested. This can be done by having the patient monitor specific thoughts and actions in the situation.

Treatment is based on the experimental method. Since all techniques will not work with all patients, an experimental method is employed. A variety of techniques may be tested until an effective one is found. Therapists must be cautious about abandoning techniques without a sufficient trial.

Principle 10: Homework Is a Central Feature of Cognitive Therapy

Cognitive therapy is geared to show patients how to apply the procedures learned in therapy to the situations they meet in everyday life outside of therapy. The primary way to ensure that patients do this is for the therapist to pay active attention to patients' homework assignments. Homework reinforces and supplements the educational aspects of cognitive therapy.

The therapist should explain to patients the practical reason for doing homework: that once-a-week visits are insufficient for overcoming long-held anxieties. Further, the rationale for particular assignments has to be explained, because patients are unlikely to carry them out if there is any doubt about their potential utility. The therapist can present homework as an experiment to prove or disprove a hypothesis, such as the patient's belief that a traumatic experience will occur if he faces the feared situation.

The therapist should take a collaborative, problem-solving approach to the process of assigning homework as he does to other aspects of therapy. The patient must agree that the assignment makes sense and that it is neither too hard nor too easy. Reactions—such as, "It's silly"; "It's busy work"; "It's too much trouble"; or, "It simply won't work"—can be tested.

The therapist looks for other blocks that could prevent the patient from carrying out an assignment. Ways of overcoming such blocks are then devised. In the remaining chapters, specific homework assignments for a variety of anxiety problems will be presented.

Now that the basic principles of cognitive therapy have been outlined, the specific strategies and techniques can be explored.

Chapter 11

Strategies and Techniques for Cognitive Restructuring

Developing Self-Awareness

An initial goal in therapy is to help a patient restructure his thinking by first becoming more aware of his thought processes. The therapist stresses that learning to catch one's thoughts is a necessary step in correcting distortions. The patient frequently finds that increasing self-awareness is sufficient to start correcting his thinking errors. Self-awareness allows him to distance himself from faulty thinking and develop a more objective perspective toward a situation. As the patient begins to collect automatic thoughts, the therapist gains a greater understanding of the patient's vulnerability and of the specific schemas that control his perception of a feared situation.

Unlike the depressed patient, who brings his depression into the office, the anxious patient is often free of anxiety in the office. For this reason, the therapist needs to be creative in helping the patient catch the thinking behind his anxiety.

A standard way for the therapist to elicit automatic thoughts is to use a marker board or a chalkboard. The patient usually gives two or three frightening thoughts when asked directly about his fears. When the therapist puts these on the board, this visual reminder triggers the patient to look for less obvious thoughts. The therapist needs to continue to probe past the first few responses. By repeatedly asking the patient for his thoughts and waiting for him to identify them, more meaningful ones will start to emerge. The thoughts can then be rated according to how much fear the patient associates with each. Often ones the patient comes up with last are the most frightening. The patient's holding back is usually due to cognitive avoidance. Most patients find that seeing their thoughts on the board is less frightening than they expected and thus are stimulated to overcome their avoidance and search out other frightening thoughts. One patient, after seeing some of her fears on the board, said, "What I'm really afraid of is getting old. If I get old, no one will want me and I'll be alone. That's what I'm really afraid of." Because people experience many of their fears in the form of pictures, patients often respond well when their fears are illustrated with stick figures or symbolic drawings.

The primary function of the board is to help enhance the patient's observing self. With this perspective, the patient is able to distance himself from his thoughts and behavior. Some comments that patients have made about the use of the board are: "I was able to get some perspective on my problems"; "I had to look at what I didn't want to face and this made it less scary"; "Laying the problem out on the board clarified it for me"; or "I can see the choices I've been making aren't in my best interests." The therapist can also use the board to conceptualize a patient's problems and choose possible strategies.

The therapist can also have mirrors in the office to help patients become aware of their thinking. Floor-length mirrors and small shaving mirrors can be used. A mirror can be a "social window" where a patient sees his presentation of his social self. Upon looking in the mirror, the patient may identify anxiety-producing thoughts that he previously was unaware of having.

The patient can be asked to free-associate at a rapid pace those thoughts that come to mind while looking in the mirror. One woman with severe social anxiety had a stream of thoughts about being ugly and unattractive —from "fat thighs" to her "odd-shaped body."

The therapist can have the patient complete sentences to help identify associations; for example, "Being rejected would mean ——"; or "Making a fool of myself would mean ——." Similarly, the therapist can ask for memory associations to the anxiety and thus can often help himself and his client to identify underlying beliefs and major concerns, which will be discussed in chapter 15.

The therapist can use other methods to help the patient catch his thoughts while they are "hot." One method is to do a behavioral task in the office, such as reading aloud.

The therapist can also use places near his office for *in vivo* exercises. He can go with the patient to restaurants and stores to help him become aware of his thinking. One patient with fears of public incompetence played video games with the therapist in a nearby fast-food store. This allowed the therapist to catch the cognitions when they were actually occurring.

A patient with a fear of driving can take a drive with the therapist. Therapy sessions can be held in a variety of places, such as a gym, the beach, a crowded area, or other situations that a patient finds anxiety provoking.

The general rule is for the patient to do as much anxiety-provoking activity as possible during the session. Such activity might include writing letters, filling out applications, and writing outlines for speeches. Because many anxious patients fear making phone calls, having to do so is a rich source of anxiety-producing thoughts. A phone call can be taped, and the patient can identify his automatic thoughts when it is played back. A businessman, for example, was putting off making a call to set up an appointment with a creditor. By reviewing the call he made in the office, he was able to identify his fearful thoughts of "not wanting to bother others" and his imagery of himself as being "a small, helpless child."

Therapists can use other technical aids, including being called by a patient when he is in an anxiety state. The use of CB radios for patients with driving phobias is a possible device. Another particularly useful tool is a set of walkie-talkies. If the patient feels safe with the therapist, he may not have any significant anxiety if the therapist goes with him. For this reason, when a patient is afraid to be out alone, walkie-talkies can keep him in touch with the therapist and allow him to report automatic thoughts.

DIRECTING PATIENTS

Merely telling patients to become more aware of their thinking can be sufficient. This is similar to the suggestion that one consciously chooses to remember one's dreams. The patient may be unaware of his thinking because he has considered it unimportant. The therapist needs to stress the effect thinking has on one's life. Automatic thoughts can be presented as being similar to subliminal advertisements: by learning to detect them, the patient can free himself from their effects.

As we have said, the anxious person does not really "own" his emotions but often attributes them to other people and to external events. This passive role makes him unable to see how he is creating his own feelings. A typical patient will say "he," "she," or "it" was making him anxious. The patient is encouraged to make such affective statements in the active ("I was making myself anxious") rather than the passive ("It was making me anxious") voice. The therapist points out this distinction throughout the therapy. (For more on owning one's emotions, see chapter 13.)

The patient is taught to replace "why" questions with "how" questions. When the patient asks himself why he is anxious or why he cannot control his anxiety, he elicits more thinking, and less awareness. By focusing on *how* he is making himself anxious, he switches out of the thinking self and into the observing self.

An overriding strategy is for the patient to approach what he fears. One reason is to provide the patient with opportunities to discover what he fears. Most patients are unable to identify their automatic thoughts and specific fears in the office but need to be in the anxiety situation to do so.

Quite often the therapist has to work with the patient to design ways for him to experience the anxiety so that he can discover his thinking. This is often the case with phobias where the patient succeeds in avoiding the fear stimulus. A patient with speech anxiety, and with no speeches on the horizon, for example, can ask questions at meetings he attends—a procedure that will usually produce the same or similar anxiety responses. One patient was able to identify his automatic thoughts by asking himself as he saw others giving speeches, "If I was up there right now, what would I be afraid of?"

The patient often attempts to block his fearful thoughts and thus achieves temporary closure; however, his frightening thoughts reappear all the stronger. For this reason, the patient is encouraged to think through unpleasant scenarios he is trying to block out of his mind. The person afraid of losing control in public is encouraged to stay with this feeling until he can identify his ultimate fear. The rationale given is, "The more you try not to think about something, the more you think about it." The patient can be asked to *not* think about his nose, and then to observe what goes on in his mind.

The patient is told that images and thoughts that cause him to "shudder" are rich sources of automatic thoughts and fear-producing beliefs. One patient shuddered at the thought of getting cancer. By thinking this through, he was able to pinpoint fears not only of dying but also of social disapproval.

In the same vein, a patient is encouraged to experience the feelings he is trying to shut off. The anxious patient often tries to divert himself from painful feelings; consequently, he is unable to see what is causing negative feelings. One patient discovered that he hummed to himself whenever he started to feel anxiety. While humming provided a temporary coping device, it hindered awareness of the thoughts behind his anxiety. Once he stopped using this strategy, he became aware of his automatic thoughts. Up until this time, he had not believed that any thoughts preceded his anxious feelings.

The therapist suggests the patient take an active approach to life instead of reacting to it. Patients who are undergoing treatment for anxiety are repeatedly encouraged to "err on the side" of inclusion rather than exclusion. One patient was anxious about going to a high-school reunion and had decided not to go. The therapist encouraged her to go so she could explore what in the situation triggered her fear. She would say No to many invitations and deprive herself of a chance to learn more about herself. After successfully going to the high-school reunion, her homework assignment was to say Yes to every social request made of her. By following through on this task, she was able to learn how many social invitations she normally turned down, and also what thoughts preceded her social anxiety.

A patient often covers up and lies to avoid the experience of anxiety. This dishonesty not only stops him from pinpointing his fears but may cause him to suffer from shame and guilt. The patient is encouraged, in a nonmoralistic way, to be more honest with others. The therapist presents the patient with the "no lose" proposition that, by becoming aware of when he does lie, he can learn more about himself and gain valuable information.

The patient is asked to question his inconsistencies by focusing on where and when his thoughts, feelings, and actions are going in different directions. One woman observed that she would tell people she would attend certain social functions, and then not show up. By looking at her inconsistencies, she was able to become more aware of how she was frightening herself; she also came to see why many people discounted her stated intentions.

A patient can increase self-awareness by voluntarily choosing to distance himself from his anxiety. The patient can do this by referring to himself as "it" or by his first name. In this exercise, the patient refers to himself as a separate entity throughout the day and comments on his anxiety from a distance: "Bill seems to be scared. His heart is beating. He seems to be concerned that others are thinking poorly of him. Bill is focusing on the impression he is making." By so distancing himself from his anxious response, the patient can gain a more objective picture of himself.

The most common method by which a patient can become aware of his thinking between sessions is the thought record. A patient can be asked to record on dysfunctional thought forms (see appendix), or in a notebook, situations where he is anxious and then to bring this into therapy. The patient uses his anxiety as a cue to write out frightening thoughts. One patient said "Thank you" to himself after pinpointing a thought; he then continued to ask himself what else was frightening him. The "Thank you" reinforced himself for identifying the thoughts.

Patients are taught to track their fears back to the original stimulus. One patient said he started to be anxious about the possibility of his being an alcoholic. He said, "This just came out of the blue, I had no reason to be afraid." After careful questioning, he discovered that his anxiety was due to seeing an alcoholic in a television movie. His anxiety stemmed from the thought, "This could happen to me," and the image of "ending up a drunk like my old man." From this experience, he learned to trace his fears back to their original stimulus and then to find out how he was frightening himself.

Strategies and Techniques

After the patient has learned to identify his faulty thinking, he learns how to correct his distortions and how to restructure his thinking. Cognitive, behavioral, and affective strategies and techniques are used to help the patient learn more realistic and adaptive thinking. The therapist chooses what he feels will be the most effective approach for a patient and then tries this out on an experimental basis; if it fails, another is tried. While many strategies and techniques are outlined in this chapter, the therapeutic goal is to find the one or two that work best.

COUNTING AUTOMATIC THOUGHTS

There are times when a patient is unable to restructure his thoughts. When he cannot slow down his mind enough to correct them or is in a situation where he is unable to write them down, the patient can simply count his thoughts. Counting allows the patient to distance himself from his thoughts, gives him a sense of mastery over them, and helps him to recognize their automatic quality, rather than accepting them as an accurate reflection of external reality. Counting automatic thoughts helps the patient see how his thoughts produce, maintain, and intensify his anxiety.

Technical aids can be used to help a patient become aware of the stereo-typed, repetitive nature of his negative thoughts. The therapist who is satisfied that a patient is correctly identifying automatic thoughts can demonstrate one of these aids. The patient may be asked to mark a 3-by-5 card each time he recognizes an automatic thought; or he may count thoughts using (1) a golf wrist counter available from sporting-goods stores, (2) an inexpensive plastic counter, or (3) a stitch counter sold in knitting shops.

Through practice with these devices, the patient learns to distance him-self: "There's another fearful thought. I'll just count it and let it go." The patient is told to accept the thoughts rather than fight them. He observes his thoughts and lets them go. The patient is asked to report the total number of thoughts at the next session.

This method has a number of variations, such as: (1) counting specific types of anxiety-producing thoughts (such as self-doubting or catas-trophic thoughts); (2) counting thoughts in the midst of an anxiety at-tack, since counting may help the patient gain mastery over the situation; (3) counting during time samples (for example, between 5 P.M. and 7 P.M.) (4) counting at random time samples of ten minutes, using a mechanical timer.

One patient used a digital watch with a buzzer set for certain times, which signaled him to stop what he was doing and count any threatening thoughts he was having. He found that this method helped to separate him from his thoughts. He said, "I now realize that my thoughts have a life of their own, and I don't have to become overconcerned with them."

Counting or recording automatic thoughts may be counterindicated. One patient was so fully immersed in anxiety-provoking thinking that he was unable to distance himself from it. He was trained to lessen its impact by focusing on the task at hand and by using other methods of concentra-tion. Again, the therapist adopts an experimental approach in applying any technique or strategy.

QUESTIONS

Therapists help patients correct faulty ideas and logic mainly through questions. Eventually patients learn to pose the therapist's questions to themselves. The following are typical questions:

1. *"What is the evidence for or against this idea?"* This is one of the most frequently asked questions in therapy, and one that patients readily learn to use. Together, therapist and patient should develop an agreement re-garding what constitutes acceptable evidence.

2. *"Where is the logic?"* Anxious patients jump to conclusions without considering their logic. One patient with a health phobia thought that his doctor was withholding information about something that was wrong with him. Once he looked for the logic in the situation, he saw that it was unlikely that his doctor was lying to him.

3. *"Are you oversimplifying a causal relationship?"* One lawyer assumed that if he made one mistake in the courtroom, his case would collapse. He began to observe other lawyers and saw that many made mistakes, and that mistakes did not automatically lead to losing a case.

4. *"Are you confusing a habit with a fact?"* A woman with social anxiety thought strangers would have the impression, "She looks funny, there's something wrong with her." She was unable to provide the therapist with any evidence that strangers reacted to her this way, but she still believed it. The therapist pointed out that she had these thoughts in many diverse situations, and that perhaps the thoughts seemed to be true simply because she had a strong *habit* of thinking along these lines. This woman learned to ask herself, "Is this thought coming from reality, or is it coming from my thinking habit?"

5. *"Are your interpretations of the situation too far removed from reality to be accurate?"* The therapist can say:

> When you become too remote from what you can perceive with your five senses, it's easy to enter into the world of fantasy and nonreality. When you stick with what you can perceive, you're usually on much safer ground.

6. *"Are you confusing your version of the facts with the facts as they are?"* Patients are told to keep in mind that the facts in their entirety can never be known, and to discriminate between the known facts and the construction they put on these facts. Facts remain the same, but opinion varies.

7. *"Are you thinking in all-or-none terms?"* The anxious person often sees his experiences as white or black and overlooks the fact that almost nothing is "either/or." One patient believed she was going to be either completely loved by others or totally rejected. In one session the therapist gave her the following explanation:

> In general, everything we know, we know by contrast; the English language is set up in such a way. We need to know "down" to understand "up." When you're anxious, you often make absolute and sharp contrasts. A useful strategy for anxiety is to lop off the extremes by considering the worst possible expectation ("Everyone there will ridicule

me") and the best possible expectation ("Everyone there will be over-joyed to see me"). Usually you end up dropping both extremes and expecting the middle course ("I'll go and see what happens").

Patients usually accept the middle possibility much more easily after the therapist has presented both extremes.

8. *"Are you using words or phrases that are extreme or exaggerated?"* Words such as *always, forever, never, need, should, must, can't,* and *every time* rarely correspond with reality. The same applies to the verb *to be:* "I am anxious" versus "I have some anxiety."

9. *"Are you taking selected examples out of context?"* Patients are often so consumed with a feared event that they do not perceive the larger context in which it takes place. One of the effects of anxiety is that a person loses touch with the general context of the situation.

10. *"Are you using cognitive defense mechanisms?"* These mechanisms may be rationalization, denial, or projection: "I'm not afraid, I just don't want to go out"; "The other people expect me to be perfect"; or, "I don't want to make the call because I don't have the time."

11. *"Is your source of information reliable?"* Is Uncle George's opinion of the situation likely to be colored by vested interest, lack of experience, preju-dice, or other factors? Patients will often give credence to unreliable sources. One patient who feared bankruptcy believed all the dire financial predictions he read or heard about without considering their source.

12. *"Are you thinking in terms of certainties instead of probabilities?"* Patients often demand a degree of certainty that is unattainable. Many anxious people want to have 100-percent assurance that what they fear will not happen. It is helpful to point out to patients that there is often a 10-percent uncertainty factor that everyone has to live with. Thus, patients con-fronted with an ambiguous situation can see it as part of this uncertain 10 percent.

13. *"Are you confusing a low probability with a high probability?"* The therapist can help patients see that a possibility differs from a probability. That one *could* go insane does not necessarily imply a high probability that one will.

14. *"Are your judgments based on feelings rather than on facts?"* Many anxious patients use their feelings to validate their thoughts and thus start a vicious cycle: "I'll be anxious when I ask for the date so there must be something to fear."

15. *"Are you overfocusing on irrelevant factors?"* One person thought, "Be-cause three people I know died of heart attacks, I know I'll have one."

When using these questions, the therapist should avoid appearing smug, or being sarcastic. An attitude that displays curiosity and minimizes threat is indicated when making inquiries into sensitive areas. Patients can be given a list of similar questions to use when they are correcting their automatic thoughts between sessions. The questions they find most useful can be used in the list.

Guidelines in asking questions are:

1. *Resist the inclination to answer questions for the patient.* When the patient seems confused about the purpose of a question, *rephrase* the question:

THERAPIST: What do you think would happen if you confronted your boss about changing your hours?

PATIENT: Oh, probably nothing would happen.

THERAPIST: Can you be more specific? What exactly do you think would happen?

PATIENT: Well, he probably would just shrug it off and say, "Well, it's just the way it is."

THERAPIST: Can you be even more specific? Maybe think about it for a moment? Can you close your eyes and imagine it?

PATIENT: Well, I imagine he might be taken aback at first. But then he would probably ask me why I brought it up, then I really think that he wouldn't carry it any farther.

THERAPIST: Can you imagine it again?

PATIENT: I can see him act another way. He's very mad at me.

THERAPIST: How are you reacting to him?

PATIENT: Well, I'm getting uptight and I can't talk. I want to leave.

THERAPIST: That's what I was wondering about. To be even more specific, what would be the worst thing about the situation? Your feeling? The way you would act? Or the reaction of your boss?

The therapist used questions to get the patient to specify what exactly he was afraid of in the situation.

2. *Ask specific, direct, and concrete questions.* Although an open-ended question such as "How have you been feeling?" is useful for obtaining general information, questions that elicit particular types of information are usually more helpful: for instance, "How anxious were you when you asked for the date?" Such questions enhance the patient's observing self in the session and, thus, improve communication, provide structure, and facilitate relief of symptoms. When a patient says his anxiety concerns the "meaning of life," the therapist asks the patient to "concretize": "What specifically concerns you about the meaning of life?" What at first appears to be a patient's existential anxiety or preoccupation with vague philosophical concepts can in nearly every case be traced to specific fears.

3. *Base each question on a rationale.* Although many new therapists ask questions without any clear intent, each question's aim should fulfill definite therapeutic functions. A question should grow out of the therapist's conceptualization of a patient's problem. For example, if the strategy is for the patient to see offsetting rescue factors in a situation ("I could call the police"), the questions would be geared to having the patient generate these factors ("What could you do?").

4. *The questions should be timed to foster rapport and problem-solving.* Poorly timed questions may increase a patient's anxiety (as would, for example, asking a patient to cognitively "rehearse" a fearful event before he has established trust in the therapist). Questions geared to enhance trust ("Do you feel nothing will happen?") need to be asked early in treatment.

5. *Avoid a series of rapid-fire questions.* Cross-examination makes a patient more defensive. The therapist needs to take time to think about the information he has elicited before he phrases the next question. A common error is for the therapist to formulate a new question instead of listening to the patient's answer.

6. *Use in-depth questioning.* The patient usually has more information than he is aware of. The therapist may stop asking questions before the patient has run dry, but the question "Can you think of anything else?" can elicit richer responses from a patient. Usually a patient's most helpful reconceptualizations come after his immediate responses. The therapist can draw out these deeper answers by saying, "Take a couple of minutes and see if you can think of anything else." Simply repeating the question often brings up new material.

In the following clinical example, a therapist uses questions to elicit information and to open up a patient's closed logic.

PATIENT: I don't think I'll ever be able to get a job.
THERAPIST: How often do you have this thought?
PATIENT: Quite often.
THERAPIST: And what do you base this thought on?
PATIENT: I just feel it. There's no use.
THERAPIST: Do you think feelings are always logical?
PATIENT: No. I guess not always.
THERAPIST: Your feelings are often wrong and are just reflecting what you're thinking. What are the advantages of this type of thinking?
PATIENT: Well, I don't have to go for the interview. I don't have to think about it.
THERAPIST: Those are real benefits. What disadvantages are there?

PATIENT: Well, I'll never get what I want. I may be making a mountain out of a molehill.

THERAPIST: On balance, is this thinking helpful to you?

PATIENT: I suppose not.

THERAPIST: What do you think you could do about this type of thinking if it's getting in your way?

PATIENT: Well, maybe look at it more closely.

Three Basic Approaches

Anxious patients in the simplest terms believe, "Something bad is going to happen that I won't be able to handle." The cognitive therapist uses three basic strategies or questions to help the patient restructure this thinking. Nearly all of the cognitive therapist's questions can be broken down to one of these questions: (1) "What's the evidence?" (2) "What's another way of looking at the situation?" and (3) "So what if it happens?" Some patients respond better to one approach than to another. Each patient, however, should develop skill in using all three approaches.

WHAT'S THE EVIDENCE?

Analysis of Faulty Logic. A standard method is to review the patient's logic in construing his experiences. For example, a sixty-seven-year old woman was extremely anxious about, and believed she would fail, a written driving exam, although she had passed a previous one. The therapist led her to concede that there was no evidence she would fail (other than her thoughts that the second test could be harder than the first), and that she could read the license manual. When the patient recognized that she was "jumping to conclusions," her anxiety subsided sufficiently to allow her to study for the test and, as a result, went down even more. When she eventually did pass the exam, this success was used by the therapist as further evidence of the futility of illogical conclusions.

Three-Column Technique. Patients can identify thinking errors by the three-column technique. In the first column, the patient describes an anxiety-producing situation; in the second, his automatic thoughts; in the third, types of errors found in these thoughts.

Data	Interpretation	Error
While I was walking by, a stranger was looking at me as he got out of his car.	I'm vulnerable. He wants to cause me trouble. Everywhere I go there's danger.	Self-focusing. Arbitrary inference. Overgeneralization.

In an adaptation of this, patients use the third column to comment on the situation as might an "objective" observer, such as the therapist or a friend.

Data	Interpretation	Observer's Interpretation
I went to the store and heard a siren.	I'm going to die. Next time it'll be for me.	This person heard a siren. That's all he can realistically say about it. These predictions are not relevant to the situation.

By doing this, the patient practices viewing his experience from the vantage point of a neutral ally rather than from that of a predictor of doom. Even if initially experienced as an "intellectual" exercise, this exercise with practice usually takes on personal meaning for the patient.

Providing Information.   Lack of information or erroneous information may exacerbate the patient's anxiety. The patient who is afraid of going insane usually is unaware of the symptoms of schizophrenia; but this fear can be alleviated if the therapist explains the difference between hallucination and delusion and the symptoms of anxiety.

When a patient exaggerates the actual odds of his experiencing a feared event, the therapist can provide realistic information to enable him to reassess the potential of danger. Thus, the therapist can point out that if a person could die only as the result of a plane crash, he would live to be a million years old; or, if he could die only because of an automobile accident, he would live to be over three thousand years old (Marquis 1976).

Hypothesis Testing.   Much of the homework between sessions involves testing hypotheses. The therapist should encourage the patient to write out his prediction of dire consequences for later evaluation, so as to accumulate a recorded body of data disproving the patient's catastrophic predictions. As one negative consequence after another fails to occur, the patient's belief in the certainty of impending disaster begins to weaken.

The patient can test many maladaptive hypotheses during the session.

1. I'm too anxious even to read.
2. I'm too anxious even to make an outline for a speech.
3. I'm too nervous to call and ask for information.
4. I can't even talk to a stranger.
5. I can't do anything when this symptom comes on.
6. I can't make any decisions.
7. I can't think or talk about this—it's too frightening.
8. I can't do anything to control my anxiety.

The therapist can set up different tests in the office. Typically, however, patient and therapist set up experiments the patient runs outside of the session. The experiments are always set up as "no lose" situations, since each experiment, no matter what the outcome, provides useful data.

WHAT'S ANOTHER WAY OF LOOKING AT IT?

Generating Alternative Interpretations. The anxious person's closed and limited view of reality excludes more neutral and more realistic interpretations. A major therapeutic aim is to teach the patient to consider possibilities other than the dire predictions. Although the therapist uses different methods to achieve this aim, the standard procedure is to have the patient write down his anxiety-producing thoughts, then search for alternative interpretations (the "two-column" technique). This strategy is modeled first during the session, often on a blackboard.

One patient's anxiety centered on his fear of being fired. When his supervisor was aloof, he would think, "He's avoiding me. He's going to fire me. That's why he's so aloof." Alternative explanations that he was able to generate included:

1. "He [the supervisor] is aloof from all the workers, not just me."
2. "There is a real status difference between our roles."
3. "He could dislike me regardless of what he thinks of my competence."
4. "Even if he does think I'm incompetent, the other supervisors there know I'm not."

The patient was eventually able to lower his anxiety by repeatedly considering alternative interpretations. He came to see that the alternatives were nearly always more accurate, and certainly more functional, than his original appraisal of the situation.

While the ideal situation is for the patient to generate believable alternative viewpoints, he often has difficulty doing so because he is so focused on the threat. The therapist who excels at divergent thinking can be most helpful. From a large list of alternative constructs, the patient is likely to find one or two useful ones. The therapist needs to ask repeatedly which alternative way of thinking is the most helpful for the patient.

Dysfunctional Thought Records. A primary strategy is to teach the patient to recognize his automatic thoughts outside of the session, and to strive for a more balanced alternative view. A special form (the Daily Record of Dysfunctional Thoughts) is used to help patients analyze anxiety-producing thoughts (see table 11.1). This is a more elaborate form than the two-column technique just mentioned and is brought by the patient to the therapy session. Because the record of dysfunctional thoughts is an integral part of treatment, the therapist needs to spend time showing the patient how best to use it.

The patient fills out the form as soon as possible after becoming anxious. Initially, he completes the first three columns of the record: (1) situation leading to anxiety; (2) emotion felt and degree of emotion; and (3) automatic thought and degree of belief in the thought. This process helps him learn how to monitor changes in level of anxiety, to recognize automatic thoughts, and to understand their relationship to anxiety. When he has mastered these skills, the patient is ready to begin providing the "rational response" and outcome ratings required by the remaining columns.

An alternative to the printed form is a notebook that the patient carries with him. (Simply giving a notebook to a patient makes it more likely that he will do his written homework.) Often the patient may try writing down his thinking and concentrate only on the threat side. The therapist needs to stress the importance of dividing the written homework into at least two parts—anxiety-producing thoughts and corrections of their exaggerations.

The patient may not want to write down his thoughts because he fears doing so will make him more anxious or because they will look "silly" or "childish." The reasons the patient has for avoiding his homework often are the same ones that maintain his anxiety. When the patient fails to bring in written homework, the therapist should probe the thoughts behind his avoidance. One patient avoided doing his homework because he believed he "would screw it up!" Another believed the therapist was incompetent. Eliciting avoidance thinking helped identify the underlying assumptions of the first patient ("I have to show everyone a flawless image of myself") and the second's general distrust of others ("I can't trust anyone").

Patients with acute anxiety may need to do written homework only while they are in treatment. Patients with chronic anxiety are told they will

TABLE 11.1

Daily Record of Automatic Thoughts

Date	Situation	Automatic Thought(s)	Questioning the Evidence	Alternative Therapy	Re-attribution	De-catastrophizing
	Describe actual event(s) leading to unpleasant emotion(s)	1. Write automatic thought(s), daydream(s) or recollection(s) that preceeded emotions 2. Rate belief in automatic thought(s) 0–100%	What is the evidence?	What is an alternative view?	In what ways am I personalizing, overgeneralizing, using either/or thinking, making false comparisons, or jumping to conclusions?	1. What's the worst that could ever happen? 2. Even if that happened, what could I do?
	Emotion(s) 1. Specify sad, angry, etc. 2. Rate degree of emotion 0–100%					Outcome 1. Re-rate belief in automatic thoughts 0–100% 2. Specify and rate subsequent emotions 0–100%

have to write up their thoughts systematically for at least a year and, afterward, when needed.

Decentering.   Decentering is the process of having the patient challenge the basic belief that he is the focal point of all events. Many patients with social anxiety report thinking that everyone is watching them, or that others are acutely aware of their tension or shyness. The patient often believes that others can read his mind. There is a variety of strategies the therapist can use to help a patient see that the social world does not revolve around him. The therapist can work with the patient to establish *concrete criteria* to determine when he is (or is not) the focus of attention, and what behavior or attributes are being attended to by others.

Since the patient is required to adopt the perspective of another person, participation in this task requires a shift in focus on the part of the patient. One young man was severely handicapped with self-consciousness and so preoccupied with his own internal reactions that he noticed little about others' reactions to him; paradoxically, he attributed keen powers of observation and utter objectivity to those around him ("Because I watch myself so closely, they must be watching me in the same way"). As he became aware of how infrequently he attended closely to others and how limited his own observations were, he came to realize that the attention of most people is similarly restricted, and he became more relaxed in social situations.

Enlarging Perspective.   The anxious patient usually takes the "worm's eye view" of his situation, and one of the functions of therapy is to provide him with a broader perspective: that is, the "long" or "bird's-eye" view of the situation. For example, a college student was homesick and afraid that her pain would last forever. The therapist helped her broaden her perspective by looking at some of the positive attributes of her homesickness. Together they generated the following list:

1. Her homesickness was a form of growing pains.
2. Her homesickness was to teach her how to accept changes.
3. She was innoculating herself against future losses she would have to deal with.
4. She was demonstrating loyalty to her family.
5. By sticking out the pain instead of going home, she was putting into practice the principle of "getting better instead of feeling better."
6. The experience was helping her increase her tolerance of frustration.
7. Her homesickness was a socially acceptable way to express a lot of fearful and depressing feelings.

8. She was learning to appreciate her family more when she did go home.

9. Because pleasure follows pain, she would probably feel very good when the pain left.

She was able to recover from her homesickness rather quickly, and most of her positive predictions proved to be true.

Reattribution. In reviewing an anxiety-prone patient's automatic thoughts, the therapist often discovers that the patient attributes to himself an excessive amount of control for a potential negative outcome. The therapist can help the patient recognize that some elements in a situation —possibly the determining ones—are inevitably beyond his control.

First, the patient should rate the degree of responsibility he feels he has for the feared outcome; it is not uncommon for a patient to give a rating of 100 percent. The therapist then attempts, through questioning, to reduce the estimate of control to a more realistic level. One approach is to have the patient list every conceivable factor that could affect the outcome, to assess the relative degree of influence of each factor (perhaps using a diagram), and finally, to evaluate the degree of control he has over each factor.

The therapist continually questions the patient to achieve more objective ratings. At the end of this process, the patient is asked to give a second rating of his degree of control, and to compare it with the invariably higher) initial rating. Through this method, the patient becomes aware of his predisposition to believe he has to control everything in the particular situation. For example, a woman sales executive experienced extreme anxiety when anticipating closing sessions with buyers. She thought, "If I don't pull off a major sale, it shows I'm inept and not aggressive enough." After a review such as the one just described, she recognized that she was hampered in her efforts by a major problem: The competitor's product was demonstrably superior to her own company's! While her persuasive skills undoubtedly played a part in the outcome, they were unlikely to be definitive. This recognition enabled her to minimize her anxiety and address herself to the real problem.

Another patient was anxious about going to a party where she knew only a few people. She felt that she was totally responsible for everything going well. Once she reflected on the fact that she was only one of twenty people who would be there, and that she could not control how the others responded, she lowered her perceived sense of responsibility and had a corresponding drop in her anxiety.

Often the patient will dislike not having more control over events. The therapist can point out the difference between responsibility and accountability. The manager of a large division is not directly responsible for those who work under him; he is, however, accountable to his boss and, if he is a successful manager, holds himself accountable for what happens in his division. A therapist is not responsible for patients but is accountable. Similarly, a patient, while not responsible for what those he interacts with do, can choose to hold himself accountable for his relationship with them: that is, he has some control, both direct and indirect, over how the relationship develops.

SO WHAT IF IT HAPPENS?

Decatastrophizing. When predicting dire consequences, the anxious patient does not utilize all of the information available to him and rarely takes into account his past dire predictions that failed to materialize. The therapist attempts to widen the range of information on which the patient bases his forecasts, and to broaden his time perspective. This method is described in detail in chapter 12.

Coping Plans. At times, the patient fears he will be unable to cope. Therapist and patient collaboratively develop a variety of strategies that the person can use to manage the anxiety. The stress is on coping with the situation, not on mastering it.

A woman anxious about socializing with groups of people developed the following plan: (1) using self-distraction (focusing on others' body posture); (2) focusing on the "task" of conversing and behaving appropriately; (3) using a coping technique with images (turning negative images into positive ones); (4) using a brief form of relaxation (deep breathing); (5) using the incident to gather evidence about her thinking. She rehearsed this plan in the therapist's office before trying it in the real situation.

Point/Counterpoint. The therapist can use all of the strategies mentioned previously in a general strategy of point/counterpoint.

THERAPIST: You seem to have a lot of reasons why you believe the feared event is going to happen, why it is so terrible, and why you wouldn't be able to handle it. Since you have those arguments down so well, let's work together to dispute them with other possibilities. I'll give you the fearful ideas, and you give me the counter ideas. When you run out of positive counterpoints, we'll switch roles and I'll give the counterpoints.

Patient and therapist switch back and forth between these roles and help each other out in developing better counterpoints. The patient often surprises the therapist and himself with the number of counterpoints he can generate.

Generally four areas are covered in this strategy: (1) the probability of the feared event; (2) its degree of awfulness; (3) the patient's ability to prevent it from occurring; and (4) the patient's ability to accept and deal with the worst possible outcome. The therapist should present his counterpoint (anti-anxiety) with strength and confidence.

Chapter 12

Modifying Imagery

Most anxious patients have visual images of danger before and during their anxiety (see chapter 6). When they are specifically questioned about their fantasies, anxious patients report visual images that have the same general content as their verbal cognitions—that is, anticipation of psychosocial or physical trauma. Like the verbal cognitions, the fantasies often represent a distortion of reality.

One thirty-six-year-old woman suffered from acrophobia. While with her husband on the top floor of a skyscraper, she had an image of falling out of the window. The fantasy was so vivid that she shouted for help. When her husband questioned her, she realized that the fall was purely in her imagination. As with other anxious patients, her feelings were more congruent with the fantasy than with reality.

Numerous clinical observations suggest that a person visualizing a scene may react as though it were actually occurring. A person's belief that a fantasy is identical with reality may be located on a continuum ranging from total conviction to total disbelief. When an unrealistic pictorial image is so powerful that one totally believes its authenticity despite contradictory evidence, it may be considered a visual hallucination. Belief in a fantasy usually varies from moment to moment: a nonpsychotic person may partially or totally confuse the fantasy with reality until he has an opportunity to reality-test it. Even though the daydream may be temporarily experienced as reality (as a sleeping dreamer experiences a dream), anxious patients are able to regain their objectivity and label the phenomenon a fantasy. A few moments later, the fantasy may recur and again will have to be tested against reality. This kind of fluctuation in vividness and credibility of fantasies may be observed in anxiety reactions, phobias, and depressions. Rarely, however, do patients disclose frightening visual images without explicit, and sometimes repeated, questioning by the therapist.

Induced Images

A growing literature indicates that *induced* fantasies have a profound effect on behavior. Such procedures as relaxation in preparation for childbirth and hypnosis induction make use of pictorial imagery. Induced imagery was used in 1895 by Freud and Breuer (1966) and is a standard feature of systematic desensitization (Wolpe 1969). Ahsen (1965) and A. A. Lazarus (1971) have reported the use of induced imagery to clarify patients' problems.

The usefulness of visualization in modifying behavior is shown by the efficacy of fantasy techniques in learning or improving motor skills. Induced imagery has been found effective in improving performance in dart throwing, in free throws with a basketball, and in other sports. Many people have discovered that they can reduce anxiety and improve performance in public speaking or in other stressful situations by repeatedly fantasizing the situation. Such observations suggest that fantasies contribute to achieving skills and overcoming anxiety in normal life situations as well as in cases of psychopathology.

In cognitive therapy, imagery-related interventions are often used. The content of spontaneous images points to the cognitive distortions in a particular problem; and imagery procedures, such as induced imagery, can help the patient alter spontaneous fantasies, reality-test, and achieve distance from anxiety.

DELINEATING MALADAPTIVE PATTERNS

Just as reporting dreams to the analyst permits an interpretation of symbols and images, so discussing spontaneous fantasies and related elaborations can better determine the content of a particular problem. Fantasies are useful when a problem remains vague despite efforts to define it through description, associations, exploration, probing, or reflection. A twenty-six-year-old patient felt rejected by his fiancée although she had done nothing to justify his reaction. He said the feeling had started the previous day when he had been at a picnic with her and his best friend. Although his fiancée and his friend had been attentive to him, he felt uncomfortable. He then recalled that during the picnic, he had the following daydreams:

"Jane and Bob began to look at each other in a loving way. They passed signals back and forth for getting rid of me. They arranged to get together later that night. I got the old feeling of being rejected—wanting to be in but kept out. They sneaked off at night, necked and had sex. Then they told me about it and I gave her up, although I felt a deep loss at the same time." After having experienced this fantasy, he had felt rejected by his fiancée even though in reality she continued to be affectionate toward him.

After recounting the fantasy in the therapeutic hour, the patient had a stream of associations: "Bob reminds me of competing with my brother——I was always second fiddle to him——He was always better than me——Everybody liked him more than me." The patient was then able to view his unpleasant reaction at the picnic as analogous to his early pattern of expecting to be pushed to one side by his brother. He visualized Bob's displacing him as analogous to his brother's earlier triumph. He saw that his current reactions of jealousy and vulnerability were unjustified, given the facts.

PINPOINTING COGNITIVE DISTORTIONS

The use of imagery is another tool for clarifying problems. The gross distortion of reality in the patient's image often provides an important clue to an excessive or inappropriate reaction.

A woman, forty-eight years old, suffered from chronic anxiety about her children, and it often escalated to near-panic. On one occasion she had severe anxiety over a cross-country trip her son had started out on. The usual questioning of automatic thoughts—calculating the probability of a mechanical breakdown or accident—had little impact. However, when the therapist asked her to picture her son on his trip and relate the image in as much detail as possible, she provided a wealth of information about the content of her anxiety.

She pictured her son sitting in a stalled car in a small town full of hostile strangers, without any idea of what to do or where to look for help. She depicted a series of horrible scenes that might take place and imagined her son's feelings of helplessness and despair. It was as though she were watching a movie of the feared event. Through this technique, therapist and patient became aware of her many fears and of the specific distortions that needed to be addressed.

Through fantasy induction, patients can recognize the specific details of a feared situation and then reality-test and correct distortions. Standard techniques or direct discussion may fail to delineate the patient's fears; fantasy expression, however, brings them into sharp focus. One method is to have the patient imagine himself in an anxiety-producing situation. Imaging allows the patient to experience his thoughts and feelings rather than just talk about them.

Often a patient's reports of his fears are different from his real fears and concerns. Many psychologically minded patients presuppose they have certain anxieties. One patient looking for a job said he had a "fear of success." As it turned out, his actual fear was of being humiliated by an interviewer.

In order to elicit images, the therapist may ask the patient the following questions:

"Do you see a picture as you're talking?"
"Would you please describe it?"
"Is it in color?"
"Is there sound?"
"Are you moving?"
"Is anyone else moving?"
"Do you smell anything?"
"Do you hear anything?"
"Do you have any tactile sensations?"
"How vivid is the image?"
"Is it like a movie image?"
"Is there a lot of emotional activity?"

Patients should be encouraged to look for, and bring to the sessions, the visual images or daydreams that precede their anxiety. The therapist should remember to ask specifically about these images, for the patient rarely volunteers information about their existence.

MODIFICATION OF INDUCED IMAGES

Once the distorted picture is fully recognized, it can be modified. The patient then generally feels better and can handle the situation more successfully. A thirty-five-year-old married man, for example, was anxious for several days because storm windows he had purchased from a local store were different from what he had ordered. He dreaded calling the manager to insist on the right windows. Yet he was unable to explain why he felt this way. The therapist suggested he imagine how the conversation would go. The patient reported the following fantasy:

"I was in the manager's office, talking to the manager. It was me, but I looked younger even though I was grown-up. I started getting smaller and younger until I was about seven. I was a little boy. I was not stating my case but was pleading and whining. The manager got bigger; he became outsized, red in the face, and started threatening me with the back of his hand. I was facing him, cringing. He was furious, yelling at me and not listening to me." The patient had an immediate recollection relating to this fantasy: "It reminds me of when my father was mad at me. I would hide behind my mother and say, 'I can't stand him.' I would stick my neck out too far and my father would come tearing after me."

The therapist then suggested that the patient "repeat" the fantasy, and he reported this second fantasy:

"This time I just telephoned the manager. He said that the storm windows were essentially the same as the ones I had ordered. I said they weren't. He said that actually they were an improvement over the sample I had seen, which had been discontinued. I said that the windows I had been shown were better. I said he had sent me inferior storm windows, and I wouldn't accept them."

The patient had less anxiety with the second fantasy, and had more self-confidence; he was optimistic that he would be able to stand up for his rights. His dread about making the telephone call was reduced, and he subsequently handled the problem effectively.

The patient initially imagined a change in both himself and the other person: that is, he became smaller and the other person larger. As is often the case, he had a spontaneous childhood recollection of an analogous scene—in his case with his father. His first visualization was shaped to a large extent by the childhood pattern. His second visualization was more realistic of himself and of the other person. Often images are of the patient as a child in a world of adults.

Techniques for Modifying Images

The following techniques should be used first in the office, and later the patient can practice them outside the office.

TURN-OFF TECHNIQUE

The turn-off technique is particularly effective with patients who are reliving a traumatic event, such as an automobile accident. The therapeutic strategy consists of training a patient to turn off an autonomous fantasy by increasing sensory input. Methods for interrupting a fantasy include blowing a whistle, ringing a cow bell, clapping hands, or simply engaging in some constructive activity.

When absorbed in fantasy, a patient is coached to concentrate on his immediate environment and to attempt to describe aloud in meticulous detail the objects around him. When a fantasy is interrupted in this way, the patient's anxiety is usually reduced. The patient may be trained at this point to substitute a pleasant fantasy for the anxiety-triggering one.

One patient, for instance, had repeated visual images of dying. The therapist offered to teach him how to stop the fantasy with the technique of hand clapping. The purpose of this maneuver was to enable the patient to gain mastery over the repetitive fantasy. The patient was then instructed to have the fantasy. He conjured up the images, again accompanied by anxiety. The therapist clapped his hands three times, thus interrupting the fantasizing, and the patient said that the fantasy had disappeared. This procedure was repeated several times, with intervals of a few minutes between the fantasy-handclapping sequences. Each time the fantasy was interrupted, the associated anxiety abated. The patient practiced this technique of fantasy reduction by clapping his own hands.

The patient was seen three more times during the next week, and each time he reported a marked reduction in his anxiety and the fantasies. He found that he could stop the fantasy (and therefore the anxiety) by diverting his attention—for example, by having his wife clap her hands, by clapping his own hands, or by watching television. He was also trained to substitute a positive fantasy as soon as he began to experience the unpleasant fantasy. At the time of the next visit a month later, he reported that he had been asymptomatic except for about one brief fantasy a week accompanied by moderate anxiety.

This case illustrates how anxiety may be reduced in intensity and duration, and may even be eliminated, by training a patient to control anxiety-producing fantasies.

REPETITION

When patients repeat in full a fantasy that they have experienced, often the content changes with each repetition to one that is more in accord with reality. Usually the change in content is followed by a persistent change of attitude.

A twenty-four-year-old patient had bought a gift for his girlfriend. Shortly afterward, he began to think that the gift was inappropriate; he had spontaneous fantasies of her reacting in a negative way. Following the fantasy, he had been afraid to give her the present. During a session, the patient was asked to repeat the fantasy: "She opens the package. She is shocked and is in utter disbelief. Then she had a look of contempt and pain. She is really disappointed. She covers it up by pretending to like it. I feel miserable just picturing this."

When asked to repeat this fantasy several times, the patient reported the following sequence: "She opens the package. She is pleasantly surprised. She has a look of surprise because she hadn't expected such a nice present ——she really likes it. She is impressed by my thoughtfulness. She looks at it and kisses me."

The last fantasy was more consistent with his knowledge of his girl-friend's preferences and with her past pattern of reaction. Later, when he presented her with the gift, the actual sequence of events followed fairly closely that pictured in this later fantasy.

With successive deliberate repetitions of a fantasy, its content often becomes more realistic. When concerned with anticipated events, a fantasy changes from having a less probable to a more probable outcome. While repeating the fantasy, the patient automatically tests the original fantasy and molds it into a more accurate reflection of reality. We have found, however, that anxiety may sometimes be eliminated or reduced with successive deliberate repetitions of a fantasy even though its content remains unchanged.

Spontaneous modification of fantasies upon repetition seems to occur only with deliberate, conscious repetition. In the natural situation, where fantasies tend to repeat themselves autonomously, the same fantasy is reproduced on each repetition, and anxiety continues to be generated. After the patient practices this procedure, the reduction of anxiety usually carries over to real-life situations.

The patient, a thirty-seven-year-old man, was anxious about an impending interview with a group of executives for a new position. His fantasy was simply: "I am in the center of the room and they keep firing questions at me." When he had this fantasy, his anxiety increased. However, with each repetition of the fantasy, his anxiety became less. By the fourth repetition, the anxiety was minimal.

The therapist then asked him how he felt about his forthcoming interview. The man said, "It doesn't frighten me any more. I guess I'll be able to handle it all right. And if I don't, it won't be the end of the world." He later said that he went through the interview with minimal anxiety.

In this case, the anxiety became markedly reduced even though there was no change in the content of the fantasy. The patient changed his attitude about the particular experience. He no longer regarded the situation as catastrophic. In each of the cases, the alleviation of anxiety persisted after the therapy session ended.

TIME PROJECTION

When a patient is upset about a particular situation, he can project himself into the future and imagine the situation months or even years away. By doing so he can derive detachment from, and gain perspective on, an event currently disturbing him.

Beck (1967) previously described the technique of alleviating pessimism in depressed patients by inducing them to have more realistic fantasies about the future. A. A. Lazarus (1968) described a similar technique which he labeled "time projection." In the following cases, this technique was used to counter a patient's unreasonable reactions to an event.

A thirty-year-old patient became anxious upon learning that his newborn child had a hernia that might require a minor operation. He was so preoccupied with this problem that he was unable to concentrate on anything else. In the interview, he started to catastrophize, not only about the psychological trauma that the operation would entail for the child, but also about other physical disasters that might result from the surgery. The therapist then asked him to imagine what the situation would be in six months. He had the following fantasy: "The baby is sitting in the family group. He has a bandage around his groin, but otherwise he seems okay. Occasionally he seems to have a twinge of pain."

The therapist then suggested that the patient imagine the situation in three years, and he had the following fantasy: "The child is now perfectly healthy, and I can picture him playing with other children." After discussing his fantasies, the patient's anxiety about the possible operation disappeared.

An attractive thirty-six-year-old woman was obsessed with the idea that her husband might be unfaithful. She viewed this as a catastrophe: "I couldn't go on if I discovered that my husband was unfaithful." The therapist then said, "Let's suppose that you do discover that your husband is unfaithful. Try to imagine what your reaction would be immediately, one week later, and six months later." She then reported the following sequence of fantasies:

Immediate reaction: "I feel terrible and I also am furious at him. I think he has a hell of a nerve. I deserve better treatment than this and I tell him so."

One week later: "I am still furious at him, but I begin to make some plans about my future."

Six months later: "I am now able to realize that I'm an attractive woman and that I can start a new marriage. A lot of men are interested in me. I am attractive and other men notice me. My husband is sorry about what he has done and comes crawling back. But I'm not sure that I want him back. I think I'll take my time and decide whether I want to continue the marriage."

After experiencing and reporting her fantasies, the patient felt better: She had a marked lessening of obsessive worrying about her husband's possible infidelity. She also felt closer and more loving toward him.

SYMBOLIC IMAGES

By using symbolic images, the therapist can suggest adaptive behavior in a more convincing way. One patient had been unable to write for the past three years. Previously, her writing had brought her a great deal of pleasure. When she started to write, she would have thoughts that her talent was gone forever.

In the office, the therapist asked the patient to begin writing whatever came into her mind. After writing several lines, she put the pencil down.

PATIENT: I can't do it. I really can't. Nothing I write is any good.

THERAPIST: The important thing is to just write something out. It's not important whether it's good or not—but to write.

PATIENT: [*After writing a few more lines*] This is shit. It's really not good. I really can't write.

THERAPIST: Don't pay attention to the quality, just the quantity. Write till you get twenty lines of writing.

PATIENT: But if it's not good, why bother to write it? Nothing will come.

THERAPIST: Writing is similar to pumping water. When a pump has not been used for three years, a great deal of rust and dirt accumulate. You have to pump water through it for a while until the dirty water runs through. What you have been doing is just that—when you start to pump after three years and you see the water comes through brown, you conclude because it's not clear, it's not good, so you turn it off. But what you have to do is let the water run until it begins to run free and clear again. The point is not quality, but quantity of writing. Give yourself a certain number of lines to write and evaluate them later. Many professional writers can't evaluate their work until a certain amount of time has passed after the actual writing. You might want to have the image of pumping water when you start to write.

The patient reported that it was indeed helpful to visualize water gushing out of a pump when she started to write.

A patient can use a variety of visual symbols to modify old images. When one patient had an image of being attacked by others, he used the symbolic image of a shield to protect him. Another visualized a medallion that warded off all evil.

DECATASTROPHIZING THE IMAGE

The therapist can push the patient to state the most extreme aspect of his fearful imagery, and then guide him through discussion to see even this outcome as less catastrophic then he had imagined.

PATIENT: I keep getting an image of myself having a heart attack.

THERAPIST: What happens after you have the heart attack?

PATIENT: I see myself dying and helpless. That's all I can see. I feel it is a premonition or ESP. Something like that.

THERAPIST: Do you have these images and nothing happens?

PATIENT: Yes, I have them all the time and nothing happens.

THERAPIST: We've seen dozens of patients with these images, and rarely does the imagined event ever occur. I suggest you keep careful track of your images and see what happens.

PATIENT: But what if it does happen?

THERAPIST: The fantasy is consistently worse than the reality. I had an interesting situation a couple of years ago. This patient had a recurring frightening image. He owns a business. In his fantasy one of his key employees dies. He sees the business go downhill and he's forced to do things that he can't do; he then falls apart and has to be hospitalized. In the fantasy he loses his business and his freedom. Well, after about six months in treatment, believe it or not, it actually happened. One of his key managers died. And almost nothing else that he saw in his images happened. It didn't occur to him that other employees could take over tasks and that he could handle this better than he thought he could. He had overlooked in his fantasy these latent positive aspects—that is, the rescue factor. Fantasy is nearly always worse than the reality when an event occurs. The point is not to treat fantasies as real data.

PATIENT: So, if by some chance I did have a heart attack, that wouldn't necessarily mean I would die.

THERAPIST: No, it wouldn't.

Usually the anxious person's fantasy stops at the point when the feared incident occurs. He does not predict the natural consequences of this incident but instead exaggerates its proportions and believes the pain will remain forever.

A medical student, with a fear of speaking in front of his classmates and appearing foolish, said "I could never live down such an experience." Rather than accept the patient's fears at face value, the therapist began questioning him about precisely what might happen if the young man's *worst* fears came true and he *did* appear ridiculous before his peers. Would his career be ruined? Would his family disown him? Would he feel devastated? For how long? And then what? During the questioning, the student realized that he was endowing the public-speaking situation with a disproportionate significance.

The therapist did not attempt to dissuade the young man from his prediction that the talk would go poorly; to have done so would have unnecessarily risked damaging his future credibility in the patient's eyes. On the other hand, through his style of questioning, the therapist conveyed his belief that the patient's discomfort and embarrassment, however intense, would not last long and would be tolerable.

The student's subsequent presentation to the class was poorly organized (perhaps due to his anxiety); and although he felt disheartened for a few days afterward, he did not perceive the affair as a catastrophe. Prior to the next talk, he experienced less anticipatory anxiety and reported feeling more comfortable during the actual presentation as well.

A number of writers, including Bertrand Russell, have recommended that, to relieve fear, a person should focus on and accept the worst possible outcome. The patient is usually reluctant to consider the worst out of the belief that if the feared event is talked about, his anxiety will increase. Initially, the patient's anxiety may increase, but after the worst has been discussed, the patient nearly always feels better.

One belief that prevents a patient from facing the worst is that talking or fantasizing about a feared event will actually bring it about. However, once the issues have been discussed, this belief rapidly disappears.

A patient afraid of being killed in an accident was asked to try *not* to think of his fear. However, he was only able to forget about his anxiety for just a few minutes. This led into a discussion about why it was important to face it rather than shutting it off.

Another idea that can be central to avoiding the issue is: "If I no longer *catastrophize* about this, then the feared event will occur." A person can be told that after facing the worst, his anxiety will be lessened and he will actually be better prepared to prevent the feared event from occurring.

Patients frequently use a personalized strategy to prevent themselves from thinking or imaging through a feared scenario. Their attempts at "thought stoppage," however, are usually unsuccessful. Instead of resolving the problem, the patient achieves only premature closure, and the thoughts reappear even stronger. To reach premature closure, patients often tell themselves: "This is stupid." These global, childish words arrest their thinking processes—but only temporarily. When a patient describes his concerns as "silly," "stupid," "dumb," "not important," or if he uses other similar expressions, the therapist should regard this as a signal to inquire further into the issue.

One method of alleviating anxiety that people have developed in childhood is the "so what if?" technique, which in effect is using decatastrophizing imaging. The therapist here has to be willing to discuss fully the consequences of a patient's worst fears, be it the death of a child, going insane, ending up on Skid Row, or being horribly disfigured. The therapist needs to wait until he has established a collaborative relationship before he uses this strategy, as it can backfire. One patient, for example, had a fear of being homosexual. The therapist's attempt to use the strategy "So what if you are a homosexual?" backfired. The patient would not return for therapy because he believed the therapist was convinced he was a homosexual.

The "so what if?" strategy is almost a cognitive-flooding procedure. For this reason, the therapist has to make sure that there is enough time for the patient to process the material and have some reduction in anxiety. A good policy is for the therapist to schedule an extended session for doing this.

The emphasis in this procedure is for the patient to see whether he can learn to accept and tolerate the experience he fears. The therapist stresses that the feared outcome is unlikely and that the patient still has some choice over how the situation turns out. To the patient, for example, who had a fear of ending up on Skid Row, the therapist pointed out that even if he did end up there (a low probability), he could work to get himself out of it (a high probability).

Another aspect of the probability of catastrophe about which patients need information is the "rescue" factor. Patients fail to realize that for every danger there are factors that could offset its potential. For example, people who are afraid of getting cancer do not recognize or accept that there are medical and surgical ways to cure or arrest many forms of cancer. People who are afraid of being attacked discount the idea that passers-by might help them or that the police could come to their rescue.

At times, the patient may be supplied with a rescue factor. One woman was afraid of having a panic attack and becoming helpless; she was given a prescription for one sedative tablet which she could take to induce sleep until the symptoms wore off, if she did have such an attack. She never needed to resort to this remedy.

IMAGES AND THOUGHTS

Undesirable visual images often stimulate verbal cognitions. For example, an image of an automobile accident may be followed by a series of automatic thoughts: "What if that happened to me? It could happen if I'm not constantly on guard against it. Even then, something mechanical could go wrong, like a blowout or a brake failure." This type of reflective thinking eventually increases one's anxiety, causing more frightening images to arise.

The identification of this cognitive process is a positive step toward gaining mastery. Patients can use the various techniques discussed in this chapter to desensitize themselves to an image. Patients can also consciously shape their cognitive responses to the image, by reviewing the facts of the situation, by substituting a positive image, which they may have rehearsed in advance, and finally by letting the image fade away like the other many innocuous thoughts and images that flow in and out of the mind.

FACILITATING CHANGE IN INDUCED IMAGES

The patient can use imagery induction to gradually shape an anxious fantasy into a neutral or positive image. Because it is often difficult for patients to do this, the therapist may begin by having them modify certain negative aspects of an image (such as someone's negative reaction to them) and then gradually reshape more elements. Any of the following metaphor-based methods may be used to communicate the idea of changing the fantasy:

1. Television set: The patient changes channels, tuning in and out of certain aspects of the fantasy.

2. Movie set: The patient takes over a movie set and redirects the action, even changing props or cutting lines.
3. Drawing or painting: The patient sees the imagery as a painting, blotting out certain portions and bringing others into sharper focus.

The therapist can suggest a fantasy that is more adaptive than the patient's fantasy (or, in some cases, than his actual behavior). A patient who imagined that he would lose all his money was asked to fantasize a specific course of action in which he was able to redirect the unfortunate outcome by his efforts. He found this fantasy brought him relief.

In another case, induced imagery was used to facilitate more assertive behavior. A thirty-five-year-old woman with teenage children was still unable to speak to her father in an assertive way. She recounted an incident a week previously when her father had criticized her at length. He ended his criticisms by saying, "Why don't you bring up your children better so that they show more respect for you?" Up to the time of the session, she still felt hurt by this exchange. The therapist suggested that she have a fantasy of the same event, except that she would assertively tell her father that she refused to discuss this issue with him.

She did this and felt better afterward. However, her fantasy stirred up further guilt and anxiety, which served as a focus for more intensive discussion of how to deal with her father on a mature level. Subsequently, she handled her father much more effectively when he criticized her.

SUBSTITUTING POSITIVE IMAGERY

The therapist works closely with each patient to find what type of imagery he finds most pleasant, comfortable, or relaxing—perhaps a scene in the country, in a forest, at the beach, or in a special room—and to develop a positive image which he can use as a coping device. Such images may be used as a diversionary tactic. When a patient experiences anxiety-producing imagery, he can first use a "stop" technique and then recall the positive imagery he has developed and practiced. Positive imagery has also been used when patients have trouble sleeping; the emphasis is on a rhythmical, and relaxing imagery.

In developing positive imagery, the therapist pays attention to all the sensual modalities: taste, smell, hearing, touch, vivid visual details. The following is an example of the type of imagery the therapist can use:

Imagine yourself on a crisp spring day. You walk into a forest, where you have been before. The sky is blue. Several clouds are floating above the high branches of trees. You find a path. You feel happy and very relaxed. Twigs and branches crack as you walk down the path. You see a small stream ahead. You remove your shoes and socks and step into it. The cold water feels invigorating on your feet, and your feet tingle as you step over rocks and across the stream. At the other side is lush, green meadow. You can hear birds singing, short rhythmic pure whistles, which you try to imitate. The sweet smell of grass is in the air. You can almost taste the freshness of spring. You see a large oak tree ahead and you walk to it and lean against the rough bark of the trunk. You feel the soft moss under you and against your bare feet. Looking up, you see patches of leaves rustling, and patches of blue sky with the white clouds floating by. You breathe slowly and deeply. You feel completely calm and safe——just enjoy this scene for a few minutes.

Fantasizing this scene at home, a patient usually finds that it becomes more relaxing and vivid with practice.

SUBSTITUTING CONTRASTING IMAGERY

The patient can use the context of a feared image to develop a contrasting outcome. A woman with images of her baby dying developed a substitute image of seeing her baby grown and graduating from college, and learned to substitute it for the image of her baby dead in the cradle.

Because the patient's image is usually of some danger lurking in the immediate future, he can imagine the feared event not occurring. A woman afraid of flying imagined herself arriving safely at her destination while still on route to the airport. A man fearful of a heart attack imagined himself finishing a marathon race in great health. And a man fearful of freezing up while talking to his boss imagined himself speaking to him in a calm and friendly way after their business meeting.

EXAGGERATION

Exaggerating images is another technique. One patient was fearful of how she would perform in a workshop she was presenting. In her exaggerated image, all the important people in her field were at the workshop. She imagined the audience becoming hostile, yelling and throwing objects at her. A patient fearful of losing money on a business deal imagined himself panhandling as a result of going broke on this deal. And a patient, fearful that others would find out he failed a licensing exam, imagined his story appearing on the front page of the newspaper and being featured on television and radio programs. In all three cases, pushing past the limits of the fears allowed the patients to put their own fears in perspective and consequently to lower them.

This procedure also works well in cases where a patient has images of harming himself or others. The therapist emphasizes that thoughts do not immediately lead to actions. And he points out that by exaggerating one's thoughts and images, one can put them in perspective and see that one has some choice both about their content and about which ones to act on.

A woman had images of stabbing her children. Her attempts to stop these images were ineffective and caused more anxiety. In the office, the therapist had her imagine stabbing her children, her husband, her friends, neighbors, and eventually everyone in the whole city. The instruction not to stop with her children but to carry this fantasy to an extreme was effective in stopping the images. Several times her fear of the images reoccurred because she had reverted to stopping her thoughts. In addition to the use of the technique of exaggeration, therapy also focused on her fear of expressing anger.

Often the patient's image does not show the feared event actually happening but shows what will happen right before the dreaded consequence. In such a case, it can help to push the patient through the feared event. A patient was fearful of having a head-on car crash. In fantasy he pushed this imagery beyond the crash to his death and what that would be like. He said he felt calm and peaceful. This procedure helped him diminish his anxiety, and he stopped having recurring anxious dreams.

COPING MODELS

Another version of coping imagery is to have patients imagine a person they know coping with an anxiety-producing situation. The patient with a fear of playing the piano in public can imagine his teacher performing and coping with the adverse reaction of the audience. A more extended version of this imagery involves the patient's imagining himself to be someone who is supremely skilled at a particular activity; for example, he could imagine himself to be Leonard Bernstein performing. A person with social anxiety can imagine himself as Johnny Carson, Mike Douglas, or Dinah Shore. This is a version of fixed-role therapy (Kelly 1963) or what Arnold Lazarus (1978) calls "exaggerated role taking." It is practiced in the office first; later, the patient practices it outside.

IMAGERY TO REDUCE THREAT

When a person is afraid of an encounter with a person who seems intimidating, the therapist may use imagery that strips the encounter of its fearsome or awe-inspiring aspects. A woman dreaded attending a court session because she felt intimidated when she imagined seeing the lawyers and other dignitaries in their authoritative uniforms or three-piece suits. She was able to overcome her awe by imagining them in tennis shorts and polo shirts with amusing sayings on the shirts. A musical performer believed the audience was waiting to catch him in any mistake he might make; he changed the image so that the audience was sitting at little tables, drinking beer, conversing, and not paying close attention to his performance but just enjoying it as part of the generally pleasant atmosphere. Another patient was fearful of an oral exam he had to take. He imagined himself as a benevolent lion and the questioners as lambs. In his coping imagery, he saw himself showing the lambs mercy by not eating them alive.

Other types of coping imagery can be used as well. In one variation, patients imagine going through the feared situation with the therapist along with them. For example, one patient who was afraid of going out in crowds imagined going to a shopping mall with the therapist and described to the therapist both the scene and what she was feeling. She practiced this imagery in the office first, describing the situation as if the therapist were in it with her. Later, she imagined doing it on her own. When the patient was actually in the situation, she imagined describing the scene to the therapist: "Well, I'm feeling anxious. Now I'm going out the door." And so on. This is a good diversion technique for some patients as they imagine performing a task.

ESCAPING A WORSE ALTERNATIVE

One effective variation is to have the patient imagine escaping a worse scenario by engaging in the feared image (A. A. Lazarus 1978). A woman fearful of going for a job interview imagined herself being chased by a motorcycle gang; she escaped them by ducking into the place she had to go for the interview. During the therapy this image was developed in great detail and the patient showed and expressed great relief at being able to escape the gang by going into the job interview. In nearly every case, the therapist can help a patient develop a worse alternative that can be avoided by escaping into the feared event. When the patient has his feared image, he is to go back and re-create the worse alternative and see the feared image as a way to escape it.

MIXED STRATEGY

In actual clinical practice, the therapist uses a mixture of these techniques. One thirty-three-year-old woman was afraid of driving on a particular freeway. The therapist first used repeated images, which brought out her fear of dying on a specific freeway at a specific time. A discussion of the odds of dying in a traffic accident followed. Then an image of herself as an eighty-year-old woman driving happily on the freeway was used and reviewed repeatedly. When she said that she was really afraid of being hit by a truck, she was given an imagery to practice in which her car was protected by an invisible shield; anyone who would hit her would simply bounce back. During this image she said, "I see now the real problem is I have no confidence in my driving." She then imagined herself going off for an intense four-week training program in Washington, D.C., where she was trained to be one of the best freeway drivers in America. This was followed by imagery of driving confidently in the Indianapolis 500 race.

She then was able to imagine herself driving on the freeway with considerably less anxiety. She said she still felt considerably relieved when she got home after driving the freeway. She was asked to imagine a chemical spill in her neighborhood which she got on the freeway to escape. The further she went on the freeway away from her home, the safer she would be. She said she could do it but would still dislike it. She then was asked to imagine a time when she felt happy while driving or moving in some way. She had an image of riding her bike on the beach, and she then imagined driving on the freeway with the same feelings she had riding her bike on the beach. She was then instructed to use this imagery when she was actually driving on the freeway. Indeed, the images helped her to cope with the actual driving.

Future Therapy

Imagery can be used to help a patient gain mastery over his future. The anxious patient dreads the future, to which he takes a reactive approach, and usually hopes just to survive. A way to help counteract this mental set is to work with the patient to develop a plan where he can create the type of future he wants. F. T. Melges's (1982) systematic form of future therapy can be adapted to cognitive therapy and used with the anxious patient. The following guidelines are used in this strategy:

Wait until the patient's anxiety is manageable before developing a future plan. A patient who is too anxious has great difficulty envisioning a positive future.

First, have the patient choose a date three months in the future. A date around a holiday or a meaningful day such as the first of January is helpful. Then ask the patient to imagine what he would like to have happen by that date. He should imagine getting up and going through the day with his new attitudes and behavior. He can note what areas give him trouble and which ones he has mastered.

The therapist should interview the patient in the present as if he were in the future. The therapist asks what he has accomplished, how he views his problems, and how he has modified his beliefs. The patient's future can be divided into external and internal goals. One patient, for example, in his external life wanted to have finished some specific projects on his job, made some new friends, bought new clothes, and be in the process of planning a trip. His internal goals included being more accepting of his flaws, more assertive, and a better reality tester.

The patient's internal goals can be placed on a scale of 0 to 10. The patient can estimate where he is currently on the scale and where he plans to be in three months. In developing the future images, Melges suggests that the patient visualize a scene that represents movement on this scale. The therapist asks the patient to make up some image to demonstrate this. One patient who wanted to be able to handle criticism better imagined being severely criticized by her boss and taking the criticism calmly, in a nonreactive way.

The patient needs to choose goals that are under his control ("I'm accepting my wife more" versus "My wife is much nicer to me"). The patient is also advised to choose realistic goals. When the patient chooses unrealistic goals or goals that involve changing other people, the therapist can discuss how the patient's expectations can set him up to experience failure.

After the patient has developed three-month goals, the therapist can help him develop ways to reach these goals. A major part of this program consists of having the patient imagine how he will spend the target day three months in the future. He practices this image daily. The patient is also asked to visualize this image on a spontaneous basis whenever possible.

In addition to using imagery, the patient is encouraged to develop the feelings associated with the desired end goals. Melges suggests that the patient use positive childhood images that evoke the same quality of feelings as the ones in the goal. The patient should choose childhood images where there were no adults around. One patient, for example, wanted to have more enjoyment in his life and tied this desire to feelings he had playing stick ball as a youth. Another patient, who wanted to be more self-confident, tied this future image to the same feeling of self-confidence he had when he got his first job as a paper boy.

The therapist stresses that one of the key ingredients in creating the future is repetition. Repetition causes one to focus on the goal and generate interest in creating it. Melges gives a variety of situations where the patient can use outside stimuli to cue himself to rehearse the goal image: these include such cues as self-stroking (touching his beard or hair), colors associated with goals (blue with calm), specific times ("On getting up, I'll think of my goals"), and behavior ("I'll think of my goal when I open my car door").

Symbols and slogans can also be used to help the patient focus on the goal. A discussion of the means used by advertisers to pursuade people can be helpful.

THERAPIST: Did you notice the billboard at the corner of Wilshire and Western? And the one a couple of blocks west on Wilshire? Both billboards use the same principles. First, there is the power of repetition. The advertisers spent thousands of dollars on these billboards because they know that people going to work day after day will look at them. Second, they use symbols and slogans. The one on the corner has a picture of a car battery with "Las Vegas" written on it. The slogan is "A big charge for a little charge." The one down the street has a picture of a loaf of bread with "Palm Springs" written on it. The slogan is "More loafing for less bread." You can use these principles of repetition, symbol, and slogan to sell yourself on reaching your goals.

The patient can be asked to develop a symbol of the goal he wants to reach. One patient wanted to be able to tolerate ambiguity better. He chose the telegram as a symbol, which he then used to cue himself to be more accepting of ambiguity.

The patient can also develop slogans that help him to keep his goal in mind. One patient's goal was to stop the compulsive spending that had put him in debt and which caused him great anxiety. He developed the slogans "Anxiety-free in '83" and "Poor no more in '84," which he wrote on blue and green 3-by-5-inch cards that he carried with him. He also wrote the slogans on posters that he kept at home. The different colors were significant. He associated green with the control of his spending, and blue with anxiety management.

Goal Rehearsal

The rehearsal of a patient's desired goal is one of the most common uses of imagery in cognitive therapy. A standard practice is to have the patient imagine new, frightening behavior, such as going for a job interview, or behavior that he has previously been avoiding, such as calling up a friend. The patient first imagines this behavior in the office and later performs it as a homework assignment (see chapter 14).

The rationale given to a patient is that he can practice in a safe place first in order to foresee potential problems and prepare to handle them. For example, one patient imagined going to a doctor's office: he imagined a variety of negative reactions from the visit and how he would handle them. This practice gave him a cognitive map to follow.

Many of the techniques and strategies of cognitive therapy employ imagery as an adjunct procedure. For example, patients who are practicing assertiveness can do so first in their imagination.

Another use of goal-rehearsal imagery is in the coping package worked out in therapy. Patients here imagine a variety of coping strategies. One patient developed the following coping package: "When I give the speech, I will practice beforehand. I will be task-relevant. If I start to get anxious, I will talk to myself to calm down. I will talk slowly." He practiced imagining this before he actually used it *in vivo*.

Therapist and patient can use the patient's imagery of the future as a guide to which of the goals the patient needs the most work on. The therapist can use the technique of future autobiography (Melges 1982), where the patient responds as if the target date has arrived ("Looking back on the last three months, what was the most difficult situation you ran into?"). The therapist can also have the patient role-play his future self with his present self to help him spot potential difficulties and see that he has a say in how he directs his future.

The patient is asked to get a notebook and keep track of his progress towards his goals. He is told that to tell too many people about his goals could weaken them. An exception to this rule is a friend or relative who is unconditionally supportive. One patient developed what she called a "credit union" with a friend. They would reinforce and support each other in reaching their goals.

The therapist helps the patient develop a feedback system so that the patient can self-correct if he is not working toward his goals. The patient often has strategies that get in the way of completing goals. One patient tried so hard to impress the therapist that she got tired of the goals before they were completed. Another patient became so involved in daily and weekly crises that she did not have the time or energy to focus on her goals. In both cases, the therapist helped the patients become aware of how they were getting in the way of themselves so that they could correct themselves. The most common problem a patient has is letting what others think of him get in the way of his goals. Through imagery and other cognitive/behavioral procedures, one can learn to overcome this self-imposed obstacle.

Chapter 13

Modifying the Affective

Component

The experience of anxiety is usually so highly distressing to a patient that it often generates a second level of fear (see chapter 6). In therapy, a patient eventually learns to reduce unpleasant feelings by correcting distorted cognitions. This approach works best in the context of the therapy session; patients need time, practice, and coaching before they can use this technique on their own. For this reason, cognitive therapists train patients in a variety of methods that help them cope directly with the immediate affective state. The goal is to provide symptom relief as fast as possible. The methods used can be broken down into five strategies: accepting the feelings, action strategies, self-observation, emotional review, and owning one's emotions. It is helpful to give patients copies of the "A-W-A-R-E" strategy, which provides specific rules to follow when one becomes anxious (see appendix II, pp. 323–24).

Accepting the Feelings

Accepting the presence of anxiety is crucial. The patient usually wants to avoid or fight anxiety symptoms. In cognitive therapy, he is encouraged instead to accept his symptoms. This strategy is based on the rationale that once anxiety reaches a certain level, the patient can no longer control the symptoms. Paradoxically, by giving up the idea of control, the patient can be taught to control his anxiety. The therapist needs to sell the patient on the idea of accepting (not being resigned to) his anxiety.

THERAPIST: There is literally nothing else that you can be aware of but feelings and sensations. Anything that you experience in life is composed of feelings and sensations. If you're afraid of making a fool of yourself when giving a speech, what you're really afraid of are your sensations of anxiety, self-consciousness, and shame. And if you're afraid of dying in an accident, you're actually afraid of the inferred sensation and panic of being out of control, as well as of the anticipated pain of the injury. By accepting these feelings, you can lessen them.

This approach has certain implications for the patient. Weinberg says, "Knowing that our only fear can be fear of ourselves, of pain of some kind, and this pain through acceptance becomes endurable, helps breed a quiet courage and sensible serenity which in turn prevents many psychosomatic ills from developing in the future" (1973, p. 187).

Patients usually find helpful the idea that all they can fear are feelings, and that acceptance of these feelings makes them bearable. The therapist can stress that one has to accept reality to deal effectively with it. If a person does not accept that he has a broken leg that needs to be set, he can make himself a cripple. But a patient may confuse acceptance with resignation, believing that if he accepts the anxiety, it will escalate and that what he fears most will occur.

The therapist should thus make it clear that acceptance is allowing what exists at the moment to be as it is. Acceptance is acknowledging the existence of an event without placing a judgment or label on it (right/-wrong, good/bad, safe/dangerous). The negative judgments and evaluations the patient places on his anxiety only deepen his distress. For this reason, the patient is encouraged to stop "value-judging" his anxiety.

REDUCING ANXIETY ABOUT ANXIETY

The patient may fear social disapproval or rejection because of his anxiety. He may also fear that he will suffer physical harm or permanent psychological damage, such as loss of control or insanity. The anxiety about the anxiety flows directly from the activation of these fears. For many patients, anxiety about anxiety may be so severe that it prevents them from attempting certain techniques of cognitive therapy. For this reason, the patient must modify his ideas about anxiety.

THERAPIST: Okay. I think we have a pretty good idea of the thoughts that you're having about your anxiety. We have to see about correcting them with more realistic and helpful ideas. I suggest we try role playing. I'll role-play your frightening thoughts about your anxiety, and you role-play with more rational responses. Shall we give it a try?

PATIENT: Okay.

THERAPIST: My anxiety is terribly painful.

PATIENT: Well, you may possibly find out if you actually rate it that it's not as terrible as it seems when you just have a general impression.

THERAPIST: It's intolerable.

PATIENT: Well——I'm having trouble answering that one.

THERAPIST: Okay. You could ask yourself if it is indeed intolerable. If you were having a hot branding iron placed on you, that would indeed be intolerable, and the chances are you would race from the room or do something equally dramatic to alleviate the distress. The fact that you have stayed in this "intolerable" state without taking dramatic action suggests that it's not truly intolerable even though it may be very uncomfortable. . . . Okay, it's back to the role playing. . . . I'll never again get myself into this situation of having this anxiety.

PATIENT: That's irrelevant. In fact, if you manage to get your way through this situation of anxiety, you may be better prepared the next time.

THERAPIST: I'm dying.

PATIENT: It's very unlikely that you're dying. The symptoms of anxiety may make you feel weakness, and you associate this with dying.

THERAPIST: You can also say, "You can test this out by moving around actively." . . . All right, I'm having a heart attack.

PATIENT: This is also extremely unlikely. By moving around actively, you can demonstrate to yourself that your physical condition is fine.

THERAPIST: Okay. That was pretty good. Are there any thoughts that you think you would have trouble answering?

PATIENT: One is, "The anxiety has started and will never stop, it will get worse and worse until I reach the breaking point."

THERAPIST: Well, anxiety generally comes in waves. It has a beginning, a peak, and an end, and even though the waves may recur, there is generally an interval relatively free of symptoms between the waves. Each person seems to have his own pattern and it's possible by exposing himself to a similar situation to be able to time the duration and intensity of the waves of anxiety.

This patient held some of the common attitudes about anxiety. Other attitudes follow, along with ways to answer them:

"This anxiety is preventing me from functioning. I can't deliver my speech, concentrate on the exam, or talk to other people because I'm so anxious." People with high anxiety are still able to perform fairly adequately. A number of public speakers, for instance, have reported that they had extreme terror during their speech although impartial observers considered the delivery and content to be highly competent. Similarly, a person can carry on a coherent conversation with others despite considerable anxiety. However, when one believes that one cannot function because of anxiety, one gives up trying to function.

"Having anxiety means that I'll lose control." It is unlikely that one would lose control as a result of anxiety. The person may become rigid and tense in a counterproductive attempt to control anxiety; he may sense that these controls are not holding and so fear "loss of control." Other more effective ways of containing the anxiety can disprove the idea of losing control.

"I may go crazy." This notion is based on lack of information. Although individuals with severe anxiety may on occasion require special medication, there is no evidence that high anxiety itself causes psychosis. (For detailed discussion of this point, see Raimy 1975.)

REDUCING SHAME ABOUT SHOWING ANXIETY

The patient may experience shame at having exhibiting anxiety in front of others—shame that stems from his belief that he is being judged as childish, weak, foolish, and inferior for exhibiting anxiety. The patient often will think, "I look like a fool. It's awful to appear this way." Because the anxious patient does not readily admit to feeling ashamed, the therapist must inquire about such feelings and demonstrate to the patient that the patient creates these feelings.

THERAPIST: Are there things you were ashamed of in the past and no longer are? Are there things you are ashamed of and others aren't? Are others ashamed of things that you are not ashamed of?

Many patients underestimate the tolerance and acceptance of others and discount their awareness. To counteract this tendency, the patient can find out others' attitudes toward people who show anxiety; usually one finds that others do not take a negative view of such people. The therapist may also inquire whether the patient himself has a low opinion of people who are anxious, as it may well explain why he expects derogatory remarks from others. If this is the case, the patient can modify his opinion.

If the patient adopts an "anti-shame philosophy" toward his anxiety, he can avoid much pain and discomfort. When a patient becomes anxious, for example, he can turn the experience into an anti-shame exercise by telling someone he is anxious, or by disclosing the anxiety he experienced to another person at a later time. If the person pursues this "open-door" policy long enough, the shame will diminish.

The following are common shame-producing thoughts and alternative ways the patient can view these concerns:

"*I'm weak.*" Anxiety is simply a symptom of a problem. The evaluative statement, "I'm weak," is accurate from the standpoint of neither the patient's physical condition nor his psychological condition. In general, "I'm weak," indicates a negative judgment based on society's image of the macho "happy warrior" who is free of anxiety.

"*I'm neurotic.*" Although this notion has been fostered by mental health professionals, the term actually has little validity as a label. The patient merely has a specific symptom which arises in particular situations.

"*Others can tell I'm anxious and are put off by it.*" The anxious patient often believes that others can readily tell that he is anxious, and therefore think less of him. This attitude is expressed in the old saying, "A thief always thinks his hat is on fire." Quite often patients show minimal anxious behavior, but have an exaggerated view of how anxious they appear. A patient can check whether this is true of himself by requesting feedback from observers or through videotaping.

If the person is showing obvious symptoms of anxiety, the therapist discusses the idea that all people do not automatically make negative judgments about anxious persons; and that even if some people do make such judgments, they are not necessarily correct; nor do their opinions automatically translate into negative consequences.

"*No one else gets as anxious as I do.*" When a patient discounts the amount of empathy and understanding other people have for anxiety, the therapist points out that nearly everyone has at times suffered from some anxiety, whether at the beginning of a party or an important meeting. In other words, the therapist normalizes the experience.

"*They will reject me.*" Rarely is a person rejected simply because of anxiety. However, people continually "write off" other individuals for a host of reasons, only one relatively minor one being that the rejected person is anxious.

"*I look ridiculous.*" "Other people may label you as appearing ridiculous; however, it is probably inaccurate and unproductive to label yourself in this way. You can let other people make their own images of you, and then you can deal with those in a mature way."

"Since I have appeared anxious (or blown my speech because of anxiety) nobody will want to be my friend, or associate with me." "This is an empirical question. You can select specific instances in the past when you have appeared anxious or have done poorly and recall which friends you actually lost."

In general, the therapist can tell the patient that it is not shameful to be anxious; it is simply a phenomenon. "If other people want to downgrade you for it, there is nothing to stop them. However, there is no reason for you to buy into their adolescent attitudes." The therapist may also have patients listen to Albert Ellis's cassette tape, "How to Stubbornly Refuse to be Ashamed of Anything."* (In chapter 14, we discuss shame in greater detail.)

The therapist can paraphrase these general ideas or he can have the patient reach this conclusion through a series of questions and answers. The best strategy is to find out what the person is thinking that makes accepting anxiety so difficult. Then the therapist can help the patient to correct the distortion.

NORMALIZING ANXIETY

One way to relieve symptoms is to help the patient become less self-absorbed with anxiety symptoms and to act in spite of them. Presenting to the patient some aspects of the evolutionary model of anxiety discussed earlier can help explain and demystify the symptoms, making them less frightening. One should bear in mind that a large part of cognitive therapy is educational.

THERAPIST: Anxiety consists of those symptoms we have talked about—dizziness, light-headedness, tightness in the throat, a variety of palpitations, sweating, and so on. You often start worrying about these symptoms. You then label them as dangerous, a warning that something terrible is about to happen. This creates more anxiety. The more anxious you become, the more the symptoms increase. It becomes circular because you are focusing too much on these symptoms. When you selectively attend to a physical symptom, it becomes stronger.

The symptoms of anxiety are like a headache: if you let them recede into the background while you continue functioning, they usually go away. The symptoms of anxiety are the result of thousands of years of evolution. In prehistoric times, these symptoms represented a physiological response to a real threat. They may have served a survival func-

*This tape is available from the Institute for Rational Living, 45 East 65th Street, New York, NY 10021

tion, preparing the body for action—primal responses such as fight or flight—but these are no longer needed.

A second normalizing approach is:

THERAPIST: Strong emotions like anxiety are not mysterious. They are simply signals from your brain that you need to correct the way you're viewing the world or responding to it. Anxiety is not painful to punish you, but rather to wake you up and get your attention. Your mind is telling you to take the situation seriously. If the pain were not sharp, you might end up ignoring the signals and so not make the necessary choices.

What message is your anxiety trying to send you? There are two possibilities: you need to *act* differently, or you need to *think* differently. When you're anxious, for example, the message is either that you're in danger and should protect yourself, or that you're exaggerating the danger and should think realistically.

Emotional pain is like physical pain: both tell you something is wrong and needs to be corrected. If you ignore either, the pain persists, and the problem usually gets worse. By acknowledging painful emotions, you send the message back to your brain that you realize something is wrong and that you will take care of it. Once you do this, the severity of the pain immediately starts to lessen.

You may try to ignore these emotions because you don't want to admit anything is wrong with you ("I shouldn't be afraid to speak up —I'm a professional," "I shouldn't feel guilty—I didn't do anything wrong"). You are disowning your emotions. But when you take responsibility for how you feel ("I'm making myself anxious"), you can make choices in your favor.

When discussing the general nature of anxiety, the therapist can point out that a certain amount of anxiety, particularly in an unknown situation, is not only appropriate but may even be functional in that it can heighten a person's awareness. In going for a job interview, for example, a certain amount of anxiety is normal and expected; and many stage performers believe that some anxiety before they perform is necessary for a good performance. They do not succumb to anxiety but let it work for them— to give their artistry an edge. In contrast, anxious patients often label even mild levels of anxiety as frightening, perhaps foreshadowing an anxiety attack. The therapist states explicitly that the goal is not to be anxiety-free, but to learn to manage the anxiety and to avoid being overwhelmed by it.

ACTIVE ACCEPTANCE

Patients need to know that acceptance is an active, not a passive, process. One can choose to accept one's anxiety. Choosing to accept it usually gives one a sense of mastery over the experience. At times patients have found helpful a procedure where they welcome the anxiety and ask for more of it. One patient with social anxiety, for example, found it helpful to say to herself, "Hello, anxiety." She would also say hello to her worst fears and to the corresponding possibility: "Hello, I might make a fool of myself," and "Hello, I might not." She found this strategy effective in accepting her anxiety when it appeared.

Admitting one's anxiety to oneself or to others is another way of accepting it. An anxious speaker is often advised to tell the audience that he is anxious, and this advice works. Many patients find it helpful to admit their anxiety problem publicly.

Patients vary in their ability to use the acceptance strategy. Those who are able to make use of it often make quick progress in lessening their anxiety symptoms. For many people, accepting their anxiety allows them to manage the whole problem. One doctor, for example, had to leave several jobs because he was unable to manage his anxiety. He would continually double- and triple-check all of his work. He labeled accepting anxiety as "eating" the anxiety. He found that by staying with the anxiety and not attempting to reduce it he was able to reduce it significantly.

Patients can be encouraged to look at their anxiety in more expanded ways and, if possible, to put it in a new, positive light. The therapist, for example, can point out that by choosing to accept and experience the anxiety the patient can reach higher levels of maturity. No anxiety, no growth.

IDENTIFYING EMOTIONS

Some patients may have trouble correctly identifying a feeling as anxiety and may, for example, call it "stress" or "tension." This problem is easily rectified. A more common problem is the mixed emotions that patients present. The therapist can discuss with a patient the four basic emotions—mad, sad, glad, and scared—and how other emotions are usually a result of some mix of these emotions: for example, hurt is a combination of sad and mad. Many anxious patients have had the glad/scared mix (thrill rides, horror movies). One of the most common mixtures that patients have is scared/mad. It is helpful for the patient to know the nature of his typical emotional mix, so that he can understand and work on both emotions.

One patient became anxious about going away for the weekend and not finishing a report that was due the following Monday. His first step was to get mad at his wife for making him go away in the first place. He then became ashamed of himself for acting so immature. Finally, he felt warmly toward his wife and apologized to her.

Many patients will be highly critical of themselves for having anxiety. This attitude produces sadness, which serves as a distraction from the anxiety and often inhibits it. Many patients swing back and forth between anxiety and depression. The therapist often has to teach the patient how to accept both emotions and how to deal with them constructively.

Action Strategies

Getting the anxious patient to *act* as normal as possible lessens anxiety symptoms.

THERAPIST: Act as if you aren't anxious. Function *with* the anxiety. Slow down if you have to, but keep going. If you're talking, finish your sentences. If you're doing something, keep moving, even though you think you can't. If you're listening, actively listen. If you're reading, read. If you're walking, walk. If you're driving, drive. Although you may act imperfectly, self-consciously, and awkwardly, keep acting.

If you run from the situation, your anxiety will decrease but your fear will increase. If you stay, both your anxiety and fear will eventually decrease.

ACTIVITY SCHEDULES

Some patients are so overwhelmed by anxiety that their normal activities are severely disrupted. One sixty-nine-year-old man, for example, was so consumed with anxiety that he was unable to perform ordinary, every-day functions. He saw the therapist on a daily basis for several weeks until his anxiety could be brought under control. Most of these sessions were spent in constructing activity schedules for the patient.

Chronically anxious patients and patients with great anxiety can benefit from planning their daily activities in detail, with the therapist's assistance.

The schedule provides the patient with a sense of direction and control. As mentioned earlier, the structure is an antidote to the patient's disorganization and feelings of being overwhelmed. The planned activities can also provide a diversion from anxiety-producing thoughts.

The following are guidelines to the development of activity scheules:

1. The therapist has to provide an acceptable rationale for the procedure.
2. The patient should focus on one task at a time and not worry about future tasks. If he finishes one task, he should engage in a pleasurable activity between tasks.
3. The goal of the procedure is for the patient to engage in activities, not to perform them perfectly.
4. The planning is done with some flexibility: if an unexpected event occurs, the patient may change his plans.
5. Activity that absorbs the patient's interest and concentration is best.
6. The activity schedule should be related to the patient's normal activities.
7. The activity should not be too specific or too general.

Developing activity schedules can be a difficult task. The therapist may have to spend the whole session with an anxious patient to schedule just one day. At a later point, scheduling is done by the patient, who is instructed to schedule one day at a time—the last activity scheduled being the scheduling of the following day.

INCREASING TOLERANCE FOR ANXIETY

One therapeutic goal is to develop the patient's tolerance for anxiety; increased tolerance decreases the amount of anxiety *about* anxiety. In response to thinking, "I can't stand this," the patient is encouraged to instruct himself, "I'm strong enough to take this." A self-challenging statement of "Who says I can't stand this?" can be helpful, or "I will time how long I can tolerate this and gradually increase the time." The therapist may state, "With practice, people can learn to increase their tolerance for nearly all forms of discomfort."

The therapist tells patients that by increasing their tolerance for anxiety, they also are strengthening and innoculating themselves against future anxiety. By observing that they actually are able to tolerate great anxiety without becoming agitated, patients develop an increased sense of mastery which can in itself arrest the spiraling effects of anxiety.

In coping with anxiety, patients frequently resort to maladaptive behavior patterns, such as smoking, overeating, excessive drinking, or excessive masturbation. Patients can increase their tolerance by increasing the time between feeling anxiety and yielding to habitual escape mechanisms. Similarly, even postponing the use of an adaptive counteractive measure (such as diversion) when they feel apprehensive helps patients increase their tolerance.

The rationale of increasing anxiety tolerance must be presented to a patient who persistently avoids anxiety-producing situations and so misses a chance to test unrealistic thoughts. The therapist explains that plunging into the experience will help him become desensitized—this is the hard/easy choice. And while avoiding short-term pain is tempting (the easy/hard choice), it is better to consider the long-term consequences of avoidance.

The therapist, when working with this problem, can keep in mind the words of Epicurus: "Pain is never unbearable or unending, so long as you remember its limitations and do not indulge in fanciful exaggeration." The therapist can point out that if pain does become intolerable, the body will die. The therapist can construct a pain hierarchy, with having one's fingernails pulled out at 99, and see where the person puts his anxiety pain level.

It is worth noting that patients can often break the hold of severe anxiety states by taking a cold shower or a brisk run. In the office we have often been able to break into such states by using shocking, dramatic, and unconventional language, as Albert Ellis (1962) has advised. The therapist has to check that this does not harm the therapeutic relationship.

ALCOHOL, STIMULANTS, DIET, STRESS

The anxious patient is cautioned against ingesting excessive amounts of stimulants, such as coffee, tea, or cola. For some patients, even a single cup of coffee can produce physiological arousal, which is often mislabeled as anxiety; and a chain reaction begins.

The anxious patient should also curtail excessive use of alcohol. The idea is to act normally without this aid. Many patients drink to control their anxiety. The drinking, however, makes the patient more susceptible to anxiety and anxietylike symptoms: again, a chain reaction may take effect.

The patient is cautioned against going too long without eating. Many of the symptoms of low blood sugar (hypoglycemia) are similar to those of anxiety and consequently can be mislabeled as anxiety. Low blood sugar can also make a person more susceptible to anxiety. If the anxious patient suspects low blood sugar, he is advised to take some protein—a glass of milk or a hard-boiled egg, for instance. Finally, stress, fatigue, or lack of sleep can increase arousal and predispose the patient to anxiety states.

MALADAPTIVE COPING BEHAVIOR

Often secondary problems—such as alcohol abuse or overeating—that originated as devices for coping with anxiety, become autonomous. In such cases, therapy focuses simultaneously on the maladaptive behavior and the anxiety. (For more specific ways of working on dependent and maladaptive behavior, see Beck and Emery 1977.) A general strategy is for patients to increase their tolerance of the anxiety by postponing the maladaptive behavior. The goal is to improve, not settle for immediate comfort.

Interventions include graded task assignments, structured success experience, assertiveness training, and assigned pleasure and mastery experiences. Patients with these secondary problems are taught how behavioral chaining develops; they are strongly encouraged to devise strategies to break such chains, with particular stress placed upon the value of delay tactics and alternative behavior. For example, one patient, when anxious, often headed straight for a bar. He would drink until his anxiety was reduced. This behavior pattern reinforced his maladaptive thinking, "I can't cope," and actually made this thinking pleasurable. Since he was strongly attached to the habit, he was instructed to engage in an active alternative behavior before permitting himself to go to a bar. He learned by direct experience that interrupting the behavioral chain at this point prevented the response chain from running off automatically and provided him with time out to change his cognitions as well.

Self-Observation

An effective way for the patient to reduce anxiety is to engage and enhance his observing self. The observing self is nonjudgmental and not caught up in the subjective drama of the anxiety. Self-awareness allows the patient to gain perspective on the situation and to see it in a larger context.

The awareness brings the person back to the present. Anxiety is a result of projecting oneself into a dangerous situation in the future. As long as the person is in the present, there is no danger. Self-awareness gives one a greater sense of control over the anxiety. Rather than thinking, "I am anxious," one sees, "I have anxiety."

As mentioned previously, the collaboration in cognitive therapy is between the therapist's and patient's observing selves. Many of the techniques and leads in cognitive therapy are geared to help form this collaboration. Probing for the patient's observing self helps to counteract his anxiety. "Why?" questions ("Why are you anxious?") provoke more thinking, while "How?" and "What?" questions ("How are you making yourself anxious?" and "What are you thinking?") provoke greater awareness.

The shape of the question or lead determines a patient's answer or response. "How come you're so mistrusting?" is likely to elicit reasons and justifications; while "You seem to be mistrusting" has a greater chance of increasing self-awareness. Similarly, a homework assignment where the patient is asked to take the role of "investigator" or "explorer" is more effective than simply having the patient perform an activity.

The therapist has to be aware of awareness. When the therapist explores early development issues or past trauma, the patient's observing self has to look at this material to restructure dysfunctional beliefs effectively. One must look at cultural distortions from the same perspective ("One needs status items or absolute success to be happy"): the patient has to detach himself from the belief to see it clearly.

One of the ways the patient can detach or distance himself from his thoughts, feelings, and actions is to "watch myself watch myself." In extremely anxiety, the person does this automatically when he depersonalizes. Doing this on purpose can also effectively lower anxiety.

A thirty-five-year-old woman, with fear of authority figures, became anxious when her boss was rude to her. On one occasion she started to get anxious, but was able to catch her thought ("He hates me and wants to get rid of me"). Her awareness allowed her to see the distortion and set the stage for substituting a more accurate thought ("He's being rude to everyone today. That's his problem. I don't have to take it personally"). Here follow some ways by which the therapist can help the patient learn to become a better self-observer.

POSITIVE SELF-INSTRUCTION

While the anxious patient cannot always control his feelings, he can direct what he tells himself. For example, the patient should tell himself, "Be alert" instead of "Don't be anxious." By focusing on what he can do (watch his anxiety), the patient is able to take away his sense of helplessness. It is important to put these self-instructions in a positive format:

THERAPIST: When you suggest to yourself, "Don't be nervous" or, "What if I'm nervous?" you are in a sense setting yourself up to be nervous. Negative statements usually contain the part you don't want. If you tell someone, "Don't spill the milk," he is more likely to spill the milk than if you put your suggestion in a positive form, "Carry the milk carefully."

When not anxious, the patient can practice the technique of self-awareness, to be prepared when an anxiety state does occur. Many patients respond positively to training in "staying tuned in to what you're doing when you're doing it."

The patient can also do a series of exercises in which he sits and practices telling himself, "I am not my body—I have a body," "I am not my thoughts—I have thoughts," and "I am not my emotions—I have emotions." Thus, the patient comes to identify more with his awareness instead of with what he may be thinking, acting, or doing at any one moment.

GRAPHS AND DIARIES

The therapist often has a patient graph the amount of anxiety he experiences during a particular period. He places *subjective units of discomfort* (from 0 to 100) on one axis, and *time* on the other, usually in half-hour intervals. He is also asked to record such situational variables as place and precipitating events. The graph provides the therapist with important information and demonstrates to the patient that anxiety is *time-limited* and generally related to external situations. This counters the patient's tendency, while in the midst of an anxiety reaction, to think that the anxiety will never cease.

The patient may also be asked to keep a diary to record the efforts he makes to face situations that he has previously avoided. In this case, he notes the situation, the degree of anxiety in the beginning, the time spent in the situation, and the degree of anxiety at the end. The purpose of both diary and graph is to produce a more objective view of one's anxiety symptoms. Self-monitoring, one of the more useful therapeutic tools, provides a simple way for the patient to develop a sense of mastery over anxiety. In addition, data gathered in self-monitoring exercises are put to use in a variety of other techniques.

CONCENTRATION (OR DISTRACTION) EXERCISES

Concentration is a common technique used for coping with anxiety. The therapist first demonstrates this technique in the office. He asks the patient to rate the current degree of anxiety; if the patient is not anxious at the moment, he can imagine an anxiety-producing situation or hyperventilate by taking forty breaths a minute for several minutes. The patient is then instructed to focus on an item in the office, such as a window shade, and to describe it in detail. What is its size? What is it made of? Is there any dust on it? What color is it? Is it colored differently where the sun hits it? What would its texture be like to touch? What would it taste like? Does it appear fragile? And so on.

The person should label the anxiety-producing thought in some way, say, "predicting," or "what if." When each anxiety thought comes to mind, he attempts to view it in a detached manner, and says "predicting." He then focuses his attention back onto the object he is looking at. After he has done this, the patient re-rates the degree of anxiety, which has usually diminished to some extent. If it has not, the therapist tries again with a different form of diversion.

If the office exercise is successful, the patient is asked to practice a concentration technique between sessions using his anxiety as a cue to begin a concentration activity. The concentration can take the form of such activities as reading, chewing gum, taking a walk, talking on the telephone, sucking on hard candy, or observing various features of his immediate environment. The patient should focus on external reality in order to break the focus on his self-created, internal reality, and should simply label his thoughts.

RELAXATION METHODS

Relaxation can be an effective form of self-awareness and can also be used to demonstrate to the patient a degree of mastery over symptoms. Standard relaxation techniques can be used. M. R. Goldfried and G. C. Davison (1976) outline a variety of active relaxation exercises. Their suggestions include presenting relaxation as a skill to be learned, warning patients that they may feel "strange" or afraid of losing control, or telling patients they are ultimately in control of the exercise and are free to move around in the chair in order to feel comfortable. They also suggest that a therapist should convey to a patient the mental set "Let go"—in order paradoxically, as we have said, to gain control.

We have also employed at times a brief relaxation method developed by Donald Meichenbaum (1974). The following therapist's instructions are adapted from Meichenbaum's manual:

THERAPIST: I'm going to go through a series of actions where you first tense muscle groups and then you let them go. I want you to tense and hold the muscles of the chest and back. You can do this by filling your chest slowly, with short deep breaths, holding each one.

At this point, the therapist models the breathing exercise while the patient is also breathing in.

THERAPIST: Fill the chest and hold. Now part your lips slightly and slowly exhale. Slowly. Good. Note as you slowly exhale the sense of relaxation and warmth you are able to bring forth. Good.

The therapist pauses, letting the patient get back to his normal, even breathing pattern.

THERAPIST: Once again, let's make the muscles of the chest and back tense by filling our chest by means of slow deep breaths. Hold the breath, feel the tenseness across the top of the chest and throughout the upper portion of your body. Bring forth a sense of relaxation by slowly exhaling, part the lips, and let the air out slowly, slowly. Good. Note the distinction between tenseness and relaxation which you've been able to bring forth.

The patient is now sitting quietly.

THERAPIST: You can relax by using your breathing. By taking slow deep breaths and by exhaling slowly, you can control any feelings of tenseness and anxiety. The breathing technique works because of its effect on heart rate and on the rest of the body. Slow breathing slows the bodily processes and lowers arousal. Try the breathing exercise again. This time try it on your own, breathing in slowly and holding each breath and then parting the lips and letting the air out slowly. Try it.

This cycle is repeated once again. The therapist can also suggest to patients:

THERAPIST: You can deepen the relaxation and relax away feelings of tension by thinking silently to yourself the words *relax* and *calm* as you slowly let out your breath. Think or picture these words to yourself as you slowly let out the breath. This will be helpful between sessions when you practice relaxing and slow deep breathing or during those times you become anxious.

The pattern of inhalation modeled by the therapist usually involves filling the chest for four or five seconds or so, and finally slowly exhaling for another ten seconds. The breathing sequence takes about twenty to thirty seconds, and can be adapted to the characteristics of patient and therapist. The patient does not hold his breath to the point of breathlessness, but rather should leave sufficient time for slow, deep exhalation. Patients are told both during and after the relaxation exercise that the difference between a sudden sharp inhalation and exhalation causes the heart rate to increase, and that a slow inhalation-exhalation cycle causes a quieting of bodily processes, including heart rate.

The therapist can make a relaxation tape that the patient can play when he is anxious or has trouble sleeping. The patient at first practices in an optimal situation. This includes a comfortable seat that supports the back, subdued lighting, average room temperature, and comfortable, loose clothing. He should avoid having in the background loud noises or music or unpleasant odors and should not be physically exhausted, which could cause him to fall asleep.

Deikman (1976) has described a technique called "quitting" that is an effective relaxation method. The following is the rationale that is given:

THERAPIST: How many hours a day are you involved in some purposeful action? This might be working, eating, playing sports, watching TV, talking. There are probably very few moments that you're not doing something. This method is to simply quit doing everything. The following are the steps you take to practice quitting.

1. Stop whatever you're doing and just sit (glance at a clock or watch).
2. For ten minutes, quit reacting to any internal or external stimuli (if a fire engine goes by outside, let it go; if you feel like moving, tell yourself, "The heck with it, let it go").
3. Ignore your thoughts. If you start a thought, don't even bother to finish it. Let it drop.
4. Stay awake and let the outside world come to you. I suggest you try this right now. Whenever you become overly focused on your fears, just quit for ten minutes, after you do this, you will have greater freedom to choose how you want to feel.

Melges (1982) has developed another self-aware relaxation method—"expanding the present." The patient is told to relax and imagine that inner time is gradually becoming slowed down and stretched out. In doing this, the therapist stretches out counting from one count per second to one every thirty seconds. The patient is told to imagine that he has much more inner time, that the past is way in the distance and the same for the future. Past and future almost do not even exist.

The patient is to imagine his mind is peacefully empty. This method is particularly helpful for anxious patients who feel overwhelmed. Although Melges recommends this method be done in conjunction with hypnosis, this is not necessary for the patient to obtain a state of alert relaxation. The patient can learn to use this as a general coping strategy when he feels too much is coming in too fast.

Relaxation is an important resource in cognitive therapy and can be viewed as an adjunct procedure—a means to an end. Relaxationlike concentration exercises and meditations are used to provide symptom relief and to facilitate the investigation of dysfunctional thinking.

Emotional Review

The review procedure is quite simple. A patient is asked to imagine a feared situation and then tell how he feels about it. The review should be done in the office at first, with a minimum of input from the therapist. As rationale, the therapist can tell the patient that this situation is like a "lump of pain": by going over it in his mind, the lump can be smoothed out.

Discussing the anxiety-producing situation often provides emotional relief; Raimy writes, "In the techniques of repeated review, the therapist has an opportunity to focus the individual attention on a particular problem, then to repeat the cognitive review until a different, more satisfactory solution is reached" (1975, p. 79).

Raimy (1975) reports using this approach successfully with a number of patients. In this procedure, the therapist simply asks the patient to close his eyes and tell "What happened (or what will happen) and how do you feel?" The therapist keeps the patient focusing on the feared event and reflects back to him what his experience is. The therapist repeats this until the patient's anxiety is lessened.

Most people use a version of this method to calm down the reverberations of their emotions. When a person has some trauma or emotional upheaval he usually wants to talk or think it out. In thinking or talking, he reviews the situation from different angles. This need for review can be seen in those people who have suffered trauma. A three-year-old boy was in a non-injurious but traumatic accident on the freeway. For several weeks after the accident he would say, "Talk the accident." He had his parents describe the accident to him in great detail several times, and he in turn described it to other people. He seemed to need to review the accident in order to process it and put it in his long-term memory.

Raimy (1975) points out how most therapies use a version of the review strategy, although each gives it a different name. The psychoanalytic school calls it "processing" or "working through." Gestalt therapy uses a variety of ways to look at the patient's symptoms, such as the "empty-chair" method by which the patient has a dialogue with a significant person other than himself, which helps him become aware of body reactions. Behavior therapy uses systematic desensitization and impulsing—that is, the patient floods himself with images of the worst possible outcomes. Logotherapy uses intentional paradox to rehearse the emotional reaction. Therapists who help patients resolve grief through flooding employ this strategy almost exclusively. By reviewing what he fears, the patient is able to start to accept the possibility of the feared event. In the reviewing process, he is counteracting his avoidance tendency. At the start of one review, the patient, who was afraid of growing old, thought, "It's too terrible to face. I can't believe this is happening." Later she was able to imagine directly, with minimal anxiety, what it would be like to be old. The reviewing process gets the patient to face the reality of the situation and makes it easier to accept.

Each time the patient reviews a situation, he usually can see it in a larger context. A patient who felt he had made a fool of himself at a meeting was starting to see, by the second review, that most of the people there were not even paying attention to him. Subsequent reviews are also more specific and more detailed. Further, by looking at the event a number of times, the person starts to imagine himself handling the situation in a better fashion, and his confidence increases.

The most useful aspect of this procedure is that it allows the patient to distance himself from the problem; he starts looking at it from the perspective of an observer instead of an actor. By identifying more with his observing self than with his anxious self, he lessens the anxiety.

Repeated review is an excellent way to test reality. The patient reviews what is real to him and experiences it in the present. Rather than have the therapist challenge the patient's conceptualization, the latter is able to do this himself by repeatedly looking at what did happen instead of what he *thought* happened, and at what is likely to happen instead of what catastrophe *could* happen. The patient's repeated review of reality can eventually disprove his distortions. A patient with a fear of "making a fool of myself" at a presentation compared this fear with what was likely to be the real situation (he would do an acceptable job). The patient's anxiety was due to the gap between what was likely to happen and the worst he was afraid would happen. By repeatedly exposing himself to this gap, he was able to close it.

One of the premises of cognitive therapy is that people are able to deal with reality; that what they cannot deal with are their fantasies of what might happen. The premise is that "reality is generally friendly." The distorted view of reality causes the problems. The review procedure gets people to look at reality in a more friendly way.

The patient may have been trying a version of this method by rumination, worry, and even dreaming about the feared event. This process is obsessive and involuntary. In contrast, the review procedure helps the patient become self-directive. By looking at his own thoughts and correcting distortions, eventually without help from the therapist, he increases independence.

People's concerns and worries diminish over time. This process is not a function of time itself; rather, new concerns replace the old ones; or, through spontaneous review, one is able to close the issue and put it in one's long-term memory. Repeated review allows the patient to speed up this process. One patient was grieving over a recent move and afraid that she could not adjust to a new city. She believed that she could get over this in a month or two. However, in two sessions of repeated review, she was able to accept her move, and her grief disappeared.

At times a patient's stated fear may cover other emotions or more basic fears. In the repeated review, the patient often finds what he really is afraid of is different from what he thought, and he learns to deal with the more basic fear. One patient said he was afraid of his wife. Repeated review enabled him to see that he was really angry at his wife and afraid to express this anger. Once the underlying fear became apparent, he was able to make plans to deal assertively with his wife.

Because of premature closure, the patient is unable to see rescue or compensating factors in the frightening situation. In the review he often brings up off-setting rescue factors. A woman was afraid that she would be fired because the boss told her to stop chewing gum. In her review she saw that she was well thought of at work by her immediate supervisor, and that he would stick up for her if this became an issue. Often the person is unable at first to see himself coping with the situation. However, after three or four reviews he can see himself coping satisfactorily. And this usually breaks the cycle.

IMAGERY METHODS

This procedure works best when the patient closes his eyes and imagines the feared situation. This helps the person who is unable to simply talk about the feared situation. A combination is often used: the patient goes through the imagery once or twice and then discusses with the therapist some of his fears and possible reconceptualizations and then has another imagery review followed by a discussion. Usually after each review, the patient discovers new distortions in his structure of the situation. (See also chapter 4.)

METAPHORS

If the patient has trouble with imagery or if discussion is unproductive, a helpful strategy is to use a metaphor to look at the problem. The focus is on sticking with the feared situation and looking at it from different angles. This allows patient and therapist to get outside the problem and consider its various aspects in a creative way.

One man was fearful about an upcoming business meeting. Since he had been an officer in the army, a military metaphor was appropriate, and many aspects of the meeting were discussed in terms of it. Selling the company: "Peace with honor." Doing this in six months: "Getting the troops home by Christmas." Management problems: "Battle fatigue" and "Life in the trenches." Needing more staff and equipment: "Needing more support troops" and "Replacing outdated artillary." After looking at the meeting from these different angles, the patient was significantly less anxious about it. An indirect result of the military metaphor was that he felt strong facing his business associates. The fact that the patient was the source of the image metaphor that enabled him to handle the situation increased his confidence in his ability to cope with the situation.

REPEATED REVIEW OUTSIDE THE OFFICE

If a patient has trouble doing a review outside the office, the therapist can use the following guidelines to help him at home:

1. Give yourself plenty of time for review—from fifteen to thirty minutes. If you're unable to find relief after thirty minutes, stop and try later.
2. If you get more anxious, consider this a good sign. Just continue to review the situation until the anxiety has diminished.

3. You can do a review with another person. It helps you stay focused and organized, and the other person can provide objectivity.
4. Use aids such as talking into a tape recorder or writing the material down. Review the situation in any way that is helpful. You may want to listen to the tape of the review you did in the office.
5. If you have several fears and concerns, clear your mind for a moment and stack all of your problems outside yourself. Then work with one at a time. Once you feel more comfortable with one, review another one.
6. It is helpful to review the problem in slow motion. Run it through as if you were watching a slow-motion movie.
7. After some of your anxiety is reduced, ask yourself what action, if any, you need to take on the problem.
8. We can do this together, through a phone call, at first. But the goal is to learn to do it on your own.

The patient's inability to use this procedure can be used as a source of material for therapy. Generally, the reason is that the patient is not pinpointing his real fears: he may go just so far toward his fear and then take a detour that leaves it untested and unexamined.

Owning One's Emotions

An important step in therapy is to help a patient see how he is responsible for his own feelings. The therapist must keep in mind that nearly all anxious patients believe to some degree that the stimulus they are afraid of—not their thoughts—is causing the anxiety. By learning how to correct this faulty reasoning, the patient benefits in two ways: first, he is in a better position to deal with his anxiety; and second, he is better able to learn how to learn.

SEQUENTIAL REASONING

The patient may believe that the fact that an event immediately precedes his anxiety means it has caused that anxiety. He hears a siren and feels anxious. The therapist can stress that anxiety makes one more vulnerable to primitive and superstitious thinking. The therapist can ask the patient about superstitions that he may have, or that he knows others have. A man wears a blue shirt and his team wins, and he starts to half-believe that the shirt plays some causal role.

THERAPIST: If I were to tell you that Dustin Hoffman is a better actor than Robert DeNiro, what would this tell you?

PATIENT: Well, I guess that's your opinion.

THERAPIST: Right. That's my opinion, and it has nothing to do with the actors. Similarly, when you say asking a girl for a date is frightening, that's all due to your opinion and has nothing to do with asking the girl out. With emotions, opinion is just about everything.

CORRELATIONAL REASONING

Patients often confuse correlation and cause. A patient may correlate his anxiety with some stimulus, such as a social gathering, and believe that one causes the other. The therapist can use a variety of ways to point out this error.

THERAPIST: Stress can provide an example of correlational reasoning. While it's true that high stress is correlated with anxiety, it doesn't necessarily cause anxiety. Many people with low stress become anxious, and many with high stress do not. The third variable here is how you handle stress, whether you let it bother you. If you know how, you can handle high stress; without any tools, low stress can cause problems.

ANALOGICAL REASONING

The patient uses an analogy to describe his anxiety, "I felt like I was going crazy," and then believes as if the analogy were fact. Physical pain is frequently used as an analogy for psychological pain.

THERAPIST: Because others can cause you physical pain, you may think that they can cause you emotional pain. Yet you are really only drawing an analogy: psychological pain is similar to physical pain, but there are also major differences. Other people can assault your body and *physically* intrude, but they can't intrude psychologically. Sticks and stones may break your bones, but others' thoughts and words can't kill you. When you're an adult, no one can emotionally harm you unless you give them such power over you.

EMOTIONAL REASONING

The patient may believe that, because he feels others cause him to be anxious, they must actually do so. The therapist has to point out that feelings are not thoughts, but only reflections of what one is thinking. The patient needs to see that his emotions are products, not causes, no matter how much they feel like causes.

THE PAYOFF

Although many patients obtain some secondary gain from their anxiety, such gain is hardly the primary motivation for the anxiety. However, the patient does need to be aware of his secondary gains so that he can expect and deal with their loss. The following is one way this can be presented (Emery 1984):

THERAPIST: You don't want to sabotage yourself. To learn how to manage your anxiety, you'll have to stop believing you'll lose something when you give up negative feelings. Ask yourself, "What am I giving up when I let my bad feelings go? Revenge? Attention? Sympathy?" Your emotions are real—you do feel bad—and you often get benefits or a payoff for them. One of the reasons you may hang on to your negative feelings is that you don't want to risk losing the payoff. This isn't to say you feel bad just for the sake of the payoff. But the payoff can prevent you from getting these feelings. Knowing what the payoff is lets you decide whether you're willing to give it up.

Your emotions influence others in the same way that advertisements sway their audience. The threefold goal of advertising is to first capture your *attention,* then hold your *interest,* and finally motivate you to take *action.* Your emotional payoff shares these characteristics with successful ads. We often use our negative emotions to try to get someone to "buy" something from us.

Your emotions can draw attention to you. This attention may be wanted ("I wanted to let them know I was mad") or unwanted ("I didn't want to let them know I was nervous"). Your emotions are a rapid and effective form of communication. You may be communicating danger, pain, or a warning. Because your emotions reveal themselves in your facial expressions, voice, and body language, they serve to call attention to you. Just as in advertising, you often have to vary the attention-seeking strategy so that it will remain effective.

Attention isn't enough in advertising: you have to keep people reading or tuned in. Your emotions are often instinctively interesting to others; most of the time people want to know what's behind your emotions.

A good way to keep someone's interest is to involve the other person. Advertisers want you to care so that they can influence you in some way. They might want you to buy their product or service, or to vote for their candidate, or send money to their cause. Your emotions often have the same effect. This emotional request can be specific ("I want you to take me out"). At other times, the expected action is vague. When someone is upset and you ask, "What do you want from me?" he often is unable to say exactly what he wants.

The secondary gains for a patient vary. Therapist and patient need to work together to see precisely what they are.

Special Treatment.   The highly anxious person often has fewer demands made on him. A patient with public-speaking anxiety said, "The teacher knows that I get real nervous when I have to talk in front of others so she doesn't call on me."

Help.   Most people have empathy for a person experiencing anxiety. The help can become an obstacle to getting better. The patient may get others to do tasks for him because he is too anxious to do them himself. The person can often use a middleman: "You call up Sears. I'm too uncomfortable on the phone." With many anxious patients this pattern started quite early and is carried on by a husband or a wife who will do the activity the patient avoids out of anxiety.

Lack of Risk.   The person's payoff may be that, with his anxiety as an excuse, he does not have to take a risk and endure the possibility of failure. A patient said that he could not teach a new course because of his anxiety. The therapist's reply was, "Everyone is scared, but the difference between those who are successful and those who aren't is that the successful ones act even though they are scared."

"If Only."   An anxious patient often is able to retain the idea that he is a superior person, and that the anxiety is the only thing holding him back. One man said that if it were not for his anxiety, he would be the best salesman in the office.

Justification.   The patient may say, "I have to smoke (drink or overeat) because I'm anxious." The anxiety becomes a rationale for some behavior he does not want to give up.

Special Privileges.   The person may use the anxiety to get freedom from those around him. One patient who wanted privacy would tell his wife and children that he had to be left alone because he was having an anxiety attack. The patient may use anxiety to avoid social duties ("I'm too uptight around those people"). Others often do give the anxious person special consideration.

Role of Victim. An extreme form of secondary gain is found in the patient who takes the *victim* role. This person uses his anxiety to manipulate and control others. The person takes little accountability for his own plight in the world and, instead, blames others and circumstances to an extreme degree. The person has well-developed skills in getting others to help him. Previous helpers are often seen as persecutors. With this individual, the therapist needs to keep firm limits and not engage in rescue behavior. The therapist has to repeatedly point out to the patient when he is taking the role of victim. Most of these people will readily agree that this is their life style; however, some are so invested in it and see so few other options that they are reluctant to give it up.

Dealing with the Secondary Gain from Anxiety. The therapist has to point out to a patient what payoffs cost in terms of lost effectiveness and poor human relationships.

THERAPIST: To manage your anxiety, you have to come to terms with the payoff. Again, ask yourself, "Is the gain worth all the pain?" Your negative emotions, considering their cost, usually give you little in return. One of the catches of the payoff is that you continually have to up the ante: you have to be increasingly more dramatic and emotional to get people's attention.

You can gain the benefits without the liabilities by being direct with people. Tell them up front what you want. This is more effective than the indirect method. Even if you fear they'll say No, it's better to put up with an occasional No than to endure painful feelings.

Most patients can see the secondary gains and are willing to give them up once they realize this is in their best interests.

Chapter 14

Modifying the Behavioral Component

One way of approaching the problem of avoidance in anxiety is to encourage the patient to visualize anxiety-producing situations in the office or to come in for a session while feeling anxious so as to record his thoughts and images and practice specific coping techniques. Nearly every patient, however, must confront the anxiety-producing situation to modify dysfunctional thoughts and beliefs. For this reason, *in vivo* homework (where the individual confronts the situation) is a crucial element in the treatment of anxiety. Whether one is afraid of interacting with strangers, driving, contracting a disease, or staying alone at home, one must be persuaded to confront the situations one fears. It is generally agreed that exposure to crowds, bus rides, open spaces, and other feared situations is a crucial element in the treatment of agoraphobia (Chambless and Goldstein 1982; Mathew, Gelder, and Johnston 1981; Mavissakalian and Barlow 1981).

Identifying Protective Mechanisms

The therapist has to find the specific protective mechanisms used by a patient to decrease anxious feelings. There are two general mechanisms. In the first, which is to directly leave or avoid the frightening situation (flight), the therapist's general strategy is to encourage the patient to approach what he fears—a process that often necessitates restructuring complex behavior patterns. One patient had to "boycott" impulses to "tell others what they want to hear," "to cave into unreasonable requests," "to lash out at others," "not to let others know I don't know," "to immediately leave unpleasant situations," and "to betray confidences in order to earn others' approval."

In the second means of decreasing anxious feelings, a person seeks reassurance by continually appraising the degree of threat. He may check on locked doors, look in the mirror for signs of disease, repeatedly visit doctors for health checkups, or ask others if they still care for and love him. The therapist's strategy is to encourage the patient to refrain from seeking such reassurance. The patient may also respond to percieved danger by freezing, which involves an involuntary tightening and tensing of muscles. The therapist's strategy is to encourage and show the patient to relax and let go in the situation.

Generally, one protective mechanism will be more characteristic of a patient than the other. When a combination of mechanisms is operating, each one has to be dealt with separately in therapy. One patient with health fears would constantly check for symptoms of disease but avoid going to the doctor for an examination. The therapist's strategy was to have him stop the checking behavior and see a doctor. The overall strategy is to have the patient do the opposite of what he is inclined to do.

Motivation

EXPLAINING THE THERAPEUTIC APPROACH TO THE PATIENT

Of the variety of methods a therapist can use to encourage the patient to act against his behavioral disposition, providing information is one of the most straightforward. The therapist repeatedly points out that the patient has to experience the anxiety to get rid of it. The patient often has some recognition that he should "face his fears," but probably has not thought through all of the reasons for doing so. By clearly spelling out the full rationale, the therapist often can persuade the patient to approach the feared event and experience his anxiety.

The therapist may present the notion that what one learns in a safe situation is often not recalled when in a frightening situation. Studies have shown that subjects who learned nonsense syllables when intoxicated forgot them when they were not intoxicated and then remembered them again when they became intoxicated again. In a variety of ways, the therapist conveys the message that the patient has to learn how to handle anxiety when he is anxious.

The anxiety-management skills the patient is learning can be compared with those of tennis or other sports. A tennis player may hit long rallies with the coach in practice, but fail to do so in competition. Similarly, the patient may feel he has mastered techniques because they come fairly easily in the therapist's office; but when he is on his own, it becomes much more difficult to do what he thinks he has learned.

Learning to manage anxiety is a developmental process: basic procedures must be mastered before the more complex ones are approached: "You have to learn to walk before you learn to run." The patient initially may learn ways to manage his anxiety in the office. Learning is enhanced when it is relevant to a specific problem confronted in the real world; and therefore, to proceed to advanced skills in anxiety management, the patient needs to try simple anxiety-management exercises in real-life situations. As the situations he confronts become more difficult and complex, repeated self-instructions and insights take on new meaning. The patient learns subtle differences in managing his anxiety in repeated exposure to different intensities of it.

Teacher's Fallacy. Nearly all patients have trouble learning to learn; if they did not, they probably would not be patients. The therapist's awareness of this problem can help prevent him from falling prey to the teacher fallacy (Raimy 1975): that is, the therapist's belief that providing the patient with the right information or right learning experiences will automatically correct the patient's misconceptions. Such cause and effect is the exception rather than the rule. The patient usually has emotional, behavioral, and cognitive strategies that protect his belief system.

BLOCKS TO LEARNING

People have many behavior patterns that prevent them from learning. When material threatening a patient's belief system is brought up, for example, he may yawn, say he is tired, let his eyes glaze over, or become bored, angry, or irritated. This behavior stops others from providing information that would correct his core misconceptions. Therapist and patient need to discover the latter's specific learning blocks so that they can be overcome.

Once a patient knows his assumptions about his assumptions, the therapist can use the same strategies that are used in modifying other misconceptions (chapter 13). Here are some of the assumptions that one patient, a forty-seven-year-old businessman, was able to recognize:

> "If I admit I'm wrong on a specific point, then my worst fear that I'm completely wrong will be true."
> "If I act in new ways, even ones that are in my best interest, I'm being a phony."
> "I have to discount what others below me in rank can teach me, because if I accept this from them, then I would be on the same level."
> "I have to avoid what's frightening, even if it's farfetched, because there's always the chance I won't be able to handle it."
> "If I let people know what I'm really like, they would use it against me, so I can never be myself."
> "If I let others lead me, I've given up my power to them."

After the patient identified these beliefs, he was able to work on correcting and acting against them.

A patient may understand new ideas but be unable to integrate them. He may verbally agree with the therapist but not modify any of his beliefs; the patient avoids learning by giving lip service to the new input—saying, "I know you're right"—and then ignoring it. When they meet no resistance, the therapist and others in the patient's life stop providing input, and the patient continues in the same old way.

The therapist can use three strategies with such a patient: (1) Stress the importance of action ("Actions speak louder than words"). (2) Stress that to learn new ways of looking at the world, one has to get one's thoughts, actions, and feelings going in the same direction. (3) Stress that learning new material is a continuous intellectual process combined with experiential learning. The person lives and learns, and learns and lives. The patient needs both to learn abstractly (books, discussions, lectures, therapy sessions) and to practice what he has learned in real-life situations.

EDUCATIONAL DEVICES

Cognitive therapy, in addition to providing corrective learning experiences for a patient, incorporates didactic techniques such as providing information, assigning reading, listening to audio tapes, and written homework, and suggesting that the patient attend a lecture. The following are useful educational devices:

Chalkboard or Marker Board. As mentioned in chapter 11, a marker board or a blackboard can be extremely helpful in the therapist's office. On this board the therapist can put up agendas, analyze problems, list and answer automatic thoughts, explore options, and assess the advantages and the disadvantages of decisions, as well as carry out many other procedures.

Audio Tapes.   As a matter of course, the therapist should tape each session for the patient to listen to between sessions. A patient may be initially reluctant to tape the sessions, but the therapist should gently insist that the session be taped and tell the patient that he always has the option of either listening to it or not. Patients most reluctant to hear these tapes often benefit most from them.

The therapist can tell the patient that most people dislike listening to themselves, but that repeated listening to himself on tapes enables him to increase his self-acceptance as well as his self-awareness. This is taping's major benefit; it also teaches him to face problems he may have been trying to avoid looking at.

Because the anxious patient has trouble concentrating, he frequently misses much of the content of a session. Taping the sessions greatly increases the efficiency of the therapy.

Potential problems with other family members (Bedrosian 1981) often can be avoided by having significant others listen to the tapes. Taping can also include significant others in therapy (having husbands and wives listen to the tape helps them and frequently prevents them from sabotaging or working at cross-purposes).

Videotapes.   Videotaping can give a patient accurate feedback on his behavior. The anxious patient usually believes that his anxiety is readily apparent to everyone. While it sometimes is, the patient usually exaggerates the extent to which others can read his anxiety. Videotaping allows such distorted thoughts to be seen for what they are. Portable video units can be used to show a patient that he is largely ignored, even if he purposely makes a scene in public.

The socially anxious patient can be videotaped role-playing various social situations. In addition to learning new social skills, the patient frequently can see that his social behavior is not as bad as he has thought. In videotaping it is a good idea to exaggerate both highly appropriate and inappropriate behavior. One patient, who was afraid of being a fool, exaggerated his obnoxious behavior in one segment and showed extremely retiring behavior in another. He was surprised to find that the two were not very different and that he had trouble when he purposely tried to act obnoxious.

Handouts and Other Educational Reminders.   The anxious patient usually has trouble using new concepts and needs repetition in order to incorporate them. The therapist can give out 3-by-5 cards with useful quotations or ideas.

Patients need repeated review to learn new concepts, and any method to achieve this is helpful. One patient wrote two opposing statements on his light switches; on the top of a switch he wrote, "I'm responsible for my feelings," and on the bottom, "Others are responsible for my feelings." He came to see that the difference between the two attitudes is the difference between being in the dark and being in the light.

FUTILITY OF SELF-PROTECTION

The patient needs to see how his avoidance and protective behavior strengthen his unrealistic, fearful thoughts. As most patients know, this is the reasoning behind the admonition that when you have been thrown from a horse, you must get right back on, or you may have trouble riding in the future.

While the principle of facing one's fears to overcome them is generally known by all patients, it still needs to be repeatedly stressed in therapy. The therapist can ask the patient if there have been traumas in his life that were not followed by avoidance in contrast to those traumas that were. A patient is usually able to provide evidence that avoidance has increased his fears and that confronting them has decreased them. George Weinberg's *Self-Creation* (1978) can help to underline this point to patients. Weinberg's thesis is that each action adds strength to the motivating idea behind the action.

The therapist needs to demonstrate repeatedly that the inclination to protect oneself from anxiety is self-defeating:

> While it is usually a good idea to follow your instincts or feelings, this is the wrong approach when you're anxious. You have to do the opposite of your instincts. That's because anxiety is paradoxical. The more you try to defend yourself, the more frightened you become. The more the miser tries to protect himself from being poor, the more he worries about being poor. The more nonassertive you are, the more you fear other people. Your efforts to protect yourself make you more vulnerable.

EXPERIMENTS

The therapist can often spark interest in approaching an activity as a scientific experiment. Within the context of cognitive therapy, persuasion and reassurance are viewed as helpful in themselves but not powerful enough to change a patient's cognitive distortions and dysfunctional attitudes. As mentioned earlier, therapist and patient are seen as co-investigators, working together to design "real world experiments" that test the validity and utility of dysfunctional cognitions.

A young man with social anxiety wanted to cancel a date because of his fear; he was encouraged to see if he could go on the date and still function even though he would be anxious. The therapist and the patient set up specific hypotheses—such as, "I won't know what to say"—that he could test out in this experiment. His actual experience, as is often the case, disproved his hypothesis. He was less anxious than he predicted, and he was able to act as if he were not anxious, even when he experienced anxiety.

The therapist presents a sound rationale for conducting the experiment. A common rationale is that experiments are needed to obtain solid data regarding central problems. A thirty-three-year-old woman anticipated rejection and disapproval from others and, as a result, isolated herself socially. Her anticipation of rejection rested on the assumption that she knew what others were thinking: that is, that they were thinking negatively about her. During a session, the therapist conducted a behavioral experiment in which, to determine the accuracy of her "ESP," she tried to guess what the therapist had written on a piece of paper and was unable to do so. She went to two social events, which she normally would avoid because of her fear of rejection, and was to look for specific incidents of personal rejection. She was unable to see any examples of clear-cut rejection. Her conclusion was, "Perhaps the real problem is that I have been rejecting others by staying away from them."

If the patient had come back with specific examples of being rejected, the therapist could have taken a number of different tacks, which would include praising her for getting the information and determining whether she had really been rejected or whether she had wrongly interpreted others' responses. If it turned out that she was indeed being repeatedly rejected, the therapist could have worked with her to see how she was contributing to this problem. Experiments are always "no lose" situations because the person always gains—whether in learning, taking risks, or strengthening will.

GRADED STEPS OR A GRADUAL APPROXIMATION

The patient must approach a feared situation gradually, with each step taken being determined by his degree of discomfort. To underline the importance of graded steps, the therapist can ask the patient if he has ever tried to approach the feared situation. Most patients have tried before, but failed because they attempted to do too much at one time. Such an "all or none" approach often fails because one is unable to stay in the fearful situation long enough to adjust to it; for this reason, smaller steps have a greater chance of success.

One patient found it helpful to repeat the therapist's catch phrase, "Little steps for little feet," in approaching fearful situations slowly. In the past she had berated herself for being a "coward" and "weak" for taking small steps.

The therapist at times may need to encourage the patient to take bigger steps by reminding him that since "fantasies are consistently worse than reality," the process will probably be easier than he imagined.

HIERARCHY

The steps in exposure can be developed systematically as a formal hierarchy ranging from least to most anxious situation. The patient is advised to stay in each situation until his anxiety diminishes, even if only slightly. If he does leave before his anxiety is reduced, he should return again as soon as possible and stay until it has diminished. If he is still unable to stay in the situation, he should drop down to a lower, less threatening situation.

The advantage of such a hierarchy is that it prevents the patient from moving ahead too quickly. Moving too quickly often backfires. One woman who was afraid of "going berserk" in a crowd did so well in a small group of friends that she decided to venture out into a large downtown crowd. However, she then had a panic attack and returned home.

By performing successive approximations to a goal ("graded approximation"), the patient can gradually work his way to the desired behavior. A patient with a fear of heights started by going up to the second floor of a building. He stayed there until he felt comfortable enough to go on to the next floor, and so on. Over a series of trials, he was able to get to the top of the building.

Merely establishing a hierarchy of steps can lead to cognitive restructuring. This patient realized that a problem he viewed as global could be broken down into concrete, manageable steps. Completion of each step allowed him to see that his goal could be reached as a result of his own effort and skill. In the course of performing graded tasks, patients often experience a "cognitive click" (Mahoney 1974)—a relatively sudden reconceptualization of the experience in the direction of greater functioning, and they are then able to make rapid progress.

An accountant was anxious about a major address he had agreed to give at a convention. A hierarchy of situations was set up and included speaking at informal gatherings, asking questions at small public presentations, and even giving the address at the convention. At a small group meeting while he was giving a talk, this man had the cognitive click: "I'm not responsible for whether these people are entertained or not." This concept had been discussed during a therapy session; but it was only later, at this meeting, that he was able to internalize it and operate from it. He was able to give the speech with a minimal amount of anxiety.

Each graded step can be seen as a separate experiment—a hypothesis to be tested. Even if he does not remain in the situation, the patient is told he can still collect data (thoughts and images) about the incident to be used in therapy. He is encouraged to view any approximation of the step as a success.

Aids to Exposure

Presenting an experimental rationale, grading tasks, and making a task "fail-proof" are all ways to motivate the patient to approach or stay with the anxiety. As the patient gets closer to the situation, his resolve to confront the feared event fades. The therapist can make use of different techniques and strategies to help the patient act against this strong behavioral inclination to avoid the anxiety.

INITIATION TECHNIQUE

The therapist can encourage the patient to take a minimal first step that will lead to direct contact with the feared situation. A secretary was anxious about confronting a fellow employee with whom she had a problematic relationship. The therapist told her:

> I know you don't feel like trying this now, but if you make some move toward confrontation, such as telling a close friend when you are going to do it, that in itself can become a powerful motivation. What you are doing is using a lower motivation, shame, to develop a higher motivation, courage.

The patient told her sister that she was going to confront to her co-worker, and later told the therapist, "I wasn't going to follow through, but I remembered what I told my sister."

The therapist has take some care with this procedure. An agoraphobic patient, who broke her stated intention to make a crosstown trip, came to think, "I let everyone down," and felt depressed. The therapist told her that commitments can never be more than *serious intentions,* and that the unexpected can get in the way of serious intentions. The therapist also said that while it makes sense to follow through on serious intentions, it is not always possible to do so.

While public commitments, or stated intentions, can motivate patients, private commitments or commitments to the therapist are also helpful. This is one of the reasons that specific homework assignments are spelled out in detail at the end of each session. The following guidelines can be used with homework:

1. *Make homework a top priority.* The therapist's attitude is the most crucial determinant of whether patients follow through on homework. Patients of a therapist who values homework are the ones who do it. If the therapist does not believe that a patient will do it, the latter probably will not do it.

2. *Stress the value of the homework to the patient.* The patient needs to know that research has found that degree of recovery is related to how much work one puts into treatment. The therapist frequently has to sell the patient on the value of homework.

3. *Always follow up on homework assigned.* Patients often will not mention completed homework if therapists fail to ask about it. A good policy when assigning homework is to write it out on NCR paper (no carbon required), with both therapist and patient keeping a copy. A common complaint of patients is that a therapist would assign homework and then never ask about it again. Failure to ask about an assigned task seriously impedes the patient's follow-through. The written assignment can remind the patient to do the homework and the therapist about what he has assigned. The therapist's attention is a powerful reinforcement for completing homework.

4. *Develop the homework on a collaborative basis.* The patient's input is necessary to make sure that homework is relevant to a current problem and neither too easy nor too difficult. Early in therapy, the therapist may take the lead; however, by the end of treatment, the patient should be designing nearly all of the homework.

5. *Present homework as a form of communication.* The homework can be a form of communication and a valuable way to cut down the therapy time spent on past behavior. In many cases, a patient can mail in written homework between sessions.

6. *Make sure the patient can do the homework.* The first step of much homework

can be done in the office, with the patient learning how to record his thoughts or role-playing an upcoming encounter. By having the patient do some homework in the office, the therapist can see potential problems and assess the patient's ability to do the work.

7. *Use the "foot-in-the-door" method.* Get the patient to do any type of homework to start with. Even before he comes to the first session, the patient can be asked to do such homework as writing down the history of his problem. This task helps develop a mental set for doing homework.

8. *Personalize the homework.* The homework needs to be tailored to a particular patient's style and concerns. Most autonomous patients, for example, like to set and develop their own assignments. Some patients do not respond well to the term *homework,* associating it with the drudgery of schoolwork. The therapist in these cases can refer to it as *tasks, assignments, self-therapy practice,* or whatever is acceptable to the patient.

9. *Experiment.* Each homework assignment is an experiment. The experiment may be one of gathering information or of testing hypotheses. Nearly all homework assignments can be framed as experiments. One patient's homework was to run an experiment of "refraining from checking up on my wife" in order to find out whether this would lessen his anxiety over time. Another patient's homework was to run an experiment of "checking out what my wife is thinking" in order to discover whether this would lower his anxiety.

10. *The homework should grow naturally out of a problem covered in a particular session.* For example, if the person is anxious about being rejected, the assignments would directly relate to reducing that anxiety. In the first few sessions, the therapist may assign standard homework; afterward, however, the specific assignment grows out of the patient's and the therapist's conceptualization of the problem and their selection of strategy and tactics.

11. *Assess obstacles to homework completion.* The therapist needs to elicit difficulties the patient may have in carrying out an assignment: "Now, I know you said you're going to do this, but can you see any problems or obstacles that might get in the way of your carrying it out?"

The therapist may have to point to potential problems he foresees: "In the past, you've had a tendency to get sidetracked with other concerns. Could this happen here?"

Another way to assess potential problems is to use the "future autobiography" method, in which the patient role-plays himself in the future, and the therapist addresses him: "Okay, it's been a week since I saw you. How did you do on the homework? Did you run into any problems?" Once difficulties can be pinpointed, patient and therapist can develop problem-solving strategies and contingency plans.

12. *Have the patient make a commitment to the homework assignment.* Getting the patient to make a verbal "agreement," "commitment," "promise," or "serious intention" increases his follow-through. Some patients respond well to the notion of "contracting." One patient even had her contract (to accumulate a specific number of anti-shame points) notarized. Going to the notary public was one of the ways she obtained anti-shame points.

13. *Use reinforcement strategy.* Research indicates that when patients are reinforced they increase their homework follow-through (Shelton and Levey 1981). The patient can do this by giving himself pats on the back ("I did well in taking that risk"). The patient can also set up a system where he is reinforced with material rewards, such as buying himself an article of clothing for completing a task. Another version is to have the patient set up a situation where significant others can act as reinforcers for completing a task. For example, a fourteen-year-old boy with a school phobia used extra free time with his mother as a reinforcer for his attending school.

When a patient expresses a desire to do the task but has serious difficulty following through, contingency contracting can be used. The patient gives the therapist a fixed amount of money, which is returned only when the task is completed. If the task is not completed, the money can be disposed of in a number of ways, such as being sent to a charity or relative the patient dislikes. The rationale is that desire + money = results. While the ideal goal is for the task to be self-reinforcing, other means of reinforcement can be used until the experiences of success become self-reinforcing.

14. *Elicit reasons and thinking behind failure to follow through on homework.* Often the same reasons a person has for not doing the homework are the ones that maintain avoidance behavior. Because the therapist is directly involved in this behavior, he can test the reality of such beliefs as "I was afraid I wouldn't do it right."

15. *Use authority.* As a last resort, the therapist can tell the patient who is not improving that he *has* to do the homework if he wants to get better. The therapist points out that the patient has a clear-cut choice: "You can not do the homework and stay the same, or you can do the homework. It's your choice."

SELF-INSTRUCTION

A patient can also help to overcome his fears of entering anxiety situations through verbal self-instruction. In this procedure, one actively repeats to oneself phrases that represent important concepts developed in therapy: "Stay with the situation"; "Stay focused on what you're doing"; "The anxiety level will go down"; "What is my purpose?"; "Don't evaluate yourself"; "Anxiety is uncomfortable but not dangerous"; or, "What others think of me is none of my business." Many patients find catchphrases helpful when they approach a feared situation. Some examples are, "The lion will disappear when I face him"; "Face what you fear"; "I need to take risks"; "This will pass"; or, "I have to accept the anxiety." The patient repeats these catchphrases in a self-confident and self-assured manner. In helping the patient develop a catchphrase or an affirmation, the therapist can point out how advertisers, politicians, and others in the mass media use such slogans as means of persuasion.

Some patients find images can serve the same purpose. One patient used the image of being tennis player John McEnroe as a way to face authority figures. When he approached his boss or his father-in-law, he imagined himself as having the same self-assurance McEnroe has in confronting a linesman at a tennis tournament.

The patient can also use symbolic items to help stay with the anxiety. One patient with severe claustrophobia carried a small rock in his pocket to remind him to be like "granite" in dealing with frightening situations. When confronted with the necessity of riding in an elevator, he would touch this stone to remind himself to carry through.

The therapist stresses that the patient has power over his body—at least over the gross motor movements, if not the finer symptoms of anxiety. By actively "talking to himself," the patient can force himself to enter and stay in situations. Self-instructions vary depending on the patient, the therapist, and the feared situation. A graduate student and his therapist devised the following set of self-instruction statements to control his anxiety in speaking to his dissertation chairman:

1. Don't give in.
2. Bite your tongue if you have to. Don't cave in or be weak.
3. Don't be a sap. Stand up for what you want.
4. Be adamant. It's a matter of who gives in first.
5. Be eternally vigilant. When you see yourself becoming passive, move toward a strong, active position.
6. Chin up. Feel tension in the neck. This is a sign you're strong.
7. Ask questions as much as possible. Be in charge of the situation.
8. Be firm and decisive.
9. Be a block of stone, an immovable object. Don't let him psychologically push you over.
10. Be decisive.

By using these, he was able to cope with the frightening situation.

The therapist can also ask a patient how he was able to face difficult tasks in the past. One patient said that he would pretend that he was a carnival pitchman and tell himself, "All right, step right up. Let me tell you what I'm gonna do. I'm gonna go right in there and knock them off their feet. All right! All right! This way, step right in."

The therapist can also disclose some of his own strategies:

At times I imitate television personality Reverend Ike to get myself motivated. Reverend Ike says if you want to have money, you have to stop saying, "I hate money" and start yelling, "I love money." In graduate school I found I was telling myself, "I hate writing this dissertation, I hate writing it." As a result, I avoided it. I started yelling throughout the house periodically, "I love writing this dissertation, I love it," and the next thing I knew, I was writing it.

In this case the therapist was giving the patient a coping model as well as taking some of the seriousness out of the problem. Self-instructions have recently been incorporated into a variety of exposure-based treatments for agoraphobia. For example, S. L. Williams and A. Rappaport (1983), working with severe driving phobias, suggested that patients cope with fear by relabeling anxious feelings as uncomfortable, rather than harmful; by substituting favorable for fearful self-statements; and by redirecting attention to the task (see also Mathew, Gelder, and Johnston 1981).

BEHAVIORAL REHEARSAL

Behavioral rehearsal (role-playing) prepares patients for potentially stressful social situations. The techniques may be used to model social responses; to elicit fearful thoughts that accompany assertive behavior; and to bolster the patient's self-confidence through such practice and problem solving. Occasionally, behavior rehearsal will identify apparent social skills deficits, which can also be addressed in this context.

One patient recognized in the role playing that he anticipated being "put down" by his date and was unsure how to respond if this happened. The therapist helped him develop and practice some retorts to "put downs," and to question his beliefs that situations involving a potential "put down" must be feared and avoided at all cost.

A businesswoman was role-playing a stronger stance that she planned to take with her more aggressive male colleagues. She identified her thinking, "They'll ignore what I say and take the discussion in whatever direction they want to. They'll make me look like a fool when I give an unpopular idea by ignoring me." Having been able to identify this specific problem, she could devise a strategy to deal with it: that is, she planned to ask directly for feedback on her previous comments, should they ignore her.

The therapist should engage in frequent role playing with the anxious patient. Rather than formally setting these up as "role plays," he can spontaneously say, "I'm your sister (or whomever the patient is talking about). What do you mean by being late? . . ." or in the case of role reversal, "I'll be you. I want to talk to you about this. . . ." In role playing, the therapist frequently overplays a role as he should present the worst fears a patient may have. During role play with a patient who feared being criticized by strangers, the therapist played a hypercritical stranger.

During the behavioral rehearsal, the patient is encouraged to practice a variety of responses. A patient was fearful that people would find out that his son was homosexual. Among other responses, he rehearsed a short, conservative response (It's true, but I don't feel comfortable talking about it") and an exaggerated one ("He sure is, and you should see the great-looking guys he goes out with"). Exaggerated role playing, by pushing the limits, allows the patient to feel more comfortable with a balanced response.

THE USE OF SIGNIFICANT OTHERS

Family members, other important persons in a patient's life, and paraprofessionals can serve as auxiliary therapists in carrying out behavioral assignments and can help a patient identify automatic thoughts. Their most important job, however, is to help the person stay in the anxiety situation until the anxiety is lowered. Gradually, the other person is removed from this process. The significant other is given the following guidelines: (1) reinforce small steps; (2) encourage, don't pressure; (3) make the process a collaborative effort ("I'll help you with this problem and you can help me with mine"); and (4) let the patient take the lead.

When possible, the therapist can accompany the patient into anxiety-producing situations. A therapist accompanied a patient who feared elevators to the elevator. At first she refused to go near it—although while in the therapist's office she estimated her chance of getting stuck and suffocating in an elevator as being "one in ten thousand." As she approached it, with the therapist's encouragement, she stated the odds were "fifty-fifty" that she would suffocate. The therapist then rode up and down with her to help her identify anxiety-producing images. After they made several trips, she no longer experienced these images. This initial data-gathering venture turned into the basis for the development of a hierarchy of exposure steps with a significant other present.

The most useful aid is the telephone. Cognitive therapy encourages the patient to practice coping methods while in the midst of an anxiety experience. By establishing telephone contact, the patient can enlist the support and encouragement of the therapist when time and distance would otherwise rule out such assistance. To overcome a patient's reluctance to impose upon the therapist's time, or to interrupt him at odd hours, the therapist should arrange with the patient that phone contacts will be considered therapy time and charged accordingly. As therapy progresses, the patient is encouraged to enter feared situations alone. Since the patient may resist this, the therapist should stress again that such protection from anxiety-producing stimuli in the long run reinforces the fear. Consider this exchange with an agoraphobic patient:

PATIENT: But I feel better when my daughter goes out with me.

THERAPIST: I understand. In fact, that's the major reason props are so hard to give up—they do make you feel better. But do they make you *get* better?

PATIENT: You mean in the long run?

THERAPIST: Yes, in the long run, do you think it's better to *feel* better or *get* better?

PATIENT: Well, I know that I would rather get better.

THERAPIST: Why do you think that it would be better to go out on your own now instead of with your daughter?

PATIENT: I guess I would believe I'm more capable if I go out by myself.

THERAPIST: That's right. If you go out with your daughter, you're likely to say you were successful *because of* your daughter not because of your own coping abilities. You want to see your success as *self-mastery*.

PATIENT: But I think I'll need help in case something happens.

THERAPIST: Okay. Let's look at that and see what we can come up with.

The patient was eventually able to start going out on her own.

Technical Aids

As mentioned before, a variety of technical aids have been employed to help patients face feared situations. In one case, a therapist obtained a dual-control car—the type used in driver's education—to facilitate treatment of a woman afraid to drive on freeways. The patient felt safer; first, because the therapist was accompanying her, and second, because he could take control of the car in case she panicked. The safety margin that this arrangement afforded permitted the woman to confront her fear.

"Walkman" tape recorders allow a patient to listen to an audio cassette while confronting a variety of fearful situations. The patient can replay tapes of the sessions, or use tapes tailor-made for confronting a fear.

COGNITIVE AVOIDANCE

Even when patients do approach a feared situation alone, many use cognitive avoidance strategies to shut out the anxiety ("Don't think about that," et cetera). While such strategies can initially allow a patient to stay in a situation, they soon lose their benefit. Patients are encouraged, in a variety of ways, to expose themselves mentally, physically, and emotionally. They are told to tell themselves to experience the anxiety and not try to avoid it through thought stoppage. The therapist can draw a triangle with thoughts, feelings, and action at the three points, and then, by drawing arrows between these points, can stress the importance of getting all three systems going in the same direction.

The Critical-Decision Technique

The critical-decision is a technique that patients can use to face their fears. The behavioral disposition in anxiety leads to a chain of behavior, which will include, at some point, a decision and self-instruction. Often the last chance at intervention occurs at the decision point. Once the patient exposed to a situation that he perceives as dangerous begins to act on this perception, it is difficult to challenge or modify the beliefs through verbal methods. When the patient is in the process of getting ready to take escape action, he is unlikely to question the original conclusion that the situation is dangerous.

THERAPIST: Going with your feelings or instincts is a good idea most of the time; however, when you're in a critical decision anxiety situation, your best decision is to do the exact opposite. For example, if you're talking to someone and you want to back away and hide, it's better to force yourself to move forword: you approach instead of avoid. When you want to protect yourself, you make yourself more vulnerable.

Patients are usually able to use this technique in different ways. One man, for example, got a letter from an angry customer. His normal pattern would have been to throw the letter away and try to shut it out of his mind. Just as he was about to do this, he remembered the critical-decision technique and called the customer. This turned out to be a mastery experience for him that increased his overall self-confidence.

The therapist tells the patient to look for those moments when he can choose to act against his strong inclination to escape. The following dialogue shows what a patient can do after beginning to recognize a critical point:

THERAPIST: You were asking what can you do once you become aware of these moments—what you can do to stay in the situation?
PATIENT: That's right.
THERAPIST: Well, it's actually quite simple. You don't need to analyze what to do. Because you have a little time to think, the second part of the critical decision technique is easy. You do the opposite of what you feel like doing. So when your instincts are to flee, you stay. If you want to stay, you go.
PATIENT: You just do the opposite of what you feel like doing, of what your instincts are? Well, how can I get myself to do this?
THERAPIST: You have to talk to yourself. You can tell yourself this is a critical point and then force yourself to do the opposite. Once you start acting on that principle, you've chosen a different path and you're on your way.
PATIENT: Well, I know what you're talking about, but I don't know if I can do it.
THERAPIST: Let's take an example—the last time you were anxious—and see if we can find that critical moment and see how you could have applied the critical decision technique to it.

The patient recalled an instant where she avoided telling her sister what was really on her mind. The therapist and the patient role-played this situation, and he had her act the opposite of her instinct.

In presenting this procedure, the therapist usually can identify problems that would prevent patients from making the adaptive choice—much as he does in the behavioral rehearsal technique. One patient stated he would feel "phony" staying in a social situation where he did not feel he should be. The therapist introduced the notion that any new behavior can produce the feeling that "it's not the real me," but that this feeling of strangeness or phoniness goes away with time—if one practices the new behavior. Another patient said, "I won't handle the situation well. I'll look foolish." The therapist may profitably review the patient's often perfectionistic criteria for performance in an unfamiliar situation. The therapist can ask, "What has worked in the past? Has fleeing worked? Would a new, radical, opposite approach have a better chance?" With one patient, the therapist said, "When you surprise yourself by doing this, you also surprise others because it's so out of your pattern. In addition to seeing yourself differently, others will see you differently."

SURPRISE

This concept of surprise can often be used as a motivational aid. When a patient is not sure whether he will carry out the approach behavior, the therapist can suggest, "Why don't you surprise yourself and see what happens?" By structuring the situation as being one where surprise is welcome, pressure is off patients to perform.

One woman attempted to approach what she feared with an "I should" strategy: "I should face my fears"; "I should have more courage to do what I want to do." She said, "I know I should do what I fear, but I can't make myself." At the end of the second session, the therapist gave her the homework "Surprise yourself."

At the next session she reported that she had surprised herself in many ways. She had impulsively flown to San Francisco with a friend even though she had previously been highly reluctant to fly. She used this strategy of surprising herself to quit her job, to have satisfying sexual experiences, and to attempt many experiences she had previously avoided.

CHOICE

This strategy often works well with the patient who has problems involving control and who avoids situations where he fears losing control. The patient has lost trust in himself and in his environment and typically wants an unrealistic degree of control. To be safe and secure, he comes to believe he has to have complete control over the environment or himself. He previews or mentally rehearses a fearful situation to ensure control over it.

One of the ways the therapist can deal with this issue is to translate the concept of control into one of choices:

Often the concept of control is an illusion. We have little direct control over other people and only a degree of control over our own thoughts, feelings, and actions. It is more helpful to think in terms of choices. I might tell you that you can only sit in one chair in this office. You may or may not go along with my command. This is your choice. On the other hand, I may take all of the chairs out of my office except one. You then only have one choice. You might think of either of these tactics as controlling you or as decreasing your choices.

The strategy of switching the issue of control to one of choices can be used whenever the issue of control comes up. One patient, for example, was afraid to speak up to other people for fear they would get angry at him and because he would not know how to respond, he would be out of control. The choices he did have in this situation were revised. His choice became to listen and stay calm, repeating his main points. This switch from control to choice allowed him to approach interpersonal situations he had had to avoid in the past.

The therapist can stress that the patient always has the choice to approach what he fears. The patient who attempts to use self-control to face his fears often feels out of control. A patient wanted to approach his wife sexually (he had been avoiding her for several months):

PATIENT: I don't have a choice. I have to do it.

THERAPIST: Let's see if we can find you a choice. You do have a decision, right?

PATIENT: I could decide to do it or not do it.

THERAPIST: Or decide not to decide. A decision is selection of alternatives. A choice is something you prefer to do instead of something else, right?

PATIENT: I guess that's it. I don't want to keep on like I have been doing and see the marriage end, and I don't want to humiliate myself by not performing.

THERAPIST: How can you make your decision to risk possible humiliation into a preferable choice?

The patient was able to generate a number of reasons this was his preferable choice. Most patients can label their approaching a feared event as a choice, rather than as something they have to do or should do.

Avoiding the "shoulds" is not an absolute rule. A number of patients respond well to self-commands. They will approach what they fear because they "should," "ought," "have to," "have no other choice," and "must." The self-instruction that it is to their advantage to do this is not nearly as powerful as their absolute commands. The clinical reality is that patients often take the right action ("I'll go for the interview") for the wrong reasons ("I don't want to let my therapist down"). Overall it is a net gain for the patient. As the therapy progresses, the therapist can help the patient develop and switch to more self-directional motivation.

TASK ORIENTATION

Because the patient feels frightened, he believes there is some danger and focuses on this rather than confronting the task at hand. Patients can be taught the "TIC/TOC technique"—namely, to differentiate between *t*ask-*i*nterfering *c*ognitions ("I've got to get out of here," "I can't stand it") and *t*ask-*o*riented *c*ognitions, in which the focus is on staying with a situation ("What do I have to do to get through this situation?" "How can I get more into the situation?").

The patient learns to become aware of his interfering thoughts and to ignore or replace them with more task-relevant ones. As in the preceding case, the therapist can help a patient identify his reasons for engaging in an activity and then get him to focus on this goal. One patient enrolled in an evening class with the idea that it would give him some pleasure and a chance to be with other people. His self-consciousness, however, interfered, and he continually had to remind himself that he was there to enjoy himself, to risk doing something different, and to be with other people.

The patient who forgets why he wants to engage in feared stimuli when he is in the midst of anxiety, can write down on a card the reasons for engaging in the activity. He can use phrases or slogans that help him to remember his goal. Patients have found the following types of catchphrase helpful: "Keep your eye on the ball"; "When you're up to your elbows in alligators, it's hard to remember you wanted to drain the swamp"; "*Pensa al fine* ('Think of the Goal')"; "The end determines the means"; "Remember what my purpose is"; "Small strokes fell great oaks"; and "A journey of one thousand miles begins with one step."

BEHAVIORAL THOUGHT

With each anxious patient, the therapist needs to ask himself what can the patient do behaviorally to reduce his anxiety. The possible steps often seem so simple that the patient overlooks them. For example, a woman with a fear of missing important calls got an answering machine; and a pilot with a fear of being caught unchecked by an air inspector got out the manuals he needed and studied the material he had to know.

Often seeking advice can alleviate a patient's anxiety. A man fearful of being sued consulted a lawyer to see where he stood. He found out that, while he might have a problem, it could be solved in a number of ways.

One strategy is for a person to stop engaging in behavior that brings on a threat. Thus, a woman fearful of getting caught using drugs can decide to stop using them; a man fearful of getting caught having an affair can stop the affair; or a man fearful of getting caught cheating on his taxes can stop cheating. The therapist helps such patients see what the potential price for their behavior might be. The patient who is unwilling to pay the price is encouraged to consider curtailing the behavior. The general strategy is "Given the consequences what is the best choice?"

The patient may overlook readily available rescue factors. A man who had to drive a long distance to work was afraid he would break down some night and have no way of getting help. His anxiety diminished when he got a CB radio and joined the American Automobile Association. Another man was afraid of dying, one of his biggest fears being that his wife and children would be left destitute. This fear was diminished somewhat by getting his financial status and will in order and by taking out life insurance. In some obsessive anxious situations, this type of protective intervention might make the person more fearful. However, with this patient and many others, developing safeguards is quite effective.

One behavioral intervention is to have the patient do what he is trying to avoid. A young girl with a cocaine addiction was afraid her family would find out. Instead of trying to hide this, she systematically told her family members. As is often the case, they already strongly suspected it. Or, an elderly couple was afraid that their friends and relatives would find out that their son had gone to prison for armed robbery. At the therapist's encouragement, they started to tell certain people about their son and found that, instead of rejection and shock, they received sympathy and support. Both spouses had a corresponding drop in anxiety.

Direct confrontation with what the patient fears can be useful. A telephone call to get more information is often one of the most effective behavioral interventions. One woman was terrified because her house insurance was canceled after she had filed her third claim, and feared that she would be unable to get insurance on her house. At the therapist's insistence, she called several insurance agencies until she found one that would insure her.

In these cases the therapist can often nudge the patient into doing something that both know is for the latter's good. This pressure should only be applied when there is sufficient trust and a high probability that the patient will carry out the action. Initially, the patient may be angry or irritated with the therapist.

After the patient completes the action, he is usually grateful. When he attributes the success to the therapist, as often happens, the therapist has to respond in a clear, strong way:

THERAPIST: It's true you did confront your husband partly because I put pressure on you. You, however, were the one who did it. In the future you can use the same process and *force* yourself to do what you don't want to do. The psychoanalytic writer Theodor Reik, when asked how he was able to write thirty-nine books, said, "I force myself!" We can learn to force ourselves much more than we tend to think we can.

Whenever possible the behavioral intervention should be done in the present. One man who was extremely unassertive put off making an appointment with a producer who was interested in a script he had written. The therapist pressured this man into making the call and appointment. When, with great reluctance, he did this, he was greatly relieved until he noticed that the appointed time conflicted with a previous appointment. The therapist put pressure on him to call the producer for the second time. After putting up a great deal of resistance, the patient complied and, afterward, had great relief and feelings of mastery. Then he realized that his second appointment time also conflicted with another appointment. (The patient's repeated conflicts with appointments were probably also due to his wanting to avoid the producer.) The therapist suggested that he call the producer a third time. The patient said, "There's no way I can do that"; but, after some strong persuasion and role playing, he called the producer for the third time. This was a significant interaction on the patient's part, and he was better able to confront authority figures afterward. The strategy the patient found the most helpful was to act on impulse. When he has an impulse to be assertive, he learned to act on it. He learned that if he waited, he would talk himself out of it.

A patient may believe that he has to confront directly, "like a man," people he is afraid of. The patient's high standards prevent him from doing what would normally reduce his anxiety. The therapist can help such a patient expand his ways of confronting unpleasant situations. For example, a patient was putting off dropping out of a self-help group because she could not get herself to deal with the leader.

THERAPIST: There are hundreds of ways to skin a cat. There's no law that says you have to tell him to his face. You could call him, send a telegram, a letter, or a card, or even get someone else to tell him for you. The goal is to let him know you're dropping out of the group.

The patient decided to call him and was able to accept her less-than-perfect way of confronting her fear.

The "As If" Technique

The anxious patient gives himself a suggestion ("What if") and then acts on it *as if* it were true. The behavioral technique of acting as if one had no fear stops the anxiety from spiraling, as the patient sees himself acting without fear. This technique may increase his self-confidence and further diminish his anxiety.

Many people use a version of this technique in their daily lives. Salesmen, for example, know that acting enthusiastically generates enthusiasm. Therapists learning their trade find that acting as if they know what they are doing leads to real confidence and eventually real competence.

The patient can use the following in employing this technique:

1. *Develop images.* The patient can describe how he would like to act if he were unafraid, and can observe others who perform without anxiety. One variation is to have the patient first develop an extreme opposite image of acting as if he were very scared, which may allow him to develop a more balanced image. One patient developed the following ideal image about meeting others:

A. I focus on the other person. I look straight at the other person. My eyes stay fixed.
B. I hold my ground and let him move more toward me, rather than rushing to him.
C. I keep my body straight and project presence. I stay balanced rather than shift my weight from foot to foot.
D. I communicate openly. I keep my arms down rather than taking a defensive position.
E. I keep my head erect rather than nodding or looking away.
F. I speak confidently in a clear direct way rather than qualify excessively, apologize, or overexplain.
G. I ask questions about the person and call him by name.
H. I'm friendly but quiet and sincere.

I. I'm dressed in a way that allows me to feel good about myself.

J. I'm really enjoying meeting the person.

He watched other people meet people on television shows and in real life to see what he could learn from them.

2. *Practice imagery.* The patient can practice imagery acting "as if" he were not afraid. The person who has anxiety from this image should continue to rehearse the image until his anxiety diminishes.

3. *Role play.* The patient can role play as if he were not scared with the therapist, with a significant other, or with himself. At times patients find that it helps to assume the role of a person such as baseball player Reggie Jackson or tennis player Billie Jean King, who have almost aggressive attitudes. The person then practices acting as if he were not anxious in real life situations. The patient can keep a diary of when he acts this way and periodically review how he is doing at it.

Shame and Other Feared Experiences

Most anxious patients are afraid of experiencing shame and—in accordance with the principle of systematically doing or confronting what one fears and what one is trying to avoid—therapy provides opportunities where one can purposely experience shame. A patient is asked to put himself in a situation where he is likely to experience shame; or when he finds himself in a shameful situation, he is to experience the shame as part of his anti-shame program. The following rationale can be given by the therapist:

> The anti-shame exercises use the same process of desensitization used in many areas of psychology and medicine. For instance, if you have allergies, the allergist can give you therapeutic doses of the pollens you're allergic to—with the paradoxical effect of desensitizing you to the same pollens. To desensitize yourself to shame, you have to give yourself therapeutic doses of shame. After you have reached the therapeutic level necessary, your shame will become noticeably less of a problem.

This procedure can be used with whatever a patient is afraid of confronting. Patients have collected experiences of "being rejected," "being separated," "authority figures," "criticism," "taking risks," "making mistakes," "displeasing others," "being in tight places," "being out of control," "being around sick people," and "approaching strangers." The therapist can set up a behavioral desensitization program with just about any avoidance patterns.

The therapist can use some of the following suggestions in developing a program for the patient:

1. *Self-monitoring.* The patient keeps a written record of his counter behavior. One patient, who had trouble receiving from others, kept a diary of the times he had asked for help and was given something, such as a compliment.

2. *Lists.* The patient can develop a list of behaviors that would qualify as therapeutic. One woman who had a fear of displeasing others made up a list of "anti-nice" behaviors, including such items as "not laughing at jokes I don't think funny" and "not telling others their cooking is great and asking for the recipes."

3. *Look for opportunities.* The person can purposely do items on his list or look for opportunities to experience what he's afraid of. Life usually offers abundant opportunities to experience what one fears. Two different patients, for example, who were concerned about shameful appearances, had to apply a conspicuous skin medicine to combat skin cancer. Both were able to turn this necessity into powerful anti-shame experience.

4. *Point system.* The patient may set up a point system, with each experience being rated from 0 to 100. For example, a patient fearful of authorities set a goal of reaching three-thousand points in six months. At the end of this period, he was significantly less intimidated by authority figures. An alternate plan would be for the person to seek out and try to have at least one corrective experience each day.

5. *Fully experience the emotion.* The patient is encouraged fully to experience and accept the feelings and sensations he has been trying to avoid. He is to stay in the situation as long as possible without props. If the person is drinking or using drugs, he gets no points.

6. *Focus on intention.* Often a patient may discover that when what he has been dreading actually occurs, it is only a minor irritation. One patient who was getting anti-respect points called the therapist and said, "I went to a meeting in informal clothes because I thought they would discount me. They seemed to respect me more than when I put on the dog—does this count?" The therapist told him that what is most important is the intention. If he intended to endure feelings of being "disrespected," this was what was important. (For a more detailed discussion of these methods, see Emery 1984.)

Developing Self-Confidence

As A. Bandura (1982) has shown, increasing a patient's sense of confidence decreases his anxiety. Patient and therapist can work together to develop ways for the patient to increase his confidence in the feared area. The patient's confidence is enhanced primarily as the result of self-attributed success experiences. One woman fearful of being alone took on more and more activities to do on her own, culminating in a two-week vacation by herself in Europe.

The patient can use educational means—such as driving lessons, speech classes, and special tutoring—to acquire skills. Books and tapes can serve the same function. One patient with social anxiety read Dale Carnegie's *How to Win Friends and Influence People* and practiced some of the principles in the book with the result that he reduced his anxiety. Knowing, even theoretically, what he could do to influence others in a positive way increased his self-confidence.

The ability to handle any risk can increase a patient's sense of confidence. Thus, it is often beneficial to encourage an anxious patient to take a risk for its own sake. The risk does not have to be directly related to the specific fear. Some may do something that they never have done before: one woman asked a man out for the first time. Another man with test anxiety took a ride in a small plane—something he had been afraid to do. The gain in self-confidence spread to other areas of his life.

The most common lack of confidence is in the social area. The therapist can help the patient develop skills in dealing with others. The patient is often afraid that he will not know what to say, particularly if the other person is angry or demanding. The therapist can say that, in a social encounter, one has basically four choices—to say nothing, to agree with others, to disagree, or to change the topic—and can expand on each of these.

The patient may believe he has to respond when others talk to him. Silence is one of the most powerful responses a person can make and has kept psychoanalysts in business over the years. Most socially anxious people make the mistake of saying too much: they overexplain and overqualify, particularly in dating situations. Silence can make a person seem more genuine and more interesting than he turns out to be.

Ernest Becker (1971) points out that catatonics receive much attention in state hospitals largely because people are fascinated about what secrets they may hide. The same holds true for the amnesia patient. Becker notes,

"With a charged commodity like silence, the most impaired persons can be skilled performers." He goes on to say, "If I were to write a manual on seduction for adolescent young men, the first and foremost precept would be: keep your mouth shut" (1971, p. 108).

A homework assignment for one overly talkative socially anxious patient was to answer questions with either a simple Yes or No. He had trouble doing this but, when he was able to pull it off, he felt much more confident and powerful.

AGREEING

The patient is often extremely anxious about having attention drawn to him. Paradoxically, his rejection of this attention usually creates more attention. He may defend himself against criticism or protest against a compliment. The therapist can show the patient how agreeing with the other is a much easier way to handle the situation. With criticism, the patient can disarm the other by saying, "Thank you for calling this to my attention." And the same applies to a compliment: "Thank you, I like it myself." The patient and therapist can role-play a variety of such situations.

DISAGREEING

Often the patient needs practice in disagreeing with others. One device is for the patient to tell the other person twice that he disagrees, and to leave it at that. The patient may well not know that one can agree to disagree and still remain friends.

DOING THE UNEXPECTED

One unexpected response a person can make is to change the subject—an option the patient often does not know he has, particularly if the other person seems to have more power. The therapist can point out the usefulness of asking questions to change the topic:

In sales, it is generally understood that whoever answers the question first loses. That's why it's interesting to watch a salesman try to sell another seasoned salesman. For example, "What would you be willing to pay for this house?" is answered with, "Well, if you were me, what would *you* pay for this house?" One way of changing a subject is to answer a question you don't want to answer with another question. Therapists are notorious for doing this.

The patient can also be taught how to change a subject by answering with a non sequitur or an irrelevant response. (This was one of the methods of the famous hypnotherapist, Milton Erickson, who seemed to be able to address just about any social situation.) The patient can memorize some irrelevant remarks to use whenever the occasion demands it.

Erickson's genius was in his ability to handle confidently whatever social situation arose. For example, one of his rules was: "Never take an insult." He tells the story of having a brilliant medical student who was specializing in pathology. The student was hostile to Erickson and did not want to take a class in psychiatry. He was to turn in a book review, but instead handled in a blank piece of paper as a way to insult Erickson. Erickson said, "Without reading your review, I notice you made two mistakes: you haven't dated it and you haven't signed it. So, turn it in next Monday. And remember, a book review is like reading pathology slides" (Rosen 1982). The student turned in a very competent book review. The point of Erickson's story is that by doing the unexpected one can gain command of a social situation.

One can take command of a situation by joining with a potential adversary. In role playing awkward social situations that the patient finds himself in, the principle of doing the unexpected can be tried out. Often just the suggestion or consideration that the patient could try some unexpected behavior provides him with new confidence. One patient, for example, had a fight with a fellow employee, a woman. He dreaded going back in to the office the following Monday because of all the "bad vibes" in the air. The therapist suggested that he experiment with treating this woman in an exceptionally friendly way. He role-played this behavior and said that he had never considered it.

The patient can be taught that when confronted with a novel situation, he should stop and reflect on it and then think of and do something unexpected. Practicing this strategy will increase his social confidence.

MAKING A MISTAKE PART OF THE SHOW

Another strategy is for patients to make any mistakes they make part of their social show.

THERAPIST: A good speaker will act as if any mistake he makes, or any unforeseen events that occur, are part of the show. Johnny Carson does this when he blows a line in his monologue. Whenever you make some slip up, act as if you planned it. For example, if you're a famous tennis player and have to leave in the middle of a nationally televised game, you can act as if this is part of your game plan. If you say something stupid or awkward at a party, act as if this was part of the show to see how others would respond. If you have an anti-shame philosophy, this works very well in that all of your social faux pas can be seen as deliberate anti-shame exercises.

This strategy works well with the overall goal of increasing one's self-acceptance.

Chapter 15

Restructuring a Patient's Assumptions and Major Issues

The anxious patient's major maladaptive assumptions often center on one of the following three issues—acceptance, competence, and control—which derive from his sense of vulnerability and may be associated with particular domains—autonomous or sociotropic, private or public (see chapter 5).

Many vague fears can be better understood when they are looked at from the standpoint of these three issues. Let us consider, for example, three different patients who all presented with fears of developing terminal cancer. The first patient's major issue concerned acceptance by others: she believed that if she developed the illness, her friends and relatives would reject her, and she would die all alone. The second patient's major issue related to competence: for him to develop cancer meant that he had lost the "good health contest" with his peers. The third patient was concerned with control: he had to control all of the factors that influenced his life; his self-esteem was tied to his ability to control his life, and to develop this illness meant he had lost control. Similarly, a fear of intimacy can be due to fear that other people will reject one if one gets too close, or that others will control one, or that one cannot live up to their expectations or standards of behavior.

Identifying Assumptions

While initially the focus of cognitive therapy is on relieving the patient's symptoms, later it shifts to modifying the underlying beliefs that predispose the patient to anxiety. In the process of collecting automatic thoughts, general themes that compose the patient's world view start to emerge.

The therapist uses a deductive method: he starts with feelings and behavior, moves to automatic thoughts and then to assumptions behind the thoughts, and finally arrives at the patient's major concern. In clinical practice, this procedure may vary. The therapist may use some inductive reasoning and go in the other direction (from major issue to assumptions, for example). However, in both methods the four types of data—*feelings, thoughts, assumption,* and *issues*—are used as checks on each other.

The patient's anxiety-producing assumptions become activated when he encounters a stressor, or a series of stressors, that impinges on one of his major concerns. The patient's assumptions may have to do with any number of issues—health, religion, relationships, or achievements—and are usually framed in extreme, all-or-nothing terms.

The following are some examples of assumptions that make up the three major issues:

ACCEPTANCE

1. I have to be cared for by someone who loves me.
2. I need to be understood.
3. I can't be left alone.
4. I'm nothing unless I'm loved.
5. To be rejected is the worst thing in the world.
6. I can't get others angry at me.
7. I have to please others.
8. I can't stand being separated from others.
9. Criticism means personal rejection.
10. I can't be alone.

COMPETENCE

1. I am what I accomplish.
2. I have to be somebody.
3. Success is everything.
4. There are only winners and losers in life.

5. If I'm not on top, I'm a flop.
6. If I let up, I'll fail.
7. I have to be the best at whatever I do.
8. Others' successes take away from mine.
9. If I make a mistake, I'll fail.
10. Failure is the end of the world.

CONTROL

1. I have to be my own boss.
2. I'm the only one who can solve my problems.
3. I can't tolerate others telling me what to do.
4. I can't ask for help.
5. Others are always trying to control me.
6. I have to be perfect to have control.
7. I'm either completely in control or completely out of control.
8. I can't tolerate being out of control.
9. Rules and regulations imprison me.
10. If I let someone get too close, that person will control me.

The patient's assumptions are supported by his family and personal experience. From the patient's point of view, his assumptions prevent something undesirable from happening and ensure that something of value will occur. A patient who believes he needs love is afraid that he cannot exist without it and anticipates that with love will come eternal happiness.

The therapist can use different methods to identify the patient's assumptions. The standard method is to form hypotheses about them and then to try these on with the patient for fit. The therapist's hypotheses are based on the patient's automatic thoughts, behavior, coping strategy, and personal history. As therapy focuses on modifying assumptions, the assumptions often are reformulated to find the correct fit.

Another method for identifying the patient's assumptions is to use an imagery technique. This is useful when the patient is having distressful experiences. The therapist asks the patient to close his eyes and picture the earliest memory he has of a distressing experience as similar as possible to the one he is undergoing. The therapist needs to give the patient time and encouragement to recall an experience similar to the present one. If he cannot come up with one, the therapist can say, "Okay, we'll go on to something else, but if one comes to mind, let me know." If the patient is unable to recall one, he can be asked to make one up.

In nearly every case, the patient will have a vivid image of some experience that is strikingly similar to his present distress. Often he will have more than one that is similar in theme. The patient is asked to concentrate on the earliest one and then to state in one sentence the underlying belief that he was operating from at that time. The formulation of this belief may take a while for therapist and patient to put together in a meaningful way. The therapist can use a blackboard (as discussed in the last chapter) to help specify the underlying belief. The patient is asked to give the feelings and body sensations associated with his early experience and to compare them with what he is presently experiencing. The patient usually reports a close fit.

One patient suffered through every Christmas holiday season with a sense of doom. He said his earliest memory of this feeling was seeing his mother taken away to a tuberculosis sanatorium one Christmas evening when he was seven. He had not put these two events together until asked by the therapist to look for an early image of an experience that was similar in feeling to his current dread of the holidays.

His belief was that "something bad was going to happen over the holidays." During the session, he expanded on his limited belief ("Just because I think I will have a bad Christmas doesn't mean I will"). Later he reported he had his most enjoyable holiday ever, and the first anxiety-free one.

A business executive with severe speech anxiety related his anxiety over an upcoming speech to an early incident when he was afraid to play sports with school kids for fear of showing up as incompetent. Identifying his basic belief ("I can't show public incompetence") helped him to modify the same fear of public incompetence he still had. In table 15.1 are some of the case examples of how this procedure identifies beliefs.

This procedure helps the patient to see how his past memories are creating problems in the present and getting in the way of his future happiness. The therapist can then suggest that the patient learned this assumption at an age and level of development when he lacked sufficient ability to see the belief's limits. Although the therapist has no way of knowing whether the patient's assumption actually developed as a result of this specific incident, it is helpful to view it as at least a contributing factor. Most patients respond well to this procedure and rationale. Patients often bring up fantasies and images of earlier incidents that are extremely similar in feeling and content to the present distress.

The patient can let go not only of the content of childhood beliefs but of the process of immature thinking as well. The therapist can show how the patient is processing experiences in an immature way whenever he acts on one of these beliefs. One patient was acting on the belief that she was nothing if she was rejected. The therapist helped her to see how she was

TABLE 15.1

Identifying Basic Beliefs

Early Memory	Present Fear	Underlying Belief
At age four being a nuisance to big brother.	Fear of approaching boss.	I can't bother those in authority.
Being ridiculed by first-grade teacher.	Fear of being intimidated by law professor.	Those in power will humiliate me.
At age six being spanked by father. At age four seeing father carried home drunk.	Fear of getting into trouble at work. Fear of becoming an alcoholic.	If I'm not perfect, I'll be punished. I'll end up just like my father.
At age five going away and having family dog die.	Fear family member will die while on trip.	When I'm not physically close to others, something bad will happen to them.
At age six being forced to work on weekend by stepfather.	Employer will make me work overtime and exploit me.	Those in authority have complete power over me.
At age five getting lost away from home.	Fear of getting lost on freeways.	I always have to know exactly where I'm going.
At age five getting caught stealing money.	Fear of being accused of dishonesty.	I have to be 100 percent honest.
At age six being told to change from left-handedness to right-handedness.	Fear of being rejected by others.	I have to change to be acceptable.
At age seven having father leave mother permanently after a fight.	Fear others will leave if assertive.	If I make others angry they will leave me.

processing this information in a concrete, global, and all-or-nothing fashion. The therapist has to keep in mind that it is the process associated with the immature belief—not simply the content of the belief—that is causing the problem.

The patient's basic assumptions are usually readily identifiable because he repeats the same patterns throughout his life. Further, his assumptions often have a long history that can be unearthed. One eighty-year-old patient was able to trace the origin of his fear of losing money back to his grandfather: a Russian immigrant who had suffered economic distress when he first came to this country. His fear of losing money was a family tradition and could be traced back to the 1800s.

Major Issues

IDENTIFYING MAJOR ISSUES

To be effective, the therapist has to address the basic issues in the patient's life. Just as the therapist lacks the time to correct all of the patient's automatic thoughts, he lacks the time to correct all of the patient's faulty assumptions. He can, however, repeatedly focus on the patient's major issues, which tend to be among the three already mentioned—acceptance, competence, and control.

The patient's major issue is a habitualized, fixed, and largely automatic way of thinking, acting, feeling, and responding to the world. A person with a major concern about self-competence has thought about his competence thousands of times, spoken about it thousands of times, and acted on these thoughts thousands of times.

E. Easwaran uses the metaphor of channels in the brain to describe how a person's major concern develops: "In the early stages, this channel may be only an inch or so deep. Thought may flow down it, but it may also flow somewhere else. Also, the walls are still soft and crumbly; they may cave in and fill the channel a little" (1981, p. 92). Patients respond well to this metaphor. The therapist can point out that the patient has a choice in the matter. For example, every time he structures his experience as one of rejection, he makes the channel a little deeper. Easwaran sums it up, "It is almost neurological; we are conditioning the patterns of thinking within the mind. And finally there is a huge Grand Canal in the mind" (p. 92). At that point just about anything at all is enough to provide a conditioned response.

The patient's major concern has been so overpracticed and overlearned that it has developed a life of its own. For one patient, the major issue was control, which manifested itself mainly in regard to her health: the thought that something was dangerously wrong with her health would often appear spontaneously, and she would become mobilized to control this danger. This intense concern dictated how she perceived the world. She saw health dangers everywhere. She would focus on the health dangers reported in the mass media and tune into any discussion of illness. She would scan her body and her internal sensations in an attempt to find some danger. Just as alcoholics will drink because the Dodgers win, because they lose, or because they do not play, the patient used any happening as a reason to focus on her concern. She would be anxious when the doctor said there was some problem (to her, this meant that she would get some fatal disease unless she controlled it), when the doctor said there was no problem ("he could have missed something"), and when she did not see a doctor ("I haven't seen a doctor about it; I have to do something about that").

The patient often develops a life style based around his major concern. One woman who was concerned with acceptance spent much of her time and energy in developing and maintaining a series of relationships where she hoped to be accepted. She maintained relationships with many people she even disliked, because she saw all of her relationships as insurance policies against being rejected. She was kept busy paying the premiums on all of her policies.

POSITIVE AND NEGATIVE REINFORCERS

These major issues provide one with benefits. As a result of one patient's fear of being incompetent, he was motivated to overachieve at his career. He worked long hours and spent his free time figuring out ways to do better work. Although frequently insecure and anxious, he was quite successful in his career.

The patient may vacillate between periods of boredom and anxiety. When there is little threat to his major concern, he is bored, and when there is, he is anxious. The threat to the major concern becomes the major motivator in his life and, paradoxically, often the greatest source of pleasure.

A major concern is frequently negatively reinforcing (reinforced by the removal of an aversive experience), so that the patient feels temporarily elated when the feared event does not materialize. One man whose major issue was acceptance by others would celebrate by eating some forbidden fattening food after he had been complimented on his appearance. The compliment removed the fear that he was old and ugly.

The patient obtains social reinforcement for his major concern. He usually belongs to some formal or informal group of people who share the same concern. One patient concerned with competence used his intelligence to bolster his self-esteem. He became a member of Mensa and other formal and informal groups that prize intelligence. The social reinforcement the workaholic receives is well documented. The person who is extremely concerned about control will be reinforced for self-discipline in dieting and exercise.

The patient's major concern frequently is *systemic* and engulfs his whole psychological system. His concern leads to physical, emotional, and behavioral responses that feed back to the original concern. One patient's major concern with control caused him to tighten up and respond ineffectively to authority figures, who he thought were trying to control him. His response, in turn, fed the original concern that he could not control his own life when it came to authority figures.

PSYCHOLOGICAL DOUBLE

A person often will be involved with significant others who reinforce and validate his concern. The person who is afraid of being controlled will start a relationship with a person who wants to control it. The person who is ambivalent about attachment because he was raised by an ambivalent parent will start a relationship with someone equally ambivalent. The person will often enter other situations that reconfirm his basic concern. For example, people who seem to have the greatest problem with rejection will enter fields such as sales, writing, or entertainment, where rejection is likely.

The patient's major concern is associated with a dual image of himself (Horney 1950), which represents extremes: one image is a despising one, revolving around a sense of inferiority or lack; the opposite is overcompensation and correction for the despising image. The image of rejection is combined with one of unconditional acceptance; the image of humiliation is combined with one of superiority; and the one of being dominated by one of being in control. The dual images are inversely related. The more despising the one image, the more grand the other has to be in order to compensate for it.

The patient will often experience these dual images in vivid fantasies. One patient whose issue was competence had images of being a bum and compensated with images of being extremely wealthy. Another patient with a despising image of being a ninety-eighty-pound weakling had contrasting images of being a star athlete. The patient's dual image system is the source of much anxiety: he alternates between fear that his despised image will come true and fear that his ideal image, which he believes he needs to feel good about himself, will not be met.

Achieving one's ideal image does not alleviate one's anxiety. One patient had a fantasy of becoming a professional singer, which compensated for an image of being unacceptable. He did have some success in this area. However, he became all the more insecure because the opposite of what he expected occurred; many people were jealous of his success, and he received more rejection after he reached his goal than before! He also became fearful of losing his new-found status.

The more intense a person's issue, the more anxiety he will have and the more he resists modifying it. A person whose life is heavily invested in one or two major issues often is the more difficult to work with because of this investment.

DEVELOPMENT OF MAJOR CONCERNS

The therapist can review with the patient how he developed his major concern and how this is related to his anxiety. It is often beneficial to do this early in therapy. Although the modification of issues may not be worked on initially, the therapist demonstrates an understanding of the patient's situation and lays out a map to help guide the therapy.

Figure 15.1 shows how one patient's anxiety about being rejected for being physically unattractive was diagrammed. She believed that she was too skinny and her breasts were too small for her ever to be fully accepted by a man. The innermost circle represented her core misconception and major area of concern. To compensate for her "flaw," the woman felt she needed to be loved and unconditionally accepted by an attractive, perfect man. However, she had several beliefs that tended to undermine her relationships with men. One of her beliefs was that all attractive men just wanted sex with her and did not really accept her. Another was that the men who did care for her were unattractive. A third belief was that she had to avoid having men see her without clothes on. For this reason, she had sex with several men but did not fully undress with them. She avoided exposing her body by not going to gyms or to the beach. She believed she would never find the "perfect man."

The therapist can use a diagram such as figure 15.1 to show a patient how his beliefs and assumptions serve to protect the misconception at the core of his major concern. All of the assumptions spiral down to seemingly prove the misconception. In this figure, the assumptions lead back to the same conclusion, "I'm physically unacceptable."

The therapist can tell the patient that one may develop an undesirable view of oneself early in life as the result of a blow to the self-image. The core misconception about the self can be considered a kind of poison that may affect the person's system throughout his life. Each experience that

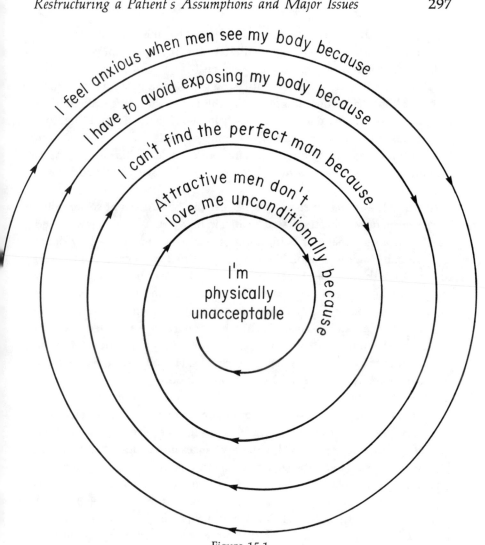

Figure 15.1
Major Concern and Downward Spiral of Beliefs and Assumptions

reaffirms the core belief reinforces the system. To combat the negative core belief, the person develops a contrasting fantasy and a plan for overcoming the initial flaw. The problem is that the overcompensation or antidote perpetuates the original misconception.

The therapist can frame this misconception as a decision the patient made about himself before he had all the information. It can be looked at as a way of adapting what is no longer useful. The therapist can use a variety of metaphors to illustrate how the attempted cure is perpetuating the problem: "If you took heroin for a headache, the side effects of the heroin would make you think you still have the illness, so you would have to take more heroin to cure the side effects."

Patients are usually able to identify the source of a core misconception or major concern. When acceptance is the issue, the source might be a critical or unaccepting parent; the core belief is, "I'm flawed and therefore unacceptable." The core belief when competence is the concern is, "I'm inferior"; it can often be traced to failure or modeled failure experiences; the conviction, "I have no control," frequently originates from a domineering parent.

At times the source of the "toxic" belief can be cultural or social influence. One man was discriminated against in his youth for being Jewish and developed a self-image of being inferior. He overcompensated by doing exceptionally well in school. He believed that he had to continue to excel to overcome the stigma of inferiority. He had many successes, but never as many as he believed he needed. His life, for the most part, was a series of anxiety and depression episodes. He was anxious when he thought he would not excell and depressed when he thought he had failed. Later in life, he needed more and more success and almost daily injections of praise and attention to fight off his negative feelings. He could never get enough of what he really did not need but thought he did.

Self-Fulfilling Prophecy. The patient often unwittingly creates real situations that reconfirm his basic assumptions about himself. The anxiety itself often brings about what he fears, as happens in speech anxiety: he is afraid that he will do a poor job, and his anxiety causes him to do so. As described by Guidano and Liotti, the patient's repetitious procedures "model" the outside environment until he creates an "environmental niche" that is adequate for his or her personal identity and life program" (1983, p. 90).

One patient, although well thought of at his job, feared that he would be fired. Eventually his suspicion that other people were out to get his job led to his being fired. Another patient, who believed that he could never have a relationship with other people, moved to a remote area with few people around. Although his reasoning was circular and he was quite lonely, he correctly assessed that there were few people around with whom he could fail at striking up friendships.

The therapist can help the patient see how he reduces the world to fit his map. The strategy here is for the patient gradually to change his life style so as to be able to learn more about himself and better ways to attain his goals.

Selective Abstraction. Repetitive thinking errors are a major block to learning (Beck 1976). When a person's method of assimilating information is faulty, he continues to believe and act on faulty assumptions. He assumes the world will turn out a certain way, and his method of taking in information reconfirms his basic assumptions.

Often a patient fails to learn because he attends only to material that supports his original assumptions. The patient who believes he lives in a hostile world will pay strict attention to news reports and have conversations that focus on dangers. Such selective focusing on crime, pollution, war, and pestilence reconfirms the belief that one lives in a dangerous world.

Arbitrary Inference. Arbitrary inference often leads to the realization of what one has originally feared; and if one expects other people to act in a certain way, they will often fulfill these expectations. For example, a person who believes he cannot trust others often acts untrustworthy. One patient was afraid his business partner was stealing from him. To protect himself, he started to steal from his partner. His partner found this out and then did start to steal from him. The fear does not have to be realized for this pattern to reinforce the false belief; a person can validate his distortion in many ways. One student got a C on his midterm and falsely assumed he would fail the class, drop out of school, and become a bum. He overstudied and ended up with an A+. His conclusion: He was saved from a life as a "bum" only by his hard work.

Failure to Test Reality. The goal of much of therapy is to set up corrective learning experiences. An overall goal is to have the patient develop the mental set of being a reality tester instead of a reality avoider. In many of these learning experiences, the patient approaches what he fears. The strategy that worked with the preceding student was to help him develop an attitude of risking and "living more dangerously." He put in less work in his studies and found he could still get good grades.

Circular Reasoning. A person who engages in circular reasoning can effectively block learning. Patients often have closed forms of logic: "I can't stand being there because I can't stand not standing it"; "I can't stand the anxiety because of the anxiety"; or, "I'm anxious because I know I'm going crazy and I'm going crazy because I'm anxious."

Dichotomous Reasoning. The patients often structure their experience in such an either/or way that they fail to learn. If a job or person is not perfect, then it is totally unacceptable.

Magical Thinking. The most common block to learning is magical thinking that is reaffirmed by superstitious behavior ("I had an image of the plane crashing so I cancelled the trip"; "I knew he would be angry at me so I never called him back"; "I sat in this chair at the doctor's office and nothing bad happened before, so I always sit in the same chair").

Overgeneralization.   Patients often will take one or two pieces of information that support a threat, and then overgeneralize. Thus, a patient fearful of mugging will overgeneralize from a reported case of mugging that "everyone is getting mugged."

Misattribution.   A person may attribute his problem to the wrong cause. One patient attributed all of his test anxiety to an approaching test when the real problem was that he had not studied enough. Another patient attributed his lack of a social life to his not liking singles bars.

The patient may lack any sense of cause and effect in his anxiety or have a fixed idea of cause and effect. One mother was anxious about the possible consequences of her parenting ("My son will become emotionally disturbed"). She exaggerated the degree of danger and her role in creating the damage. She believed that if there was a negative outcome, she was the cause. Her underlying belief was that there was a direct causal link between her action and the outcome.

Fixed Ideas.   Lack of flexibility can keep one from learning. The therapist can point out that all beliefs are to some extent limiting: they exclude more of reality than they include.

THERAPIST: If you say, "I'm an American," you're excluding much about yourself. And if you give too much emphasis to this one belief at the expense of others, it could become self-defeating in that you could become a fanatic about being an American.

The goal is to let a patient see that, in the long run, holding onto rigid beliefs is not a strength but a weakness, in that they prevent one from dealing more effectively with reality. An indirect approach stressing the benefits of flexibility often works. To one rigid patient who held onto the belief that she had to keep all commitments or chastize herself, the therapist said:

Almost any virtue, if carried to an extreme, can become a vice. Often people lost in the desert will drink themselves to death when they find water. At one time you may have needed this structure in your life, but do you still need it now?

When a patient sees his obstacle to learning as a virtue, it is helpful for therapist and patient to rename the virtue. The patient may see his block as being "principled," "consistent," or "strong." The therapist who has a good relationship with the patient can substitute the term "stubborn."

Fortune Telling. The anxious patient nearly always assumes a negative outcome, which may be rationalized with the thought, "This way I won't be disappointed." The real result is that if the feared event does not happen, the patient attributes this to luck or to his worry about it beforehand. An occasional bad result supports the whole process of worry and assumption of threat.

A patient may not learn from experience because he attributes the nonoccurrence of the catastrophe to some lucky break. A man who feared "ending up on Skid Row" said, "I wouldn't have been successful if I hadn't by sheer chance found the perfect location for my business."

Self-Propaganda. People often become prisoners of their own doomsaying, creating a climate where one starts to believe one's own propaganda. One patient, for example, discussed health threats with so many people that he had difficulty distancing himself from this topic of conversation when others brought it up.

Shame and Pride. Shame is one of the strongest emotional blocks to learning. Learning new skills often involves using them in imperfect ways, and many people refuse to try because of the shame involved. Often patients will not even tell a therapist some of their deepest concerns out of shame. Teaching the patient to overcome his shame is a major way to help him to become a better learner.

One patient was painfully self-conscious about his hairpiece and believed that "everyone will reject and humiliate me if I go without it." Because of his shame, he was unwilling to test this assumption.

Pride, the other side of shame, is an equally common block to learning. One of the most remarkable features of people with emotional problems is that often they have fixed ideas of what they need to do to solve their problems. The ideas can be exaggerated in the patient who has the special-person syndrome (Raimy 1975): that is, he believes in his natural superiority. Often he is intelligent and successful in some area, while his pride usually prevents him from learning in his problem area. The therapist can discuss shame and pride in practical terms and point out that the person who does not learn from his experiences is destined to repeat them. The therapist can also model humility (the willingness to accept that he can learn from anyone).

Greed. A person's desire for ever more security creates more insecurity. One patient, for example, wanted absolute assurance that he was healthy. The doctor's clean bill of health had the consequence, if not the intent, of making him even more insecure.

One patient had developed a pattern of not completing jobs or carrying out plans. Once he would get to a part he felt he could not do, he would switch jobs with the rationale of, "There is more money, opportunity, creativity in the new job or plan." His greed compounded his fear of being inadequate.

A person who feels incompetent may have trouble accepting himself and feeling accepted by others; he may also feel "out of control." Despite this interrelationship, patients do prominently exhibit one issue more than others. For this reason, the major issues will be discussed separately.

Acceptance

The core belief of the person concerned with acceptance is that he may be flawed in some way and thus be unacceptable to others. The development of this concern may be the result of lack of acceptance by one parent or of having some stigma or flaw that makes him unacceptable to his peers. One woman, for example, lost an eye as a child and felt unacceptable most of her life because of this loss.

The patient uses a variety of strategies to get others to accept and love him. His overcompensation is usually a desire to get others to accept and love him unconditionally. He often is terrified of being rejected. This is the reason such a person is concerned with being liked and pleasing others. Because he feels unacceptable, he is terrified of being alone. He is often bothered by separation and is constantly seeking attachment.

This person is often anxious about his flaws and afraid others will discover them. One woman had trouble accepting herself and used her weight and lack of a good job as reasons for being unacceptable. She believed others would reject her as well. Her attempts to overplease had the effect of driving others away.

The patient exaggerates the extent and significance of social acceptance and rejection. He *overgeneralizes* and *homogenizes:* that is, he sees everyone's acceptance as essential and equally important. Acceptance by a mailman, a salesman, by all members of a social group, by a passer-by on the street, is as important as acceptance by people close to him. The consequences are seen as *absolute.* Acceptances or rejections are thought to be forever.

Because other people's opinions directly affect his self-esteem, he is highly dependent on feedback from others. He continually checks to see whether the other person is accepting him. If the other person appears to be accepting him, he becomes more confident and generally performs better.

If another person appears to reject him, his confidence goes down and his performance deteriorates. Because his self-esteem is sensitive to cues, especially when his performance is variable, he experiences an increase in inhibition. This indicates that his self-esteem is basically unstable—at least in this context. Part of his dependency is designed to authenticate whether "I am on the right track." If he receives corrective signals that are friendly or interpreted as such, he can correct his performance without losing self-esteem.

One of the reasons he cannot shrug off other people's opinions is his conviction that mass acceptance is essential for his well-being if not for his existence. Admiration and social success may increase his self-esteem temporarily and fortify it; however, his self-esteem is not stable because of its dependency on social input. Others' input will affect his self-esteem in either direction. In other words, his self-confidence is based on sand.

For example, a young man was hurt because he was not invited to a party. He thought he had been deliberately excluded and that the people who organized the party consciously discriminated against him. On further exploration, it became clear that the party was for people who had contributed money to a particular charity, and he was not even in the relevant pool of people who might be invited. The therapist used this incident as a chance to provide the client with an alternative point of view:

> All people have their frame of reference. When your frame of reference is out of kilter with social reality, it leads to a variety of symptoms —hurt feelings, anxiety, sadness, depression. When your frame of reference differs from the generally recognized way of interacting, this leads to problems with other people—to overconcern, nonassertiveness, and avoidance, for example.
>
> It is a difficult lesson in growing up to learn that there is an outside world that has nothing to do with you. Many people in their own tunnel vision tend to fix on a wide range of external events and relate them to themselves. They may, for example, do as you did in this case, draw conclusions regarding the power of other people's actions over your well-being, when in reality, these actions are totally irrelevant to you.

Patients like this young man intrude themselves into events that are remote from their existence—like a meteorite falling in Siberia. Why do they relate these events to themselves? Because one's large investment in being accepted leads to a pathological mode of scanning the social environment for signs of acceptance or rejection. The focus on acceptance is also determined to some degree by a relatively immature frame of reference. The person has not progressed to the point of decentering his universe to where he can judge social events completely separately from himself.

This excessive concern with acceptance is often manifested in the desire to be treated as a favorite child. If the person fails to receive special treatment in social situations, he believes he has been slighted or rejected. If he is not actually involved in the situation, he expects that others *should* take him into consideration in any event; and he believes that their failure to do so will have dangerous consequences.

When such perceived slights do occur, he attributes negative motivations or intentions to the other people concerned—even though, logically, the others have no motivations toward him at all, since he was not within their immediate area of consideration. For example, a practicing tax lawyer heard that one of the professors at the local university had been appointed to a chair in taxation at a distant university. Even though the patient himself had never been involved in academic work, he was frustrated and anxious: "Why didn't they take me? After all, I'm an expert on taxes. Perhaps this means they don't like me. What will this lead to?"

The person is continuously vigilant to gratify, or protect others' opinions of him. He has specifically incorporated an idiosyncratic set of rules for protecting his social images. Since he has his own set of rules that are inconsistent with normal behavior, he is likely to fear that other people are damaging his interests in some way.

Since his future depends on an assumption such as, "If I am going to get anywhere, I must be accepted by others," he is likely to be fearful of situations where another person might slight him. He often has considerable difficulty in dealing with authority figures because he fears the consequences of rejection. He interprets a particular policy or action by an authority as endangering him; when in reality, such actions do not affect him. He misinterprets attempts to bring order out of a chaotic situation, to regulate behavior in a logical way, as dangerous to his self-esteem. At the same time, he gains pleasure from pleasing the authority figure.

He frequently operates according to rules that suggest that others are better judges of his interests. In this sense, he assumes a child's role toward his peer group, spouse, children, or students. For example, one man would not make any plans without first consulting his wife. His reason was that she knew what was best for him. He believed not consulting her would lead only to unnecessary messiness or delay.

A striking feature of such a person is his frequent excessive empathy for other people. Because of this sensitivity, he believes that he must always be considerate, kind, sensitive, and generous. When this excessive concern is brought to his attention, he rationalizes it as others needing his attention to survive.

Competence

The patient whose major issue is competence fears that he does not measure up. His core belief is that he is inferior. Often he was raised in a family that, because of race, religion, or social class, felt inferior to others. At other times, the sense of inferiority comes from comparison with siblings, or from real shortcomings, such as doing poorly at athletics or in school, or from a parent who told him that he couldn't "do anything right." He also may have had few mastery or success experiences. Any major setback he experiences reinforces the belief.

On the other hand, the patient may be fearful of being unable to do the work required to reach his goal. His solution may be to induce others to help him, and he often develops work-related dependency. The person has many fears of being unable to finish projects. He is often bothered by procrastination and may have problems taking risks.

Such patients are afraid that their incompetence will be exposed—for example, in the course of contact with an authority figure. If an authority indicates the person is wrong, to some extent he believes the authority to be correct. Bill's (an insurance adjuster) boss accused him of not having filled out a report as he had promised. Even though Bill believed he had carried out what he had promised, he had a nagging doubt about it. His immature part believed his boss was right—even though the evidence against his being so was overwhelming. Bill felt overwhelmed in trying to present his case to his boss. The boss "smothered him with words," and Bill could not get in a word in his own defense. At the end of the interview, the patient was summarily dismissed. When he returned home, he felt a huge rage and had wishes that the boss would die. On the other hand, Bill was attracted to the boss; he felt that he could draw on some of the boss's strength, self-confidence, and status and offset his own weaknesses. He could not envision himself doing anything actively against the boss.

When the therapist suggested that he confront the boss, Bill became extremely anxious. He could not pinpoint the cause of his anxiety. However, he experienced an overwhelming, smothering feeling, which made him feel weak, helpless, and incapable of speaking. He compared his feelings with those of Melville's Billy Budd. Bill could not even envision the possibility of his having an open discussion with his boss. It is interesting that Bill functioned well in his various relationships—except for those with authority figures. He was the youngest of three brothers, and his oldest brother resembled an authority figure in many ways, having mocked and criticized the patient throughout his youth. The therapist suggested to Bill the possibility that he still retained the constellation of attitudes and reactions from childhood, which were mobilized by the presence of the authority figure and had become autonomous.

Therapy consisted of having a series of cognitive rehearsals, with Bill talking to the authority figure and exploring his attitudes about him. The therapist pointed out that even though Bill believed he was unable to speak up to the boss and would make a fool of himself, it was possible for him to speak articulately, even when anxious. Bill saw that, as long as he was in the grip of his own involuntary withdrawal and submissive, self-abnegating behavior, he validated his view of the boss as an all-powerful force and of himself as a helpless incompetent.

Patients concerned with such issues often report feeling like a phony or an imposter when they speak up to an employer, a supervisor, or a person whom they perceive as competent. One believes that one is really inferior, smaller, and less worthy: when one acts differently from the way one usually acts, one has a sense that one is trying to fool others. The sense of imposture is carried into many social situations.

One successful businessman, age 56, for example, said he always felt as though he was conning other businessmen when he was with them, and dreaded being found out. He often thought, "I'm not competent enough to handle the situation," or that he was not grown up enough to handle interactions with others.

Many patients report having images of themselves as small children in a world of giant adults. They may believe that later, when they have grown up, they will be able to handle the situation. However, avoidance of the situation prevents them from gaining experience that would give them more confidence.

Because the person often thinks he lacks competence and is putting on an act, he is constantly on the lookout for signs that others can see his incompetence. At this point, he is likely to take what others say literally —even statements intended to be humorous and non-evaluative. The anxious patient tends to be extremely literal about sensitive areas. A woman's friend made a joke about her driving: she took this literally and thought she was being criticized for being a "flake."

Some patients have images of themselves as frightened animals. One person thought, "I'm a scared rabbit, weak and passive." He saw himself as subhuman. One man saw himself as a frightened dog and had images of others picking him up by his ears. The therapist, as mentioned earlier, needs to inquire about the possibility of such images.

In social situations, the patient concerned with competence often feels unsure of himself, as if he does not belong. He exaggerates the demands of the situation and minimizes and overlooks his social skills and abilities. The person usually uses feedback from others to assess whether or not he is being perceived as competent. If the feedback is negative, his functioning is likely to go down. He becomes disabled, impaired, possibly even mute, because of the symbolic meaning of the negative feedback. In actuality, he can function if he believes himself to be capable of functioning. In other words, the negative feedback from others makes him believe that he cannot function adequately. The power of the perceived downgrading by others can be likened to that of a hypnotist over a subject. The socially anxious person can be hypnotized into believing that he cannot open his mouth, that he cannot think clearly, that he cannot stand erect. He is, in a sense, hypnotized into believing that his brain and organs of articulation are paralyzed.

The individual often engages in circular reasoning. One young man said that the idea of going to parties frightened him because he would not know how to act and because he was frightened he would be even more awkward; so he did not go to parties. The more he avoided social gatherings, the more frightened he became of them. The following are examples of the automatic thoughts he had when interacting with others: "I won't be able to do it. I will fail, falter, be mute"; "They are judging me as inadequate, inept, inappropriate"; "They are disapproving of my nervousness and my talking"; "Disapproval means not only loss of approval but also a clear prediction that I'm unable to be with others"; "I'll be unable to carry on"; "I'm not functional."

The strategy with this patient was (1) to help him separate his worth from his social performance and his achievements, (2) to help him accept himself and those within his domain as they were, (3) to separate what he was responsible for from what others were responsible for. The therapist had to correct not only personal distortions but cultural ones as well. The overall goal is to have the patient do a job for its own sake instead of as a way to bolster his self-esteem.

Control

The fears of the person concerned with control center on the possibility of being dominated by others or by events outside of his control. This fear can take many different forms. It may have to do with losing control to authority figures or significant others, with illness, or with loss of control over money. The patient usually develops this concern as the result of being in a situation where he perceives himself as having little or no control. This may have been a relationship with a domineering parent or being raised in an environment where lack of control was a significant issue. Another pattern we have observed is that of the person who has been unable to get a consistent response from his parents and is forced to live with ambiguity. He overcompensates by trying to control his own life, which often includes those around him. He is unable to tolerate ambiguity because he cannot control the outcome.

The patient is often afraid that he will go "out of control." Anxiety attacks are particularly frightening because he has no control over his feelings. The patient may focus on a fear of going crazy or losing control over financial or health matters. He often has problems with other people because of his excessive concern with control. Others see him as "controlling" and "manipulative" and, as a result, are less cooperative with him.

The patient usually does not present his problem as fear of losing control, but describes it as being caused by the situations or events themselves —crowds, teachers, dentists. However, the therapist can readily observe that it is not object, event, or situation that the patient fears as being dangerous, but the consequences of being out of control. For example, a patient who identified his problem as "fear of crowds" did not actually believe that danger in some mysterious way emanated from crowds and focused on him. What he actually feared was how he might behave in a crowd: that he would lose control in some way—faint or vomit, become vociferous or hysterical. In therapy, it then became necessary to discover the kernel of primitive logic that lay at the core and to devise strategies for counteracting its effects.

Like the person concerned with acceptance or competence, the person with a fear of being controlled may be afraid of authority figures. However, in this case the fear is that the authority will attempt to dominate him and make him do something he does not want to do. The person believes the dominance hierarchy determines whether one is "master" or "slave." It is easy to see how this belief system would lead to anxiety. For example, one patient, who had to get a recommendation from his professor, had to exert great effort to overcome his fear enough to ask for the recommendation. He thought the professor's attitude would be, "You're applying to the wrong school. You should go to the one I recommend to you."

The senses of control, effectiveness, and individuality are as important in interactions as receiving social supplies—nurturance, affection, approval. To a given individual, rejection may imply the loss of control as well as of supplies: "I have no control unless the other person acknowledges that I have control." The problem here is the perceived attitude of the other person: "If he does not give in to my request, it means I'm not in control of my own life." The patient's self-image is threatened by the perceived lack of control.

People must be able to open their mouths and speak intelligibly to function socially. If one cannot do this, it means that one has no control over body functioning—a devastating phenomenon. Further, if one has an involuntary postural sway and trembling, it is further evidence of a lack of control. This demonstration of lack of control is perceived by others. The person then has the fear of his being unable to function, plus the greater fear that others will see him as weak and continue to control him.

The patient concerned with control will usually show his concern in the first interview. He will make specific requests (such as adjusting the lighting, setting, or some other adjustment), interviewing the therapist ("What are your qualifications?"), not answering questions, and putting limitations on therapy. One woman said, "I have to be careful because most therapists try to get their hooks into patients." The person may also show anxiety over lack of self-discipline. One patient was highly anxious because she was not able to control her smoking. Paradoxically, her attempt to control herself made her feel more out of control, and her attempts to force herself to relax when anxious made her more anxious. Similarly, the more one tries to control another person, the more out of control one feels.

Anorexia, for example, appears to be fear of obesity, when more often the real fear is of loss of control. Often when a person feels out of control in one area of his life, he will overcompensate by extreme control in other areas. One patient whose personal and business life was in great disorder became obsessed with running.

A person concerned with control will use different strategies to regain control: one is to get angry at the person he believes is trying to control him; another is to give up all control. One patient was concerned about losing control of his finances. When he felt he had spent too much money and was out of control, he would spend more money. This gave him a temporary sense of being in control.

Human socialization seems to dictate that if people treat one in a specific way, one has to respond in kind to keep face. For this reason, some people feel boxed in by social interaction. Becker has described this process. "The parents' early enjoinder 'Say thank you to the man' is not an inculcation of obsequiousness. It is an exercise in control: it is now up to 'the man' to frame an appropriate response or to end the social situation gracefully" (1971, p. 97). Even inferiors in a social hierarchy can control the superior with the right verbal expressions. Becker describes this process: "An army officer may exclaim to his sergeant, 'Stop sirring me!' It is a protest against being manipulated by an overly constrictive definition of one's identity. One is too easily being put in another's box" (p. 97).

The person concerned with control is highly sensitive to these forms of control. Although rarely verbalized, fear of being controlled is the reason he avoids social gatherings and is uneasy at them. As with the other major issues, the patient often sets up a self-fulfilling prophecy: one's attempt to control others before one is controlled often causes others to use counter control.

Motivation and Major Concerns

Given the nature of the patient's major concerns, the therapist needs to have realistic expectations in helping him modify them. The patient is often reluctant to let go of his major concern. He wants to get rid of the anxiety, or product, of the major concern, but not of the concern itself. The patient, for example, wants to get rid of his fear of rejection but not of the wish to be fully accepted and approved of by nearly everyone. The necessary ingredient for helping him to modify his concern is persuading him to want to abandon this wish.

The patient can be shown that the benefits of his major concern are outweighed by its costs. Often the person concerned with competence will not stop overworking until he has a heart attack or has to pay some other high cost, just as some people will not stop smoking until they develop cancer. The therapist helps the patient see that he can lead a better life by making his major concern into a minor one ("I want to be accepted" versus "I need to be accepted"), or by switching priorities ("I have to be a success" versus "I'm going to focus on enjoying my life").

When a patient is not be willing to modify the major concern, such as a need to be successful, the therapist can point out the consequences of this choice and even perhaps help him obtain what he believes he "needs" to be happy. One woman, for example, said that she had to be a successful writer to be happy. She needed this achievement to compensate for very low self-esteem. She had a twenty-year history of anxiety and depression involving her need to be a successful writer. The therapist's attempts to make this a minor instead of a major concern and to switch the focus onto "writing for it's own sake" had little effect. The focus of therapy then switched to how she could most effectively reach her goal. The rationale for the switch was that she had to have either some success or more failures before she would be willing to modify her major concerns.

Once the patient sees the benefits to modifying the major concern and wants to, the therapist has available certain strategies and techniques. The following are some of these:

1. *Role of repetition.* The therapist has to avoid the "teacher's fallacy": telling the patient the correct assumption is rarely sufficient to make him discard the old one. The therapist has to repeatedly have the patient focus on the assumption. The therapist has to attack it from a variety of different angles: at times, it can be a direct attack ("Let's look at the costs and benefits of this belief"), and at other times it can be indirect (use of metaphors and teaching stories). As a general rule, the therapist should never be afraid of repeating himself.

The therapist also needs to elicit the patient's help in the use of repetition. One patient with a series of fixed concerns about self-competence that led to social anxiety ("I always have to look better than others") wrote a series of more adaptive beliefs on 3-by-5 cards and reviewed these beliefs at least once a day for six months. This, along with other repetitive strategies, allowed her to become more reasonable in judging herself.

2. *Choice versus change.* Since a patient has learned his assumptions so well, it is nearly impossible for him to change them, even if he wants to.

THERAPIST: You think, "I'll try to change," and then when the same beliefs reappear, you become discouraged about change. A better strategy is to think of choice. Your overriding problem is difficult because you've so overlearned it that it automatically reappears. However, you always have the ability to choose different points of view; you can become aware of what you are doing. So when the old belief reappears and you catch yourself, you can simply choose to replace it with a new belief. If you continue to choose the new belief, this choice will eventually become automatic.

3. *Role of action.* Each major concern leads to a series of behaviors that reaffirm it. The therapist needs to stress the importance of action in maintaining old roles, and can point out that by repeatedly acting the opposite of his inclination, the patient can undermine the old belief. One woman who was afraid of being rejected by men was given the assignment of approaching men in some way at least one hundred times. She would say hello to men in her office, sit next to a man on a bus, and so on. She took eight months to complete the assignment and reported it as being helpful in modifying her belief that being around men was dangerous.

4. *Life-style changes.* The therapist can suggest that a patient modify his major concerns by adjusting his life style. A therapist persuaded a person overly concerned with his health to stop reading health books, listening to "wellness" tapes, going to faith healers, seeing countless nutritionists, and having endless conversations about health and sickness. Or, the therapist can encourage a patient to associate with people who do not share the same major concerns. A patient with a major concern about controlling death stopped going to genealogy meetings and joined groups with other interests.

The restructuring of assumptions and major concerns follows naturally from earlier stages of cognitive therapy, such as the identification of automatic thoughts and imagery and of maladaptive behavior. The process of restructuring assumptions reflects the therapist's and the patient's growing understanding of the anxiety reaction in relation to the latter's goals, strategies, and life choices. At the same time, the process may open up new challenges to his habitual ways of thinking and behaving.

Postscript

Although cognitive therapy has received considerable research attention and support as a treatment for depression, there have been relatively few studies of its effectiveness in the treatment of anxiety disorders. Results of these studies have been generally encouraging. A. O. DiLoreto (1971) compared the effects of systematic desensitization, client-centered treatment, and rational-emotive therapy (a close relative of cognitive-behavioral therapy), and a placebo control, on interpersonal anxiety. While all treatments reduced anxiety more effectively than the placebo, rational-emotive therapy produced the largest increase in interpersonal activity outside the treatment setting. Rational-emotive therapy and client-centered therapy were approximately two thirds as effective as systematic desensitization in reducing anxiety.

Another cognitive approach to social anxiety was evaluated by N. J. Kanter and M. R. Goldfried (1979), who concluded that systematic rational restructuring more effectively reduced anxiety and irrational beliefs than did self-control desensitization, although the treatments produced equivalent effects on behavioral and physiological measures.

A study by F. L. Gardner, et al. (1980) compared five cognitively and behaviorally oriented strategies in the reduction of moderate to severe levels of social anxiety. On every measure except pulse rate, all treatments were superior to a waiting-list control. However, the cognitive therapy, rational-emotive therapy, and stress-inoculation training procedures were generally more effective in reducing self-reported negative affect, fear, and avoidant behavior. Three treatments—cognitive therapy, behavioral assertion training, and interpersonal cognitive problem-solving skills training—produced equivalent and superior effects on a behavioral measure of anxiety (timed behavior).

Cognitive approaches to test anxiety have been studied by Goldfried, Linehan, and Smith (1978) and by Holroyd (1976). Goldfried and his fellow researchers found that systematic rational restructuring outperformed prolonged exposure in decreasing test anxiety. Similarly, Holroyd demonstrated that cognitive therapy was more effective than systematic desensitization in reducing test anxiety and improving grade-point average. Additional studies of cognitive-behavioral interventions in anxiety-related conditions have been reviewed by P. C. Kendall and M. R. Kriss (1983).

Although the utility of cognitive therapy in the treatment of generalized anxiety seems promising, its contribution to the treatment of phobias is not well defined in current research. For example, Williams and Rappaport (1983) found that providing coping self-statements did not enhance the effectiveness of exposure therapy for severe driving phobics. Emmelkamp (1982), treating agoraphobics, found superior results at post test for exposure *in vivo* as compared to a cognitive restructuring procedure, although the differences between these groups diminished at one-month follow-up. However, these studies do not reflect the actual practice of cognitive therapy. Like other trials of cognitively oriented treatment strategies reported in the recent literature, these phobia studies test the efficacy of artificially contrived and restricted variants of cognitive therapy procedures.

More adequate trials of the approach to treatment of anxiety disorders described in this volume would be based on the manual developed by Beck and Emery (1979). Although controlled clinical studies of this type have been initiated, we must conclude that at this time the definitive research has not been conducted. We suggest, on the basis of available data and extensive clinical experience, that cognitive therapy for treatment of anxiety and phobias is an important and potentially rewarding area for clinical research.

Appendix I

The following self-help agenda can be given to anxious patients when they come for treatment. Reading this will give them a better understanding of how cognitive therapy can help them.

Coping with Anxiety

To be human is to have emotional problems. Sometimes you can deal with these problems by yourself or with the help of family and friends. But just as you would not wait until a physical illness reached the critical stage before consulting a physician, you sometimes can benefit from professional help in overcoming emotional problems before they become so severe as to be disabling. The decision to get help is a sign of wisdom, common sense, and faith in one's own creative potential. To make the most of your experience with therapy, read this pamphlet before your first session. You might find answers to some of your questions; and the suggestions will prove helpful.

SIGNS OF ANXIETY

"What if I fail this exam? My career will be ruined before it starts. I feel so sick just thinking about it that I can't study. But I *have* to study, or——."

"I can't give that speech tomorrow because I know I'll be so nervous I'll forget what I was going to say. I can just see what it will be like—all those eyes looking at me, all of them knowing how nervous and inadequate I am."

"That job was just *made* for someone with my qualifications. I should apply for it. But it's on the thirty-second floor. I can't stand the idea of going up in an elevator every day. If I get panicky, I might scream or be sick. It will be terrifying and humiliating."

"Every time I leave the house, my heart starts to race. I'm sure I'll have a heart attack. Just like my father, who died of one."

Such are the thoughts and emotions that sweep over those who suffer from anxiety and phobias. Since both anxiety and phobias are rooted in fear, both indicate the dread of some type of danger or threat to one's wellbeing. This sense of threat is manifested by a wide range of physical symptoms—anxiety's "body language"—which are distressing in themselves: rapid breathing, accelerating heart rate, dizziness, nausea, headache, sweating, dryness of mouth, tightening of throat, pain in various sets of muscles, and, so on. When the state of anxiety is prolonged—or chronic —these frightening, uncontrollable symptoms may take the form of what seems to be a real disease or disability.

One of the most important facts for a severely anxious person to learn —and to recall to mind at critical moments—is that the symptoms he is experiencing are *not* dangerous. The racing pulse or pounding heart, the dizziness or nausea, the desire to scream or cry or pound the table—none of these physical or emotional reactions indicates that the person is dangerously ill or "going crazy." They are unpleasant. They are uncomfortable. But they can be tolerated until they go away. And they *will* go away.

The Nature of Anxiety and Phobias

While phobias cause intense anxiety, accompanied by its various physical and emotional symptoms, the phobic individual is reacting to a specific object or situation which can, to some extent and without great inconvenience, be avoided. As long as the feared event, object, or situation is not an integral part of the person's life, he can remain free from the anxiety effects of phobia. For instance, someone who has an intense phobic fear of flying, can plan to travel by means of earthbound transportation.

The anxiety sufferer, however, cannot always pinpoint the source of his anxiety. And even if he can identify the cause, he cannot avoid encountering it; either the demands of his life situation force him to confront the feared circumstance, or he has so completely internalized his fear that the source of it is within himself.

Sometimes it is necessary for a person to experience fear in order to acknowledge the threat of a real danger and to prepare himself to meet it. A certain degree of anxiety may accompany such fear. But the person who suffers from excessive anxiety or phobic reactions is not responding to the realities of the situation. He may be anticipating a threat to his wellbeing when there is little likelihood that it will occur. If he is facing a challenge of some sort—an exam or job interview—he will magnify the difficulties and dwell on the horrors of a negative outcome. At the same time he will underestimate, overlook, or discount his own ability to cope with whatever he fears. In other words, he misinterprets and distorts reality so that he feels anxious about dangers either which do not exist or which he could cope with effectively if he were not so disabled by his own anxiety reactions.

To make matters worse, when the severely anxious person becomes intensely aware of his own unpleasant physical and emotional reactions, he may begin to dread and fear the symptoms themselves even more than the situation that triggers them. The more upset he gets, the more exaggerated his symptoms become, and he is involved in a self-perpetuating spiral of increasingly intense emotional and physical suffering.

NEW UNDERSTANDING FROM RESEARCH

Since this form of anxiety is based on a misinterpretation of reality, studies have revealed that certain thoughts and mental pictures automatically accompany the experience of anxiety. These thoughts, or *cognitions,* are usually focused on the future: "I will be fired"; "I will lose control of myself and be humiliated"; "I'll die from a heart attack"; "If I go to the hospital, I'll faint from fear."

The connection between these automatic thoughts and the experience of unwarranted anxiety suggested to those studying the problem that if these cognitions were monitored and then reshaped to conform with reality, the anxiety itself would be modified and even eradicated. Experience with patients has borne out the effectiveness of this method, which is called *cognitive therapy* because it is concerned with the way one's thought patterns affect one's emotions and behavior.

THE COGNITIVE METHOD APPLIED

In the following anecdote, you may recognize the way in which one's "inner voice" of anxiety destroys one's ability to function adequately. A lonely young man wants to ask a girl for a date. But every time he has the opportunity to do so, anxious thoughts rise up: "She'll think I'm stupid to be so nervous. She'll turn me down, and I'll feel so miserable that it will show. I might even cry. More disgrace!" As these thoughts flood his mind, his throat tightens, his mouth is dry, and he can't utter a word even if he tries. The opportunity for a date goes by, and the young man now hates himself for failing again. "I'm a loser," he thinks.

How would cognitive therapy help this young man and those of you whose anxious thoughts and imaginings interfere with your ability to live the kind of life that is rewarding to you? By helping you learn to recognize the mistakes in your thinking about what would happen if you dared to act as you really wish. Through therapy you will learn to apply your reasoning skills and powers of observation to situations in your life that are causing anxiety. Like a scientist, with your own self as a "guinea pig" and life as a laboratory, you will learn how to "test out" your ideas to determine how realistic they are. When you can gradually eliminate the distortions and inaccuracies in your own thinking, you will develop a workable, anxiety-free approach to dealing with life situations.

STEPS IN COGNITIVE THERAPY

The *first step* is to recognize your automatic thoughts whenever you feel anxious. To help recognize them, keep these characteristics in mind:

1. These thoughts seem to come out of nowhere. They are not summoned by conscious recollection or by an attempt to reason or develop a logical pattern.

2. The thoughts are unreasonable, as you will realize when, with the help of your therapist, you learn to challenge them with logic and facts.

3. Even though the thoughts are unreasonable and inaccurate, they probably *seem* plausible and reliable at the time you are experiencing them. You tend to accept them as readily as a realistic thought, like "The phone is ringing—I should answer it."

4. These thoughts serve no useful function and interfere with your ability to control your own behavior. Therefore, the more you accept them, the more anxious you feel.

Try to remember what you said to yourself and what mental pictures or fantasies you had in your mind when you began to feel anxious. Your automatic thoughts may have been triggered by an immediate challenge —the need to take an exam, participate in a social event, keep an appointment for a job interview—or they may relate to the possibility of an event in the distant or indeterminate future, such as a heart attack, an accident, or becoming the victim of a crime.

The second step, after you have learned to recognize these cognitions, is to keep track of them in a notebook. With your therapist's help, you will learn to challenge them, to consider them in the light of your own logic and specific knowledge of reality. Your therapist may also show you how to record the frequency and duration of your anxiety on a graph. When you realize that *each anxiety experience is time-limited,* you will not be panicked by the mistaken notion that you will always feel like this.

The third step is to develop and carry out strategies for testing your thoughts and beliefs about what might happen. For instance, the young man in the anecdote will plan to ask a girl for a date, not in order to actually get a date, but to test his ability to ask her, his exaggerated ideas about the probability of being rejected, and his sense of how rejection will affect him.

The fourth step is to discuss the results of the test. The young man may find that because he was just "testing, one, two, three," his anxiety about the result was almost nil, and that even a negative result was not as disastrous as he had expected.

A fifth step, or corollary technique, will be role playing. To help you practice various ways of coping with difficulties, your therapist will assume the role of "Anxious You" so that you will find yourself on the "other side of the fence" where you can challenge some of your own statements and ideas about what will happen to you in a particular situation. When you are well on your way to applying the methods learned in therapy, your anxiety-producing thoughts will subside, and you will experience a sense of confidence and pleasure in your ability to manage your own responses and to meet life as it comes.

THINKING ERRORS

When you keep track of your anxiety-producing thoughts, you may find that your thinking errors fall into these general categories.

1. *Exaggerating:* A woman was convinced that her husband was going to leave her, that she was too old to be attractive to him. Her anxiety caused her to notice all the new wrinkles in her face and neck, all the gray hairs in her head, and to compare herself unfavorably with every younger woman she met. She could not recognize any of her own merits and became too upset to make the most of them. Furthermore, she underestimated the extent of her husband's love and loyalty and did not even think about the fact that he, too, was showing signs of getting older.

2. *Catastrophizing:* When the anxious person anticipates danger or difficulty, he perceives total disaster as the probable outcome. An anxious

patient facing a relatively simple surgical procedure fears that death or prolonged incapacitation will be the result.

3. *Overgeneralizing:* One negative experience, such as being turned down for a promotion, will be translated into a law governing one's entire existence ("I'll never get anywhere in life. I can't make the grade").

4. *Ignoring the positive:* The anxious person overlooks all the indications of his own ability to cope successfully, forgets all the positive experiences of the past, and anticipates only unsurmountable problems and unendurable suffering in the future. For example, the anxious student will ignore his record of high grades on past tests; he will also forget that this is one of many exams and will not of itself "make or break" his career.

HOMEWORK

An important part of therapy is the homework assigned. Since you will be learning methods for coping with anxiety which will be applicable throughout life, carrying out your homework assignments not only strengthens your ability to use the strategies developed in therapy but also provides a way to test your ideas in real-life situations. In addition to monitoring and recording your automatic thoughts, you will learn how to confront anxiety-producing situations in a way that enables you to control your anxiety reactions, even to "nip them in the bud." Here are some of the ideas you can keep in mind as you practice your new techniques.

1. Before confronting the anxiety-producing situation, consider what we call "rescue factors." What do you have going for you? The anxious student may concentrate on remembering his good grades, his faithful preparation for many months, his past good record on exams.

2. To avoid catastrophizing, think through the situation to the worst possible outcome. For instance, if the student fails, will it really mean the end of his career? Will he have more opportunities to prove his basic ability? Usually you will find that you can tolerate or "live through" the worst. And since the worst is unlikely, you will be able to take what comes.

3. If your mind begins to flood with images of disaster or pain or humiliation, make a list of them and consider each image or fantasy in the light of logic and degree of probability. When you begin to see how illogical or improbable these images actually are, you will learn to challenge them as they come without writing about them.

4. If you have a few basic beliefs at the root of your anxiety, make a point of getting facts to test them, for knowledge is the antidote to fear.

If you have a phobia about elevators, get all the facts you can collect about elevator safety: construction, inspection, accident rate, alarm systems, and the like. If you are anxious about a heart attack, have a physical check-up and follow a physician's recommendation for an exercise routine.

5. If you feel overwhelmed at the thought of actually confronting an anxiety-triggering situation, do it gradually. For instance, if a man is too anxious to ask for a date, he can first ask someone who has a valid reason for turning him down (such as, being already engaged or married) and can tell her he is just "practicing." Someone with fear of going up in tall buildings can go up a few floors at a time, first with a friend, then alone.

6. When you are already in the midst of a challenge-situation and anxiety begins to take hold, practice the technique of diversion. Concentrate on various details that have no relation to your anxiety. If you are in an exam, read the name on your pen or notice the shoe styles of various students. In a social situation, study fabric patterns, furniture styles, or random superficial facts about other persons in the group.

Your therapist will help you apply these techniques to your own situation and will encourage you to try more ways to control anxiety, such as increasing sensory input by ringing bells or hand-clapping, substituting a pleasant fantasy for an upsetting one, practicing your ability deliberately to summon up an unpleasant fantasy in order to tune it out, as you would a TV show you didn't enjoy. In therapy sessions, you will rehearse these techniques so that you can rely on them when you are on your own.

Since you are just starting therapy, here are some general ideas to keep in mind.

Beginnings are important. Once you get started, once you make the decision and begin to carry it out, you will become aware of more power and control already within yourself.

Setting goals gives impetus to your program. If you have in your mind a clear picture of how you would like to change and what you imagine your life could be like if you were free of anxiety, you will know what you are working toward. Share your ideas with your therapist so that he or she can help you reach your goal.

Remember that "you can only get out what you put in." Effort is required if significant changes are to take place. You have been prey to anxiety responses for a long time. It will take time and effort to isolate old thought patterns and to develop ways to counteract and eradicate them.

Remember there are others who can lend a helping hand if you need them. Your own extended family, relatives, friends, business associates, fellow church members, physician, and others interested in your well-being are all potential participants in your progress. Learn to call upon them for understanding and help. Usually these "significant others" experience favorable changes in their own lives when they are called upon to help another.

Be conscientious in the use of techniques learned in therapy. Although *therapy itself is time-limited,* the methods you learn are applicable throughout life. No one is forever free of emotional problems, but you will find that the anxiety they create need not dominate your existence.

And, finally, permit yourself the pleasure of feeling excited about exploring new ways to meet life's challenges. The very fact that you have shown enough initiative to seek help indicates that there is a lively spark of hope and expectation within you. As therapy progresses and anxiety recedes, that spark of hope will kindle a new enthusiasm for daily living. Believe it, and be prepared to work for it.

Appendix II

To Cope with Anxiety, Remember A–W–A–R–E

The key to switching out of an anxiety state is to accept it fully. Remaining in the present and accepting your anxiety cause it to disappear. To deal successfully with your anxiety, you can use the five-step *AWARE* strategy. By using this strategy, you'll be able to accept the anxiety until it's no longer there.

1. Accept the anxiety. Webster defines accepting as "giving consent to receive." Agree to receive your anxiety. Welcome it. Say "Hello" out loud or to yourself when it appears. Say, "I'll gladly accept this."

Decide to be with the experience. Don't fight it. Replace your rejection, anger, and hatred of it with acceptance. By resisting, you're prolonging the unpleasantness of it. Instead, flow with it. Don't make it responsible for how you think, feel, and act.

2. Watch your anxiety. Look at it without judgment—not good, not bad. Don't look at it as an unwelcome guest. Instead, rate it on a 0-to-10 scale and watch it go up and down. Be one with your observing self and watch the peaks and valleys of your anxiety. Be detached. Remember, you're not your anxiety. The more you can separate yourself from the experience, the more you can just watch it.

Look at your thoughts, feelings, and actions as if you're a friendly, but not overly concerned, bystander. Dissociate your basic self from the anxiety. In short, be in the anxiety state, but not of it.

3. Act with the anxiety. Normalize the situation. Act as if you aren't anxious. Function with it. Slow down if you have to, but keep going. Breathe slowly and normally.

If you run from the situation your anxiety will go down, but your fear will go up. If you stay, both your anxiety and your fear will go down.

4. Repeat the steps. Continue to (1) *accept your anxiety*, (2) *watch it*, and (3) *act with it* until it goes down to a comfortable level. And it will, if you continue to accept, watch, and act with it. Just keep repeating these three steps: accept, watch, and act with it.

5. Expect the best. What you fear the most rarely happens. However, don't be surprised the next time you have anxiety. Instead, surprise yourself with how you handle it. As long as you're alive, you will have some anxiety. Get rid of the magical belief that you have licked anxiety for good. By expecting future anxiety, you're putting yourself in a good position to accept it when it comes again.

References

Agras, S.; Sylvester, D.; and Oliveau, D. 1969. "The epidemiology of common fears and phobias," *Comprehensive Psychiatry* 10:151–56.

Ahsen, A. 1965. *Eidetic Psychotherapy.* Lahore, Pakistan: Nai Matbooat.

Alcock, J. 1979. *Animal Behavior: An Evolutionary Approach.* 2nd ed. Sunderland, Md.: Sinauer Associates.

American Psychiatric Association, 1980. *Diagnostic and Statistical Manual of Mental Disorders (DSM-III),* 3rd ed. Washington, D.C.: American Psychiatric Association.

Amies, P. L.; Gelder, M. G.; and Shaw, P. M. 1983. "Social phobia: A comparative clinical study," *British Journal of Psychiatry* 142:174–79.

Angelino, H.; and Shedd, C. I. 1953. "Shifts in the content of fears and worries relative to chronological age," *Proceedings of the Oklahoma Academy of Science* 34: 180–86.

Appleby, I. L.; et al. 1981. "Biochemical indices of lactate-induced panic: A preliminary report," in D. F. Klein and J. G. Rabkin, eds., *Anxiety: New Research and Changing Concepts,* pp. 411–23. New York: Raven Press.

Assagioli, R. 1973. *The Act of Will.* New York: Viking Press.

Bandura, A. 1977. "Self-efficacy: Toward a unifying theory of behavioral change," *Psychological Review* 84:191–215.

Bandura, A. 1982. "Self-efficacy mechanism in human agency," *American Psychologist* 37:122–47.

Beck, A. T. 1967. *Depression: Clinical, Experimental, and Theoretical Aspects.* New York: Harper & Row. Republished as *Depression: Causes and Treatment.* Philadelphia: University of Pennsylvania Press, 1972.

Beck, A. T. 1970. "Role of fantasies in psychotherapy and psychopathology," *Journal of Nervous and Mental Disease* 150:3–17.

Beck, A. T. 1971. "Cognition, affect, and psychopathology," *Archives of General Psychiatry* 24:495–500.

Beck, A. T. 1976. *Cognitive Therapy and the Emotional Disorders.* New York: International Universities Press. Paperbound edition published by New American Library, New York, 1979.

Beck, A. T. 1983. "Comparison of sociotropy and autonomy in agoraphobics and other psychiatric patients." Unpublished study.

Beck, A. T. 1984a. "Cognitive approaches to stress," in C. Lehrer and R. L. Woolfolk, eds., *Clinical Guide to Stress Management.* New York: Guilford Press.

Beck, A. T. 1984*b*. "Cognitive therapy of depression: New perspectives," in P. Clayton, ed., *Treatment of Depression: Old Controversies and New Approaches*. New York: Raven Press.

Beck, A. T.; and Emery, G. 1977. *Cognitive Therapy of Substance Abuse*. Philadelphia: Center for Cognitive Therapy.

Beck, A. T.; and Emery, G. 1979. *Cognitive Therapy of Anxiety and Phobic Disorders*. Philadelphia: Center for Cognitive Therapy.

Beck, A. T.; Laude, R.; and Bohnert, M. 1974. "Ideational components of anxiety neurosis," *Archives of General Psychiatry* 31:319–25.

Beck, A. T.; and Rush, A. J. 1975. "A cognitive model of anxiety formation and anxiety resolution," in I. D. Sarason and C. D. Spielberger, eds., *Stress and Anxiety*, vol. II, pp. 69–80. Washington, D.C.: Hemisphere Publishing.

Beck, A. T.; et al. 1979. *Cognitive Therapy of Depression*. New York: Guilford Press.

Beck, A. T.; et al. 1983. "Development of the sociotropy-autonomy scale: A measure of personality factors in depression." Unpublished manuscript.

Becker, E. 1971. *The Birth and Death of Meaning: An Interdisciplinary Perspective on the Problem of Man*. 2nd ed. New York: Free Press.

Bedrosian, R. C. 1981. "Ecological factors in cognitive therapy: The use of significant others," in G. Emery, S. Hollon, and R. C. Bedrosian, eds., *New Directions in Cognitive Therapy*. New York: Guilford Press.

Berecz, J. M. 1968. "Phobias of childhood: Etiology and treatment," *Psychological Bulletin* 70:694–720.

Bowlby, J. 1970. "Reasonable fear and natural fear," *International Journal of Psychiatry* 9:79–88.

Bowlby, J. 1981. "Cognitive processes in the genesis of psychopathology," Invited Address to the Biannual Meeting of the Society for Research in Child Development. Boston, April 1981.

Burton, R. 1927 [1621]. *The Anatomy of Melancholy*. Edited by Floyd Dell and Paul Jordan-Smith. New York: Farrar & Rinehart.

Buss, A. H. 1980. *Self-Consciousness and Social Anxiety*. San Francisco: W. H. Freeman.

Cannon, W. B. 1929, *Bodily Changes in Pain, Hunger, Fear and Rage: An Account of Recent Researches into the Functions of Emotional Excitement*. 2nd ed. New York: Appleton-Century-Crofts.

Carnegie, D. 1936. *How to Win Friends and Influence People*. New York: Simon & Schuster.

Chambless, D. L.; and Goldstein, A. J., eds., 1982. *Agoraphobia: Multiple Perspectives on Theory and Treatment*. New York: John Wiley.

Costello, C. G. 1982. "Fears and phobias in women: A community study," *Journal of Abnormal Psychology* 91:280–86.

Crowe, R. R.; et al. 1983. "A family study of panic disorder," *Archives of General Psychiatry* 40:1965–69.

Darwin, C. R. 1872. *The Expression of the Emotions in Man and Animals*. London: John Murray.

Deikman, A. 1976. *Personal Freedom*. New York: Grossman.

Deikman, A. 1982. *The Observing Self.* Boston: Beacon Press.

DiLoreto, A. O. 1971. *Comparative Psychotherapy: An Experimental Analysis.* Chicago: Aldine.

Dixon, N. F. 1981. *Preconscious Processing.* New York: John Wiley.

Doctor, R. M. 1982. "Major results of a large-scale pretreatment survey of agoraphobics," in R. L. DuPont, ed., *Phobia: A Comprehensive Summary of Modern Treatments,* pp. 203–14. New York: Brunner/Mazel.

Doctor, R. M.; Gaer, T.; and Wright, M. 1983. "Success at one year follow-up for agoraphobia treatment," Paper presented at the Fourth Annual Phobia Conference, White Plains, N.Y.

DuPont, R. L., ed. 1982. *Phobia: A Comprehensive Summary of Modern Treatments.* New York: Brunner/Mazel.

Easwaran, E. 1981. *Dialogue with Death: The Spiritual Psychology of the Katha Upanishad.* Petaluma, Calif.: Nilgiri Press.

Ellis, A. 1962. *Reason and Emotion in Psychotherapy.* New York: Lyle Stuart.

Emery, G. 1984. *Own Your Own Life.* New York: Signet.

Emery, G.; and Lesher, E. 1982. "Treatment of depression in older adults: Personality considerations," *Psychotherapy: Theory, Research, and Practice* 19:500–505.

Emmelkamp, P. M. G. 1982. *Phobic and Obsessive-Compulsive Disorders.* New York: Plenum.

Emmelkamp, P. M. G.; Kuipers, A. C.; and Eggeraat, J. B. 1978. "Cognitive modification versus prolonged exposure *in vivo:* A comparison with agoraphobics as subjects," *Behaviour Research and Therapy* 16:33–41.

Engel, G. L. 1962. *Fainting: Physiological and Psychological Considerations,* 2nd ed. Springfield, Ill.: Charles C Thomas.

English, H. B.; and English, A. C. 1958. *A Comprehensive Dictionary of Psychological and Psychoanalytical Terms: A Guide to Usage.* New York: Longmans, Green.

Epstein, S. 1972. "The nature of anxiety with emphasis upon its relationship to expectancy," in C. D. Spielberger, ed., *Anxiety: Current Trends in Theory and Research,* vol. II, pp. 291–337. New York: Academic Press.

Feather, B. W. 1971. "A central fear hypothesis of phobias." Presented at the Louisiana State University Medical Center Spring Symposium, "Behavior Therapy in Theory and Practice," New Orleans.

Fowles, D. C. 1982. "Heart rate as an index of anxiety: Failure of a hypothesis," in J. T. Cacioppo and R. E. Petty, eds., *Perspectives in Cardiovascular Psychophysiology,* pp. 93–126. New York: Guilford Press.

Fox, N. A.; and Beck, A. T. 1982. "Communication anxiety and personality factors: Results of a pilot study." Unpublished manuscript.

Freud, S. (1915–1917) *Introductory Lectures on Psychoanalysis,* in *The Standard Edition,* vol. 16, pp. 243–96. J. Strachey, trans. London: Hogarth Press, 1963.

Freud, S. (1926) *Inhibitions, Symptoms and Anxiety,* in *The Standard Edition,* vol. 20, pp. 75–175. J. Strachey, trans. London: Hogarth Press, 1959.

Freud, S.; and Breuer, J. 1966. *Studies on Hysteria.* New York: Avon Books. Originally published in 1895.

Friedman, P. 1959. "The phobias," in S. Arieti, ed., *American Handbook of Psychiatry,* vol. I, pp. 292–305. New York: Basic Books.

Furse, M. L. 1981. *Nothing But the Truth?: What It Takes to Be Honest.* Nashville, Tenn.: Abingdon.

Gallup, G. G., Jr. 1974. "Animal hypnosis: Factual status of a fictional concept," *Psychological Bulletin* 81:836–53.

Gardner, F. L.; et al. 1980. "A comparison of cognitive and behavioral therapies in the reduction of social anxiety." Poster session, Annual Meeting of the Association for Advancement of Behavior Therapy, November 1980.

Gellhorn, E. 1968. "Attempt at a synthesis: Contribution to a theory of emotion," in E. Gellhorn, ed., *Biological Foundations of Emotion,* pp. 144–53. Glenview, Ill.: Scott, Foresman.

Gilson, M. L. 1983. "Depression as measured by perceptive bias in binocular rivalry." Ph.D. dissertation, Georgia State University.

Gittleman, R. "The relationship between childhood separation anxiety disorder and adult agoraphobia." New York State Psychiatric Institute, for presentation at the 14–16 September 1983 conference.

Goldfried, M. R.; and Davison, G. C. 1976. *Clinical Behavior Therapy.* New York: Holt, Rinehart & Winston.

Goldfried, M. R.; Linehan, M. M.; and Smith, J. L. 1978. "Reduction of test anxiety through cognitive restructuring," *Journal of Consulting and Clinical Psychology* 46:-32–39.

Gorman, J. M.; et al. 1983. "Effect of acute B-adrenergic blockade on lactate-induced panic," *Archives of General Psychiatry* 40:1079–82.

Graham, D. T. 1961. "Prediction of fainting in blood donors," *Circulation* 23:901.

Griffith, S. B., 1982. *Sun Tzu: The Art of War.* London: Oxford University Press.

Grosz, H. J.; and Farmer, B. B. 1972. "'Pitts' and McClure's lactate-anxiety study revisited," *British Journal of Psychiatry* 120:415–18.

Guidano, V. F.; and Liotti, G. 1983. *Cognitive Processes and Emotional Disorders.* New York: Guilford Press.

Heider, F. 1974. *Thought and Feeling: Cognitive Alteration of Feeling States.* H. London and R. E. Nisbett, eds. Chicago: Aldine.

Hibbert, G. A. 1984, "Ideational components of anxiety: Their origin and content," *British Journal of Psychiatry* 144:618–24.

Hoch, P. 1950. "Biosocial aspects of anxiety," in P. Hoch and J. Zubin, eds., *Anxiety,* pp. 105–16. New York: Grune & Stratton.

Holroyd, K. 1976. "Cognition and desensitization in the group treatment of test anxiety," *Journal of Consulting and Clinical Psychology* 44:991–1001.

Horney, K. 1950. *Neurosis and Human Growth: The Struggle toward Self-Realization.* New York: W. W. Norton.

Jannoun, L.; et al. 1980. "A home-based treatment program for agoraphobia: Replication and controlled evaluation," *Behavior Therapy* 11:294–305.

Jersild, A. T.; Markey, F. V.; and Jersild, C. L. 1933. "Children's fears, dreams, wishes, daydreams, likes, dislikes, pleasant and unpleasant memories," *Child Development Monographs,* no. 12. New York: Teachers College, Columbia University.

Kanter, N. J.; and Goldfried, M. R. 1979. "Relative effectiveness of rational restructuring and self-control desensitization in the reduction of interpersonal anxiety," *Behavior Therapy* 10:472–90.

Kelly, G. A. 1963. "Theory of Personality," *The Psychology of Personal Constructs.* New York: W. W. Norton.

Kendall, P. C.; and Kriss, M. R. 1983. "Cognitive-behavioral interventions," in C. E. Walker, ed., *Handbook of Clinical Psychology,* vol. 2, pp. 770–819. Homewood, Ill.: Dow Jones-Irwin.

Klein, D. F. 1981. "Anxiety reconceptualized," in D. F. Klein and J. G. Rabkin, eds., *Anxiety: New Research and Changing Concepts,* pp. 235–63. New York: Raven Press.

Klein, D. F.; and Rabkin, J. G., eds. 1981. *Anxiety: New Research and Changing Concepts.* New York: Raven Press.

Klein, D. F.; Rabkin, J. G.; and Gorman, J. M. "Etiological and pathophysiological inferences from the pharmacological treatment of anxiety," in A. H. Tuma and J. D. Maser, eds., *Anxiety and the Anxiety Disorders.* Hillsdale, N.J.: Lawrence Erlbaum Associates, in press.

Kraepelin, E. 1907. *Clinical Psychiatry.* A. R. Diefendorf, trans. New York: Macmillan. Reprint, Delmar, N.Y.: Scholars' Facsimiles and Reprints, 1981.

Kraft, T.; and Al-Issa, I. 1965a. "The application of learning theory to the treatment of traffic phobia," *British Journal of Psychiatry* 111:277–79.

Kraft, T.; and Al-Issa, I. 1965b. "Behavior therapy and the recall of traumatic experience—A case study," *Behaviour Reserach and Therapy* 3:55–58.

Lader, M.; Gelder, M.G.; and Marks, I. 1967. "Palmar skin conductance measures as predictors of response desensitization," *Journal of Psychosomatic Research,* 11:283–290.

Lazarus, A. A. 1968. "Learning theory and the treatment of depression," *Behaviour Research and Therapy* 6:83–89.

Lazarus, A. A. 1971. *Behavior Therapy and Beyond.* New York: McGraw-Hill.

Lazarus, A. A. 1978. *In the Mind's Eye.* New York: Rawson.

Lazarus, R. S. 1966. *Psychological Stress and the Coping Process.* New York: McGraw-Hill.

Leventhal, H. 1982. "The integration of emotion and cognition: A view from the perceptual-motor theory of emotion," in M. Clark and S. Fiske, eds., *Affect and Cognition: The 17th Annual Carnegie-Mellon Symposium on Cognition.* Hillsdale, N.J.: Lawrence Erlbaum Associates.

Levitt, E. E. 1972. "A brief commentary on the 'psychiatric breakthrough' with emphasis on the hematology of anxiety," in C. Spielberger, ed., *Anxiety: Current Trends in Theory and Research,* vol. 1, pp. 227–34. New York: Academic Press.

Lewis, A. 1970. "The ambiguous word 'anxiety,'" *International Journal of Psychiatry* 9:62–79.

Liebowitz, M. R.; and Klein, D. F. 1982. "Agoraphobia: Clinical features, pathophysiology, and treatment," in D. L. Chambless and A. J. Goldstein, eds., *Agoraphobia: Multiple Perspectives on Theory and Treatment,* pp. 153–81. New York: John Wiley.

Lorenz, K. 1981. *The Foundations of Ethology.* K. Z. Lorenz and R. W. Kickert, trans. New York: Springer Verlag.

Mahoney, M. J. 1974. *Cognition and Behavior Modification.* Cambridge, Mass.: Ballinger.

Marks, I. M. 1969. *Fears and Phobias.* New York: Academic Press.

Marks, I. M. 1981. *Cure and Care of Neurosis: Theory and Practice of Behavioral Psychotherapy.* New York: John Wiley.

Marks, I. M.; and Lader, M. 1973. "Anxiety states (anxiety neurosis): A review," *Journal of Nervous and Mental Disease* 156:3–18.

Marquis, S. N. 1976. "Estimating the probability of catastrophes: Basic arithmetic for therapists." Paper presented at the Tenth Annual Meeting of the Association for Advancement of Behavior Therapy, New York, December 1976.

Mathew, A. M.; Gelder, M. G.; and Johnston, D. W. 1981. *Agoraphobia: Nature and Treatment.* New York: Guilford Press.

Mavissakalian, M.; and Barlow, D. H., eds. 1981. *Phobia: Psychological and Pharmacological Treatment.* New York: Guilford Press.

Meichenbaum, D. 1974. *Cognitive Behavior Modification.* Morristown, N.J.: General Learning Press.

Meichenbaum, D. 1977. *Cognitive Behavior Modification: An Integrative Approach.* New York: Plenum Press.

Melges, F. T. 1982. *Time and the Inner Future.* New York: John Wiley.

Miller, L. C.; et al. "Factor structure of childhood fears," *Journal of Consulting and Clinical Psychology,* 39 (1972):264–268.

Montague, A. 1981. *Growing Young.* New York: McGraw-Hill.

Nichols, K. A. 1974. "Severe social anxiety," *British Journal of Medical Psychology* 47:301–6.

Öst, L-G.; Sterner, U.; and Lindahl, I-L. 1984, "Physiological responses in blood phobics," *Behavior Research and Therapy* 22:109–17.

Oxford English Dictionary. 1933, vol. 4, p. 114. Oxford: Clarendon Press.

Peterson, C.; and Seligman, M. E. P. 1984, "Causal explanations as a risk factor for depression," *Psychological Review* 91:347–74.

Pitts, F. N., Jr. 1969. "The biochemistry of anxiety," *Scientific American* 220:69–75.

Pitts, F. N., Jr.; and McClure, J. N., Jr. 1967. "Lactate metabolism in anxiety neurosis," *New England Journal of Medicine* 277:1329–36.

Polanyi, M. 1964. *Science, Faith, and Society.* Chicago: University of Chicago Press.

Rachman, S. J. 1978. *Fear and Courage.* San Francisco: W. H. Freeman.

Raimy, V. 1975. *Misunderstandings of the Self.* San Francisco: Jossey Bass.

Rank, O. 1932. *Art and Artist: Creative Urge and Personality Development.* Charles Francis Atkinson, trans. New York: Alfred A. Knopf,

Raskin, M.; et al. 1982. "Panic and generalized anxiety disorders: Developmental antecedents and precipitants," *Archives of General Psychiatry* 39:687–89.

Rosen, S. 1982. *My Voice Will Go with You: The Teaching Tales of Milton H. Erickson.* New York: W. W. Norton.

Rush, J.; and Watkins, J. T. 1981. "Cognitive therapy with psychologically naive depressed outpatients," in G. Emery, S. Hollon, and R.C. Bedrosian, eds., *New Directions in Cognitive Therapy.* New York: Guilford Press.

Sarason, I. G. 1972. "Experimental approaches to test anxiety: Attention and the uses of information," in C. Spielberger, ed., *Anxiety: Current Trends in Theory and Research,* vol. II., pp. 381–403. New York: Academic Press.

Sarason, I. G.; and Stoops, R. 1978. "Test anxiety and the passage of time," *Journal of Consulting and Clinical Psychology* 46:102–9.

Seligman, M. E. P. 1971. "Phobias and preparedness," *Behavior Therapy* 2:307–20.

Sewitch, T. S.; and Kirsch, I. 1984. "The cognitive content of anxiety: Naturalistic evidence for the predominance of threat-related thoughts," *Cognitive Therapy and Research* 8:49–58.

Sheehan, D. V. 1982. "Current concepts in psychiatry: Panic attacks and phobias," *New England Journal of Medicine; Medical Intelligence,* 15 July 1982, pp. 156–58.

Shelton, J. L.; and Levey, A. 1981. *Behavioral Assignments and Treatment Compliance.* Champaign, Ill.: Research Press.

Singer, J. 1974. *Imagery and Daydream Methods in Psychotherapy and Behavior Modification.* New York: Academic Press.

Snaith, R. P. 1968. "A clinical investigation of phobias," *British Journal of Psychiatry* 114:673–98.

Standard College Dictionary. 1963. New York: Funk & Wagnalls.

Staniforth, M. 1964. *Marcus Aurelius Meditations.* Middlesex, England: Penguin Books.

Stevenson, I.; and Hain, J. D. 1967. "On the different meanings of apparently similar symptoms, illustrated by varieties of barbershop phobia," *American Journal of Psychiatry* 124:399–403.

Sullivan, H. S. 1953. *Interpersonal Theory of Psychiatry.* New York: W. W. Norton.

Terhune, W. B. 1949. "The phobic syndrome: A study of eighty-six patients with phobic reactions," *Archives of Neurological Psychiatry* 62:162–72.

Thorpe, G. L.; and Burns, L. E. 1983. *The Agoraphobic Syndrome.* New York: John Wiley.

Torgersen, S. 1983. "Genetic factors in anxiety disorders," *Archives of General Psychiatry* 40:1085–89.

Webster's Third International Dictionary. 1981. Springfield, Mass.: G. & C. Merriam.

Weinberg, G. 1978. *Self Creation.* New York: St. Martin's.

Weinberg, H. L. 1973. *Levels of Knowing and Existence.* Lakeville, Conn.: Institute of General Semantics.

Weissman, M. M.; Myers, J. K.; and Harding, P. S. 1978. "Psychiatric disorders in a U.S. urban community," *American Journal of Psychiatry* 135:459–62.

Westphal, C. 1871–72. "Die agoraphobie: Eine neuropathische erscheinung," *Archiv fur Psychiatrie und Nervenkrankheiten* 3:138–61.

Williams, S. L.; and Rappaport, A. 1983. "Cognitive treatment in the natural environment for agoraphobics," *Behavior Therapy* 14:299–313.

Wolpe, J. 1969. *The Practice of Behavior Therapy.* New York: Penguin Press.

Zimbardo, P. G. 1977. *Shyness.* New York: Jove Publications.

Index